Date Due

Brussels	MAR 1 1990	
Oct.25	DEC 22 92	
July		
SEP 28 1982		8234

j917.1   Canada: the land
Can   and its people.

                                   950

		Oct. 25
Dawn		
renewed		
Boynton	July	

j917.1   Canada: the land and its people [By]
Can   Doreen Margaret Tomkins [and others]
             [n.p.] Gage, 1975.
                372 p.   illus., maps.
                Includes bibliography.

             1. Canada - Description and travel.
          I. Tomkins, Doreen Margaret.
0771582897   B-1907

6

Canada: The Land and its People

Canada: The Land and its People

Doreen Margaret Tomkins
Vernon Rout
Colin Vincent
David Walker
Victor Last

GAGE EDUCATIONAL PUBLISHING LIMITED

ISBN 0-7715-8289-7
1 2 3 4 5 6 7 8 9 10 RCS 79 78 77 76 75
Written, printed, and bound in Canada

Maps and diagrams by James Loates Illustrating
and Kennedy Art Studio Limited.

ACKNOWLEDGMENTS

The publisher is grateful to many persons and organizations for assistance in the preparation of this book. In particular, Gage Educational Publishing Limited wishes to express appreciation to Dr. George Tomkins of the Faculty of Education, University of British Columbia, for his role as advisory editor; to Dr. J. Lewis Robinson of the Geography Department, University of British Columbia, for editorial advice on the Canadian Shield; to Mr. Vernon Rout, Head of Geography, Etobicoke Collegiate Institute, for critical guidance on manuscript drafts; and to various Nova Scotia members of Le Projet des Francophones d'Atlantique for information and help on lobster fishing in Yarmouth County, Nova Scotia.

CONTENTS

PREFACE

This book is a blend of the thematic and the regional. Unit I establishes the themes of physical and cultural diversity. First, there are descriptive examinations of the differences in physiography, climate, vegetation, and soils that characterize Canada's main geographic regions. Then, there is a part-descriptive, part-investigative account of the different ethnic groups that compose the mosaic of people called Canadians.

Basic to the thematic-regional nature of Unit II is a search for geographic universals. Hence this largest portion of *Canada: The Land and its People* deals with major economic activities in roughly historical order of development: fishing, the forest industries, agriculture, mining, manufacturing, and transportation. The introductory chapter sets the scene with an overview of energy sources and their role in all these activities.

The concluding Unit analyses the effects and implications of the development of these activities on the land and the people. Indeed, one common factor underlies all three Units: the interaction between human beings and their environment.

Geography comes alive through the application of the kinds of questions, viewpoints, and techniques a trained geographer uses. Hence the many "Study" and "Study and Research" sections in the book. These enquiry sections have been designed to be relevant and challenging as well as informative.

VERBAL EQUIVALENTS OF NUMERICAL DATA

These tables will help you to translate more precisely certain basic measurements in geography.

CLIMATE
(a) Temperature
very cold	Under −20°C
cold	−20°C to −1°C
cool	0°C to 9°C
mild	10°C to 19°C
hot	20°C to 29°C
very hot	30°C and over

(b) Range of temperature
small	Under 10°C
moderate	10°C to 19°C
large	20°C to 29°C
very large	30°C and over

(c) Precipitation (annual)
sparse	Under 25 centimetres
light	25 cm to 49 cm
moderate	50 cm to 99 cm
heavy	100 cm to 199 cm
very heavy	200 cm and over

(d) Pressure[1]
very low	Under 100.0 kilopascals (Under 1000 millibars)
low	100.0-100.9 kPa (1000-1009 mbar)
average	101.0-101.9 kPa (1010-1019 mbar)
high	102.0-102.9 kPa (1020-1029 mbar)
very high	103.0 kPa and over (1030 mbar and over)

[1]For use in climatic descriptions

POPULATION DENSITY

Almost uninhabited	Under 1 per square kilometre
Sparsely populated	1-9/km²
Lightly populated	10-49/km²
Moderately populated	50-99/km²
Densely populated	100-499/km²
Very densely populated	500 and over

LANDFORMS

Generalized Landform[1]	Relief[2]	Slope	Elevation[3]
Plain	up to 150 metres	gentle to rolling	Under 500 metres
Plateau	variable	gentle to rolling	Over 500 m
Hills	150 to 500 m	moderate to steep	Over 150 m
Mountains	Over 500 m	steep	Over 500 m

[1]Landforms are infinite in their variety but can be classified in general terms as shown.

[2]The difference in height between the highest and the lowest points of the locality in question.

[3]The general height above sea level of the landform.

A WORD TO THE READER

International Metric System (SI) units have been used throughout the book. However, where background historical information is presented, original measures have been retained. Conversion in these cases would distort history. To report CPR track laying in metres almost denies the reality of how railway construction was measured in the nineteenth century.

Canada is a large, complicated mosaic. To help you find information on the different pieces of the mosaic — geographical, social, economic, etc. — a list of reference materials is included on page 375. This list is divided into two parts: general reference works and enrichment materials; and sources that relate more specifically to chapter topics.

Some questions in the Studies specifically direct you to certain sources (the *Canada Year Book*, *The National Atlas of Canada*, etc.). Others are left open for you to choose your own reference (although, for many of these, the *Canada Year Book* is a good resource). With the research skills you have acquired, you can use these and other materials listed as sources for specific information, and also as a means for supporting, refuting, qualifying, and extending the topics presented in this book.

Chapter 1

Where we live:
A land of physical diversity

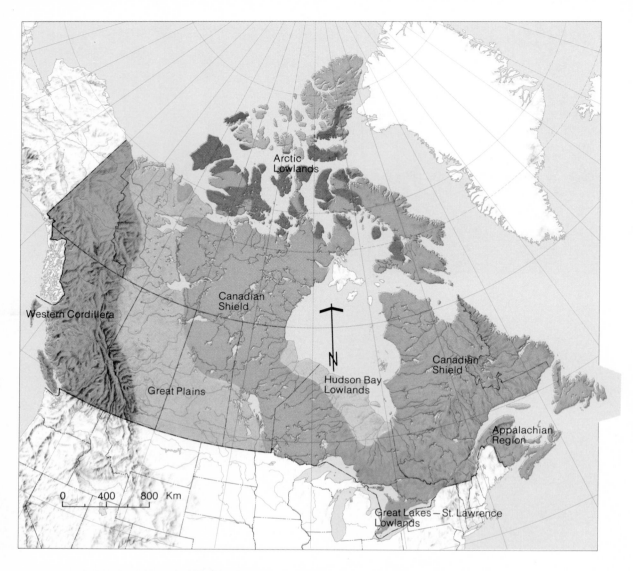

CANADA: GENERALIZED PHYSIOGRAPHIC REGIONS

To most of the world, the word "Canada" conjures up images of frozen wastes, abundant forests, endless prairies, and craggy, snowcapped mountains. In a world that is rapidly becoming urbanized, Canada is thought of as one of the few places left where there is game hunting and fine fishing. All this is perfectly true. But the land that is renowned for fir, jackpine, and balsam also has cacti and even a few palms. Although Canada is famous as a major producer of wheat, there is also a significant rice harvest. And while some of the lowest temperatures in the world have been recorded in Canada, on a July day many locations across the country are as hot as some places in the tropics.

Many Canadians know that they live in the second-largest country in the world, but do they understand what this means? How many realize that, for Newfoundlanders, a journey to Europe is considerably shorter

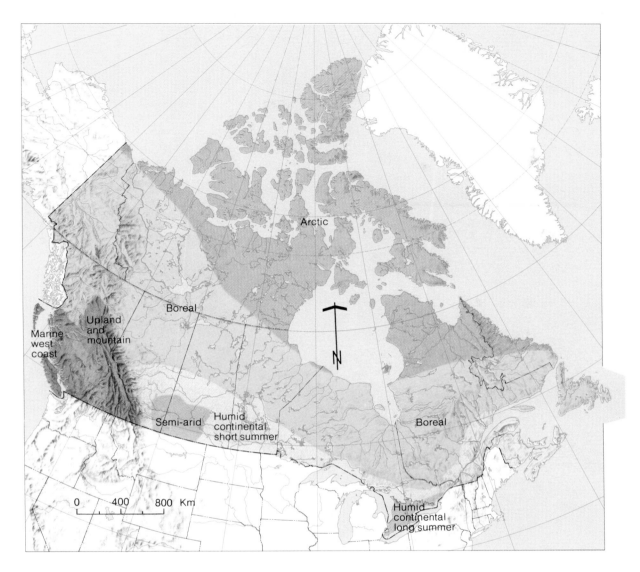

CANADA: GENERALIZED CLIMATIC REGIONS

than a trip to the British Columbia coast? How many Canadians are aware that the north-south extent of their homeland, from the northern tip of Ellesmere Island to Middle Island in Lake Erie, is just as great as the east-west extent from Cape Spear, Newfoundland, to Mount St. Elias in the Yukon?

In such a vast, sprawling country, it is not surprising that there is great variety of landscape and climate.

Shaping the variety

For millions of years natural forces have interacted to shape the landscape of Canada. Some rock formations were produced when the earth's crust cooled and hardened, or when molten lava was spewed forth from deep beneath the surface. Others were formed as sediment dropped to the floors of ancient seas and was gradually com-

5

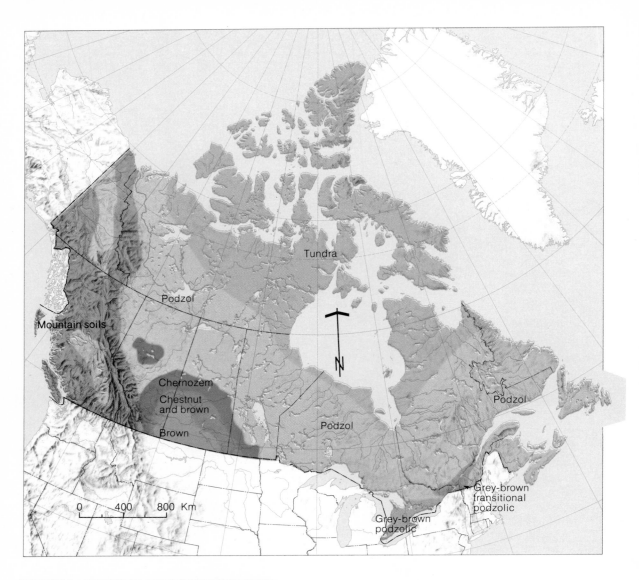

CANADA: GENERALIZED SOIL REGIONS

pressed into rock. Slow, steady stretchings and squeezings and, occasionally, violent earthquakes crumpled the outer crust. Layers of rock were tilted and twisted, crunched together or wrenched apart.

And all the while, battles were raging in the atmosphere. Huge air masses, cold or hot or humid or dry, struggled for supremacy. Water, wind, glaciers, and extremes of temperature have shattered, scoured, smoothed, and sculptured the surface of the land. Ice sheets, glaciers, and rivers

have transported various forms of debris — from enormous boulders to the finest sand and silt — all over the country. When eventually dumped, these materials gave rise to widely different scenes, from the table-top flatness of dried-up lake beds, to sloping hills, to steep ridges, to towering mountains.

Somewhere along the way, life appeared. In tiny crannies in the rocks, in sand and clay near and under water, seedlings took root; and animal life was born. In time, par-

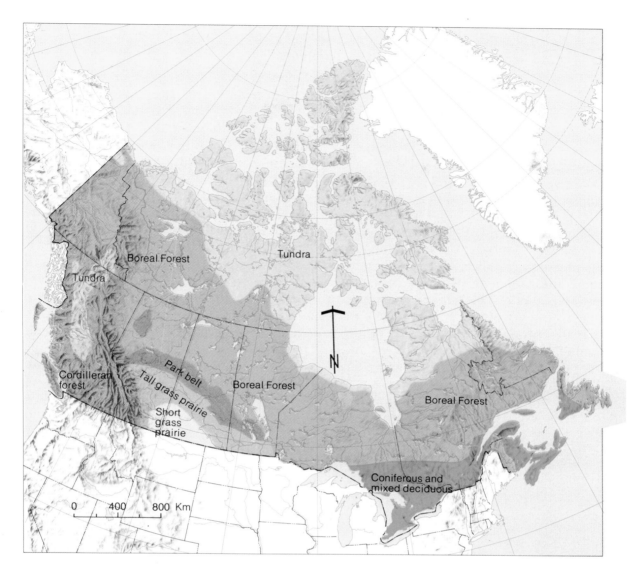

CANADA: GENERALIZED NATURAL VEGETATION REGIONS

ticular vegetations and animal groups developed in particular areas. Different kinds of soils were created by different conditions of climate, rock, and plant and animal remains.

To begin to understand such a huge, diverse land, it is necessary to divide Canada into fairly distinct regions. Some criteria that can be used to do this are shown in the maps on pages 4-7. Note that the *boundaries* of these divisions do not always coincide. For example, the physio-

graphic region known as the Western Cordillera contains several different types of climate; and the region of humid continental, short summer climate includes many different soil types. Furthermore, any one of these divisions contains within itself many physiographic, climatic, soil, and vegetative differences. So, while these divisions are useful, they must be handled carefully. The six physiographic regions can be used as a basis to get some idea of Canada's incredible physical diversity.

The Canadian Shield: A legacy of the ice ages

The Canadian Shield is by far the largest region. This immense, U-shaped sweep of rock, lake, muskeg, and forest covers close to 50 per cent of the mainland. This is the landscape immortalized in paintings by the Group of Seven. This is the region that challenged those most rugged of folk heroes: the voyageur, the lumberjack, and the prospector. This is the natural home of our traditional symbols: the beaver and the maple leaf. This is the sanctuary to which millions of Canadians escape each year for rest and relaxation. The Shield is so often written about in novels and magazines, so often photographed and filmed, that it has given many a Canadian a strong sense of national identity.

The Shield is a geologist's paradise. Almost every type of rock in the world can be found somewhere here. Its complex formations contain some of the oldest rocks on earth. There are **igneous** intrusions — granites and basalts — formed when magma thrust up into the earth's crust. Forces within the crust caused great cracks and fissures beneath the surface. With the release of pressure at these points, the hot, solid masses beneath the crust changed to magma and flowed up into these cracks and fissures. (Geologists examine igneous intrusions with particular care; these are frequently rich in metallic ores.) There are massive **sedimentary** deposits — sandstones and limestones — laid down on the floors of long-gone lakes and seas. There are **metamorphic** rocks, formed as the result of intense heat and earth movements — slate (altered shale), marble (a compressed and highly heated limestone), and gneiss (a metamorphosed, or changed, granite).

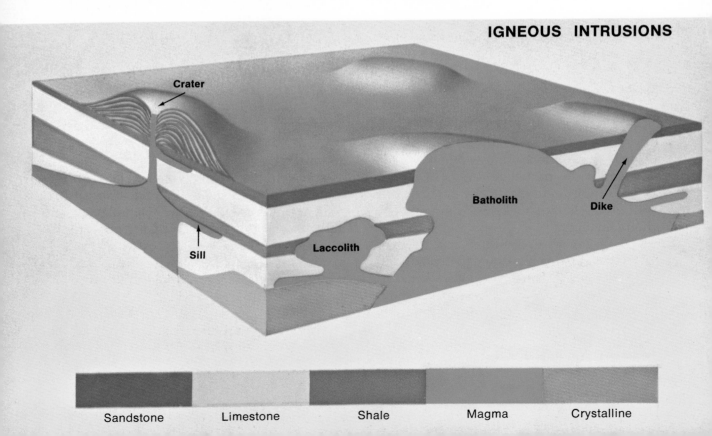

IGNEOUS INTRUSIONS

Crater

Batholith

Dike

Sill

Laccolith

Sandstone   Limestone   Shale   Magma   Crystalline

Shield landscape is unmistakable—lake, river, forest, and rock. Add to these characteristics, muskeg. Indeed, an historian has described the region in even more basic terms. "The country is four-fifths drowned and when not frozen is half-hidden by mosquitoes and black flies."

Geologists and other Shield workers have to contend with the extremely rugged nature of the region. The land surface has been partly reshaped by the movement of mighty ice sheets of past ages. Thousands of metres thick, they spread, century after century, over the northern half of the continent. As the glaciers moved over the land, boulders, stones, and pieces of gravel embedded in the ice "sandpapered" the land and gouged and deepened hollows of all shapes and sizes.

The ice advanced and retreated several times — scouring away almost all the soil — before it shrank back to polar regions. The result is, in general, a jumbled, rocky countryside rising to fairly level horizons.

As the ice sheets slowly melted, millions of tonnes of sand, gravel, and boulders carried along by the ice were dumped in haphazard fashion. Thus, streams and rivers twist and turn through all this debris as they seek a route down to sea level. Where water has not yet had time to carve out gently sloping river beds, there are falls and rapids. In valleys dammed by glacial material, the water has backed up, forming long, narrow lakes. Innumerable lakes, ponds, and pools dot almost one-third of the entire region. And in the low-lying stretches of muskeg, water is trapped in countless swamps and bogs.

Study 1

1. You are a surveyor searching for a railway route from Ryde Lake to Southwood. Which of the following will be your major problems?
   (a) detours around lakes and ponds,
   (b) trestles to maintain an even gradient across rough and rugged terrain,
   (c) shortages of lumber for rail ties and telegraph poles,
   (d) a firm foundation for the roadbed across swamp and muskeg,
   (e) elevating the roadbed to avoid spring floods in large areas of low-lying land,
   (f) long, steep gradients,
   (g) cuttings through rocky outcrops,
   (h) major tunnels through high mountains.
2. Make a short report describing the character of the country.
3. What evidences of glaciation are illustrated on pages 9 and 10?

◀ *Extract from the Orillia, Ontario, sheet (31 D/NW) of the National Topographic System. Scale 1:125,000. Courtesy Surveys and Mapping Branch, Department of Energy, Mines, and Resources, Ottawa.*

PLEISTOCENE GLACIATION

Sea ice

Greenland centre

Junction of Alpine and

Continental glaciation

Alpine glaciation

Keewatin centre

Glacier ice

Areas of post-glacial marine submergence

Sea ice

N

Labrador centre

Post-glacial lakes

0   400   800 Km

Glacier ice

Glacier ice

Climate, soil, and vegetation

Imagine for a moment that you are in the Shield countryside near Gravenhurst, Ontario. What do you see? Snow-covered slopes for skiing and snowmobiling? Frozen lakes for ice-boating? The refuge of shady trees and cool waters in the sizzling heat of summer? Hiking trails winding through the brilliant reds and golds of a crisp fall day?

All of these images reflect the diverse seasons of the Shield.

Although such an enormous region experiences considerable climatic variations, conditions over most of the Shield are sufficiently similar to allow some generalizations. Most of the Shield experiences a **boreal** climate: long, cold winters and short, cool summers. For well over two-thirds of the year **average temperatures** are below freezing. Daily minimum temperatures often drop to −45°C in northern areas and to −35°C in southern parts. For about 90 per cent of the region, average temperatures in January are below −18°C. When boreal blizzards blast out of the Arctic, the region is gripped in a miserable cold indeed. Even in summer, average temperatures reach only the mid teens. However, there are rare climatic oddities. Some places experience a few very hot days when the mercury soars into the thirties, and Chicoutimi, Quebec, once set a record of 40°C.

Why are low temperatures the dominant factor in this type of climate? For one thing, in high latitudes the sun's rays are dispersed over a wide area, not concentrated as in tropical latitudes. And the little heat that does accumulate during the short winter days escapes from the earth during the long hours of darkness, the more so since there is little soil to retain this warmth.

Nonetheless, long summer days can cause quite a build-up of heat, and when there are influxes of Gulf air, the weather can become very hot indeed. However, since Arctic air can pour in at any time, a rapid drop in temperature is not an infrequent summer occurrence.

Because of the vastness of this region, the Shield experiences some of the world's most extreme temperatures. This is clearly indicated in the climagraph for Kapuskasing below.

KAPUSKASING, ONT.

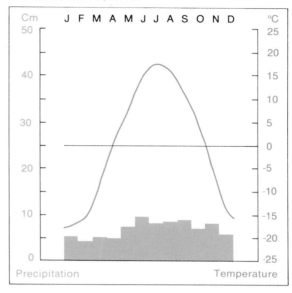

The sheer size of the region also influences the precipitation pattern. The western section of the Shield occupies the centre of a great land mass, far from sources of moisture. So this region receives only small

For about half the year, the Shield is blanketed by snow. What are the advantages of this kind of climate?

amounts of precipitation, varying from 25 to 46 centimetres annually, 40 per cent of which is snow. In the eastern part, however, moisture conditions are quite different. Total precipitation averages about 84 centimetres per year. Heavy snowfalls are experienced when low-pressure "cells" draw in great quantities of moisture from the Great Lakes and move out over the eastern Shield. Forced to rise by the upland elevation, they drop their condensed moisture in heavy concentrations of snow. Some of the heaviest snowfalls in the world occur north of Quebec City.

Large sections of the Shield have little plant cover except for mosses, lichens, and small flowers. Others are covered with evergreen, open-crown forest (thin spreads of spruce and balsam). South of 50°N, however, the forest is quite dense. It is in this forest that a great deal of Canada's lumbering industry is carried on. The long hours of weak sunlight have produced tall, thin trees well suited to the production of pulp and paper. Northward, the forest thins out to the treeless tundra. Southward, more and more **deciduous** (fall leaf-shedding) trees appear alongside **evergreens.** Maple, birch, and aspen – the favorite food of the beaver – are common Shield trees.

Soil does not form easily in the Shield. How can it? In low temperatures, plant and animal matter decomposes slowly. Thus Shield soil tends to be a surface layer of only partly decayed organic matter on top of a pale-colored, nutrient-poor layer. Why is it nutrient-poor? A low evaporation rate, due to low temperatures, leaves a great deal of moisture in the ground. So where soil does form, it is well-**leached,** acidic, or "sour." Leaching involves two simultaneous processes: mineral salts that plants need as food are carried away below the surface in solution; a chemical reaction in the solution converts these soluble salts into insoluble salts useless to plants.

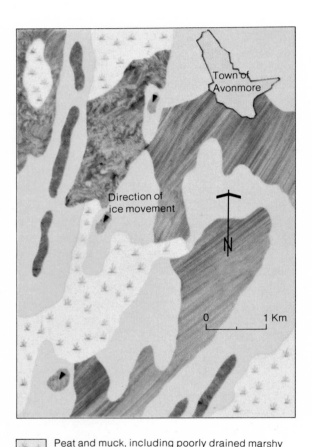

Town of Avonmore

Direction of ice movement

N

0   1 Km

Peat and muck, including poorly drained marshy areas

Boulder beach gravel
Marine sand
Marine clay and silt
} Deposits of the Champlain Sea

Sandy till, clay till, and bouldery till
Drumlinized till
} Deposits of retreating ice

SURFACE GEOLOGY NEAR CORNWALL, ONTARIO

You have only to glance at the map on page 4 to realize that the Shield does not merge gradually with the landscape of the Great Lakes-St. Lawrence Lowlands. The change is abrupt. Gone are the many lakes, tumbling streams, and twisting watercourses. To the west of Kingston, Ontario, gently rising escarpments divide the rolling countryside into valleys. Surface materials consist mainly of debris dumped by the ice sheets.

Around the edges of present-day lakes, the remnants of post-glacial beaches exist as clay and sand plains.

Study 2

1. The geology map on page 14 is a sample of the type of surface material found throughout the Great Lakes-St. Lawrence Lowlands. What types of material cover the land surface of the Lowlands? With what event do you connect these deposits?
2. Look at the topographic map of Orillia on page 10 and the geology map on page 14 How do they reveal the direction of ice movement?
3. The photograph below shows a **drumlin** (the whale-backed mound of material in the centre of the photograph) similar to those near Avonmore, as indicated in the landform map. What materials form drumlins?

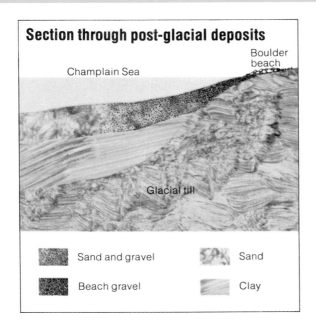

Section through post-glacial deposits

Champlain Sea

Boulder beach

Glacial till

Sand and gravel

Beach gravel

Sand

Clay

Victor C. Last

15

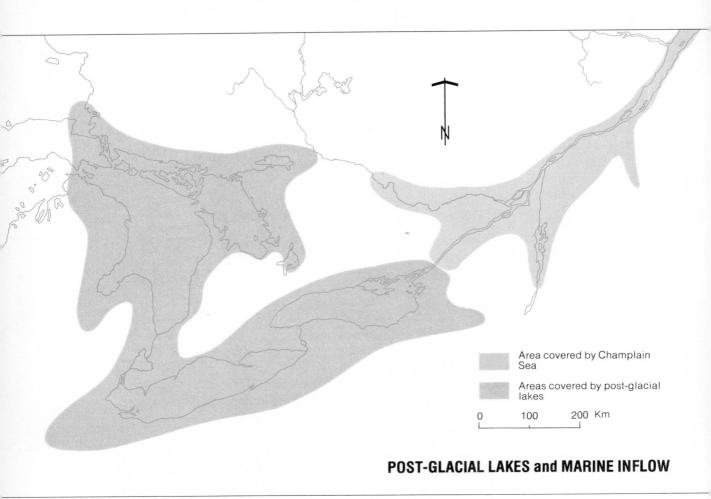

Areas covered by post-glacial lakes

0   100   200 Km

POST-GLACIAL LAKES and MARINE INFLOW

Furthermore, as the ice sheets retreated northward, water accumulated between the melting edges and **moraines** — ridges of **glacial drift**. These meltwater pondings soon dried up. Their beds remain as patches of clay and sand plains. Ice sheets gouged the valleys of huge preglacial rivers into giant basins that are now occupied by the five Great Lakes.

East of Kingston, a spur of the Shield divides the Lowlands: the Great Lakes Lowlands on one side, and the St. Lawrence Lowlands on the other. East of the spur, the Lowlands are truly named, for here is some of the flattest land in Canada. When the great weight of the ice was removed,

and before the Lowlands slowly began to rise, a gulf of the Atlantic Ocean, known to geologists as the Champlain Sea, spread as far inland as the modern Thousand Islands district. As the continent rose, the sea retreated, revealing its bed — rich deposits of silt and clay.

Some of the more remarkable physical features of the Great Lakes-St. Lawrence Lowlands are terraces and beaches, now high and dry above present water levels. Montreal is divided by a striking bluff, 45-55 metres high, that is part of the shoreline of the Champlain Sea. A conspicuous ridge running through the city of Toronto marks the shoreline of ancient Lake Iroquois.

A zone of climatic conflict

One word pretty well sums up the main characteristic of the climate of the Great Lakes-St. Lawrence Lowlands: variety.

Situated as the region is in the funnel between the uplands of the Shield and the Appalachians, cell after cell of low pressure is channelled through by the westerly flow of air. Warm-front conditions — rain or snow falling from monotonous grey skies — can go on for days. After a slight clearing, heavy precipitation from a blustery cold front heralds a high-pressure cell. Then come clear skies, announcing in summer, refreshing cooler temperatures, and in winter, an invigorating, dry cold spell. Arctic air can sweep down in fall, winter, or spring, and temperatures then drop rapidly. When warm, moist air from the Gulf of Mexico makes its way up the Mississippi and Ohio valleys and over the Great Lakes, summer days become horribly hot and humid. The interaction of these two major air masses, Arctic and Gulf, can create some of the most vicious weather in eastern Canada. In the zone of conflict between them, storms are generated, and when unstable air passes over the Lowlands, thunderstorms, ice storms, and heavy snowfalls occur. In fall and spring, dense fogs can form. One such fog stopped the final minutes of play of a Grey Cup game in Toronto.

Temperatures in the Lowlands are less extreme than those of the Shield, as indicated by the statistics for Toronto, a typical station. This region experiences the highest average temperatures in Canada and has recorded some of the hottest days — Toronto 40.6°C, London 41.1°C. Winter days, however, are not the coldest, mainly because of the latitude. Record lows are around −32°C, and winter averages are −4°C. Temperatures generally become cooler from Windsor to Montreal due to

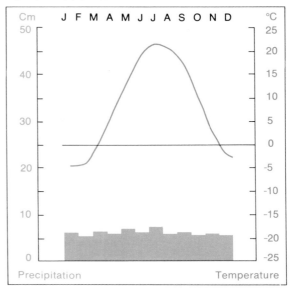

TORONTO, ONT.

the southwest-northeast trend of the St. Lawrence Valley.

The constant procession of low-pressure cells across the region ensures that precipitation is evenly distributed throughout the year. Each month has a total precipitation of between 5.1 and 7.6 centimetres, with yearly totals of about 76 centimetres. There are fewer such cells in summer, but the amount of precipitation remains steady because of **convectional rain** caused by the cooling of air that rises from the overheated land surface.

Soils are as varied as the factors that produce them. **Parent material** of sand, clay, and till is enriched by bark, leaves, and roots. With adequate precipitation and relatively warm temperatures, hosts of soil-forming micro-organisms are present. The result is a variety of soil patterns, but in general, soils are "forest brown," or transitional "grey-brown podzolic." These are quite fertile and have given rise to the most varied and the richest (in dollar value) agricultural section of Canada.

Extract from the Lumsden, Saskatchewan, sheet (72-1/10, Edition 2 MCE, Series A 742) of the National Topographic System. Scale 1:50,000. Courtesy Surveys and Mapping Branch, Department of Energy, Mines, and Resources, Ottawa.

The Great Plains

French and English trader-explorers have left us accounts of their travels on the Plains in the late seventeenth and early eighteenth centuries. Although born and raised in the much gentler environments of France and England, they had become accustomed to the rugged terrain and harsh climate of the northern forestlands. Suddenly, they broke through into a totally unfamiliar environment. It bewildered and frightened them. They called it "barren," to describe the lack of trees rather than to denote a lifeless wasteland.

Anthony Henday of the Hudson's Bay Company was one of the first Europeans to cross the Plains. In 1754, he was sent westward to persuade more Indians to bring fur pelts to the Bay. After travelling southwest for forty-five days through the familiar Shield landscape, Henday learned from Indian contacts that he was "on the Confines of the dry inland country." From mid-July to late October, Henday moved steadily westward through the Plains. The vast, apparently endless extent of the prairies overwhelmed him. Again and again he noted in his diary: "We are still in the Muscuty plains."

Extracts from Henday's diary for August, 1754

11. Sunday. Travelled 11 miles S.W. by W. Level lands, short grass; no woods; and no water but what is salt.
12. Monday. Travelled 7 Miles W.S.W. Level land, with small black Cherry trees, yielding plenty of fruit. Nothing but salt lakes.
13. Tuesday. Travelled 7 Miles W.S.W. Level land, short grass, Dry-woods, and several salt-water lakes. We are now entering Muscuty plains, and shall soon see plenty of Buffalo, and the Archithinue [Blackfeet] Indians hunting them on Horse-back. ...
19. Monday. Travelled 10 Miles W.S.W. in Muscuty plains; fine land, no woods; several salt-water lakes; have passed but 4 places of fresh water, these five days past.

Study 3

Anthony Henday journeyed through country similar to that represented in the map on pages 18 and 19.

1. How does the map indicate that the land surface of the Plains is generally very level? How is minor unevenness of the surface indicated?
2. Draw a section, or calculate the gradient, of the hill down to the Qu'Appelle River. Comment on the width of the valley floor and on the size of the Qu'Appelle. Henday must have crossed several such valleys. Why then did the land *appear* so flat to him?
3. Henday travelled in August. Does the map indicate a shortage of fresh water in that month?
4. Is this part of the Plains treeless? Why did the explorers and early settlers emphasize the "barren" appearance of the Plains?

Flat and monotonous?

The Great Plains of North America are often thought of as huge expanses of flat land, clearly edged by mountainous areas. There are, in fact, marked differences in the local **topography** or surface features.

Flattest of all are those areas that were once covered by post-glacial lakes. North of the morainic hills, water backed up over large sections of the Plains to form huge glacial lakes — Lake Agassiz, for example.

These then drained away very, very slowly, leaving behind **lacustrine plains**. However, when the ice retreated, it left behind rock material ranging from boulders to finely-ground particles. This glacial drift or **till** forms much of the surface **mantle** of the Plains. Streams and rivers flowing eastward from the western mountains dumped loads of sand, silt, and gravel. Local winds picked up fine particles of these materials and deposited them as sand dunes and **loess** (fine-textured earth) plains. The overlay of loess on glacial till has developed

excellent soils. All these plains are very recent, geologically speaking, little disturbed by earth movements and erosion.

However, the thick layers of horizontal, sedimentary rocks, which underlie most of this region, have been tilted very gently westward. Ancient rivers eroded the softer rock in these **strata**, producing a series of east-facing **scarp-slopes**. The most prominent scarp-slopes in the Canadian section of the Plains are the Manitoba Escarpment and the Missouri Coteau. They divide the region into three distinct levels: the Mani-

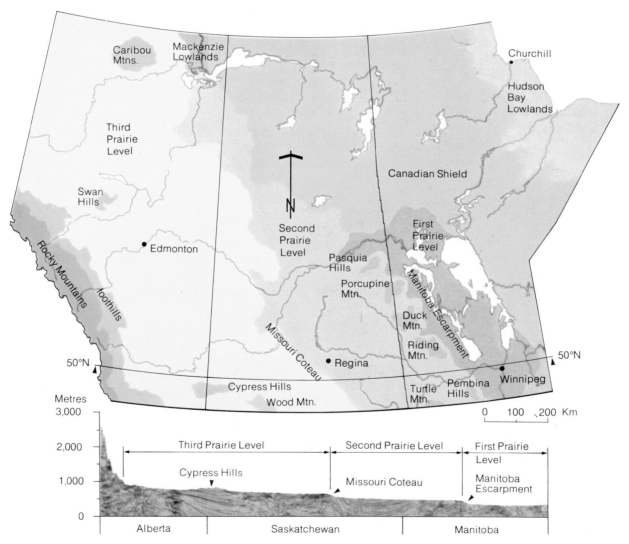

RELIEF AND ELEVATION OF PRAIRIE PROVINCES

21

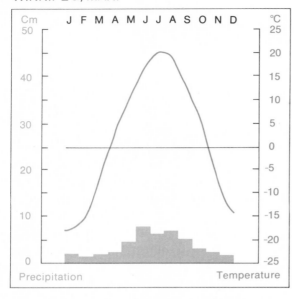

Cm — JFMAMJJASOND — °C

Precipitation — Temperature

areas. Calgary receives an annual average of only 43 centimetres, Saskatoon, about 33 centimetres. Despite the popular image of snow-swept prairie, most locations actually receive less snow than do the Great Lakes-St. Lawrence Lowlands. This is because there are few sources of moisture in the middle of a large continent, and the air is too cold to absorb what moisture there is. Nearly all the air masses passing over the Plains are dry. Moist air from the Gulf of Mexico becomes steadily drier as it moves northward over the Great Plains. The winds from the Pacific Ocean are warmed as they descend the eastern side of the Rocky Mountains, thus picking up moisture instead of dropping it.

As the land cools in winter, cold air "sits" heavily over the Plains, and a high-pressure system of bright sunny weather, with little or no moisture, develops. In an effort to equalize pressure, sooner or later winds flow outward towards surrounding low-pressure areas. In summer, heated land produces a low-pressure system and outside air is drawn in. While relatively moist, this air brings only light precipitation to the Plains. Luckily, it comes during the

This landscape near Drumheller, Alberta, is another prairie scene. Why is it so different from the prairie landscape shown two pages earlier?

Sandra Tomkins

Extract from the Lumsden, Saskatchewan, sheet (72-1/10, Edition 2 MCE, Series A 742) of the National Topographic System. Scale 1:50,000. Courtesy Surveys and Mapping Branch, Department of Energy, Mines, and Resources, Ottawa.

The Great Plains

French and English trader-explorers have left us accounts of their travels on the Plains in the late seventeenth and early eighteenth centuries. Although born and raised in the much gentler environments of France and England, they had become accustomed to the rugged terrain and harsh climate of the northern forestlands. Suddenly, they broke through into a totally unfamiliar environment. It bewildered and frightened them. They called it "barren," to describe the lack of trees rather than to denote a lifeless wasteland.

Anthony Henday of the Hudson's Bay Company was one of the first Europeans to cross the Plains. In 1754, he was sent westward to persuade more Indians to bring fur pelts to the Bay. After travelling southwest for forty-five days through the familiar Shield landscape, Henday learned from Indian contacts that he was "on the Confines of the dry inland country." From mid-July to late October, Henday moved steadily westward through the Plains. The vast, apparently endless extent of the prairies overwhelmed him. Again and again he noted in his diary: "We are still in the Muscuty plains."

11. Sunday.   Travelled 11 miles S.W. by W. Level lands, short grass; no woods; and no water but what is salt.
12. Monday.   Travelled 7 Miles W.S.W. Level land, with small black Cherry trees, yielding plenty of fruit. Nothing but salt lakes.
13. Tuesday. Travelled 7 Miles W.S.W. Level land, short grass, Dry-woods, and several salt-water lakes. We are now entering Muscuty plains, and shall soon see plenty of Buffalo, and the Archithinue [Blackfeet] Indians hunting them on Horse-back. ...
19. Monday.   Travelled 10 Miles W.S.W. in Muscuty plains; fine land, no woods; several salt-water lakes; have passed but 4 places of fresh water, these five days past.

Study 3

Anthony Henday journeyed through country similar to that represented in the map on pages 18 and 19.
1.   How does the map indicate that the land surface of the Plains is generally very level? How is minor unevenness of the surface indicated?
2.   Draw a section, or calculate the gradient, of the hill down to the Qu'Appelle River. Comment on the width of the valley floor and on the size of the Qu'Appelle. Henday must have crossed several such valleys. Why then did the land *appear* so flat to him?
3.   Henday travelled in August. Does the map indicate a shortage of fresh water in that month?
4.   Is this part of the Plains treeless? Why did the explorers and early settlers emphasize the "barren" appearance of the Plains?

Flat and monotonous?

The Great Plains of North America are often thought of as huge expanses of flat land, clearly edged by mountainous areas. There are, in fact, marked differences in the local **topography** or surface features.

Flattest of all are those areas that were once covered by post-glacial lakes. North of the morainic hills, water backed up over large sections of the Plains to form huge glacial lakes – Lake Agassiz, for example.

These then drained away very, very slowly, leaving behind **lacustrine plains.** However, when the ice retreated, it left behind rock material ranging from boulders to finely-ground particles. This glacial drift or **till** forms much of the surface **mantle** of the Plains. Streams and rivers flowing eastward from the western mountains dumped loads of sand, silt, and gravel. Local winds picked up fine particles of these materials and deposited them as sand dunes and **loess** (fine-textured earth) plains. The overlay of loess on glacial till has developed excellent soils. All these plains are very recent, geologically speaking, little disturbed by earth movements and erosion.

However, the thick layers of horizontal, sedimentary rocks, which underlie most of this region, have been tilted very gently westward. Ancient rivers eroded the softer rock in these **strata,** producing a series of east-facing **scarp-slopes.** The most prominent scarp-slopes in the Canadian section of the Plains are the Manitoba Escarpment and the Missouri Coteau. They divide the region into three distinct levels: the Mani-

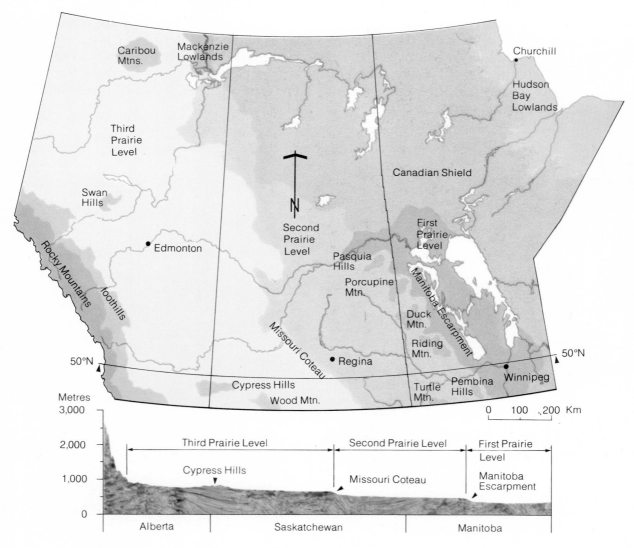

RELIEF AND ELEVATION OF PRAIRIE PROVINCES

toba Lowland, or First Prairie Level; the Second Prairie Level; and the High Plains, or Third Prairie Level. Riding Mountain on the Manitoba Escarpment rises as much as 300 metres above the level expanse of plain to the east. Most of the topmost layer of these sedimentary beds was probably removed by the erosive power of rivers that no longer exist. Wood Mountain, Turtle Mountain, and the Cypress Hills, which rise from less than 100 to almost 600 metres above the general level of the Plains, were likely formed in this manner. However, in most districts even the scarp faces are now crumbled and poorly defined.

Most surface deposits on the Plains are easily eroded. Rivers flow through them in **entrenched** (deeply cut) **valleys.** Driving across the Plains, you often find that the seemingly endless, level, straight highway suddenly dips to plunge down a steep hill,

only to climb up again once a river has been crossed. Some valleys are those of major waterways, such as the North and South Saskatchewan rivers. Many are swampfloored, with only small rivers. All were carved out of the earth by enormous numbers of meltwater streams and rivers at the end of the last ice age. The tiny watercourses in huge valleys are appropriately known as **misfit streams.**

Local variations in the generally level nature of the Plains are greatly valued for recreational purposes — shady, wooded areas, swimming places, ski slopes, and so on. However, the Plains image of billiard-table flatness is sometimes justified. The landscape of the lacustrine plains is so level that in clear weather you can see for miles in any direction. Many a person has likened the experience to that of being in the middle of an ocean.

This view of part of the Manitoba Escarpment shows that the landscape of the Plains is by no means flat and featureless.

Rosy visions and harsh realities

Word of the Plains filtered back to eastern Canada and, in time, was vigorously promoted in the overcrowded countries of late nineteenth- and early twentieth-century Europe. "Acres of level land!" "Deep, fertile soil!" Obviously, land that supported luxuriant natural grasses would be ideal for raising wheat and other cultivated grasses. Livestock would thrive in the environment that was the natural home of mighty herds of bison. Above all, there was more than enough space for everyone, and land was available free to any family willing to plough 160 acres of it. Thousands of immigrants, attracted by the promise of rich soil and abundant pasture, spread out over the Plains.

Why then did some colonists, disillusioned and embittered, leave this land of promise after a season or two? Why did those who persisted — and finally prospered — tell grim stories of their struggle to survive?

Most of their troubles were caused by the weather. The Canadian Prairies* experience some of the most extreme temperatures on earth. Regina has a record high of 43°C, and Prince Albert a record low of −57°C.

In the heart of a great continent the land heats and cools quickly. Furthermore, skies are often clear for weeks on end, and heat radiates freely. Winter days are short in these northerly latitudes, and the little heat that builds up during the day escapes rapidly during the long hours of darkness.

*Strictly speaking, a prairie is a treeless plain. But Canadians have acquired the habit of using the term "Prairies" to refer to the entire southern sections of Manitoba, Saskatchewan, and Alberta.

Temperatures below −18°C are common, and the coldest spot in Canada is said to be the corner of Portage Avenue and Main Street in Winnipeg — the temperature about −35°C, the wind blowing about 65 km/h, and not a bus or cab in sight. **Diurnal** (twenty-four-hour) averages in winter are much lower than in the Lowlands.

Average summer temperatures, however, run only about 3° lower than those in the Lowlands. Summer days are usually very hot indeed, because the sun's heat radiates freely through the long daylight hours. But the rapid escape of heat during the night results in lower average diurnal temperatures.

The general pattern is one of long, cold winters and short, hot summers. However, within the general pattern of this large region there are strange and intriguing oddities, for example, the average winter temperatures of Winnipeg, Calgary, and Edmonton. The strip of land along the foothills of the Rocky Mountains is greatly influenced by a local wind known as the Chinook, an Indian word for "Snow Eater." As this wind descends from the Rockies and rolls down onto the Plains, it is subject to continual pressure. This raises its temperature so much that, within a few hours, the warmth of a Chinook can clear away several metres of snow. (In summer, this same wind produces dusty, dry, choking conditions.) Thus, amazingly, Winnipeg has a winter average of −18°C, while that of Calgary, 113 kilometres north, is −10°C and that of Edmonton, 322 kilometres north, is −14°C.

If the climagraph for Winnipeg makes you think that precipitation is generally low on the Plains, you are absolutely right. In fact, Winnipeg is one of the more favored

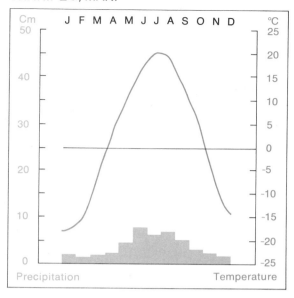

areas. Calgary receives an annual average of only 43 centimetres, Saskatoon, about 33 centimetres. Despite the popular image of snow-swept prairie, most locations actually receive less snow than do the Great Lakes-St. Lawrence Lowlands. This is because there are few sources of moisture in the middle of a large continent, and the air is too cold to absorb what moisture there is. Nearly all the air masses passing over the Plains are dry. Moist air from the Gulf of Mexico becomes steadily drier as it moves northward over the Great Plains. The winds from the Pacific Ocean are warmed as they descend the eastern side of the Rocky Mountains, thus picking up moisture instead of dropping it.

As the land cools in winter, cold air "sits" heavily over the Plains, and a high-pressure system of bright sunny weather, with little or no moisture, develops. In an effort to equalize pressure, sooner or later winds flow outward towards surrounding low-pressure areas. In summer, heated land produces a low-pressure system and outside air is drawn in. While relatively moist, this air brings only light precipitation to the Plains. Luckily, it comes during the

This landscape near Drumheller, Alberta, is another prairie scene. Why is it so different from the prairie landscape shown two pages earlier?

Sandra Tomkins

growing season, when it is most needed. Averaged out over many years, the Plains receive between 25 and 50 centimetres of precipitation annually. But this is a long-term *average*. Year-to-year conditions can be very different. Some years are so wet that crops rot in the ground; others are so dry that wheat can be harvested with a lawnmower! What is more, precipitation can come in the form of damaging hailstorms or thundershowers. There is seldom as much precipitation as the Prairie farmer would like, and it is *never* a reliable and even source of supply.

This precipitation pattern has greatly influenced the development of vegetation and soils.

Around the edge of the Plains to the west, north, and east is a huge horseshoe of black earth, **chernozem.** Here, precipitation is sufficient to produce a natural vegetation of scattered groves of small trees, mainly aspen and elm. This is where the much-publicized long grasses grew in abundance. Grasses and their roots, decaying animal remains, and countless microorganisms produced a rich, deep humus layer high in organic content. The light rainfall percolated slowly through the thick grasses and tangled mat of roots, so leaching was well-nigh non-existent. Thus was developed some of the richest soil in the world. Inside this outer horseshoe, precipitation lessens, the humus is not as deep, and the result is a soil color that is chestnut and brown, rather than black. Here, the original grass was neither as long nor as thick. However, the soil is still rich. In fact, this inner horseshoe is the famous Canadian wheat belt.

Inside this inner horseshoe is a roughly triangle-shaped stretch of land where precipitation is quite light and most unreliable. Here, the natural grass was short, very often clumpy with bare patches in between. This is the zone of brown soils, a region of marginal farming. These soils are still quite fertile, but rather shallow. Rains are sparse and uncertain. Overgrazing and deep ploughing, combined with prolonged droughts, turned much of this land into a dustbowl. Where it can be irrigated, however, the soil produces in abundance.

The Western Cordillera

The valley of the Fraser River, British Columbia. What obstacles to railway construction (and maintenance) can you spot in this photograph?

The more or less level surface of the Plains has long been a great advantage to surveyors and engineers. In the summer of 1882, during the construction of the Canadian Pacific Railway, Van Horne's trackmen once laid a record-breaking 5 miles of line between dawn and dusk. That same day, in the Fraser River canyon, Andrew Onderdonk's work gangs, struggling with almost insurmountable natural obstacles, advanced only *6 feet*. Indeed, for months on end, the men in the Cordillera section were unable to lay any track at all. Steep cliff walls, described by the fur-trading Simon Fraser as places "where no human being should venture," rose high and sheer from the water's edge. No less than twenty-seven rock tunnels had to be blasted through their mass. It took eighteen months to drill just four of these. Furthermore, the flanks of the mountains hemming in the Fraser are grooved by deep canyons, which necessitated the construction of six hundred bridges and trestles.

About two hundred miles northeast of Onderdonk's weary work crews, a hardbitten, hard-swearing surveyor began climbing eastward through the Rockies. The "Railway Pathfinder," Major A. B. Rogers, was struggling back to civilization with the epic news of his discovery of Eagle Pass. For years, surveyors had been searching for just such a breach in the frustrating barrier of the Selkirk Mountains.

"Now ain't that thar a pretty sight!"

The Cordillera was a massive engineering obstacle to Onderdonk's men, but what a magnificently beautiful obstacle it is! Tourists who travel the transportation lines laid down by the sweat and struggle of engineers and surveyors will agree with Major Roger's favorite comment: "Hell's bells, now ain't that thar a pretty sight!" Sparkling blue-and-green lakes mirror towering rock crags and tumbling glaciers. Shady woodland paths, alpine meadows, and sun-warmed lake beaches beckon holiday-makers. Where the mountains meet the sea, there are majestic fiords, all quiet and still, and sweeping panoramas of cliff, cove, and pounding ocean breakers.

The Cordillera is what geographers term a region of **high relief**. Summits tower 3000 metres or more above valley floors. This complex, jumbled mass of mountains and valleys, plateaus and canyons is of recent origin, geologically speaking. In a period of intense disturbance of the earth's crust, rock formations were crumpled, slowly pushed upward, folded, and fractured. The Rocky Mountain Trench, a **fault valley** about 1500 kilometres long that separates the Canadian Rockies from the other western ranges, is an awesome example of Nature's handiwork. There are many spectacular peaks in the Rockies, notably Mount Robson at 3954 metres and Mount Assiniboine at 3618 metres.

Between the Selkirks and the coastal ranges is a region of plateaus and ranges. Summits are much less jagged and seldom exceed 1200 metres. There are no glaciers here today, but the area was at one time subjected to alpine glaciation. The beds of major lakes, Okanagan, for example, were created by the gouging action of glaciers. And the several plateaus here have been deeply dissected by the vigorous down-cutting action of glacier-fed rivers. Constructing a roadbed in this country is almost as difficult as in the mountains.

The coastal ranges consist of some of the most magnificent, uplifted intrusions on earth. They boast even higher peaks than the Rockies. Mount Waddington is 4042 metres, and Mount Logan, at 6050 metres, is the highest peak in Canada.

Between the fiord coast and the Island Arc of mountains lies the Inner Passage of island-dotted waters.

Mountainous areas are quickly attacked by the various agents of erosion. Icefields and their offshoots, glaciers, are eternally at work grinding pieces off underlying mountainsides in the form of boulders, stones, and gravel. Moisture seeping into cracks and crannies alternately freezes and thaws; contractions and expansions gradually shatter rock into jagged fragments. Wind, rain, and gravity then carry these as **talus** or **scree** to lower levels. The "arm-chair hollows" of **cirques,** the knife-edged ridges of **arêtes,** and the sharp-pointed **horned peaks** are formed when rocks, torn out of hollows by glacial ice, act as chisels to gouge these hollows even more deeply. Glaciers moving down into valleys scour out great U-shaped troughs. These tongues of ice are now melting back faster than they are being formed. Thus, spectacular mounds of morainic material are being dumped along the forward edges of glaciers and along their flanks, too.

In regions of high relief, vegetation and soil zones are very clearly determined by different altitudes. If you were to climb a mountain, you would progress from thick forest through alpine meadows to everlasting snow and ice.

The S.S. Queen of Prince Rupert *in the Grenville Channel (near Prince Rupert), British Columbia. A fiord coastline like this offers several advantages to residents of the province. How many can you think of?*

Study 4

The photograph on page 28 was taken from the Banff-Jasper highway near Sunwapta Lake, looking directly south up the tongue of the Athabasca Glacier to the mountains beyond. Try to match the map, the photograph, and the diagram by identifying common points.

1. What is the elevation of the peaks shown?
2. How do the contours on the map indicate the cirques? Why is a special type of contour needed to indicate the arêtes between the cirques?
3. Note that the map uses special shading to indicate the lateral moraine on the east side of the Athabasca Glacier. Locate this feature in the photograph. Of what type of material is it formed? Account for the presence of a large spread of similar material on the flat ground between the tongue of the glacier and the highway.
4. Why is the water of Sunwapta Lake and the stream that drains it milky colored?
5. Draw a section across the Sunwapta Valley west of Wilcox. Describe and account for the shape of the valley.
6. The thin orange line indicates a road that used to lead to the departure point for snowmobile tours on to the tongue of the Athabasca Glacier. Since the ice is retreating rapidly and the tongue has become too steep, the departure point is now located about 1.6 kilometres south, high on top of the moraine. Describe a trip down the moraine and out onto the glacier, noting and explaining the features you would see.

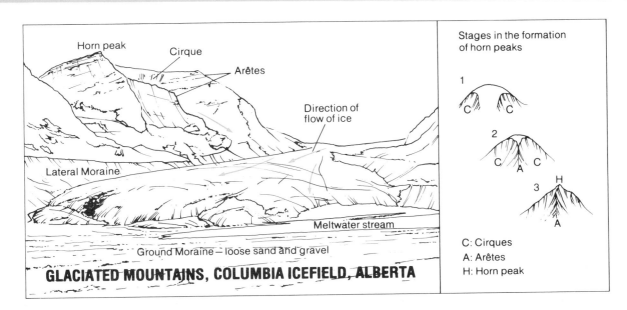

GLACIATED MOUNTAINS, COLUMBIA ICEFIELD, ALBERTA

Extract from the Columbia Icefield, Alberta — British Columbia, sheet (83 C/3, Edition I MCE, Series A 741) of the National Topographic System. Scale 1:50,000. Courtesy Surveys and Mapping Branch, Department of Energy, Mines, and Resources, Ottawa.

The Pacific Coast

The Pacific coast is the only section of Canada that enjoys *average* winter temperatures above freezing. All summer long the Pacific Ocean gathers in the sun's heat, which is released slowly during the winter and carried landward by the prevailing Westerlies. Thus there is little difference in average winter temperatures along the entire British Columbia coast. Prince Rupert has winter averages only 3° lower than those of Clayoquot, about 650 kilometres to the south. (Compare this with a difference of 14° between Kapuskasing and Toronto, which are about the same distance apart.) In summer, the tempering effect of Pacific waters, cooler than the sun-warmed land, is likewise brought shorewards. The tremendous moderating influence of the Pacific Ocean (and the prevailing westerlies) makes **temperature ranges*** very small: 15° at Vancouver, 8° at Clayoquot

*The difference between the *average* temperatures for the highest and lowest months

CLAYOQUOT, B.C.

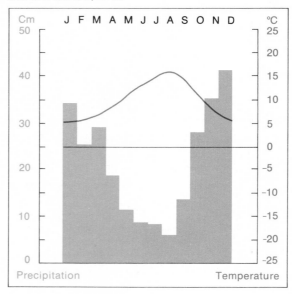

(compared with 39° at Winnipeg, 26° at Toronto, and 36° at Kapuskasing). In addition, the Cordillera acts as a great barrier to the waves of cold air that are brought

The semi-arid landscape of the Okanagan Valley in south-central British Columbia.

south by polar Easterlies. However, once every fourteen years or so, the British Columbia coast does experience the shock of a very cold snap — witness the record low for Vancouver of −18°C.

Although temperatures are very similar throughout the coastal area, there is considerable variation in precipitation. Exposed parts of the coast experience the heaviest rainfall in Canada — Clayoquot 264 centimetres, Prince Rupert 239 centimetres. However, sheltered behind high mountains, Victoria receives one-third of that amount — 69 centimetres. There is also tremendous local variation. Vancouver International Airport, in the Fraser delta to the south of the city, receives only 104 centimetres, but the mountainsides of the north-shore suburbs receive slightly more than 200 centimetres — with considerable snow at higher elevations.

With Westerlies blowing across the Pacific and spilling themselves against the Coast Range all year long, you might ex-

pect even precipitation throughout the year. Not so. All places on the B.C. coast have much more rain in winter than in summer. In fact, anything from four to six times more. Victoria experiences a near drought in July and August, with less than 3 centimetres of rain, and Vancouver is not much better. Why? The dominant climatic control is not the ocean, the winds, or the mountains. It is a series of intense low-pressure cells that are generated all winter long in the vicinity of the Aleutian Islands far to the northwest. Like a giant vacuum cleaner drawing in great masses of moisture, each cell swoops down upon the coast, is carried against the mountains by the Westerlies, and dumps its moisture. In summer, these low-pressure cells are largely dispersed, so there is little rain.

The coastal area has the longest growing season in Canada. Winters are mild, and residents are only too eager to tell you that it was warm enough on Christmas Day for a game of golf or a ride in a sailboat. (They

Mountains next a coastline make for considerable variations in climate. Thus, in the month of December, Vancouverites can sail or ski without leaving the metropolitan area.

Brian Kent, *The Vancouver Sun*

are somewhat less eager to admit that it was probably wet enough for a raincoat and an umbrella.) Summers are pleasantly cool in comparison with the heat of the interior. This combination of plentiful moisture and moderate temperatures is exceptionally good for plant growth. Vancouverites take pride in having flowers blooming in their gardens every month of the year. (Are they as pleased about not having to put the garden tools away for the winter?) More significantly, this environment supports a forest growth of almost tropical luxuriance. Douglas fir, red cedar, and western hemlock soar as much as 100 metres upward, and trunk diameters of 3 metres are not exceptional. Mosses, ferns, shrubs, and vines complete the jungle-like impression. Growth of such proportions is, of course, confined to the coastal strip. Inland, trees gradually become smaller. At the summit of the Coast Range, this forest peters out altogether.

The interior plateaus are covered by a much more open vegetation, because temperatures are much more extreme and precipitation is low. In appearance, the pla-

teau country varies from true desert, where sagebrush, rough grasses, and occasional cacti are the only plant life, to stands of scattered Ponderosa pine and coarse grasses. To the north, where moisture increases, mixed conifers and richer grasses replace the pines.

PENTICTON, B.C.

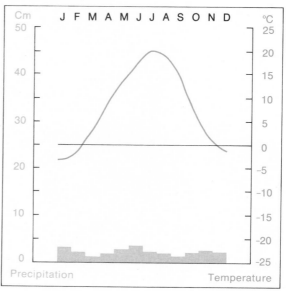

32

D. Scrimger

Desert-like conditions near Kamloops in the British Columbia interior contrast strongly with the jungle-like vegetation of the west coast shown on the opposite page.

Appalachian Canada

Like the Western Cordillera, Appalachian Canada is also a region of mountain structure. Here, too, are complex geological formations, huge igneous outpourings, a highly indented coastline, and much evidence of glaciation. Yet the landscape is very, very different. The highest elevation anywhere in the region is Mont Jacques Cartier (1268 metres), about 650 kilometres northeast of Montreal. Rarely does the rocky coast rise more than a few hundred metres above the indented shoreline. As well as rock formations thrust up as mountain ridges, there are extensive areas of sedimentary rocks occupying sizable basins between the zones of mountain structure. The key to the different appearances of the two regions is in their geological history.

The earth's history is an alternation of long periods of relative peace and quiet, when sedimentary deposits were laid down on the floors of ancient seas or lakes, and shorter periods of intense activity, when rock formations were broken up and highly compressed. The Western Cordillera was formed in the most recent of these periods of **orogenesis,*** a few million years back. The Appalachian system, however, was created somewhere between 200 million and 350 million years ago. After hundreds of millions of years, the forces of erosion — wind and water — have made considerable progress in levelling the landscape of the Appalachian region. Most of the mountain

*From the Greek *oros*, mountain, and *genesis*, creation

Countryside near Stanstead, Quebec. How does this landscape compare with that of the Rocky Mountains?

How does this photograph help to explain why Prince Edward Island has a greater proportion of its land in agricultural use than any other province?

Quidi Vidi is a fishing outport near St. John's, Newfoundland. This fiord-like inlet provides easy access to and from the sea, plus a shelter from storms.

34

structures have been ground down to a few hundred metres above sea level. Outlines are therefore much rounder and smoother than those in the Cordillera. Furthermore, there has been time for newer sediments to accumulate in the shallow basins between zones of uplift. Thus were born the lowlands of Prince Edward Island and eastern New Brunswick with their characteristic red rock and soil formations. Thus was born the Annapolis Valley of Nova Scotia.

Like the Great Lakes-St. Lawrence Lowlands and the Great Plains, the Appalachian region was once on the edge of the great Pleistocene ice sheet. Thus it received large quantities of glacial drift. Some of the soils of the glacial sands and clays offer better agricultural possibilities than those of granitic uplands. In other places, glacial deposits have disturbed the natural drainage pattern, which explains many of Atlantic Canada's swampy areas.

Where mountain structures meet the sea, the Atlantic coast is characterized by numerous coves and inlets. Like the famous fiord coast of British Columbia, Canada's eastern shore was "drowned" when arms of the sea invaded valleys depressed by the great weight of the ice. Submerged extensions of the land area form a **continental shelf.** In the shallow waters covering this formation are the greatest cod-fishing grounds in the world — especially where material dumped by melting icebergs from Greenland has been deposited on the sea floor to form the famous **banks.**

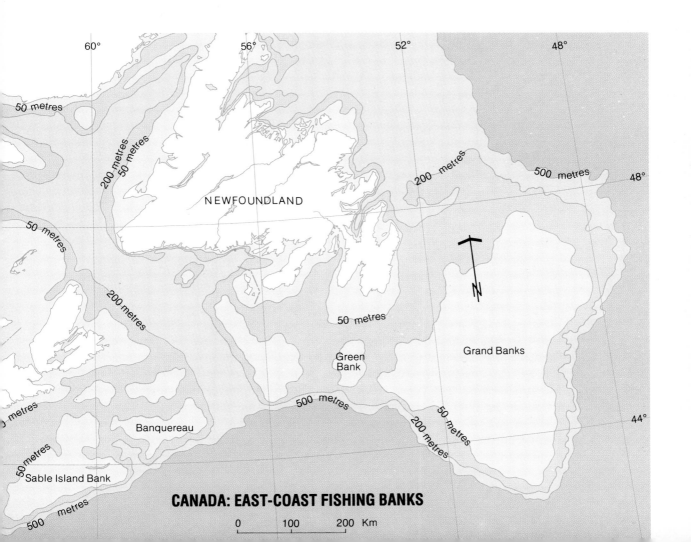

CANADA: EAST-COAST FISHING BANKS

0   100   200 Km

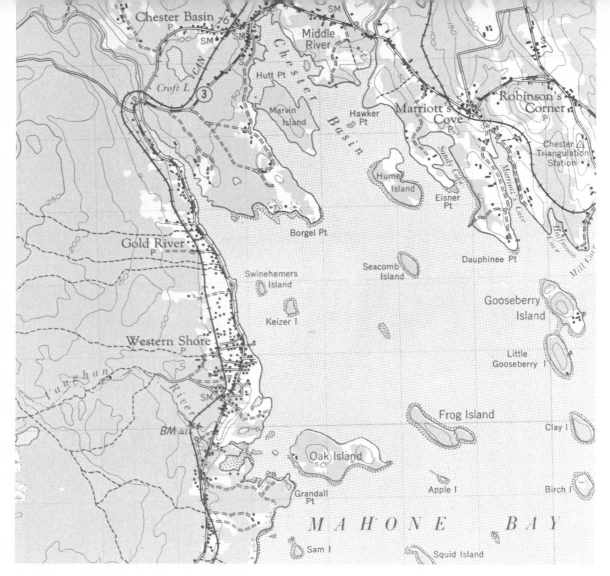

Extract from the Chester, Nova Scotia, sheet (21A/9 W, Edition I MCE, Series A 791) of the National Topographic System. Scale 1:50,000. Courtesy Surveys and Mapping Branch, Department of Energy, Mines, and Resources, Ottawa.

Study 5

1. How do the elevations, relief, and gradients compare with those of the Rocky Mountains shown on page 28?
2. The Chester area is noted for its drumlins. (You may wish to refer back to material on page 15.) Locate contour lines near Chester that indicate the presence of drumlins. What other evidences of glaciation do you see on the land surface?
3. How can you tell that this coast has been drowned?
4. Suggest why the slopes of this long-settled area are thickly forested, not farmed.

Winter gales and summer fogs

As on Canada's west coast, the combination of maritime and mountain influences makes for a great deal of variety in local climates. However, the winds that so greatly influence climate in these latitudes are westerly; they arrive in the Atlantic region from the interior of the continent. Thus the moderating influence of the sea is minimized, and the climate can generally be classified as extreme, or continental, in character. Still, temperature conditions are somewhat gentler than those closer to the heart of the great continental air mass. Halifax, for example, has a temperature range of 23°, compared with one of 36° at Kapuskasing, Ontario.

Harbors and ports on the Atlantic coast remain open all year, thanks to these mild conditions. But the prevailing drift of air from the land to the ocean also helps increase summer temperatures. This results in frequent summer fogs along the coast, created when warm air from the interior is chilled by cold coastal waters. June, July, and August are the foggiest months. Actually, the constant mixing of the warm air over the North Atlantic Drift and the cold air over the Labrador Current makes sea fog a hazard at all seasons. The meeting of these strongly contrasting air masses creates considerable turbulence and frequent precipitation. Atlantic Canada is noted for winter gales and summer breezes, for sudden heavy snowfalls and equally rapid thaws.

Boreal forest predominates on upland areas. There is a mixed forest cover on lowlands and in Nova Scotia, where conditions are generally more moderate. Under these climatic and vegetative conditions, soils tend to be podzolic and acidic.

ARCTIC BAY, NWT

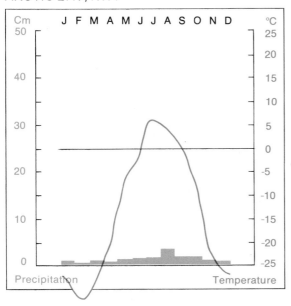

Frozen, limitless expanses, home to the Eskimo, icy grave for many an explorer who sought the Northwest Passage to the riches of Cathay — these images represent for most people the "Arcticscape." A few scholars and scientists have endured the rigors of the Arctic to pursue research on climate, ice conditions, and native cultures. Prospectors, geologists, and oilmen have searched — and still search — for mineral deposits beneath the Arctic's muskeg and

37

permafrost. Military personnel have moved in to construct and maintain defence installations. Still, very, very few people have any detailed or first-hand knowledge of the far north.

Farley Mowat has described the Canadian Arctic as "a land of undulating plains that have no horizon." Much of this landscape of ice and snow is actually part of the Canadian Shield. Unless you were to examine and identify its rock outcrops, you would never suspect the connection. Arctic Canada is practically treeless. With a permanently frozen subsoil and the harshest of climatic conditions, this northernmost section of the Shield presents the distinctive vegetation of stunted grasses and shrubs called **tundra.**

Virtually all of this portion of the Shield was once covered by sedimentary rocks, principally limestone. Millions of years of erosion have worn these down. Some layers still remain in such basins as Hudson Bay and Foxe Basin, where they form lowlands or lie beneath shallow waters. In the western Arctic, deep, wide sea channels have carved limestone plains and plateaus into a jumbled jigsaw of islands and peninsulas. (These channels are thought to be drowned river valleys that were deepened by ice erosion.) This part of the Arctic was near one edge of the Pleistocene ice sheet and is therefore littered with glacial drift — drumlins, glacial lakes, and massive morainic deposits. Raised beachlines, together with broad clay and sand plains, indicate that the region was submerged in post-glacial times but is still slowly rising — despite the great length of time since the removal of the enormous weight of the ice. Victoria Island is a striking example of this type of terrain.

The stark landscape of the Arctic. This is the area European explorers named the "Barren Lands."

Information Canada Photothèque

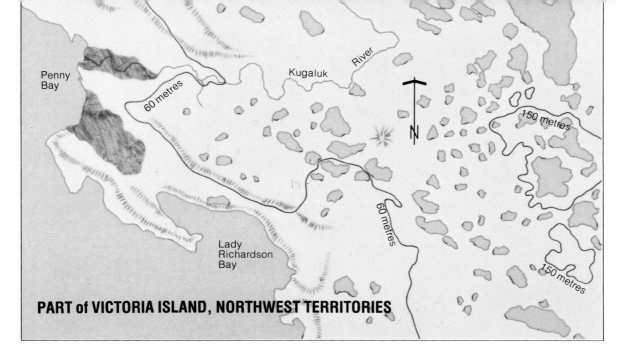

PART of VICTORIA ISLAND, NORTHWEST TERRITORIES

Lakes, pools, and ponds connected by numerous small streams

Contours

Ancient shore line and terraces

Pingo

Sand

0   2   4 Km

Study 6

1. Imagine you are going from the beach on Lady Richardson Bay to the high ground to the east.
    (a) Is the climb very steep, moderately steep, or gradual?
    (b) How does the map indicate that this area has a very uneven surface?
    (c) Account for the presence of so much surface water.
    (d) What evidence is there that this area is gradually emerging from the sea?

2. **Pingos** are cone-shaped mounds that rise 30 metres or more. They consist of a massive core of solid ice, protected by a thick covering of organic matter. Pingos are thought to be remnants of unfrozen lake beds which, when the insulating effect of the ice sheet was removed, became surrounded by permanently frozen ground. The freezing remnant expanded and could only move upward, thus forming a pingo.

    Do you think this area may develop other pingos? Explain your answer.

Winter nights in polar regions are very long indeed. Locations in high latitudes receive but a few hours of daylight in midwinter. At the North Pole, the sun disappears altogether for about three months. Thus there is little warming sunshine to moderate the low winter temperatures of the far north. Wind, its force unbroken by trees, intensifies the cold. In the climagraph for Arctic Bay, just look at the chilly difference between a January and a July day!

By contrast, summer is a balmy season of perpetual daylight. Averaged over a long period, July temperatures do not exceed 6 or 7°C, although recordings in the low forties are by no means uncommon. Yet the generally low temperatures are partially offset by the long hours of daylight. This is the season when the tundra blossoms with brightly-colored flowers and resounds with the cries of birds and small mammals — and the baleful buzzings of mosquitoes and blackflies. Only about two months are frost-free, however, and the brief summer interlude is once again succeeded by the long, frigid winter.

In the Arctic, only a surface layer of ground thaws during summer. A few decimetres — sometimes only centimetres — below ground, everything remains frozen solid. This **permafrost** prevents drainage, and the excessively wet soil tends to slide off even moderate slopes. The Arctic's hummocky terrain is pitted with boggy hollows and shallow pools. Grim outcrops of bare rock accentuate the bleakness of the landscape.

Despite the water, ice, and snow that are such prominent features of the far north, this is a region of very low precipitation. The Arctic receives barely as much precipitation as parts of the drought-prone prairies. In fact, the Arctic is a frozen desert.

The distinctive tundra vegetation is determined by three factors. Lack of warmth discourages organic processes of soil formation. Permafrost keeps the surface soil wet and badly drained. Above all, there is an extremely short growing season. Thus the tundra can only support the hardiest of small plants — coarse grasses and bushes, various lichens and mosses — all of which have tiny leaves and shallow root systems suited to the rigors of this environment.

*   *   *

Canada is a land of extreme variations. Its climates range from blinding desert sunshine to drenching fogs. Its landscapes have some of the most jagged peaks and some of the flattest places in the world. There are ocean-like lakes and tiny tundra pools. There are tens of thousands of square kilometres of naked rock and vast areas of rich soil. Vegetation includes hundreds of species, from gigantic Douglas firs to dwarf junipers, from showy orchids to shy mosses. The variety of size and species of fauna ranges from bowhead whales to prairie gophers. In a word — diversity.

Study and Research

The Shield

Chicoutimi

	J	F	M	A	M	J	J	A	S	O	N	D	Annual
Temp.	−14.7	−12.8	−5.6	2.9	9.4	15.6	18.9	17.7	12.9	6.6	−1.1	−10.9	3.2°C
Precip.	5.18	4.83	4.37	5.36	6.86	10.82	11.30	9.19	10.16	8.00	6.88	6.07	89.02 cm

Frost-free period, May 21-September 30: 132 days

Kapuskasing

	J	F	M	A	M	J	J	A	S	O	N	D	Annual
Temp.	−17.8	−15.4	−9.3	0.2	7.9	14.3	17.3	16.0	10.5	4.6	−4.9	−14.0	0.8°C
Precip.	5.49	4.47	5.41	5.28	7.98	9.45	8.51	8.71	8.99	7.19	8.31	6.02	85.81 cm

Frost-free period, June 10-September 5: 87 days

Schefferville

	J	F	M	A	M	J	J	A	S	O	N	D	Annual
Temp.	−23.0	−20.6	−14.2	−6.2	1.6	9.2	12.8	10.9	5.7	−0.9	−9.3	−18.4	−4.4°C
Precip.	4.65	4.14	4.11	4.09	4.04	9.04	9.19	9.53	8.00	7.37	6.48	4.04	74.68 cm

Frost-free period, June 19-September 2: 75 days

The Great Lakes-St. Lawrence Lowlands

Quebec City

	J	F	M	A	M	J	J	A	S	O	N	D	Annual
Temp.	−10.6	−9.7	−3.7	3.9	11.3	16.9	19.9	18.8	13.9	7.7	0.3	−8.1	5.1°C
Precip.	8.94	7.19	7.70	8.13	8.74	12.19	11.91	11.79	10.95	9.22	9.78	9.25	115.79 cm

Frost-free period, May 7-October 11: 157 days

Montreal

	J	F	M	A	M	J	J	A	S	O	N	D	Annual
Temp.	−9.7	−8.8	−2.7	5.7	13.0	18.6	21.3	20.4	15.6	9.0	2.0	−6.6	6.5°C
Precip.	8.28	8.08	7.80	7.24	7.21	8.48	8.92	7.67	8.15	7.80	8.46	8.92	97.01 cm

Frost-free period, April 25-October 21: 179 days

Toronto

	J	F	M	A	M	J	J	A	S	O	N	D	Annual
Temp.	−3.9	−3.8	0.2	7.0	13.2	19.0	21.9	21.1	16.6	10.6	4.3	−1.8	8.7°C
Precip.	6.65	5.89	6.73	6.63	7.01	6.32	7.37	6.07	6.50	6.02	6.30	6.12	77.61 cm

Frost-free period, April 23-October 27: 187 days

St. Catharines

	J	F	M	A	M	J	J	A	S	O	N	D	Annual
Temp.	−2.9	−3.2	0.7	7.3	13.4	19.3	22.2	21.6	17.4	11.4	4.9	−1.2	9.2°C
Precip.	5.03	5.16	5.89	5.99	6.88	5.23	5.77	7.14	7.19	5.79	5.69	5.28	71.04 cm

Frost-free period, May 1-October 20: 172 days

The Great Plains

Edmonton

	J	F	M	A	M	J	J	A	S	O	N	D	Annual
Temp.	−14.1	−11.6	−5.5	4.2	11.2	14.3	17.3	15.6	10.8	5.1	−4.2	−10.4	2.7°C
Precip	2.41	1.96	2.11	2.79	4.65	8.00	8.48	6.48	3.43	2.29	2.24	2.51	47.35 cm

Frost-free period, May 21-September 16: 118 days

Saskatoon

	J	F	M	A	M	J	J	A	S	O	N	D	Annual
Temp.	−17.2	−15.4	−7.9	3.7	11.3	15.4	19.2	17.5	11.6	5.2	−5.7	−13.3	2.0°C
Precip.	1.88	1.85	1.65	2.36	3.40	5.18	5.13	4.78	3.35	1.73	2.06	1.83	35.20 cm

Frost-free period, May 25-September 15: 113 days

Calgary

	J	F	M	A	M	J	J	A	S	O	N	D	Annual
Temp.	−9.9	−8.8	−4.4	3.6	9.8	13.0	16.7	15.1	10.9	5.4	−2.2	−6.6	3.6°C
Precip.	1.73	1.98	2.57	3.45	5.16	8.76	5.84	5.92	3.48	2.26	1.60	1.55	44.30 cm

Frost-free period, May 27-September 11: 107 days

Regina

	J	F	M	A	M	J	J	A	S	O	N	D	Annual
Temp.	−16.9	−14.8	−8.1	3.4	11.2	15.3	19.3	17.8	11.9	5.1	−5.4	−12.3	2.2°C
Precip.	1.93	1.73	2.06	2.13	4.04	8.33	5.49	4.90	3.38	1.78	1.98	1.70	39.45 cm

Frost-free period, May 29-September 15: 109 days

Winnipeg

	J	F	M	A	M	J	J	A	S	O	N	D	Annual
Temp.	−17.7	−15.5	−7.9	3.3	11.3	16.5	20.2	18.9	12.8	6.2	−4.8	−12.9	2.5°C
Precip.	2.62	2.08	2.74	2.97	5.00	8.10	6.88	7.01	5.49	3.66	2.90	2.24	51.69 cm

Frost-free period, May 27-September 18: 114 days

The Western Cordillera (southern interior)

Kamloops

	J	F	M	A	M	J	J	A	S	O	N	D	Annual
Temp.	−5.9	−2.9	3.3	9.5	14.4	17.8	20.9	19.4	15.1	8.4	1.8	−2.2	8.3°C
Precip.	3.56	2.16	0.91	0.64	1.52	3.96	2.06	2.21	1.80	1.55	1.85	2.44	24.66 cm

Frost-free period, April 23-October 6: 166 days

Cranbrook

	J	F	M	A	M	J	J	A	S	O	N	D	Annual
Temp.	−9.2	−5.6	−0.3	6.2	11.0	14.2	18.0	16.8	12.2	5.9	−2.1	−5.5	5.1°C
Precip.	4.50	3.89	2.16	2.16	3.71	5.64	2.31	3.15	2.69	3.45	3.53	4.50	41.69 cm

Frost-free period, June 4-August 27: 84 days

Penticton

	J	F	M	A	M	J	J	A	S	O	N	D	Annual
Temp.	−2.6	−0.7	4.0	9.2	13.7	16.9	20.2	19.1	14.8	8.7	2.9	−0.1	8.8°C
Precip.	3.30	2.34	1.73	2.24	2.95	3.76	2.59	2.31	1.78	2.34	2.69	2.67	30.70 cm

Frost-free period, May 3-October 4: 154 days

The West Coast

Prince Rupert

	J	F	M	A	M	J	J	A	S	O	N	D	Annual
Temp.	1.8	2.4	3.8	6.3	9.5	11.7	13.4	13.9	12.1	8.7	5.2	2.8	7.6°C
Precip.	22.43	17.68	19.58	17.30	12.98	10.85	11.73	14.91	21.69	33.60	29.29	27.76	239.80 cm

Frost-free period, April 20-November 7: 201 days

Clayoquot

	J	F	M	A	M	J	J	A	S	O	N	D	Annual
Temp.	5.5	6.1	7.0	9.0	11.4	13.6	14.9	15.6	14.2	11.4	7.8	6.1	10.2°C
Precip.	34.39	25.53	29.13	18.97	11.66	8.94	8.81	6.38	13.94	28.47	35.76	42.11	264.09 cm

Frost-free period, March 24-November 20: 241 days

Victoria

	J	F	M	A	M	J	J	A	S	O	N	D	Annual
Temp.	4.1	5.2	6.8	9.6	12.3	14.1	15.6	15.6	14.2	11.0	7.2	5.6	10.1°C
Precip.	11.18	8.18	5.72	3.05	2.41	2.69	1.45	1.80	3.18	7.24	9.96	12.78	69.64 cm

Frost-free period, March 5-December 9: 279 days

Vancouver

	J	F	M	A	M	J	J	A	S	O	N	D	Annual
Temp.	2.9	4.1	6.2	9.1	12.8	15.8	17.7	17.6	14.3	10.2	6.2	4.2	10.1°C
Precip.	14.02	12.04	9.55	5.84	4.88	4.67	2.64	3.48	5.41	11.73	13.82	16.36	104.44 cm

Frost-free period, April 3-October 28: 208 days

The Atlantic Provinces

St. John's

	J	F	M	A	M	J	J	A	S	O	N	D	Annual
Temp.	−4.3	−4.6	−2.9	1.2	5.6	10.3	15.4	15.4	12.0	6.7	2.9	−1.6	4.7°C
Precip.	15.29	16.26	13.49	12.12	9.86	9.45	8.86	10.16	11.96	13.79	16.26	17.40	154.90 cm

Frost-free period, June 6-October 9: 125 days

Halifax

	J	F	M	A	M	J	J	A	S	O	N	D	Annual
Temp.	−3.3	−3.6	−0.1	4.8	9.9	14.4	18.5	18.8	15.5	10.3	5.3	−0.9	7.5°C
Precip.	14.05	11.86	11.25	11.23	10.87	9.37	9.37	9.55	11.71	11.99	14.30	12.60	138.15 cm

Frost-free period, May 2-October 28: 179 days

Fredericton

	J	F	M	A	M	J	J	A	S	O	N	D	Annual
Temp.	−9.2	−8.6	−2.8	4.3	10.8	15.8	19.2	18.3	13.8	7.8	1.4	−6.9	5.3°C
Precip.	9.93	8.26	8.13	8.81	8.46	9.60	8.86	8.10	9.30	9.86	11.02	9.27	109.60 cm

Frost-free period, May 19-September 26: 128 days

The North

Arctic Bay

	J	F	M	A	M	J	J	A	S	O	N	D	Annual
Temp.	−28.7	−32.9	−27.3	−19.9	−7.2	1.9	6.3	4.9	−1.1	−9.8	−21.2	−27.1	−13.5°C
Precip.	0.99	0.58	0.99	0.69	1.45	1.60	1.65	3.71	1.78	1.78	1.09	0.99	17.30 cm

Frost-free period, June 26-August 10: 45 days

Coppermine

	J	F	M	A	M	J	J	A	S	O	N	D	Annual
Temp.	−28.6	−30.1	−25.8	−17.2	−5.6	3.4	9.3	8.4	2.6	−6.9	−19.9	−26.3	−11.4°C
Precip.	1.24	0.79	1.32	1.04	1.17	2.03	3.40	4.37	2.79	2.59	1.52	1.14	23.40 cm

Frost-free period, June 27-August 20: 54 days

Whitehorse

	J	F	M	A	M	J	J	A	S	O	N	D	Annual
Temp.	−18.1	−14.1	−7.6	−0.2	7.5	12.6	14.2	12.4	7.9	0.7	−8.2	−15.1	−0.7°C
Precip.	1.78	1.42	1.50	1.09	1.27	2.69	3.45	3.66	2.49	1.85	2.31	2.01	25.52 cm

Frost-free period, June 5-August 31: 87 days

Yellowknife

	J	F	M	A	M	J	J	A	S	O	N	D	Annual
Temp.	−27.7	−25.9	−17.8	−7.9	4.1	11.8	15.9	14.1	7.2	−1.3	−13.8	−23.9	−5.4°C
Precip.	1.30	1.24	1.30	0.99	1.68	1.63	3.61	3.53	2.95	2.79	2.34	2.06	25.42 cm

Frost-free period, May 30-September 18: 111 days

To obtain a clear picture of the climate at each of these selected Canadian stations, note in particular the average temperatures for January and July, the annual temperature *range*, the *total* annual precipitation, and its distribution throughout the year.

1. Canadians have learned to adapt to seasonal conditions. How is this obvious with regard to clothing, housing, transportation?
2. Rule three columns in your notebook. Use the first to list those parts of Canada you think are the hottest, coldest, driest, wettest, most extreme, and snowiest. Use the second column to check your answers against the information supplied in the statistics. In the third, note down any information you can obtain from other sources — such as the *Canada Year Book* — about record temperatures and so on. How many surprises did you get?
3. The Shield is of major importance as a source of fresh water. How do the climate statistics help explain this fact? What other natural advantages does this region have as a water-storage area?
4. Compare the April-July temperature and precipitation figures for the Great Lakes-St. Lawrence Lowlands region with those recorded elsewhere. What are the climatic advantages for farmers in this region?

5. Describe and account for the temperature pattern in the five Plains cities.

   Although some of the average monthly temperatures resemble those for cities of the Lowlands and the Shield, the daily weather is often very different. What characteristics of Plains weather are not revealed by these temperature and precipitation statistics?

   How do you account for the fact that, although the monthly average temperature may only be about 15°C, daytime temperatures often exceed 30°C?

   Why is the precipitation pattern a constant source of worry to Prairie farmers?

6. Account for the marked differences between the weather patterns of Kamloops and Clayoquot, which are only about 400 kilometres apart.

7. What are the climatic advantages of the West Coast as an agricultural area?

8. Why are the climate statistics for Halifax and St. John's very similar? Why do the statistics for Fredericton show marked differences from those for Halifax?

   The average January temperature at Halifax is about half a Celsius degree lower than that for Toronto. Why? Why then can the former's port remain open to shipping all year?

9. How does precipitation for stations in the North compare with that for other Canadian regions? Why are water and mud major problems in the North?

10. Imagine you are a guide to a party of visitors to Canada. Explain to them which major regions will have snow for skiing in December. (For months with below-freezing temperatures, multiply rainfall figures by ten in order to get a clearer indication of depth of snow.) Which areas get the heaviest snowfalls?

11. Each station in these seven regions shows a similarity of climatic pattern. This is what makes a climatic region. However, what differences can you see within each region?

12. Select the station nearest your home. Do its statistics give an accurate picture of your weather? Why — or why not?

13. There are two desert areas in Canada. See if you can spot them from the statistics.

Chapter 2 Where we live: A land of cultural diversity

POPULATION DENSITY

Dense
Moderate
Light
Sparse

Although Canada has a gigantic land area, its population is positively tiny. Great Britain, with about one-fortieth of Canada's land mass, has almost two and a half times as many people. The People's Republic of China, whose size is only 260 000 square kilometres less than that of Canada, supports a population thirty-five times greater. Little wonder that sparse settlement is a recurring theme in Canadian geography.

The combination of a small population and a huge country gives Canada one of the world's lowest population **densities**: about two people per square kilometre. Look at the map on pages 46-47 and you will see that this figure has little meaning, because the population is distributed so unevenly across the country.

The Great Lakes-St. Lawrence Lowlands contain the greatest **concentration** of people. Density of population in this region averages thirty-five persons per square kilometre. However, this figure soars to 7,000 in the downtown areas of the region's two largest cities, Montreal and Toronto. Each has about a million more residents than the total population of the three Prairie Provinces. Each houses a population larger than that of all four Atlantic Provinces.

East and west of Ontario and Quebec, the two-persons-per-square-kilometre population density is also misleading. Most people in the Prairies live in the southern parts of Alberta, Saskatchewan, and Manitoba. The population of the Atlantic Provinces is concentrated along the coasts. Both in the interior and along the coasts of mainland British Columbia and Vancouver Island are clusters of settlement. However, two-thirds of the province's population resides in Vancouver, Canada's third-largest **metropolis** (an urban centre with over 100,000 population).

At the beginning of this century, most Canadians lived in small rural communities. Today, Canada is one of the world's most highly urbanized nations. About 75 per cent of the population lives in cities, towns, and villages of 1,000 inhabitants and over. Indeed, 55 per cent of Canada's total population lives in only twenty-two cities.

The Canadian people

Canada is a multicultural country made up of people with different languages, religions, and social customs. As you can see in the table on page 49, the nation's ethnic composition has undergone tremendous changes since the first census was taken in 1871. Although the proportion of Canadians of French ancestry has remained relatively stable, the proportion of Canadians of British ancestry has declined steadily. To a large extent, this decrease is due to lower rates of emigration from the British Isles and higher ones from continental Europe and other parts of the world. Excluding those of French and British descent, Canadians of European ancestry now comprise 23 per cent of the population. Within this group, people of German origin are by far the most numerous, followed by those of Italian, Ukrainian, Dutch, and Scandinavian descent. Since 1951, there has been a noticeable increase in the numbers of people of Greek, Yugoslavian, Hungarian, and Asian origin. Canada's native peoples have also increased in numbers, from 0.7 per cent of the population in 1871 to 1.4 per cent in 1971.

Population by Ethnic Group* (In this table, "0.0" indicates a percentage less than 0.05.)

	1871	1911	1921	1931	1951	1961	1971
	per cent						
French	31.1	28.6	27.9	28.2	30.8	30.4	28.7
British	60.5	55.5	55.4	51.9	47.9	43.8	44.6
Austrian	—	0.6	1.2	0.5	0.2	0.6	0.2
Belgian	—	0.1	0.2	0.3	0.3	0.3	0.2
Chinese	—	0.4	0.4	0.5	0.2	0.3	0.6
Czech and Slovak	—	—	0.1	0.3	0.5	0.4	0.4
Dutch	0.8	0.8	1.3	1.4	1.9	2.3	2.0
Finnish	—	0.2	0.3	0.4	0.3	0.3	0.3
German	5.8	5.6	3.4	4.5	4.4	5.8	6.1
Greek	—	0.0	0.1	0.1	0.1	0.3	0.6
Hungarian	—	0.2	0.2	0.4	0.4	0.7	0.6
Italian	0.0	0.6	0.8	0.9	1.1	2.5	3.4
Japanese	—	0.1	0.2	0.2	0.1	0.2	0.2
Jewish	—	1.1	1.4	1.5	1.3	1.0	1.4
Lithuanian	—	—	0.0	0.1	0.1	0.2	0.1
Native Indian and Inuit	0.7	1.5	1.3	1.2	1.2	1.2	1.4
Polish	—	0.5	0.6	1.4	1.6	1.8	1.5
Portuguese[1]	—	—	—	—	—	—	0.4
Roumanian	—	0.1	0.2	0.3	0.2	0.2	0.1
Russian	0.0	0.6	1.1	0.8	0.7	0.6	0.3
Scandinavian[2]	0.1	1.6	1.9	2.2	2.0	2.1	1.8
Ukrainian	—	1.0	1.2	2.2	2.8	2.6	2.7
Yugoslav	—	—	0.1	0.2	0.1	0.4	0.5
Other Asiatic	—	0.1	0.1	0.1	0.1	0.2	0.6
Other European	0.1	0.1	0.2	0.1	0.3	0.5	0.4
Other and not stated	0.9	0.7	0.4	0.3	1.4	1.3	0.9
Total in thousands	3,689	7,207	8,788	10,377	14,009	18,238	21,568

[1]Included with "Other European" prior to 1971
[2]Includes Danish, Icelandic, Norwegian, and Swedish
*Adapted from *Perspective Canada: A Compendium of Social Statistics*, Statistics
Canada, 1974

Population by Ethnic Groups, Canada and the Provinces 1971[*]

	New-found-land	Prince Edward Island	Nova Scotia	New Bruns-wick	Quebec	Ontario	Mani-toba
	per cent						
British Isles	93.9	82.7	77.5	57.7	10.8	59.3	41.9
French	3.0	13.8	10.1	37.1	79.1	9.6	8.9
Austrian n.e.s.[1]	—	—	—	—	—	0.2	0.3
Belgian	—	0.1	0.1	0.1	0.1	0.3	0.9
Chinese	0.1	—	0.1	0.1	0.2	0.5	0.3
Czech	—	—	0.1	—	0.1	0.3	0.4
Danish	—	0.1	0.1	0.3	—	0.2	0.4
Dutch	0.1	1.1	1.9	0.8	0.2	2.7	3.6
East Indian	0.1	0.1	0.2	0.1	0.1	0.4	0.3
Estonian	—	—	—	—	—	0.2	—
Finnish	—	—	—	—	—	0.5	0.1
German	0.5	0.9	5.2	1.3	0.9	6.2	12.5
Greek	—	—	0.2	0.1	0.7	0.9	0.2
Hungarian	—	—	0.1	0.1	0.2	0.9	0.5
Icelandic	—	—	—	—	—	—	1.3
Indian (native)	0.2	0.3	0.6	0.6	0.5	0.8	4.4
Inuit	0.2	—	—	—	0.1	—	—
Italian	0.1	0.1	0.5	0.2	2.8	6.0	1.1
Japanese	—	—	—	—	—	0.2	0.1
Jewish	0.1	0.1	0.3	0.2	1.9	1.8	2.0
Latvian	—	—	—	—	—	0.2	0.1
Lithuanian	—	—	—	—	0.1	0.2	0.1
Norwegian	0.1	0.1	0.3	0.2	0.1	0.3	0.9
Polish	0.1	0.1	0.4	0.1	0.4	1.9	4.3
Portuguese	0.1	—	0.1	—	0.3	0.8	0.4
Roumanian	—	—	—	—	—	0.1	0.1
Russian	—	—	—	—	0.1	0.2	0.4
Slovak	—	—	—	—	—	0.2	0.1
Spanish	—	—	0.1	—	0.2	0.1	0.1
Swedish	—	—	0.1	0.1	—	0.2	0.9
Syrian-Lebanese	0.1	0.2	0.3	0.2	0.1	0.1	0.1
Ukrainian	—	0.1	0.3	0.1	0.3	2.1	11.6
West Indian	—	—	0.1	—	0.1	0.3	0.1
Yugoslav	—	—	—	—	0.1	0.9	0.3
Others and unknown	1.3	0.2	1.3	0.6	0.5	1.4	1.3
Total Number	522,105	111,645	788,960	634,560	6,027,765	7,703,105	988,245

[1]not elsewhere specified

[*]*Perspective Canada: A Compendium of Social Statistics,* Statistics Canada, 1974

Population by Ethnic Groups, Canada and the Provinces 1971*

	Saskatch-ewan	Alberta	British Columbia	Yukon	Northwest Terri-tories	Canada
	per cent					
British Isles	42.1	46.7	57.8	48.5	25.2	44.6
French	6.1	5.8	4.4	6.7	6.5	28.7
Austrian n.e.s.[1]	0.4	0.4	0.5	0.6	0.2	0.2
Belgian	0.4	0.3	0.2	0.3	0.2	0.2
Chinese	0.5	0.8	2.0	0.5	0.3	0.6
Czech	0.5	0.6	0.4	0.4	0.2	0.3
Danish	0.6	1.2	1.0	0.8	0.5	0.4
Dutch	2.1	3.6	3.2	2.8	1.0	2.0
East Indian	0.2	0.3	0.9	0.1	0.2	0.3
Estonian	—	0.1	0.1	0.1	—	0.1
Finnish	0.2	0.2	0.5	0.5	0.1	0.3
German	19.4	14.2	9.0	8.5	3.8	6.1
Greek	0.1	0.2	0.3	0.1	0.1	0.6
Hungarian	1.5	1.0	0.8	1.1	0.3	0.6
Icelandic	0.3	0.2	0.3	0.2	0.2	0.1
Indian (native)	4.4	2.7	2.4	14.0	20.6	1.4
Inuit	—	—	—	0.1	32.8	0.1
Italian	0.3	1.5	2.5	0.9	0.7	3.4
Japanese	—	0.3	0.6	0.2	—	0.2
Jewish	0.2	0.4	0.6	0.2	0.1	1.4
Latvian	—	0.1	0.1	0.1	—	0.1
Lithuanian	0.1	0.1	0.1	0.1	—	0.1
Norwegian	3.9	3.2	2.4	2.6	1.5	0.8
Polish	2.9	2.7	1.4	1.3	0.8	1.5
Portuguese	—	0.1	0.4	0.1	0.1	0.4
Roumanian	0.6	0.3	0.2	0.4	0.1	0.1
Russian	1.1	0.6	1.1	0.4	0.2	0.3
Slovak	0.1	0.2	0.1	—	0.1	0.1
Spanish	—	0.1	0.1	0.1	0.1	0.1
Swedish	1.6	1.5	1.5	1.7	0.5	0.5
Syrian-Lebanese	0.1	0.1	—	—	—	0.1
Ukrainian	9.3	8.3	2.8	3.3	1.8	2.7
West Indian	—	0.1	—	0.1	—	0.1
Yugoslav	0.2	0.5	0.7	0.8	0.3	0.5
Others and unknown	0.8	1.6	1.6	2.4	1.5	1.0
Total Number	926,245	1,627,875	2,184,620	18,390	34,810	21,568,310

[1]not elsewhere specified

*Perspective Canada: A Compendium of Social Statistics, Statistics Canada, 1974

Study 7

1. What is the main ethnic composition of the following regions: British Columbia, the Prairie Provinces, Ontario, Quebec, the Atlantic Provinces, the Northwest Territories, and the Yukon?
2. Who do you think "Others and unknown" are?
3. (a) How would you define "ethnic group"?
   (b) Might any groups fit under more than one classification? If so, how does this affect interpretation of the figures in the table?
4. Do you agree with the classification of ethnic groups in the official chart? Explain why you do or do not.
5. What is the ethnic composition of your community?

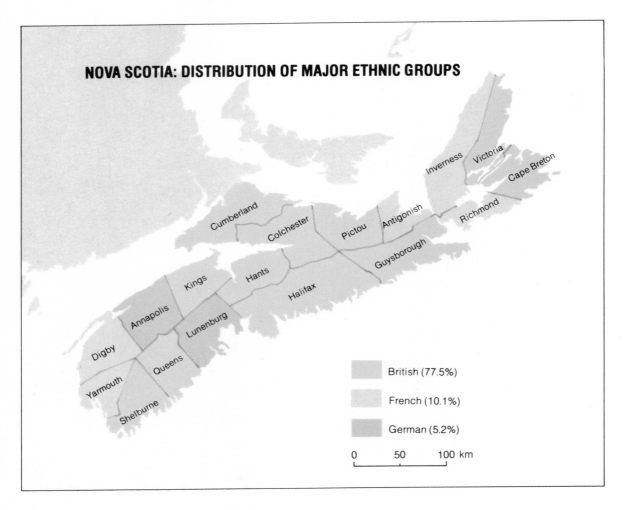

NOVA SCOTIA: DISTRIBUTION OF MAJOR ETHNIC GROUPS

British (77.5%)

French (10.1%)

German (5.2%)

0   50   100 km

Ethnic groups are unevenly distributed across Canada and within each province. Canadians of British descent live in all the provinces, the greatest numbers of them being in Ontario and British Columbia. Canadians of French ancestry show a much higher degree of concentration. About 75 per cent of them live in the Province of Quebec, 11 per cent in Ontario, and 5 per cent in New Brunswick.

Ontario has a **heterogeneous** population of *many* and *varied* immigrant groups. More Germans, Italians, Dutch, Poles, and Ukrainians, for example, live there than in any other province. Prince Edward Island, on the other hand, has a much more **homogeneous** population: 80 per cent of its residents are of the *same* descent.

People of North American Indian ancestry are well distributed throughout the country, though most are found in Ontario and the western provinces. Most of the Inuit (Eskimo) population lives in the Northwest Territories (65 per cent) and Quebec (21 per cent).

Within any one province, population groups show considerable variation in distribution. The proportion of a particular ethnic group in certain parts of a province is much higher than the average for the province. For example, in Nova Scotia, 10.2 per cent of the total population is of French descent, but French Canadians account for 52 per cent of the population of Richmond County. Although the German population forms only 5.2 per cent of the province's population, 36.6 per cent of Lunenberg County is of German descent.

A cultural mosaic

Canada is often described, socially, as a **cultural mosaic.** The pieces that make up the mosaic are the different nationalities, languages, religions, customs, and values — in other words, the different cultures — of the people of Canada. Each piece affects, and in turn is affected by, the other pieces, and yet each piece remains distinctive. When immigrant groups settle in a community, they are not immediately, and never really completely, assimilated into it. They keep certain parts of their culture, modify other parts, and abandon those customs they cannot continue, for various reasons, in their new homeland. The character of the community, in turn, is changed by the different cultures of the ethnic groups. So the Canadian mosaic is a dynamic process of creating identity through diversity.

The cultural mosaic of Canada can be most clearly seen in the distribution of ethnic communities in large cities.

With the great influx of immigrants after World War II, interesting population trends became evident. Immigrant groups tended not only to settle in urban rather than rural areas, but to prefer large cities rather than small towns. And when the distribution of ethnic groups in cities was mapped, interesting patterns showed up. Certain groups tended to settle in clusters in particular parts of a city. Often the size of the group was so great that it formed an enclave or community within a community. The map of Toronto on pages 54-55 shows where a number of different ethnic groups located in 1961.

It is not surprising that many newcomers to Canada prefer to settle in a community where most of the residents belong to their particular ethnic group. For many immigrants, making a home in a new country is difficult and painful. They are "strangers in a strange land." They cannot speak the language. They do not know how to look for a job or find a place to live. They feel lost in streets where glass-and-concrete buildings offer services they do not understand in signs they cannot read. No wonder they prefer to live in a community where they can talk to their neighbors in their own language and ask them how to find a job, how to enrol their children in a school, how to use the public transit system. Thus many immigrants choose to live in a particular section where they can shop in their own language, where they can find the food they are familiar with, and where there are community associations that can help them adjust to a new way of life.

For immigrants who come from villages and farms, the adjustment is not only to a new country but to a new life style in a city. Children usually adapt faster than their parents do, because they learn the new language more quickly and make friends with children outside their ethnic group. This lag in adapting sometimes creates conflicts between young people who want to be part of a new way of life — dating, school dances, and other extra-curricular activities — and parents who try to preserve the values and customs of the old life they knew. Finding a place in the Canadian mosaic can be slow and painful — a strange language, a new life style, different values and social customs, family conflicts — and all in an unfamiliar environment.

The first group of immigrants usually settles in a downtown section of a city. In time, the newcomers open up butcher shops and grocery stores, and set up cultural centres for language and religious classes and for social events. And so a com-

Highways

Railways

Adapted from *Economic Atlas of Ontario*

munity is established where later immigrants can settle in and feel "at home." As the first group prospers and becomes more comfortable with the new way of life in the city, many of its members move. Some locate in a "better" neighborhood and establish a "higher-class" ethnic community. Others disperse throughout the

British > 70%

British > 55%

British > 40%

British > 30%

Italian > 10%

Italian > 30%

Polish > 10%

Ukranian > 10%

German > 10%

0   2   4 km

N

city and suburbs in districts of mixed populations. However, family ties are so strong and cultural festivities (religious holidays, wedding celebrations, christenings, etc.) so numerous that, even for those who have moved away, their social life remains closely linked to the ethnic community. In the meantime, a new wave of immigrants — sometimes of different ethnic origin — comes into the original community.

Although many minority groups are concentrated in particular sections of cities, others — German, Japanese, Dutch, and Scandinavians, for instance — tend to avoid clustering and are found throughout a city.

55

Note the different use made of backyards in a Toronto suburb. What cultural groups can you detect here?

Communities and cultures

The character of any community is formed by the people who live and work there. In addition to the language and ethnic origin of the people, this character or personality is defined by the variety of age groups, the proportion of males to females, the kind of housing, the major industry, and so on. Facilities and services for "retirement towns" will be quite different from the saunas, gyms, swimming pools, and other recreational facilities of high-rise communities. A planned suburb settled by families with young children will be a more stable and organized community than a northern mining town that has a transient, predominantly male, population.

A Laurentian ski resort is quite different from a pulp-and-paper town in the St. Maurice Valley.

A country's culture is formed over a long period of time by the interaction of peoples and their physical environment. Groups of people living and working together develop laws, social customs, food habits, religions, recreational interests, and so on. French immigrants brought their culture with them, as did the British. Thus the cultures of Upper and Lower Canada were quite different. Other European immigrants came, and the mixing of the different groups has helped shape a Canadian culture that has elements of all the different groups — and yet each group has also kept many of its ways and customs. Thus Canada is described as a cultural mosaic rather than a melting pot, as is the case in the United States.

In an age of jet travel and mass communication, it is difficult to keep the diversity of the different pieces of the mosaic. In the horse-and-buggy age, ideas spread slowly because people did not travel long distances. There was little contact and exchange of ideas between communities that were far apart. So local cultures changed slowly, and there was a great variety of communities. Today, people can breakfast at home and lunch a thousand kilometres away, so contact between cultures is easier, faster, and more frequent. In fact, you do not even have to leave home to be exposed to new ideas. You can experience other cultures via the mass media — TV, movies, radio, newspapers, magazines. These are subtly but definitely influencing our way of life. We have been almost hypnotized into trying to conform to what we see, hear, and read. The variety that once seemed to distinguish communities across North America is being replaced by a monotonous sameness. Mass communications are supposedly changing the character of Canadian communities, producing a homogenized North American culture. Or are they?

Despite the American culture that is being imported via television, records, movies, etc., our way of life is still Canadian. The history of the confederation of Canada, our system of laws and government, our strong ties with Europe, the vitality of the traditions and customs of ethnic groups — all of these have helped to form a Canadian culture and keep it distinct from that of the United States. The mass media have not even levelled out differences in regional and community cultures. Despite the fact that audiences all across Canada watch the Saturday-night

Victor C. Last

Cemeteries are good places to uncover information on ethnic groups. Not too surprisingly, this gravestone is in Bruce County, Ontario.

hockey game or the Wayne and Shuster special, communities remain distinct. Certainly, skyscrapers, plazas, take-out food places, and so on are to be found all across Canada, and they make for a certain sameness of landscape. But the industrial bustle and cosmopolitan mix of Toronto is different from the historical flavor and French-Canadian culture of Montreal. Both are different from the leisurely pace and sedate tone of Victoria. And a small town in the Maritimes is different from a small town in Quebec or the Prairies.

How would you add up the similarities and differences in cultures across Canada? What makes up Canadian culture? How would you define and explain the differences in Canadian and American culture?

57

Study 8

1. What factors changed Canada from a rural to an urban society?
2. Many people commute considerable distances each day to work in a city, yet continue to reside in the country. Why?
3. Which way of life, urban or rural, do you feel is more attractive? Explain your answer with examples.
4. Give at least six examples of "mass" or "homogenized" culture.
5. (a) Where have ethnic groups located in your town or city?
   (b) If there are distinct ethnic communities, how have they developed?
   (c) What features distinguish the different communities?
6. (a) Compare the ethnic composition of Halifax, Montreal, Toronto, Winnipeg, and Vancouver.
   (b) What historical and geographical factors help to explain other differences in these centres?
7. "There is a greater variety of communities today, despite mass communication, than there was in the horse-and-buggy age." Debate this statement using criteria arrived at by class discussion.

The settlement of the Prairies: Heterogeneous communities

Communities, whether rural or urban, can be defined by their degree of **homogeneity** or likeness. In a homogeneous community, the members speak the same language, practise the same religion, and share a common culture. **Heterogeneous** communities are composed of people with differing national, linguistic, religious, and cultural backgrounds. The settlement of the Prairies by people of different ethnic origins formed a region of heterogeneous communities.

Around 1900, Canadian, American, and European immigrants began to pour into western Canada. Under the energetic direction of Clifford Sifton, federal Minister of the Interior, the population of the Prairies increased tremendously. During the period 1901-1911, about 1.7 million people arrived from the United States, Ontario, Great Britain, and central Europe. Immigrants from east European countries were particularly encouraged to accept Ottawa's offer of free land because of their experience in farming the steppe (grasslands). The expansion of farming in western Canada happily coincided with a growing demand for wheat in Great Britain. Thus the CPR served as the means for both settling farm families and transporting prairie wheat to Canadian seaports for shipment overseas. These immigrants helped to shape the cultural diversity of Canada.

Study 9

Birthplace of People by Province, 1901: Manitoba*

British Isles	33,093	Japan	13
Austria/Hungary	11,570	Norway/Sweden	1,772
Belgium	790	Roumania	110
China	209	Russia	8,854
Denmark	318	Spain/Portugal	16
East Indies	14	Switzerland	134
France	1,470	Syria	63
Germany	2,285	Turkey	6
Greece	3	United States	6,992
Holland	57	West Indies	32
Iceland	5,403	Others	58
Italy	125	Not given	611

*Census of Canada, 1901, Canada. Dominion Bureau of Statistics. Vol. I, Population

Use the table above, the map on pages 60-61, and an atlas to answer the following questions.

1. (a) What groups on the map are represented by "British Isles" in the table?
    (b) What place names in Manitoba show that it was settled as a heterogeneous community?
2. While some people from what is now the Soviet Union did emigrate to the Prairies, what particular group of these people is probably being referred to on this map?
3. Rank by size of population the ethnic groups in Manitoba in 1901.
4. Rank by size of population the ethnic groups in Manitoba in 1971. (Refer to the table on page 50.) What conclusions can you draw about the ethnic composition of Manitoba in 1901 compared to that in 1971?
5. What are the advantages and disadvantages of members of the same ethnic group settling in the same township or area?

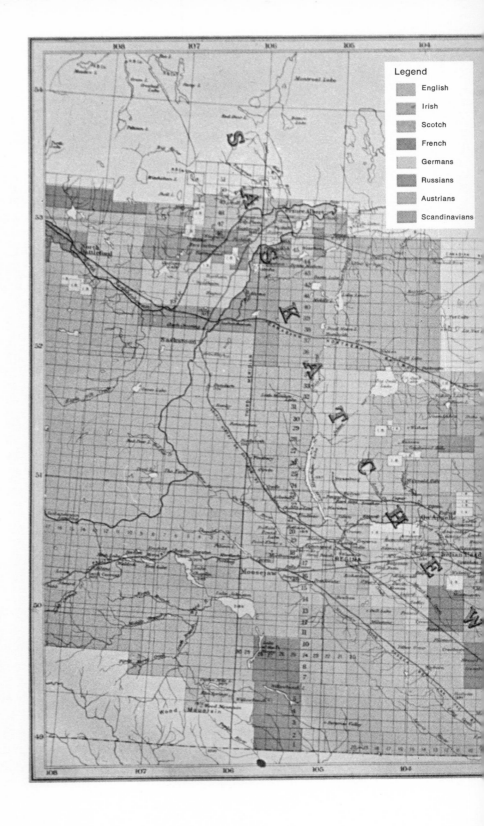

Extract from the ATLAS OF CANADA, prepared by the Department of the Interior, Ottawa, and published in 1906.

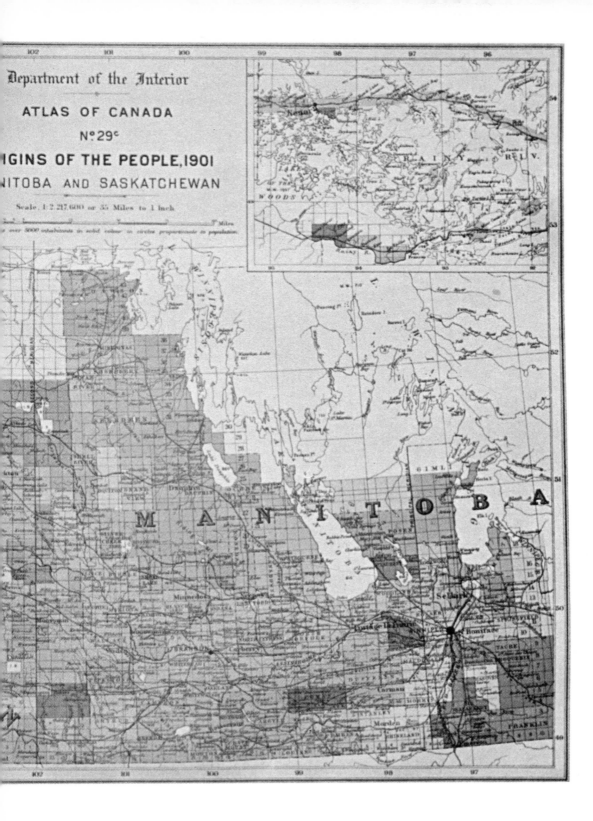

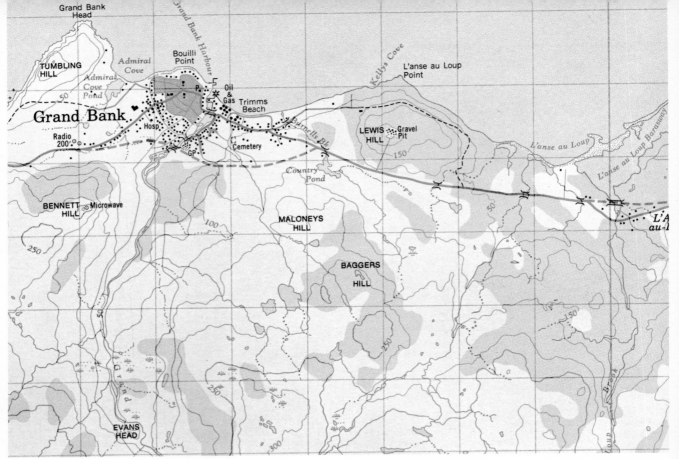

Extract from the Grand Bank, Newfoundland, sheet (1 M/4, Edition 2 MCE, Series A 781) of the National Topographic System. Scale 1:50,000. Courtesy Surveys and Mapping Branch, Department of Energy, Mines, and Resources, Ottawa.

Grand Bank, Newfoundland: A homogeneous community

Grand Bank is a small outport on Newfoundland's Burin Peninsula, situated close to one of the world's richest fishing grounds. It is a homogeneous community, largely isolated from Canadian social and economic activity. Most of its inhabitants share a common ancestry (British), language (English), religion (Protestant), occupation (fishing), and level of education (only 35 per cent have been to high school, and 2 per cent are university graduates).

The economy of Grand Bank is, and has always been, based on the fishery. In the days of dried cod, before fish processing plants, fishing was an individual effort; merchants operated vessels on the Grand Banks, and inshore fishermen set out daily in their dories. When the catch was brought in, cleaned, and salted, the fishermen's wives "made the fish." They spread the cod on flakes (platforms) to dry, turning them through the day so they would not be burned by the sun. In the late afternoon, the fish were piled up on the flakes and covered with birch or spruce bark so they would not be wetted and spoiled by

Grand Bank Harbor. Note the vessel's port of registry.

the dew. The next morning, the women spread out the fish again, and continued the process until the cod was properly dried and cured.

Individual fishing enterprise is almost a thing of the past. Today, most of Grand Bank's fishermen work for the fish processing and freezing plant, which employs about 40 per cent of the town's labor force. Fish are brought to the plant by the company's offshore fishermen, who operate its draggers and trawlers, and by self-employed inshore fishermen (who account for an additional 10 per cent of the work force). The plant processes a variety of species — cod, haddock, halibut, and ocean perch — and ships its products to markets on the North American mainland.

While Grand Bank has a population of only 4,000, it is the second-largest town on the Burin Peninsula and acts as a marketing centre for a number of smaller outports.

Canadian National Railways maintain a weekly passenger and freight service of two vessels, which operate between Argentia and Port aux Basques. The Blue Peter Line runs ships into Grand Bank to collect the products of the fish plant. There is no regular air service, though seaplanes can land at the harbor entrance. A highway links the town with St. John's, the nearest city, some 370 kilometres away.

Grand Bank is a well-organized community, with medical and dental services, schools, a library, sports and recreational facilities. Its stores provide goods for the local population and also for the residents of smaller settlements along the coast, who come "to town" for special purchases. There is active citizen interest and pride in the town. Unlike many Canadian communities of similar size, Grand Bank has a municipal plan and has taken measures to improve land use, roads, and garbage disposal. The plan recognizes the dangers of a one-industry town and recommends the establishment of other industries. But, lacking forest, soil, or mineral resources — and being located far from major markets — Grand Bank will continue to depend on its fisheries for some time to come.

The main street of Grand Bank. In the background is one of the town's vital links with other communities, a radio-communication tower, which is located close to the post office.

A view of the town along Grand Bank Brook, with a microwave tower in the background.

The outskirts of Grand Bank. The large white building on the right, a maritime museum, originally housed exhibits in Montreal during Expo '67.

Study 10

1. Try to match the map and the photographs by identifying common points.
   (a) What are the names of the hills shown in two of the photographs?
   (b) Describe the landscape surrounding Grand Bank. What factors could limit the expansion of the town?
   (c) What features on the map and in the photographs indicate something about the climate?
   (d) What evidence on the map suggests that the area was once frequented by non-Britishers?
2. Grand Bank has always been a one-industry town. It has become a one-company town. What does this mean in terms of economic security for the people of Grand Bank?
3. What are the advantages and disadvantages of living in a homogeneous community?

Toronto: A heterogeneous community

Ontario's capital has been transformed from "Hogtown" and "Waspville" into a remarkably cosmopolitan city. Yet, not too long ago, there was a popular joke, made about any and all contests, that the first prize would be a week in Toronto; second prize, two weeks. What brought about the transformation?

Since the end of World War II, immigrants from just about every country in the world and from every province in Canada have poured into Toronto. They brought with them their crafts and customs, their foods and fashions, their trades and talents, their language, their religion, their sports — in short, their culture.

Drive around the city and you find the churches, synagogues, and temples of various religions from Chinese Buddhist to Syrian Orthodox. Walk along downtown streets and you see restaurant and store signs in Greek, Italian, Portuguese, etc., as well as in English. On the streets running through the Kensington Market, you will hear half a dozen or so languages. Open the telephone directory and there are thirty pages of restaurant listings offering every kind of cuisine, from good old English roast beef and Yorkshire pudding to exotic dishes ranging from Armenian shish kebabs to Yugoslavian stuffed peppers. Stroll through a park and see a game of

Highways
----- Railways

baseball, Canadian football, or soccer; you may also catch sight of a game of cricket or boccie. Twist the radio dial and you can tune in a program in French, Macedonian, or Ukrainian, as well as in English. It is even possible to pick up a newspaper and read the news in German, Italian, or Yiddish.

It is this rich mixture of peoples that has given Toronto much of its cosmopolitan culture.

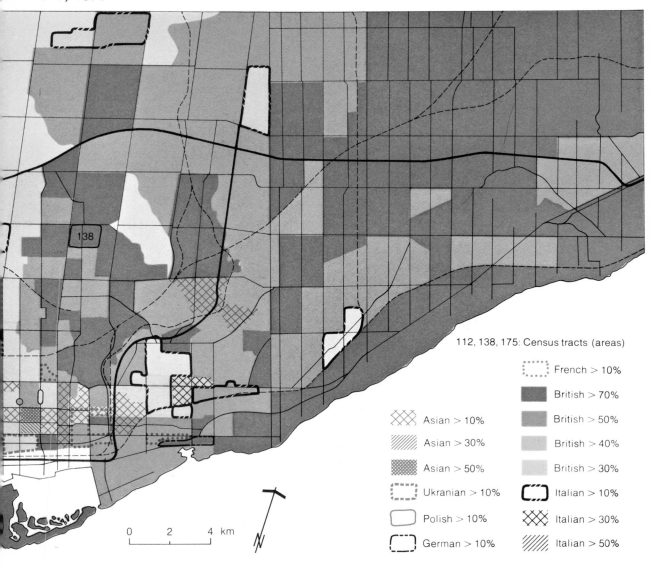

112, 138, 175: Census tracts (areas)

French > 10%
British > 70%
British > 50%
Asian > 10%   British > 40%
Asian > 30%   British > 30%
Asian > 50%
Ukranian > 10%   Italian > 10%
Polish > 10%   Italian > 30%
German > 10%   Italian > 50%

0 2 4 km

N

Population by Ethnic Group for Census Metropolitan Area, Toronto, 1971*					
British Isles	1,495,300	Hungarian	23,350	Polish	51,180
French	91,975	Italian	271,755	Russian	5,270
Austrian	7,880	Japanese	11,690	Scandinavian	18,355
Chinese	26,285	Jewish	109,910	Slovak	4,490
Czech	9,975	Native Indian	6,475	Ukrainian	60,755
Finnish	8,920	Negro	12,335	West Indian	15,625
German	116,640	Netherlands	44,425	Other and unknown	235,535

*Census of Canada, 1971 Population, Ethnic Groups, Catalogue 92-723, Vol. I, Part 3, Statistics Canada, October 1973

RELIGION, LANGUAGE SPOKEN IN THE HOME, AND HIGHEST LEVEL OF SCHOOLING FOR CENSUS TRACTS (AREAS) 112, 138, AND 175: METROPOLITAN TORONTO, 1971.

Census Tract 112

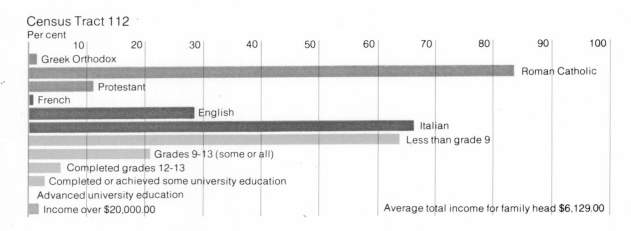

Per cent

- Greek Orthodox
- Roman Catholic
- Protestant
- French
- English
- Italian
- Less than grade 9
- Grades 9-13 (some or all)
- Completed grades 12-13
- Completed or achieved some university education
- Advanced university education
- Income over $20,000.00

Average total income for family head $6,129.00

Census Tract 138

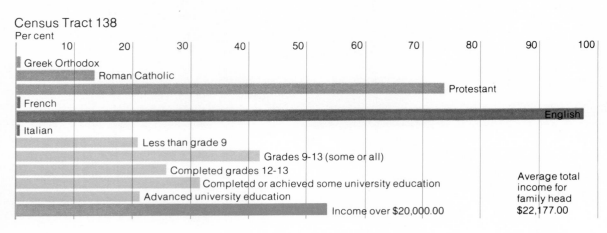

Per cent

- Greek Orthodox
- Roman Catholic
- Protestant
- French
- English
- Italian
- Less than grade 9
- Grades 9-13 (some or all)
- Completed grades 12-13
- Completed or achieved some university education
- Advanced university education
- Income over $20,000.00

Average total income for family head $22,177.00

Census Tract 175

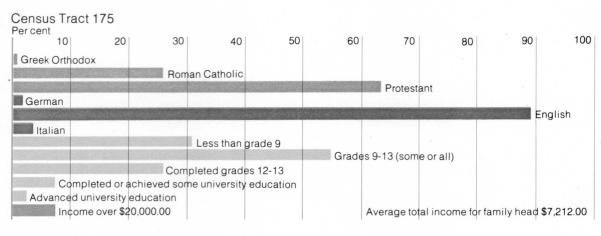

Per cent

- Greek Orthodox
- Roman Catholic
- Protestant
- German
- English
- Italian
- Less than grade 9
- Grades 9-13 (some or all)
- Completed grades 12-13
- Completed or achieved some university education
- Advanced university education
- Income over $20,000.00

Average total income for family head $7,212.00

- Religion
- Language spoken in the home
- Level of schooling
- Percentage of families with incomes over $20,000.00

Study 11

Examine the map and the table on pages 66-67.

1. On a census-tract basis, what areas have an ethnic concentration of 10 per cent or more?
2. (a) Rank in order the ethnic groups in Toronto.
   (b) What groups do you think are represented by "Other and unknown"?
3. In what parts of the city are the greatest concentrations of Ukrainians, Italians, and Britons?
4. What ethnic groups represented in the 1971 map did not appear on the map of Toronto's ethnic composition, 1961, on pages 54-55?
5. Compare the 1961 and 1971 maps of Toronto. How do they support the information in this chapter in terms of immigrant settlement and movements of ethnic communities?
6. Study the bar graphs on page 68.
   (a) What language groups are highly concentrated in census tracts #112, #138, and #175?
   (b) Compare the educational level of the residents of these three census tracts. Is there a connection between level of education and income? Explain your answer.

Québec : une province pas comme les autres

In a confederation dominated by English-speaking Canadians, Quebec, the heart of French culture in Canada, is a province "not like the others." It is this French fact that has added a distinctive element to the Canadian identity.

While both French and English are spoken in Quebec, French is the language of the overwhelming majority of the population. Consumer articles have to be labelled and described in French and English. (Because of this Quebec law, most packaged goods distributed in Canada have bilingual packaging. In most cases, it would be too costly to design and print two separate sets of packages.) Advertising and promotion campaigns also have to be carefully created to take into account the French and English markets. How much easier it would be for business firms in the United States if Quebec were not a French-speaking province! They might be tempted to reduce — in some cases, even eliminate — the advertising and marketing staffs of their Canadian subsidiaries. In fact, many Canadians — English- and French-speaking — feel that Quebec is the last best hope against complete economic domination by the United States. Some would go so far as to suggest that the French fact and strong stand of Quebec have saved Canada from political as well as economic absorption.

The definition of Canada as a bilingual nation means that both English and French

The community of Charlesbourg, near Quebec City. The common settlement pattern in New France was the famous "long lot" that edged a major waterway. However, there were very early attempts to establish a different type of settlement, of which this is an example. Explain the intent of this particular land use.

are recognized as official languages — the languages of federal government offices, agencies, publications, courts, laws, etc. However, apart from these political and legal areas, bilingualism seems to operate as a one-way practice. Quebec has been described as "a Francophone island surrounded by an Anglophone sea," and so, of necessity, most Québécois learn to speak English. The rest of Canada, for several reasons, is not motivated to become bilingual: at least 70 per cent of Canadians know little, if any, French. So les Qué-bécois feel *chez eux* only in their own province. When they travel almost anywhere else in Canada, they feel like foreigners in their own country. In most places, they cannot buy a French newspaper, or watch a French TV program, or hear a French radio program. Because they feel culturally threatened, les Québécois are determined to protect their language and culture so they will not drown in the Anglophone sea.

Without the French fact of Quebec, would it not be much more difficult to define and maintain a Canadian identity?

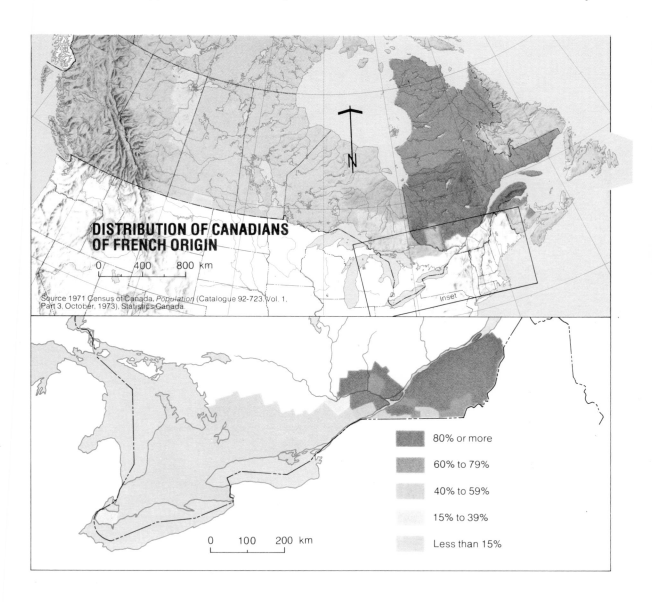

DISTRIBUTION OF CANADIANS OF FRENCH ORIGIN

0   400   800 km

Source 1971 Census of Canada, *Population* (Catalogue 92-723, Vol. 1, Part 3, October, 1973), Statistics Canada.

inset

0   100   200 km

80% or more

60% to 79%

40% to 59%

15% to 39%

Less than 15%

Study 12

1. Where does most of Quebec's non-French-speaking population live?
2. Other than Quebec, identify and name areas in Canada that have populations of French origin in concentrations greater than 15 per cent.
3.

Mother Tongue[1] and Language Spoken in the Home, 1971

	Mother Tongue	Language of the Home	% Change
English	12,973,810	14,446,235	+11.3
French	5,793,650	5,546,025	− 4.3

[1]The language first spoken and still understood

Using the statistics above, answer the following questions.

(a) Why are more people speaking English in the home than there are people who are listed with English as their mother tongue?
(b) How can you account for the decrease in the number of French Canadians who speak French in the home?
(c) If you were a French Canadian, would you be concerned about these statistics? Explain why or why not.

Forgotten, neglected people

Indian pictographs near Nephton, Ontario. No one knows how old these are. Estimates of their age range from 400 to 3,500 years.

The history of native peoples in Canada has been written (and therefore in many cases miswritten) from a non-native point of view. Their contribution to Canadian culture has generally been recorded and evaluated only in terms of its effect on European settlement. And so there are the innumerable references to snowshoes and moccasins and birchbark canoes. (What other items are usually included in the list?) The cultures of native peoples have usually been viewed in light of European values, rarely in their own terms. Thus Inuit (Eskimo) sculpture and Indian masks are "valuable" as examples of "primitive" art. But Inuit sculpted and Indians carved long before their work was recognized by North American and European art markets. Their work had value in itself.

For too long "the Indian" and "Indian culture" have been referred to as though all Indians were the same — held the same values, spoke the same language, shared the same culture. This was not the case. There was cultural diversity in Canada long before Europeans came.

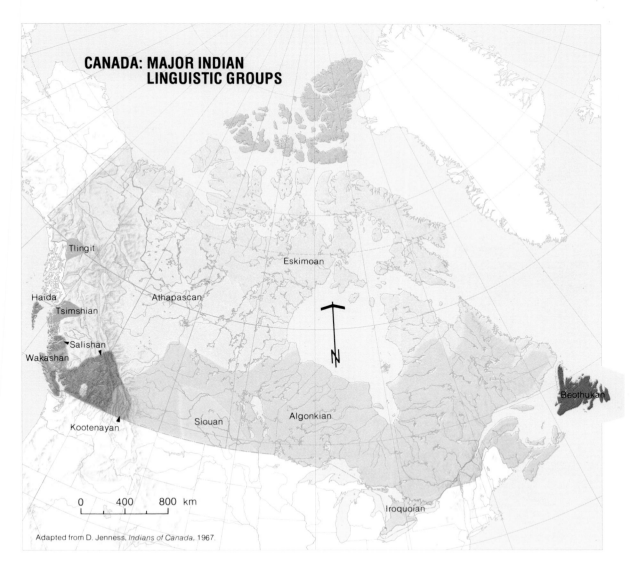

CANADA: MAJOR INDIAN LINGUISTIC GROUPS

Tlingit

Eskimoan

Haida

Athapascan

Tsimshian

Salishan

Wakashan

Kootenayan

Siouan

Algonkian

Beothukan

0   400   800 km

Iroquoian

Adapted from D. Jenness, *Indians of Canada*, 1967.

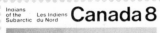

Indians
of the
Subarctic   Les Indiens
du Nord   **Canada 8**

Canada 8

Indians of   Les Indiens
the Subarctic   du Nord

Canada 8

Indians of   Les Indiens
the Subarctic   du Nord

Indians
of the
Subarctic   Les Indiens
du Nord   **Canada 8**

Canada 8

Indians of the   Les Indiens de la
Pacific Coast   Côte du Pacifique

Canada 8

Indians of   Les Indiens
the Plains   des Plaines

Canada 8

Indians of   Les Indiens
the Plains   des Plaines

Canada 8

The   Les
Algonkians   Algonquins

Indians of   Les Indiens
the Pacific   de la Côte
Coast   du Pacifique   **Canada 8**

The   Les
Algonkians   Algonquins   **Canada 8**

Indians of   Les Indiens
the Pacific   de la Côte
Coast   du Pacifique   **Canada 8**

Indians of   Les Indiens
the Plains   des Plaines   **Canada 8**

The   Les
Algonkians   Algonquins   **Canada 8**

Canada 8

Indians of   Les Indiens
the Plains   des Plaines   **Canada 8**

Indians of the   Les Indiens de la
Pacific Coast   Côte du Pacifique

Canada 8

The   Les
Algonkians   Algonquins

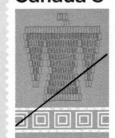

74

Study 13

1. Which of the Indian groups opposite were nomadic and which were settled? Give reasons for your answers.
2. Why was the buffalo so important to Plains Indians? List at least six reasons.
3. Make a table in your notebook listing the Indian groups down the left-hand side of the page and the following headings across the top: location, language, food, clothing, shelter, weapons, social organization. Use this table and the map on page 73 to describe the cultures shown on the stamps. Explain any differences and similarities.

Indians and Inuit have long been forgotten, neglected minorities. It is only in recent years that governments and Canadians generally have become concerned about the well-being of native peoples. That these groups have cause for complaint is well documented in the infant-mortality chart. Look at the 1960-62 death rates. Compare them with those for the total Canadian population for the same years. Then examine the two graphs on page 76.

What might explain the high infant-mortality rate for Inuit and Indian? What percentage of houses on reserves have fewer rooms than your home has? What connection might there be between the rooms per house and the mortality rates? How do the percentages on the facilities graph compare with those for your neighborhood? What does the facilities graph indicate about the standard of living of reserve Indians? How might this help explain the high infant-mortality rate? If you did not include "housing conditions" in your response to the first question, how and why would you revise your answer?

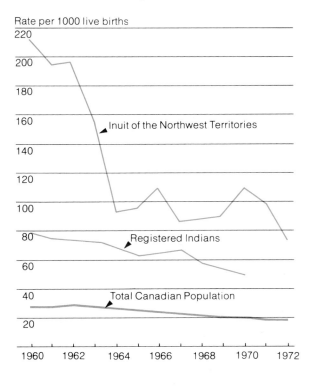

INFANT MORTALITY, 1960-1972

Rate per 1000 live births

- Inuit of the Northwest Territories
- Registered Indians
- Total Canadian Population

1960 1962 1964 1966 1968 1970 1972

HOUSING ON INDIAN RESERVES BY NUMBER OF ROOMS PER HOUSE

Per cent

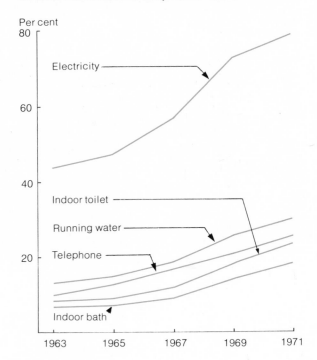

HOUSING ON INDIAN RESERVES WITH SPECIFIED FACILITIES, 1963-1971

Per cent

Housing and facilities are one way to measure standard of living. "Standard of living" is a measure of the physical comfort and well-being of a society. In North American culture, it is based on money and the things money can buy — income, housing, cars, electrical appliances, food, clothes, etc. These criteria are used as a measure in highly industrialized societies, but they are not absolute criteria. They cannot be used for all societies — for example, agricultural, pre-industrial — or for all time. Did the nobility of the sixteenth century, who lived in draughty castles without central heating or indoor plumbing or electricity, have a low standard of living?

"Standard of living" should not be confused with "culture" or "way of life." Cul-tures are different around the world. So different criteria have to be used to measure the standard of living in different cultures. The importance of such things as indoor plumbing or electricity will vary among Indians and Inuit depending on the way of life they choose. Some want to stay on the land and preserve their hunting and fishing culture; others want to stay on reserves but take advantage of modern technology to establish co-operatives and native industries. Still others want to live and work in towns and cities. What all native peoples want is the freedom to *choose* their own way of life and to determine *their own* standard of living within whichever culture they select.

The freedom to choose is being challenged from several directions. The industrial development of Canada's north is cutting into lands occupied by native peoples and disrupting hunting and fishing patterns. Indians and Inuit who desire to stay on the land feel that their way of life is being threatened. If the machines of modern industry destroy the hunting and fishing environment, what will happen to those who choose to stay on the land and preserve their age-old way of life? Those who want to acquire the skills to work in a technological culture have to attend schools located hundreds of kilometres away from their families. But if Indians and Inuit are educated far from their home environment, how will they preserve the language, customs, and values of their culture?

In order to be truly free to choose their own way of life, Indians and Inuit are struggling with such issues as land claims, treaty rights, development programs, environmental protection, and educational opportunities. When two cultures come together, conflict and change are inevitable.

Mother Tongue of Persons of Indian and Inuit Ethnic Groups*			
	1951 per cent	1961	1971
Indian and Inuit languages	82.6	71.4	53.9
English	15.4	26.7	40.5
French	1.5	1.7	4.3
Other	0.5	0.2	1.3

*Perspective Canada: A Compendium of Social Statistics, Statistics Canada, 1974

In the words of an Inuit, Adamie Angiyou:

"We are changing, but the pull to the land is still very strong on us. There is much hardship to being on the land, but we do not feel it when we are there because we feel free. We want to feel the freedom when we are in the villages, too, and not feel dominated by the whites as we do now. We feel hardship in the villages when we are told what to do. Conditions must be created where the Inuit can run his own affairs in the villages.

In this atmosphere of change, there are many who will want to stay with the old ways, but there are many who will want to go the other way. Both must be able to do as they wish, but both must be able to do so without losing their freedom. It is a question of being able to choose one's future way."

*   *   *

Perhaps this last statement is the strength of our cultural diversity — different groups of people choosing their future ways within the Canadian mosaic.

Study and Research

1. Define the following: standard of living, culture, ethnic group, income level.

2. The question of native rights and land claims has been widely reported in the media. It will continue to be newsworthy because of mining exploration and hydro-electric development in the north (which are discussed in Chapter 10). Keep a file of newspaper and magazine articles to help you in your study of the subject.

3. "The growing migration of Indians to the cities has raised the fundamental issue of whether the reserves have helped to preserve traditions or have kept the Indians isolated from the mainstream of Canadian society and made them dependent on the government for their existence."* Discuss.

4. Canada's two official languages are recognized in Parliament and in federal courts and offices across the country. Discuss whether they should also be recognized in provincial and municipal government courts and offices.

   To what extent can bilingualism be implemented as a practical policy?

5. The policy of the federal government is based on the definition of Canada as a "bilingual, multicultural nation."
   (a) Explain this definition.
   (b) How should this affect federal funds for education, language programs, manpower training, etc.?

6. Debate the advantages and disadvantages of living in a "cultural mosaic" versus a "melting pot."

7. Immigrants have come to Canada at different times and for different reasons.
   (a) What reasons for immigrating are common to all groups?
   (b) What reasons are specific to certain groups and certain times?

*Perspective Canada: A Compendium of Social Statistics, Statistics Canada, 1974, p. 237.

8. One way of stereotyping people is by occupation — for example, Indian trapper, Ukrainian farmer, Italian construction worker, etc. How true are such ethnic stereotypes? Using Table 13:24 in *Perspective Canada*, rank the different occupations listed for each ethnic group. Any surprises?

    In which ethnic groups do the following occupations rank highest: medicine, forestry and logging, sales, mining?

9. If you were Minister of Immigration, what would be your immigration policy and why? (Consider such questions as "open door" policy, quota system, residence restrictions, political and economic considerations, refugee relief, etc.)

10. One example of the difference between mosaics and melting pots is the difference in official treatment of minority language groups. Research the historical experience in the United States and Canada for the following:
    (a)   the French in Louisiana since 1805,
    (b)   the Spanish in New Mexico, Colorado, etc. since 1850,
    (c)   the French in Quebec since 1774.

11. "Science and technology more than any other factors determine the degree of cultural variety." Evaluate this statement with reference to means of transportation, employment opportunities, housing, food, clothing, recreation, religion, etc.

12. Using what you have learned in this chapter, together with any other ideas you have gained from your personal experience and reading, develop criteria for evaluating societies by comparing different cultures around the world.

    Apply these criteria to (a) a particular society today and the same society a hundred years ago, (b) a comparison of two societies today.

    If you find reason to modify these criteria as you read through this book, add appropriate notes to your reports on (a) and (b).

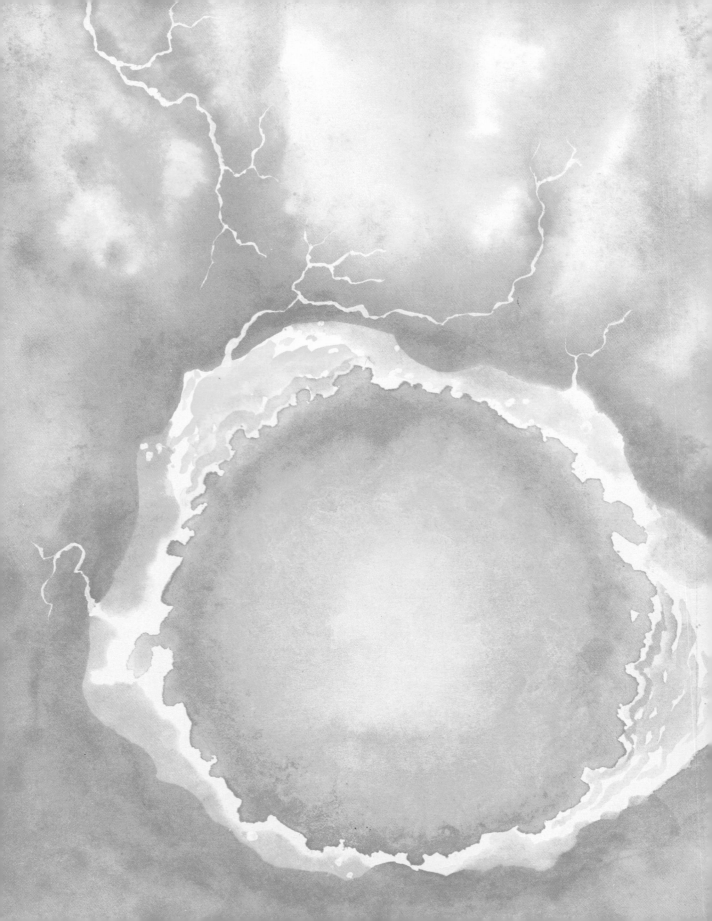

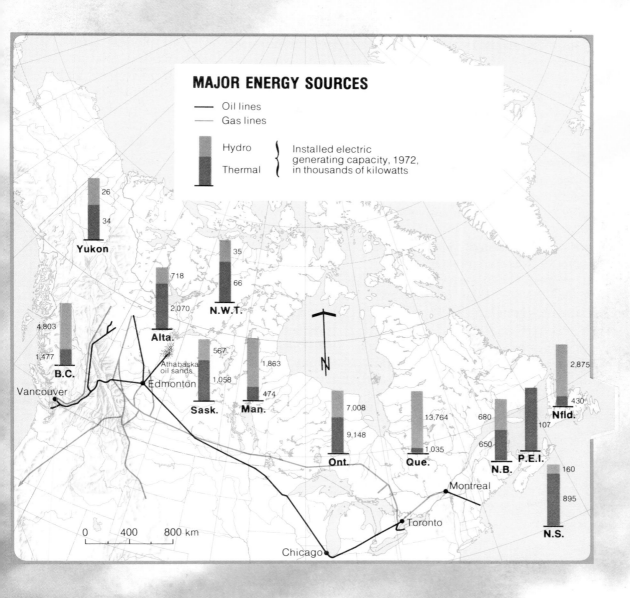

MAJOR ENERGY SOURCES

— Oil lines

— Gas lines

Hydro

Thermal

} Installed electric generating capacity, 1972, in thousands of kilowatts

Yukon 26 / 34

N.W.T. 35 / 66

Alta. 718 / 2,070

B.C. 4,803 / 1,477

Athabaska oil sands

Edmonton

Vancouver

Sask. 567 / 1,058

Man. 1,863 / 474

Ont. 7,008 / 9,148

Que. 13,764 / 1,035

N.B. 680 / 650

P.E.I. 107

Nfld. 2,875 / 430

N.S. 160 / 895

Montreal

Toronto

Chicago

0   400   800 km

Chapter 3 **Storehouse of energy**

To be of any use at all, raw energy must first be harnessed and then converted or refined before it can be used as power. In such fashion Egyptian pharaohs built the pyramids, using the energy of hundreds of thousands of slaves that the whips of their taskmasters harnessed and converted into power. A hockey player rushing relentlessly down the ice and slamming the puck past the goalkeeper is one of the most exciting, entertaining examples of the conversion of energy into power.

For tens of thousands of years, the only *realized energy* was the muscle *power* of men and women. Then people harnessed animal energy to help them do their work — pulling loads, ploughing fields. But still the work was hard and slow. The pioneers who came to Canada spent long, laborious hours felling trees, breaking sod, building homes, spinning wool, weaving cloth, and so on. However, even in pioneer times, there was some harnessing of Nature's sources of energy. Water from streams and rivers turned the huge water wheels of flour and lumber mills. (The ruins of these old mills can still be seen in a number of small towns throughout rural Canada.) On the Prairies, windmills were used to pump water from wells; in fact, some enterprising farmers used this converted energy to create electricity for lighting their homes.

Even in today's world, the energy of human and animal muscle is still a widespread source of power. But the machines of the industrialized world need much more powerful sources. It is the conversion of the raw energy of water into hydro-electric power and the refining of crude petroleum into oil and fuels that have revolutionized fishing, farming, forestry, mining, manufacturing, and transportation.

Hydro-electric power

So great is the raw energy of running water that the whole world is constantly being reshaped by it. Water is the greatest erosive force on earth. When its energy is harnessed and converted, it is one of the most widespread sources of power: hydro-electricity. Take a look at the diagram of hydro-electric power production to see how this is done.

A dam has been built to back up an enormous "head of water," which is held in the forebay. (Fish, silt, and other debris trapped by the screen racks are removed periodically.) Thus the raw energy of water has been harnessed. Now to control the flow. If the water just ran over the dam, nothing would happen. So a tunnel is built to channel the flow of water. Gates in the dam are raised, and down the huge tube of the penstock cascades the water to hit the fins of the turbine. (The higher the dam, the faster the water falls and the greater is the force it exerts.) The force of the rushing water causes the turbine to spin, which in turn spins the generator. In the generator, the action of magnets turning at terrific speed near metal coils creates electric current. From the generator, the current is sent to the transformer, which converts it into 110 volts. The control room then sends supplies of electricity along the transmission lines to farms and factories,

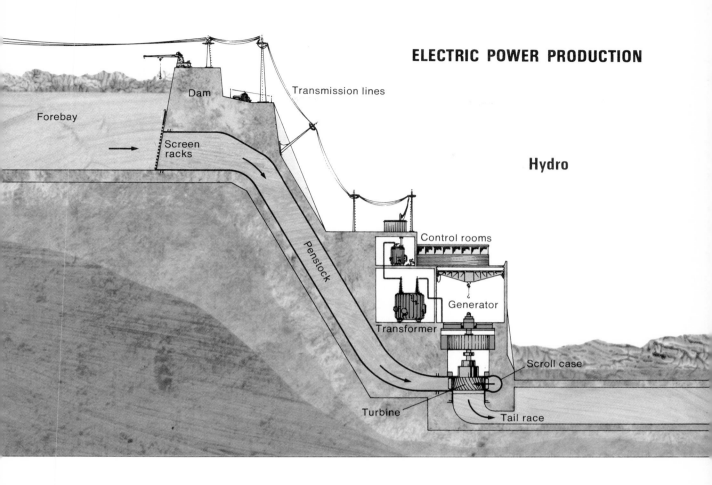

Dam

Transmission lines

Forebay

Screen racks

Hydro

Penstock

Control rooms

Generator

Transformer

Scroll case

Turbine

Tail race

to stores and offices, to your home, and from the fuse box there to electrical outlets all over the house.

Canada ranks second in the world in the production of hydro-electricity. Why? First of all, the enormous quantities of water needed are provided by a vast system of rivers and lakes. Many rivers, particularly in the Shield and the Cordillera, are fast-flowing, and several have the greatest energy potential in the world. Lakes act as natural storage basins and, together with the forest cover, serve to regulate the natural flow of water. A steady and reliable annual precipitation guarantees an adequate water "bank." To the hydro-electric industry, all this water is like having money in the bank. It is borrowed — for a

few seconds at a time — to drive turbines and then, via Nature's hydrologic cycle, is paid back. (And all without interest charges!) So the next time you are held up by drizzle, rain, snow, or sleet, remember that this water is the "fuel" that stokes many of our factories and homes.

Just think of how things would be without electricity. There would be no television or radio, no telephone, and we would be reading by candlelight or oil lamp. All the laundry would have to be done by hand, and we would be using carpet sweepers instead of vacuum cleaners, coal or wood stoves instead of electric ranges, iceboxes instead of refrigerators, and so on.

Electrical energy is the lifeblood of Canadian industries. In fact, increased electric

KINDS OF RAINFALL

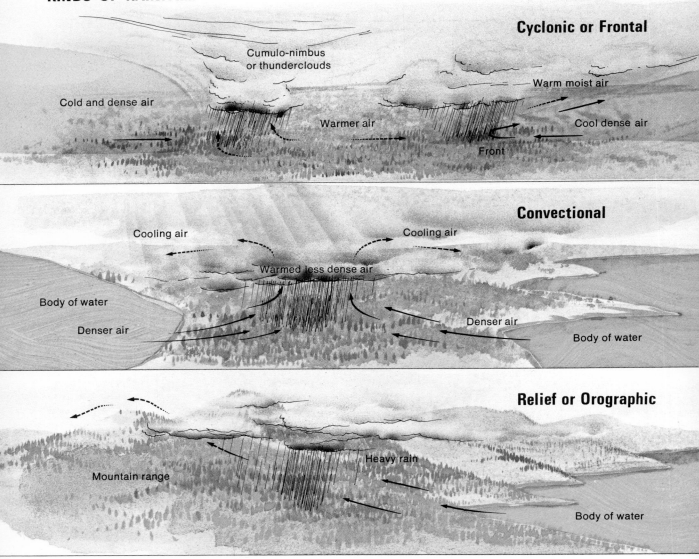

Cyclonic or Frontal

Cumulo-nimbus or thunderclouds

Warm moist air

Cold and dense air

Warmer air

Cool dense air

Front

Convectional

Cooling air

Cooling air

Warmed less dense air

Body of water

Denser air

Denser air

Body of water

Relief or Orographic

Heavy rain

Mountain range

Body of water

Two types of frontal precipitation, warm and cold, are shown in the top diagram. At the warm front, warmer air is flowing up a gentle wedge of denser air: the result is long, monotonous precipitation from a huge, continuous nimbo-stratus cloud formation. In contrast, at the cold front, a wedge of colder, dense air is thrusting vigorously into less dense air, forcing it up. From a long line of threatening, cumulo-nimbus clouds, sudden squalls drench the countryside with short, heavy showers.

In the middle diagram, convectional rainfall occurs as denser air pours into an area of warmer, less dense air. The dense air forces up the less dense, which cools, condenses, and precipitates.

In the bottom diagram, moving air has met uplands. Consequently, it has been forced up, cooled, and condensed. The result is relief or orographic precipitation.

power in Canada and a marked growth of industrial development had simultaneous beginnings around 1900. It is the *availability* of low-cost hydro-electric power that

has made possible many of our most important industries. The mining industry alone consumes 20 per cent of all the hydro-electricity produced in Canada. Such enormous amounts are used by pulp-and-paper plants that many have their own dam and powerhouse facilities. Canada leads the world in aluminum and asbestos production, which depends entirely on electricity for power.

The production of aluminum, the "magic metal" that can be stretched and rolled into almost any shape from airplane fuselages and wings to chewing-gum wrappers, is a remarkable example of the importance of water and hydro-electricity. Aluminum is locked in its ore, bauxite. To get it out, an enormous quantity of heat is necessary, and the only economical way to provide this is by using hydro-electric power. (Even so, the amount of electricity needed to free one tonne of aluminum would light a home for fifteen years.) A variety of materials is necessary to manufacture aluminum, and these are scattered around the world. Bauxite, the ore containing aluminum, is mined in Jamaica and in Guyana, South America. From Texas comes petroleum coke, used to filter out impurities from the ore. Cryolite, a flux used to help aluminum form into a mass, comes from Greenland. (A white material, it looks so much like ice that natives of Greenland call it "the ice that does not melt in summer.") All in all, seven tonnes of various raw materials are required to help make one tonne of aluminum. The cheapest way to transport them? Water.

A big problem for the manufacturer of aluminum is finding the right plant site. There must be both fast-running water dropping from a height to provide energy to produce electricity and calm waters in which to navigate ships. There are not too many places on earth that combine these two requirements. One such site is to be found in Quebec's Saguenay Valley. Glaciers gouged out this valley to a great depth, leaving its walls steep and smooth. For 48 kilometres after the Saguenay River leaves Lac St. Jean, it is a mad torrent of foaming water. Swirling and plunging, it races down a drop of 100 metres. Then it levels out to become a wide, deep waterway flowing calmly along to join the St. Lawrence. Here, then, is the right combination of a rushing river that can be harnessed to produce hydro-electricity and a deep-water anchorage near this power site.

The construction of power facilities at Shipshaw on the Saguenay is the story of how engineers found ways to get around the impossible. Building the powerhouse was no problem. But diverting the water from its natural river bed to flow through the powerhouse most certainly was. The river was moving at such terrific speed in its 48-kilometre rock trench that it would sweep away any material dumped in the water as the foundation of a dam. Eventually, the difficulty was tackled in a manner no one had ever thought of before. At a particular point on the river, soundings were taken of its bed in order to learn its exact shape. On either side of the river, where the water was flowing less swiftly, huge, steel-reinforced cement abutments were constructed and anchored to the rock walls of the valley. Then, on one abutment was built a 27-metre-high chunk of concrete, flat on one side and shaped on the other to fit the contour of the river bed. In other words, the engineers were producing the dam by constructing it on its side straight up into the air! When the day came to drop the dam into place, the cement blocks holding it upright were dynamited away. For a breathless moment, the tall, oddly shaped structure just hung there. Then, with tantalizing slowness, it began to fall across the river. It crashed into the waters, fitting exactly into place like the last piece of a giant jigsaw puzzle. The dam held solidly, and the Saguenay's rushing torrent turned aside to go through the powerhouse.

Power and more power

All this happened in the 1920s and was just one incident in the creation of one of the most gigantic power developments on earth. In the years since, several dams have been built on the headwaters of the Saguenay River to store water in reservoirs and control the annual flow of energy through powerhouses on the river. So much hydroelectricity is now produced in this drainage basin that there is more than enough to meet the power needs of aluminum, copper-refining, and pulp-and-paper plants. The

In the foreground is the Shipshaw powerhouse and dam, and in the background those of Chute-à-Caron. These power developments feed electricity to an aluminum plant at the nearby town of Arvida, Quebec. About 32 kilometres downstream is Port Alfred, where aluminum is shipped out to manufacturing centres on the Great Lakes and on the east coast of the United States.

surplus is fed into the Quebec Hydro net and thence to factories and homes.

The entire complex of installations on the Saguenay is just one of several major hydro-electric developments in the Canadian Shield. In Quebec, there are dams, powerhouses, and transmitting towers in the valleys of the St. Maurice, Outardes, and Manicouagan rivers. A massive power project is under construction in James Bay. Another huge development is on the Churchill River in Labrador, where the energy of the awesome Churchill Falls — half again as high as those at Niagara — is harnessed and utilized. The technology of hydro-electric power is so advanced today that the operation of the Kelsey Dam on Manitoba's Nelson River is controlled by a solitary engineer in a building 48 kilometres from the dam. Great though these

The aluminum plant at Kitimat, British Columbia. Deep inside the mountain on the left of the photograph, Nechako River waters, diverted to flow westward, plunge down a penstock half a mile long to spin the turbines and generators of a powerhouse also blasted out of solid rock.

major projects are, hundreds of smaller, equally important, hydro-electric sites are scattered over the Shield. Installations at Baie Comeau and Island Falls serve pulp-and-paper plants. Others on the Mattagami, English, and Wanapitei rivers supply power to mines. Dams on the Trent, Otonabee, and Winnipeg rivers heat and light nearby cities.

Elsewhere in Canada our ever-increasing demands for energy have created other vast hydro-electric schemes. In northern British Columbia, the W. A. C. Bennett Dam at Portage Mountain on the Peace River holds back a brand-new lake that is 1600 square kilometres in extent. This head of water, named Lake Williston, drops down into a powerhouse located inside a huge underground cavern. Some of the hydro-electricity generated here is used in Vancouver, 924 kilometres away. Far to the north at Kemano, a powerhouse deep in-

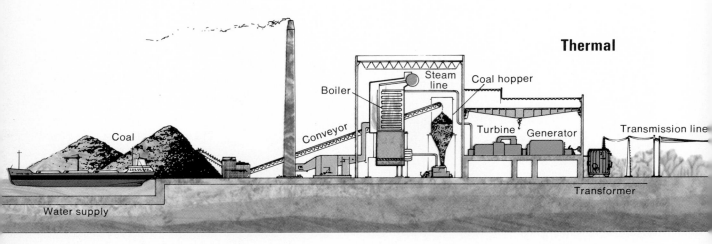

Used primarily at peak hours as a supplementary source, thermal electricity may well be a major source from which to meet the ever-increasing demands for energy today and tomorrow. The world's largest thermal generating station is located next to the shoreline of Lake Ontario on the western edge of Toronto.

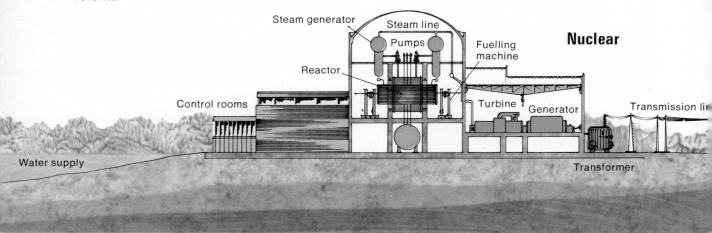

A nuclear reactor is powered by such radioactive materials as uranium and thorium. Canada's first, full-scale, nuclear-power station went into operation at Pickering, Ontario, in 1967. Four years later, 8 per cent of the electricity supplied by Ontario Hydro was being generated by the Pickering facilities and by those of another nuclear-powered installation at Douglas Point on the shore of Lake Huron.

side a mountain powers the aluminum plant at Kitimat. In the southern interior of the province, an installation at Trail generates electricity for one of the largest copper-smelting operations in the world.

As for the entire drainage system of the Great Lakes-St. Lawrence, about 75 per cent of the nation's total hydro-electric production is generated in this region. The Beauharnois and Robert Saunders stations on the St. Lawrence, together with the Sir Adam Beck-Niagara generating stations, comprise some of the greatest hydro-electric developments in Canada. In fact, when you look at the entire drainage system of the St. Lawrence — the river itself, plus its Ottawa, Gatineau, St. Maurice, Péribonca, Saguenay, Betsiamites (Bersimis) and Manicouagan-Outardes tributaries — you are looking at what is possibly the mightiest concentration of hydro-electric power developments in the entire world.

Study 14

1. Kitimat and Churchill Falls are both remote from concentrations of industry and population. What circumstances led to hydro-electric developments in these locations?
2. About 75 per cent of Canada's hydro-electric production is generated in the Great Lakes-St. Lawrence drainage system.
   (a) What are the locations of hydro-electric developments?
   (b) What use is made of their output?
3. On an outline map of Canada, indicate by appropriate symbols
   (a) hydro-electric developments already mentioned
   (b) major developments elsewhere in Canada.

   List all these developments below the map and beside each indicate the approximate output, the use made of the output, and the reasons for the location of the development.

   Now mark on your map regions that have the greatest potential for development.

   List these potential developments (below the actual developments) and explain the factors that determine their location.
4. Where in Canada are thermal-electric operating plants located?
5. (a) Use the *Canada Year Book* to find out what fuels are used by electrical utilities to generate power.
   (b) Using the dollar value of each fuel, calculate the percentage of each fuel for each province.
   (c) Rank by dollar value the use of these fuels nationally.
6. (a) Where in Canada are nuclear-powered generating plants located?
   (b) What part does water play in these plants?
   (c) What is the potential for further development of nuclear-powered plants?
7. What proportion of Canada's output of hydro-electricity is used within Canada? To what regions and for what purposes is the remainder exported?

"Black Gold"

In its crude form, petroleum is practically useless. It must be refined to provide the energy that powers engines, the oil that lubricates machines, and the fuel that heats buildings. Without oil and gasoline the wheels of industry and transportation would grind to a halt. To begin to understand the tremendous importance of petroleum — which we commonly call "oil" — take a look at the map below. Oil is a commodity that almost every nation sells or buys. It is the single most important item of international trade. In fact, the fuels derived from crude petroleum provide half the world's supply of energy.

No one knows how oil was formed, but most scientists accept what is called the organic theory. Hundreds of millions of years ago, enormous numbers of tiny marine plants and animals, some of them

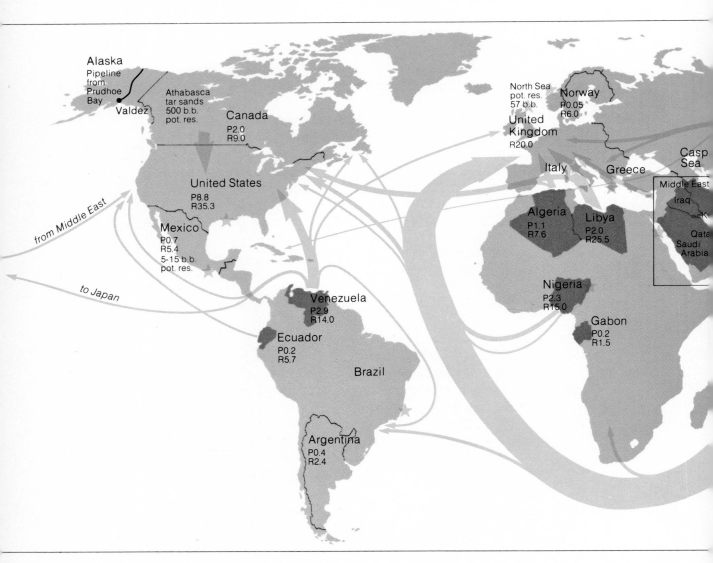

microscopic in size, lived in huge, shallow seas. In countless billions, these plants and animals died and sank into the mud and sand of ocean floors. There, even smaller forms of life – bacteria – caused them to decay. The earth revolved endlessly in its orbit, and the sun rose and set in equally endless repetition. And all the time incomprehensible numbers of dead or dying plants and animals dropped to ocean floors, and **sediments** (fine sand and mud) drifted down to cover the lifeless plant and animal matter. With climate changes, these ancient seas disappeared and reappeared several times, and more and more layers of mud and sand accumulated, one on top of the other.

In the course of millions of years, sediments piled up, their great weight pressing lower layers into hard, compact **strata** of sedimentary rock. Mud was compressed into shale, sand into sandstone, and skeletal remains into limestone. Plant and animal remains are rich in carbon and hydrogen, the chemical building blocks of petroleum. Probably by bacterial action, heat, pressure – or all three – these remains were transformed into the hydrocarbons that

Middle East

Saudi Arabia P8.5 R132.0		
Iran P6.1 R60.0	Kuwait P2.2 R64.0	
Iraq P2.0 R31.5	United Arab Emirates P1.8 R24.0	
Qatar P0.5 R6.5	Bahrain P0.07 R0.4	Oman P0.3 R5.3

WHERE THE OIL IS: AND WHERE IT GOES, 1975

■ OPEC (Organization of Petroleum Exporting Countries)

✴ Major oil discoveries in 1974

→ Movements of major oil exports

P Daily production in millions of barrels

R Reserves in billions of barrels

U.S.S.R. P9.0 R75.0

China P1.0 R19.6

Japan

India

to U.S.A.

Brunei & Malaysia P0.3 R1.6

Indonesia P1.5 R10.5

Australia and N.Z. P0.4 R1.7

Adapted from *Time,* 1975

91

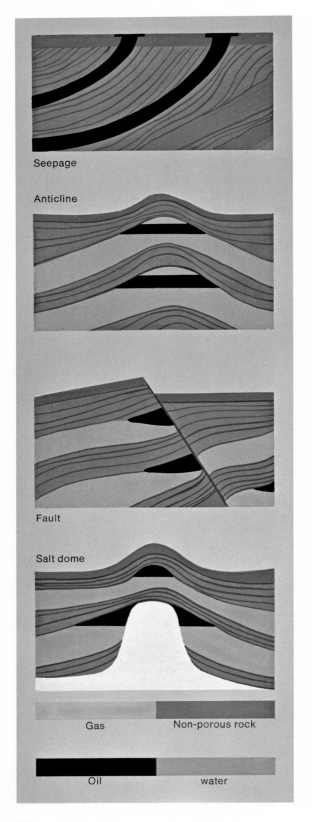

Seepage

Anticline

Fault

Salt dome

| Gas | Non-porous rock |

| Oil | water |

make up oil. That is why petroleum (and natural gas) is called a "fossil" fuel.

As the rock layers shifted and folded, the oil was squeezed upward to collect into "traps." Sometimes, oil was forced to the earth's surface and formed pools and tar pits. Some ancient people burned oil for light. Some North American Indians used tar to caulk canoes. However, during the first half of the nineteenth century, the lighting used in Canadian and American houses was a product of the sea, not the land. Men hunted whales – the sperm whale in particular – whose blubber was rendered into candles and oil for lamps. By mid-century, this source of oil had become quite scarce. And with new machines coming into use and increasing the demand for lubricants, a fresh source of oil had to be found.

There is no absolutely accurate technique to determine where petroleum deposits are located. The only way to find out if there is oil in a given location is by drilling. Exploration in the latter half of the nineteenth century consisted of drilling near sites of surface oil seepage. The first oil-producing well in North America was drilled by James M. Williams near Oil Springs in Lambton County, Ontario, in 1858. A year later, Colonel E. L. Drake drilled the first United States' well in Titusville, Pennsylvania. It was not long until, in certain parts of North America, you could hardly see the ground for oil derricks. Early oil explorers relied on guesswork and played hunches. Gadgets called "doodlebugs" were used to discover oil deposits in much the same way that a water-

Common oil traps. Petroleum can be imprisoned wherever earth movements have fractured layers of rock. Which diagram shows this?

diviner uses a forked twig to find water. Most of the time, the doodlebugs did not work.

With underground exploration, science took over. Today oilmen do not go looking for oil; they look for indications of where oil might be located. Thus prospectors concentrate their attention on rock strata formed by sand, salt, clay, lime – in fact, wherever there are geological signs that suggest the floor of an ancient sea. In their efforts to locate petroleum-bearing structures, oilmen have worked in swamps, on Arctic tundra, in dense forests, and even on offshore drilling platforms erected above the ocean's surface.

In areas where rock strata are not exposed enough to give an idea of underlying subsurface layers, new geological and geophysical techniques have been developed. The chief instruments used are the gravimeter, the magnetometer, and the seismograph. Of these three methods, the last is the most laborious and the most expensive, but also the most accurate. Yet, no matter how promising the oil-bearing potential of a given location, only by drilling can you discover if oil is actually there; and a modern drilling operation is expensive. It involves the installation of a complex rotary drilling rig, powered by diesel engines and worked by round-the-clock drilling crews. The risks are always high. Even in proven oil fields, a new well may not produce oil. About 25 per cent of field wells are dry; the percentage is considerably higher in new, unproven territory. Even if oil is found, production may not be profitable. The

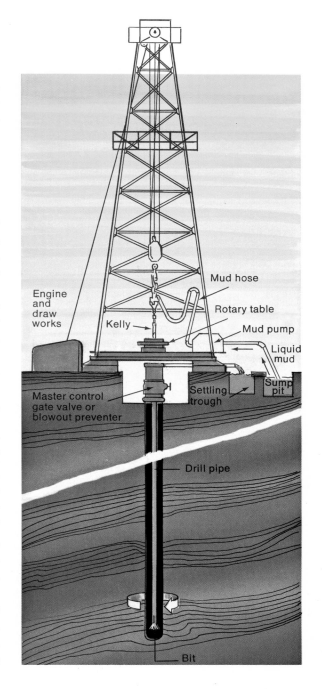

The "bit" is attached to a nine-metre length of hollow steel called a drill pipe. When the bit has cut deep enough into the earth that the drill pipe has almost disappeared from sight, another length is added. Each time a bit is changed, _all_ the drill pipes must be lifted out, unscrewed, and stacked. When the new bit is in place, all the lengths of pipe have to be re-inserted down the hole.

"Drilling mud" is an important factor in the rig's operation. This mixture of clay, chemicals, and water is pumped through the drilling pipe and then returns to the surface. It brings up what oilmen call _cuttings_, fragments of rock ground loose by the bit. Drilling mud also helps to lubricate and cool the bit, coat the inside of the hole, and prevent cave-ins of unstable rock layers surrounding the drill hole.

Shell's first service station in the city of Montreal opened in 1925. An outstanding feature of stations of that era was the hand-operated pump, which required considerable muscle and caused many a backache. Few outlets had more than two pumps on a single island. A minimum of merchandise was available, and lubrications were done outside. Note the car on the hoist at the left, probably one of the first hoists in the city because pits and ramps were more common.

quality of the oil may be too low or the volume too small for the discovery to be commercially exploitable. All in all, oil exploration is a risky and expensive business.

Crude petroleum is composed of hydrocarbons combined in molecules of various sizes and arrangements. The smallest molecules constitute the gases, and the largest make up the heavy fuels, waxes, and as-

phalts. In between are gasoline, kerosene, light fuels, and lubricating oils. These **fractions** boil at different temperatures — gasoline at lower temperatures; kerosene, higher; diesel fuels and lubricating oils, still higher. In the refining process, crude petroleum is separated into fractions by **distillation.** This is done in a fractionating tower, which is divided into levels of different temperatures, the lowest at the top, the highest at the bottom. After the crude petroleum has been heated to a vapor, it is piped into the tower. As the vapor rises in the tower, it condenses. Each fraction condenses at a different temperature level and is drawn off — gasoline at the coolest top level, heavy fuel oils at the hottest bottom level.

The amount of different fractions produced in the refinery can be varied by conversion processes that change less valuable fractions into products that are more in demand. **Catalytic cracking,** for example, cracks (breaks down) the heavier diesel- and lubricating-oil molecules into the lighter ones of gasoline. **Polymerization** does the reverse; it combines the lighter molecules of waste gases into heavier gasoline fractions. By such conversion processes, production of gasoline, kerosene, heating oil, and diesel fuel fractions can be geared to market demands.

Supply and demand

The refining of crude petroleum converts this raw source of energy into fuels that power automobiles, trucks, tractors, trains, ships, and airplanes. The term "oil" is used loosely to refer to crude petroleum and its derived products. So references to an "oil shortage" can mean anything from diminishing supplies of crude petroleum to a shortage of particular fractions — gasoline, heating oil, diesel fuel, etc.

In the early days of the oil industry, there was a great demand for kerosene and lubricating greases. The parts of crude petroleum that could not be distilled into these fractions were simply discarded as waste. (Refineries often got rid of "waste" gasoline by dumping it into rivers and streams.) Then came the automobile. At first, enough gasoline could be produced by distillation. With greater use of automobiles and increasing demand for gasoline, conversion processes have been developed to step up gasoline production. But with growing numbers of oil furnaces to heat buildings and an increasing need for power for factories, railways, smelters, etc. there is greater demand for fuels. With the increase in the number of jet aircraft there is an ever-growing demand for kerosene. With more and more grinding and drilling machines needed for mass production there is a steadily increasing demand for lubricating oils.

The production of particular fractions can be increased to meet demand, but oil is a **non-renewable resource.** Supplies cannot be replenished. The supply of crude petroleum is finite. How long before there is an absolute "oil shortage"?

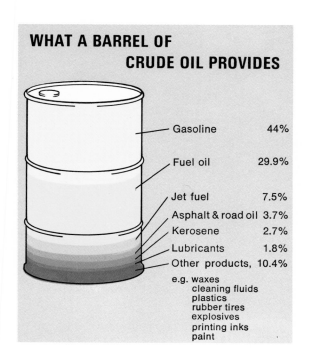

WHAT A BARREL OF CRUDE OIL PROVIDES

Gasoline	44%
Fuel oil	29.9%
Jet fuel	7.5%
Asphalt & road oil	3.7%
Kerosene	2.7%
Lubricants	1.8%
Other products,	10.4%

e.g. waxes
cleaning fluids
plastics
rubber tires
explosives
printing inks
paint

96

Study 15

1. Define and explain the following: gravimeter, magnetometer, seismograph. How is each used in oil exploration?
2. Describe the operation of a rotary drilling rig.
3. What are the prime and subsidiary products of petroleum and what uses are made of them?
4. The exploration and production of natural gas is closely related to the exploration and production of oil.
   (a) How is gas recovered from the earth?
   (b) What goes on in a gas-processing plant?
   (c) What uses are made of natural gas?
5. On an outline map of Canada, mark the oil and gas fields, the oil refineries, and the gas-processing plants.
   (a) Account for the location of all of these.
   (b) Look at the map at the beginning of the chapter. What regions do the pipelines serve? From where do those regions not served by pipeline get their oil and gas?
6. Explain the factors that determine the method used to transport oil.
7. Canada's role as an oil producer dates from the discovery of oil in Leduc, Alberta, in 1947. Write a report on the development of the oil industry in Canada since that date.

*   *   *

There is much, much more to the subject of energy — the location of individual sources of energy, their exploitation, transportation, processing, by-products, and marketing. The subject is vast and complex. This chapter has simply concentrated on the major forms of energy we use in industry, commerce, transportation, and in our homes. What an impact they have had on our lives! Thanks to them, we can do many more things much more efficiently and much more profitably than our ancestors could.

When homes were converted from gas lighting to electric, many a person who had used, first candles, then oil lamps, then gas stood at a light switch and happily turned a light on and off for the longest time. To

them, it was a miracle. Another delight was the simple act of turning up a thermostat. To be able to heat a home with a twist of the wrist instead of shovelling coal into a furnace several times a day (and night) was truly a miracle. Today's energy resources have revolutionized society to an extent only dreamed of even fifty years ago. Travel to Europe or Asia in a matter of hours! Men on the Moon! World events appearing in one's living room at the very moment they happen!

We take these things for granted. But what happens when there are more people wanting electric power than there are stations to produce it? What happens when all the oil and gas supplies run out?

◀ *Petroleum and natural gas deposits are only found in certain parts of Canada and have to be transported thousands of miles to major markets.*

Study and Research

1. Coal is still an important source of energy.
   (a) Where are Canada's principal deposits of this fuel?
   (b) What uses are made of the mined coal?
   (c) What factors will influence the future development of coal mining in Canada?

2. Write a report on hydro-electric development in the Peace River district. Include in your report
   (a) the reasons for the development
   (b) the benefits to the region and to the Canadian economy
   (c) the effects on the physical environment and the way of life of the inhabitants of the region.
   How do you evaluate the net results?

3. Draw up a list of what you consider to be (a) necessary and (b) wasteful uses of hydro-electric power in industry, transportation, retail services, and private homes. Justify the items you have listed. What restrictions, modifications, and alternatives, if any, would you propose?

4. (a) Rank Canada among the oil-producing nations of the world.
   (b) What are the markets for Canada's oil production?
   (c) Why does Canada both export and import oil?
   (d) What factors will determine the future distribution of Canada's oil production?

5. Oil is a non-renewable resource. Apply this statement to an analysis of *current* uses of petroleum and recommendations for *best* uses of this resource.

6. Write a brief report on current research into alternative sources of energy.

7. The jurisdiction over natural resources has been a subject of continuing debate at federal-provincial conferences.
   (a) Outline the federal position.
   (b) Outline the positions of the different provinces.
   (c) What special problems are posed by offshore exploration and development?
   (d) Evaluate the conflicting arguments with proposals for possible resolution and/or compromise.

8. Debate the motion: "Natural resources should be publicly owned."

9. Our need for coal, oil, gas, and hydro-electricity is beyond dispute. However, there are prices exacted for benefits gained.

   Write a report detailing the impact on the environment of the development, transportation methods, and use of these energy sources.

   What criteria can we use to determine the point at which the price becomes too high?

10. It is energy that turns the wheels of industry and transportation. Make a pie graph of the value of production of the different energy sources used in Canada. As you read the following chapters, refer to this pie graph and add to it information that gives a more complete picture of the role of particular energy sources in the Canadian economy.

Chapter 4 Wealth from the waters

Canadian Government Office of Tourism Photo

North America's oldest industry

What first attracted many Europeans to North America? Gleaming gold? Fine furs? Rich farmland? None of these – at least, not until much later. In the beginning was the cod. Why cod? In times when fish was eaten much more commonly than meat, the cod's firm, protein-rich flesh could be easily preserved by salting or drying in the sun. Storage was no problem. Cod could be kept, layer upon layer, in barrels, or just stacked in piles like firewood. Above all, supplies of cod were abundant, particularly in Gulf of St. Lawrence and Newfoundland waters.

Fishing settlements were established on the Atlantic coast in the seventeenth century, and **inshore** fishing grew and prospered. Using simple gear such as traps, handlines, or gill nets, fishermen operated small open boats within a few miles of the shore, returning nightly to clean their catch, salt it, and spread it on **flakes** (platforms) to dry in the summer wind and sun. Dried cod was exported from all the coastal areas of Atlantic Canada. For three hundred years it was by far the most important product of Newfoundland and accounted for almost half of the exports of Nova Scotia. After the small operations of inshore fishing came the development of **offshore** fishing with large dory schooners that set out from coastal villages and fished the Grand Banks for days at a time.

The village of Bay de Verde is typical of many tiny outports on the island of Newfoundland. The life of these communities revolves around the dories, docks, and flakes.

Inshore fishing and the drying of cod declined as ice refrigeration and powered boats opened up higher-priced markets for fresh fish in the United States and central Canada. Today, trawlers drag huge, bag-shaped nets along the ocean floor. The catch is hauled aboard the dragger and stored in ice in the holds.

Study 16

1. Assuming two men per boat and five persons per household, what percentage of the population of this outport would depend directly on the fishery for its livelihood?
2. What might be the occupations of the rest of the population? How might this explain the movement of many people from outports to larger centres?
3. From the table on page 124 and the *Canada Year Book*, calculate the percentage of the labor force in Newfoundland that is directly employed in the primary fishing industry.
4. From the photograph, give at least three pieces of evidence that show that in this village fishing (catching and curing) is an individual rather than a co-operative activity.

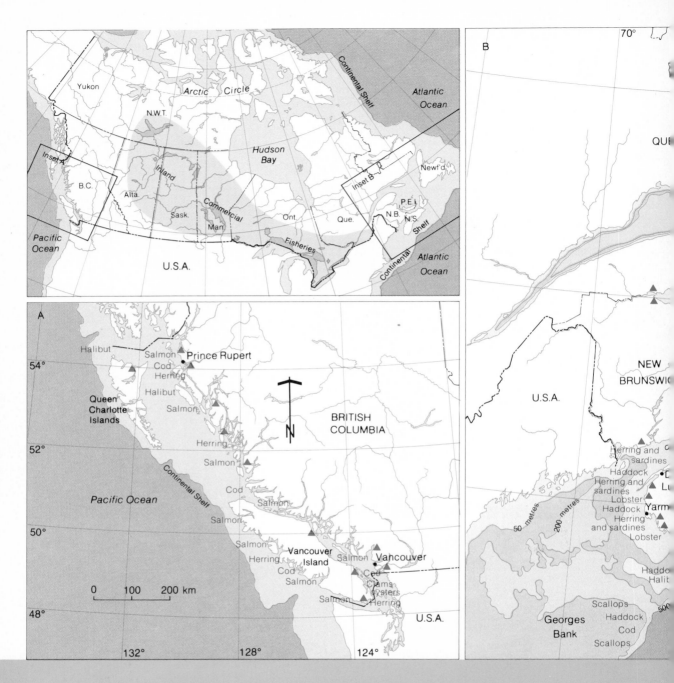

Study 17

1. Why are the Grand Banks such rich fishing grounds?
2. Dories, schooners, and trawlers are three types of vessels that have been used in the Atlantic fishing industry. Describe the operation of each. What other types of vessels have been used? In what branch of the fishery did each operate?

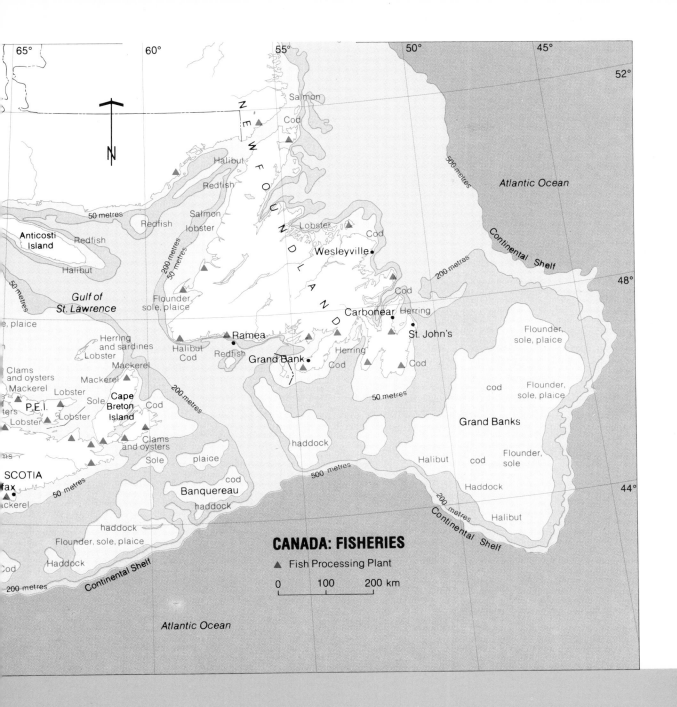

65°   **60°**   **55°**   **50°**   **45°**

52°

Salmon

Cod

N E W F O U N D L A N D

Halibut

Redfish

Atlantic Ocean

500 metres

Continental Shelf

50 metres

Salmon
lobster

Redfish

Lobster

Cod

Anticosti
Island

Redfish

Redfish

200 metres

50 metres

Wesleyville•

200 metres

48°

Halibut

*Gulf of
St. Lawrence*

Flounder,
sole, plaice

Cod

Carbonear

Herring

Flounder,
sole, plaice

e, plaice

Herring
and sardines

Ramea

•

St. John's

Lobster

Halibut
Cod

Redfish

Herring

Cod

Clams
and oysters

Mackerel

Grand Bank •

Cod

Cod

cod

Flounder,
sole, plaice

Mackerel

Mackerel

200 metres

50 metres

ters

Lobster

Sole

**Cape
Breton
Island**

Cod

Grand Banks

P.E.I.

Lobster

Lobster

Clams
and oysters

haddock

Halibut

cod

Flounder,
sole

ns

Sole

plaice

500 metres

Haddock

SCOTIA

cod

200 metres

Halibut

ax

•

Banquereau

Continental Shelf

44°

ckerel

50 metres

haddock

Halibut

haddock

CANADA: FISHERIES

Flounder, sole, plaice

▲ Fish Processing Plant

od

Haddock

0   100   200 km

200 metres

Continental Shelf

Atlantic Ocean

3. Draw a time chart of the Atlantic fishing industry, from the sixteenth century to the 1930s. Divide the chart by centuries. The headings for your chart should include the following: dates, fishermen's country of origin, type of vessel used, type of gear and equipment, principal species caught, principal processing methods, markets.

The lobster fishery of Yarmouth County, Nova Scotia

The most valuable of all Atlantic species now caught is lobster. All counties in Nova Scotia and Prince Edward Island, all coastal counties of New Brunswick, and all coastal districts of Newfoundland and Quebec engage in lobster fishing. An astounding 2½ million traps are used each year.

When the summer herring-fishing season is over, the fishermen of western Nova Scotia put away their gear and get down to the business of preparing for the lobster season. Lobster fishing requires a good deal of gear, most of it made at home: lobster traps (up to a legal maximum of four hundred); marker buoys; boxes to store the catch; and bait. Pegs — pieces of wood put between each captured lobster's pincers — are all-important. If a fisherman fails to take these along, he may find that his catches have torn claws off each other before he gets them home! Finally, he must check that his licence is in order and make

sure that he has a regulation measure to size his catch. Lobsters in this district can be kept only if the carapace measures 8.1 centimetres or more.

During the fall, the wharves and jetties hum with movement and activity. Thousands upon thousands of lobster traps are assembled and stacked all over the place. Finally, boats piled high with gear and engines ticking over, the fishermen wait impatiently for the government inspector to blow his whistle, signifying that the season is open. Boats are eager to be away to place their traps in the best positions on the lobster fishing grounds.

Once the traps are in place they must be tended almost every day. Each trap is hauled up and its catch removed and sorted. (Smaller lobsters, egg-bearing females, and any other creatures that have strayed into the trap are thrown back.) Many lobster boats are now equipped with

What four items of lobstering gear have been assembled on this pier?

motors for hauling in the traps. And no wonder. Imagine standing in a pitching open boat and hauling in a heavy trap with a handline. Then imagine repeating the process 399 times. Every day!

Most fishermen in the Yarmouth district base themselves near their traps, living in cottages on one of the many islands off the coast and returning to the mainland on weekends only. Buyer boats (lobster smacks) travel round the islands and gather up the daily catch. If weather conditions are exceptionally bad or if the fisherman wishes to hold his catch for a higher price, the lobsters can be stored for some weeks in floating wooden "cars" moored to a wharf or pier.

Lobsters can live for several days in cool, moist air, and most of them are shipped live to market. They are picked up by truck from the mainland wharves. Some are taken to the airport at Halifax for shipment to Europe; others are taken by daily ferry service from Yarmouth to Portland or Bar Harbor, Maine, for sale in the United States. The Nova Scotia lobster that was lured into the trap on Monday may well be tempting a diner in Paris, New York, or Chicago on Tuesday or Wednesday.

Yarmouth is one of the most productive of all the lobster-fishing counties of the Maritime Provinces. Although lobstering can mean anything from a full-time job to "moonlighting" with a dory and a dozen traps, for most Yarmouth fishermen it is their main source of income — but not their only source. Fishermen are very versatile people. When the lobster season is over, the Yarmouth fisherman, towing a dory astern his boat, goes out after Irish moss. This seaweed is used in the manufacture of paints, varnishes, toothpaste, and, would you believe, ice cream. The fisherman simply gathers up the seaweed from the shallow water, stows it in the dory, and sells it for a quick, easy profit. In summer, he gets out the nets and goes after herring. And then it is lobster time again.

The opening of the lobster season has everyone wading knee-deep in traps and other equipment.

OPEN SEASONS

District No.	Minimum Size* Limit	Season
1	8.1 cm	Nov. 15-June 24
3	8.1 cm	Oct. 15-Dec. 31 Mar. 1-July 31
4	8.1 cm	Last Tues. in Nov. to May 31
5	8.1 cm	Apr. 10-June 30
6a	8.1 cm	May 20-July 20
6b	7.0 cm	May 16-July 15
7a	8.1 cm	May 1-June 30
7b	6.4 cm	May 1-June 30
7c	6.4 cm	May 1-June 30
8	6.4 cm	Aug. 10-Oct. 10
9a	7.6 cm	May 10 to July 10
9b		No open season in lagoons
10a	7.6 cm	May 20-July 31
10b	7.6 cm	June 15-Aug. 15
10c	7.6 cm	May 10-July 27
10d	7.6 cm	May 1-July 17
11	8.1 cm	Apr. 20-July 5
12	8.1 cm	May 5-July 10
13	8.1 cm	Apr. 20-July 15
14	8.1 cm	Apr. 20-June 30
Offshore A	8.1 cm	No closed season

*Minimum length measured from rear of either eye socket along a line parallel to the centre line of the body shell, to the rear end of the body shell.

Study 18

1. Draw diagrams of the items of gear used in lobstering.
2. The Atlantic lobster fishery has been divided into districts by government regulation. For what purposes was the fishery so divided? Have these been achieved? Why or why not?
3. What might explain the fact that there is no open season in district 9b?

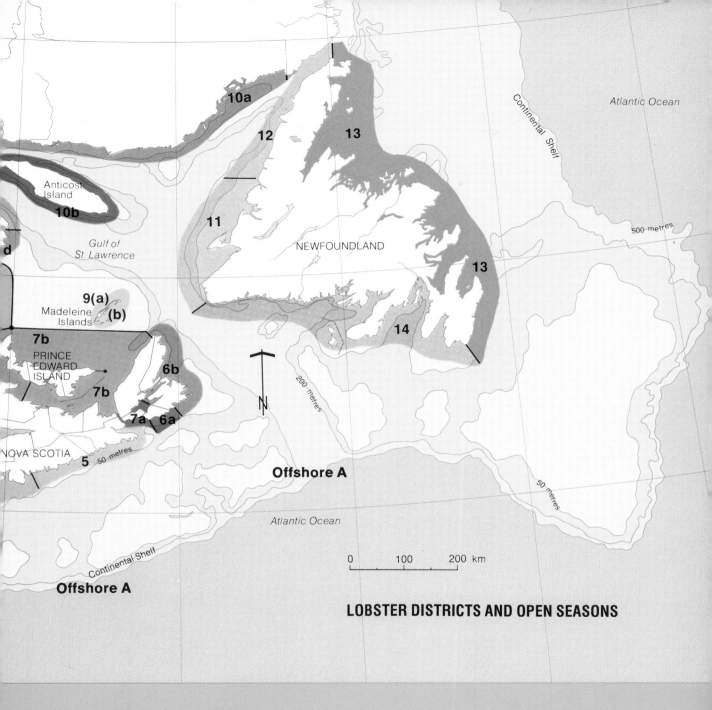

Map labels:
Atlantic Ocean
Continental Shelf
500 metres
10a
12
13
Anticosti Island
10b
13
Gulf of St. Lawrence
11
NEWFOUNDLAND
d
9(a)
(b)
Madeleine Islands
14
7b
PRINCE EDWARD ISLAND
6b
7b
7a 6a
200 metres
N
NOVA SCOTIA
5 50 metres
Offshore A
50 metres
Atlantic Ocean
Continental Shelf
0   100   200 km
Offshore A

LOBSTER DISTRICTS AND OPEN SEASONS

4. Fishermen in all these districts are only allowed to fish for lobster in specified open seasons. How do they earn a living when they cannot go lobster fishing?

5. In the Yarmouth district, there is a "devil take the hindmost" race to reach the best fishing grounds. What are some other ways in which to decide which fisherman gets which grounds?

The varied wealth of the Atlantic fishery

The Atlantic fishery is rich not only in the quantity of fish available but in the great variety of species, ranging from giant blue-fin tuna to tiny sardines. The inshore fisherman, however, can harvest only the fish that come to the shallower waters nearer to shore. This explains his dependence on cod, which move into the warming coastal waters in June when they follow capelin to their spawning grounds on the beaches. Capelin are taken for use as bait, fertilizer, or pet food. Herring, mackerel, and sometimes haddock are also available to inshore fishermen. Salmon, a high-value fish, has declined greatly in recent years, due to overfishing and the pollution of many of the streams in which the salmon spawn.

The offshore fisherman has a much wider choice. But where in the deep and broad Atlantic should he cast his net? It depends on what he is fishing for. Different species seek out particular water temperatures and feeding grounds. Cod, for example, spend the winter 160 kilometres or more offshore in the deep, relatively warm water beneath the cold layer. Haddock, redfish, and plaice are **groundfish**; they live and feed near the ocean floor. Redfish like to be at least 180 metres down and are found on the slope of the continental shelf and in deep channels. The place for plaice is cold water, like that of the Labrador Current on the northern slopes of the Grand Banks. (Longlines set for cod often come up loaded with plaice if the fisherman has underestimated the coldness of the water.) Halibut and grey-sole also turn up occasionally in offshore catches.

George S. Tomkins

Inshore or offshore, haddock or herring, the catch is usually taken directly to one of the many processing plants on the Atlantic coast. These vary from enormous multi-purpose factories with hundreds of employees to weathered buildings on village wharves. At peak periods the skeleton staff of permanent employees is augmented by numbers of local people, for the catch must be dealt with quickly.

National Sea Products, Ltd.

Left-hand photograph: What fish were probably unloaded from the larger dragger in the foreground? The smaller vessel is a scallop boat. Why is special equipment needed to harvest scallops? Right-hand photograph: Within a few feet of the dockside, the catch is speedily processed and packaged.

Study 19

1. How do you explain the co-existence of the flakes for drying cod in the photograph on page 103 with methods used in modern, integrated fish plants?
2. What fish were likely unloaded from the large dragger in the foreground? The smaller vessel is a scallop boat. What equipment is needed to harvest scallops?
3. Why have many inshore fishermen given up their boats and taken jobs in plants like this one at Lunenburg, or on company-owned vessels? Why do some still prefer the old way of earning a living?

Fish must be sorted and cleaned, and the waste material removed. They are then shipped fresh to market or processed — cured, canned, reduced to fish meal, or frozen. If rapid, efficient transportation is available, they may be packed and sent fresh to consuming centres. Via the overnight ferry from Yarmouth, fish from Wedgeport, Nova Scotia, can be in the dining rooms of New England the next day.

Certain species are almost always processed. Herring, for example, may be cured by being marinated in great wooden tanks of brine. These foul-looking herring, when cut, washed, spiced, and attractively packaged, become a most appetizing hors d'oeuvre. Large catches of herring may go directly to reduction plants, where they are made into meal and oil. Sardines are most often canned. Most fish, however, are marketed frozen. They may be fresh-frozen ready for cooking, or they may be completely cooked, ready to "heat and serve." Some plants concentrate on only a few simple processes. Others, like that at Lunenburg, which can process 22 700 kilograms of fish per hour, produce everything from fresh-frozen fillets to fish sticks.

The fishing industry makes use of every part of the catch that is marketable. Not even the waste is wasted. Skins, fins, bones, and entrails are used in the manufacture of fertilizers, drugs, animal feed, nail varnishes, and various other surprising products.

The Atlantic Provinces also benefit in an indirect way from their fisheries: tourism. Hordes of summer visitors head for uncrowded sandy beaches and picturesque fishing coves, for the Tuna Fish Tournament at Cape St. Mary and the Lobster Festival at Shediac. All of these tourists spend money on goods and services, which boosts the Atlantic economy: picture postcards and souvenir lobster traps; gasoline for the car and film for the camera; deepsea fishing excursions and seafood dinners. Just think of all the industries and commercial services that benefit from the influx of tourists! Every visitor must be lodged, fed, and served in many and various ways, thus creating jobs and income for the people of Atlantic Canada.

WHAT A FISH CAN YIELD

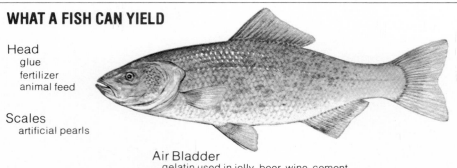

Head
glue
fertilizer
animal feed

Scales
artificial pearls

Air Bladder
gelatin used in jelly, beer, wine, cement

Bones, Fins, Entrails
fertilizer
animal feed

Shark Skin
leather
metal smoothing
and polishing

Food Products
From flesh and roe:
human food
protein
minerals
vitamins
poultry and livestock feed

Industrial Products
Oils expressed from body, used in:
soap
paint
tanning
lubricants

printing ink
metal plating
steel tempering
shortening

Drugs
From entrails:
vitamins
medicinal oil
amino acids
insulin
hormones
enzymes

Weighing tuna on a Prince Edward Island dock. (A whale of a catch?) Canadian Government Office of Tourism Photo

Study 20

1. Name the different occupations of people who will serve the needs of any one tourist in this crowd at Prince Edward Island.
2. Now take just one service — dinner in a restaurant. How many industries benefit from serving dinner to a tourist? How many different occupational groups?
3. Resolved: "Sport fishing is not the best use of the tuna fishery." Debate this motion.

Although fishing is no longer the predominant occupation on Canada's eastern shores, the economy of the Atlantic Provinces still depends heavily on this industry. This is a region of limited resources. So, with some of the world's best fishing grounds close at hand, with coastlines studded with coves and harbors, Canada's Atlantic Provinces continue in their long tradition as a sea-oriented society.

QUANTITY OF FISH LANDED ON THE ATLANTIC COAST, 1953-73, BY SPECIES

Only those landings in excess of 18 000 kg are shown. Smaller quantities of other species, including hake, halibut, catfish, salmon, crab, oysters, and scallops are also landed.

Study 21

1. (a) Which species accounted for the largest landings in 1973?
   (b) Which species declined in landings between 1963 and 1973? Why is this a matter of acute concern, considering that landings in some others species show a marked increase?
   (c) How do you account for the marked increase in herring and redfish catches?
2. How would you interpret the graph if you were
   (a) a member of the Newfoundland legislature?
   (b) a lobster fisherman in Prince Edward Island?
   (c) an official of the Department of Regional Economic Expansion (DREE) in Ottawa?
   How will the information presented affect your future plans and actions?

Fishing Pacific waters

In British Columbia, one looks in vain for graceful, low-lying boats, or fleets of dories in picturesque coves, or stacks of lobster traps piled on wharves. Here are large vessels with tall trolling poles standing high above their decks, or with deckspace almost totally occupied by a gigantic spool onto which yards and yards of netting are wound.

The boats are usually moored alongside floating wooden platforms in sheltered arms of the sea rather than in coves and harbors on the open coastline. For this fishery is very different in character from that of the Atlantic coast. The continental shelf is much narrower, and there are no great "banks" to attract fish and fishermen. The waters are warmer, and there are no lobsters or haddock found off these shores.

However, the Pacific waters, too, yield a rich and varied harvest. There are clams, shrimp and oysters, herring, halibut and sole, and, above all, the five species of Pacific salmon: sockeye, pink, coho, chum (or keta), and spring (chinook).

George S. Tomkins

Fishing boats moored at Steveston, British Columbia.

Pacific salmon – Canada's most valuable marine resource

Salmon begin life far from the ocean in nests hollowed out in the gravel beds of the headwaters of freshwater streams. The newly hatched salmon may be silted over and choked, or scoured out and scattered, or uncovered and dried out in very low water. But most survive to begin the long journey to the sea. Sockeye and coho usually spend one, even two years feeding on tiny organisms in lakes en route, but pink, chum, and spring proceed immediately to seawater. The little fish are exposed to every kind of attack. They may survive their underwater enemies only to fall prey to fishing birds or mammals. They may perish trying vainly to find their way down a stream that has become blocked or dried out. They may be swept into the turbines or spillways of a power project or poisoned in polluted water. Only 2-3 per cent of the young salmon are likely to survive the journey.

John A. Niemi

An Indian netting salmon from the Fraser River at Lytton, British Columbia.

Once in salt water, salmon spend most of their lives in the shallow waters of the continental shelf. They feed on plankton, herring, needlefish, and the abundant shrimp that drift north with the ocean current. After a few years, compelled by instinct and guided by a mysterious memory that defies human understanding, adult salmon begin the return journey — not only to their own river system, but unerringly back to the actual gravel beds in which they themselves had hatched. Swimming against swift currents, jumping rapids and waterfalls, struggling up man-made fish ladders, they travel hundreds of kilometres upstream. Battered, discolored, and exhausted, they lay their eggs and die.

It is during the journey back to the parent streams that great quantities of the fish, varying in average weight from 2.7 kilograms for sockeye to 18 kilograms for spring, are caught by large commercial vessels waiting for the salmon run. Nearly all the fish harvested today are taken by commercial vessels. These vary from one-man gill-netters, which operate in the silt-laden waters of river mouths, to powerful trollers and large seiners fishing the high seas.

TYPICAL FISH LADDER

Study 22

1. For thousands of years before Europeans arrived in British Columbia, Indians had been harvesting the salmon.
    (a) How did they catch and cure the salmon?
    (b) How dependent were they on salmon as a source of food?
    (c) What special rights do they still have in salmon fishing?
2. How do fish ladders operate? Why has it been necessary to construct fish ladders? To what extent have they solved the problem?

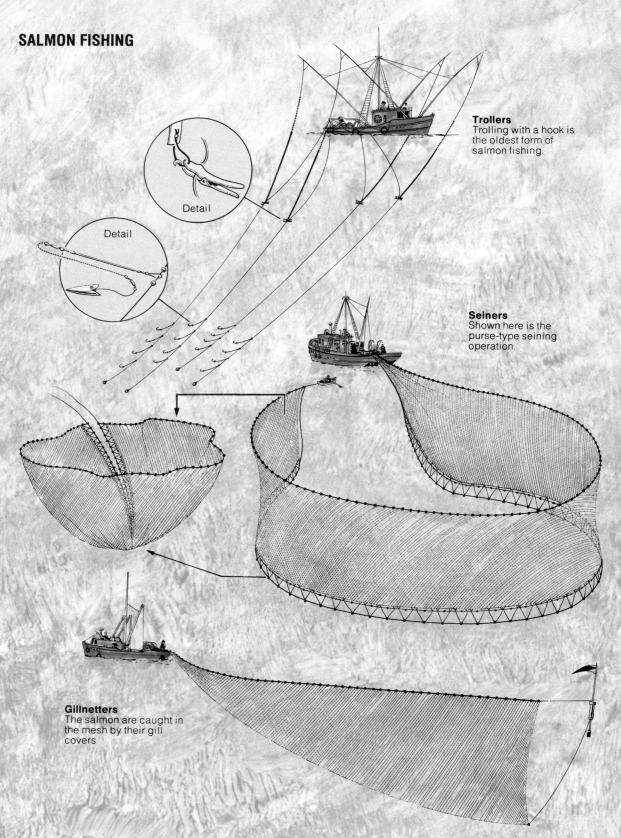

SALMON FISHING

Trollers
Trolling with a hook is the oldest form of salmon fishing.

Detail

Detail

Seiners
Shown here is the purse-type seining operation.

Gillnetters
The salmon are caught in the mesh by their gill covers

Pacific salmon mature at different times. Sockeye from Stuart Lake usually start their run in July; by the end of September, those bound for Shuswap Lake are passing through the Fraser mouth. And about a week after the last sockeye, the early pink salmon run begins. Then later in October or November come the chum. Quantity varies from year to year. In September, 1971, the sockeye run was so heavy that purse seiners were called in to the Fraser mouth to help gill-netters handle the run. (Biologists have discovered that if too many fish reach the spawning grounds, the next year's run is usually a poor one.) When the run is heavy, a fisherman can make a handsome income for a month's work. Figures, however, can be misleading. This exceptionally high income is seasonal; it is earned only during the peak of the salmon run. Furthermore, a fisherman's income fluctuates not only from month to month through a given year, but from one year to another, depending on the quality of the run.

The commercial salmon fishery is only about a hundred years old. Europeans arriving in the nineteenth century were faced with the age-old dilemma of "some good news and some bad news." First, the good news: an abundance of fish. Then the bad news: markets were far, far away. Drying and salting were never successful commercially, and it was not until canneries began to appear in the 1860s that commercial fishing became practicable. Improved trans-

portation links by both land and sea helped establish salmon as a major export of British Columbia and one for which Canada is world renowned.

Some salmon are frozen, and some have even been flown fresh to markets in eastern Canada and in Europe. But the bulk of the catch is canned. In earlier times, about ninety canneries were scattered all over the province, near the fishing grounds. However, during peak periods of production they were unable to handle the volume of salmon, and in slow periods both labor and machinery were idle. Only about twenty canneries are operating today, concentrated in the Vancouver area, but they pack a larger quantity of fish, and more efficiently and systematically. Speedy boats with plenty of ice can carry fish long distances to large canneries in urban centres. Here, there is a plentiful supply of labor, and cold-storage facilities allow fish to be fed gradually through the plant, making optimum use of machinery and labor.

There is one group of people for whom British Columbia salmon is measured in centimetres not dollars. These are the sport fishermen, who eagerly offer proof of the one that didn't get away in snapshots of themselves alongside a fish nearly their equal in size. Whether they go for a casual outing on the weekend or come for an expensive fishing vacation, sport fishermen generate many jobs and bring many tourist dollars to both coastal and inland areas of British Columbia.

The winner and the loser in the 1974 Salmon Derby, an event organized each year by The Vancouver Sun newspaper.

Study 24

Products, Quantity, and Value of British Columbia Salmon, 1973		
	'000 kg	$'000
Fresh, round or dressed	4173	9,834
Frozen, round or dressed	22 416	58,756
Frozen fillets	56	146
Fresh and frozen steaks	691	1,737
Smoked, round or dressed	478	2,482
Pickled	222	1,208
Canned	33 750	127,063
Industrial Oil	802	152
Meal	6122	800

1. Rank the salmon products by value.
2. How does the value of the Pacific salmon fishing industry compare with that of the five major industries in British Columbia?
3. What percentage of the income from the total B.C. fishing industry is earned by the salmon fishery?

Vancouver Sun Photo

One day in an integrated fish plant

Although salmon outrank all other fish in commercial value, large, integrated fish plants make maximum use of all the various marine resources. British Columbia Packers' Imperial Plant in Steveston, British Columbia, is one of Canada's largest integrated fish plants. It processes fish of all shapes and sizes disgorged from a varied assortment of fishing vessels anchored in the Fraser River.

Let's take a typical June day at Imperial. Down on the wharf, giant suction hoses and conveyor belts are unloading a mixed catch of groundfish from the holds of large seiners. The fish, mainly sole, cod, and snapper, are immediately sorted into bins. After being filleted by hand and skinned by machine, they are packed into large cartons for freezing. Pieces of fish that are too small to be used as fillets are set aside to be chopped up, spiced, and made into fish cakes. Frozen fish are stored and used as needed throughout the year for the manufacture of prepared products (fish and chips, fish sticks, and so on). Although the major emphasis is on salmon canning, it is the steady supply of groundfish that keeps the plant in production all year round.

On this June day, a troller has just unloaded a catch of salmon. These splendid, undamaged specimens are normally marketed as fresh fish, although they may also be quick frozen and sawn into steaks. Salmon is a popular fish food, and despite the high price, there is a ready year-round market.

Herring, another catch just unloaded, is not a popular food in North America, and has usually been processed into fish meal as high-protein feed for cattle, hogs, and poultry. In the 1960s, however, a conservation measure banned catching herring for reduction to fish meal and oil. So at Imperial Plant on this June day, the roes are "popped" from the herring and then salted for sale in Japan (thus satisfying the terms of the measure that permit catching herring for human consumption). The remainder of the herring can then "legally" join all the other fish waste – fins, tails, heads, and skin from all over the plant – for reduction to meal and oil.

Meanwhile, blocks of groundfish that were frozen weeks or months ago are making their way into the prepared-products section. Here they are sawn into serving pieces, breaded, fried, and packaged to provide a ready-cooked meal for a busy household.

Imperial Plant employs about 550 people regularly, but may have as many as 1800 people working round the clock at peak times. In the spring months, the emphasis is on halibut, for the year's quota must be caught and frozen in a short season of about eight weeks. Up until June, the whole canning section is idle. But when the large salmon catches come in from the gillnetters and purse seiners, the ovens are heated and millions of cans clank through the machines. Shrimp, clams, oysters, and crab are processed when available, but they form only a small part of the total enterprise.

B.C. Packers prepares some three hundred fish products in its plant, which has an annual capacity of about 18 million kilograms of fish. This is a far cry from the cannery operation of 1870 when the plant operated for only a few months of the year, and when the fish caught, including sockeye, that could not be handled were thrown back as "nuisance fish."

MONTHLY ACTIVITIES AT IMPERIAL PLANT, STEVESTON, B.C.

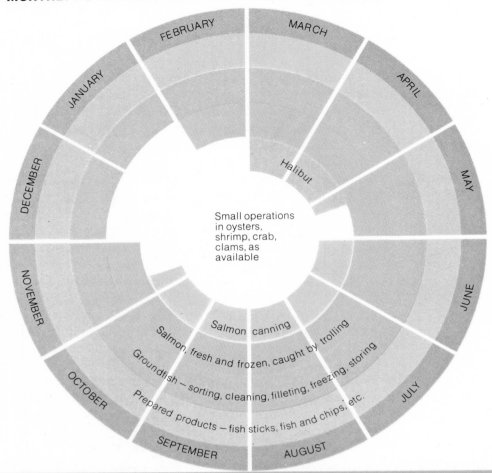

Study 25

1. Which months have the widest variety of activities in this plant?
2. Choose one month and describe the various operations in progress at the plant. Explain why they are being done at that time.
3. Account for the fact that certain species are processed only at specific times of year whereas other species are processed on a year-round basis.
4. Trace a catch of salmon from the time it is unloaded at the Steveston plant until it ends up as
   (a) salmon sandwiches
   (b) salmon steaks.

Fishing the inland waters

In addition to the great wealth of its Atlantic and Pacific waters, Canada is fortunate to have some of the richest inland fishery resources in the world. They range from tiny brine shrimp for aquariums to fine lake trout and whitefish for gourmet restaurants. They come from tiny ponds and from sea-sized lakes; from narrow, rushing streams and from deep, wide rivers; from the shallow, sun-warmed fishing grounds of southern lakes and from deep beneath the ice-covered surface of northern ones.

On a summer day in places such as La Ronge in Saskatchewan, Port Dover and Wheatley in Ontario, and Gimli in Manitoba, it is difficult to believe that one is 2000 kilometres or more from the ocean. Along the shores of the lakes are fish-processing plants. Gill-netters and trawlers lie at anchor, and wharves are piled high with gear.

During the winter, when fish are taken from the deep, warmer water beneath the ice of the northern lakes, the picture is quite different. Winter fishing requires the use of a "jigger," a device by which a net can be strung out beneath the ice. A team of men string eight or ten 30-metre lengths of net, leave these overnight, and then re-open the holes the next day to haul in the fish. In the past, winter fishing accounted for the largest portion of the inland commercial catch because of natural freezing facilities and relatively low-cost transportation by cat-train.* However the construction of more roads and processing plants is swinging the emphasis toward summer fishing.

Whitefish, yellow pickerel, lake trout, yellow perch, and goldeye command high prices in the fresh- and frozen-fish market, most of the catch being exported to the United States. In recent years there has been a marked increase in the harvesting of coarse, freshwater fish — for example, cisco — for use as animal feed and bait.

Although Canada's inland fisheries contribute significantly to the national economy, their commercial catch is much less

*A chain of loaded sleds hauled over the ice by caterpillar tractor — a slow but relatively cheap form of transportation over the fast-frozen land and water surface

Nets being paid out through holes in the ice of Last Mountain Lake, Saskatchewan.

in quantity and value than that of the salt-water fisheries. In sport fishing, however, inland waters are far ahead. Streams and lakes are easily and cheaply accessible to almost any Canadian. Their recreational value to anglers, whether "fly-in" types seeking highly prized Arctic grayling and char in the far north or small boys taking shiners and bullheads off local wharves and rocks, cannot be measured. Furthermore, sportsmen pay gladly for accommodation, gear, transportation, guides, and numerous other services and thus support the tourist and sporting-goods industries and services. But perhaps the greatest value of the sport fisherman is that he fishes as an individual, for personal needs. It is not the angler who is depleting our fishery resource and endangering the ecosystems of lakes and streams and, even, oceans. We must look elsewhere for those who are overfishing and, in some cases, destroying the wealth of our waters.

Study 26

Quantity and Value of Sea and Inland Fish Landed by Province, 1972

	'000 kg	$'000
Newfoundland	295 196	35,723
P.E.I.	25 785	9,540
Nova Scotia	286 914	66,375
New Brunswick	162 177	19,923
Quebec	83 226	11,138
Ontario	19 593	8,119
Manitoba	11 103	4,523
Saskatchewan	4865	1,634
Alberta	2203	727
British Columbia	153 091	75,128
N.W.T.	1602	839
Yukon	24	27
Canada	1 045 779	233,696

Persons Employed in Primary Sea and Inland Fishing Industry by Province, 1972

Newfoundland	14,452
P.E.I.	3,210
Nova Scotia	11,735
New Brunswick	5,161
Quebec	5,843
Ontario	2,097
Manitoba	*
Saskatchewan	1,800
Alberta	1,547
British Columbia	9,902
N.W.T.	*
Yukon	87
Canada	49,643

*figures not available

1. (a) Rank the provinces in *quantity* and *value* of fish landed.
   (b) How does the British Columbia fishery compare in quantity and value with the Atlantic fishery?
2. Discuss the factors that account for these rankings.
3. (a) Which three provinces have the largest numbers of people engaged in primary fishing?
   (b) British Columbia has a total labor force of 1,002,000 people, whereas the Atlantic Provinces combined have only 742,000 people in the labor force. What does this mean in terms of the importance of the fishing industry in those provinces? Discuss how these factors affect policies in the Canadian fishing industry.

Refer to the map on pages 104-105 to answer the following questions.
4. Describe the distribution pattern of fish plants on inland waters and on the Atlantic and Pacific coasts.
5. Account for this distribution in terms of: history, fishing grounds, variety of species, technology, and markets.

The case for conservation:

Gone are the days when European mariners could come to the rich fishing grounds of the Grand Banks and haul up their catch by the basketful. These waters are no longer swarming with fish. Greater effort and greater investment are now necessary to maintain the same number of landings. In fact, at the very time when the importance of fish is increasing because of a diminishing world food supply, the actual quantities of fish landed in Canada show an average decline – in some cases an alarming decline. Pacific halibut and Atlantic haddock, for example, have both dropped from annual landings of about 32 million kilograms in the early 1960s to a little over 13 million kilograms in 1973. To regard these as "endangered fisheries" may not seem too dramatic if we reflect that several Great Lakes' fisheries that flourished well into this century have collapsed completely. In addition, the size of individual specimens caught is declining. Lobsters have dropped in average landed weight from 1.4 kilograms in 1870 to 0.5 kilograms today.

Why are Canadian fishermen landing fewer and smaller fish?

The clue of the disappearing fish

We really know very little about the ecosystems of lakes, rivers, and oceans. But we do know that human actions cause changes in the quality of water that destroy fish, affect their normal eating and spawning habits, or contaminate them so that they are unfit for human consumption. Mercury pollution from textile mills on the St. Lawrence River, chemical plants on the St. Clair River, and lumber mills on the British Columbia coast has caused the closure of several Canadian fisheries. Industry is not the only culprit. Pollutants come from washing machines and toilets, from garbage dumps and city incinerators, from rock salt on the roads and from chemical fertilizers and pesticides on the fields. Pollution is caused by everybody, everywhere.

In addition to the direct contamination of the environment, pollution can cause far-reaching disturbances in the ecosystem that upset natural cycles. Too late it was realized that the disappearance of the mayfly (due to lack of oxygen in polluted waters) was a powerful factor in changing fish species in Lake Erie — which, in turn, may cause even greater changes. Too late we realized that algae in Lake Erie were flourishing on the wastes of civilization — and choking out almost all other forms of life.

Not all of the disturbances in ecosystems are caused by pollution. People also upset natural environments by actions whose implications are not foreseen and whose effects sometimes cannot be undone or repaired. Too late we realized that the opening of the Welland Canal allowed the parasitic sea lamprey to enter the upper Great Lakes — and destroy the lake trout. Only now do we realize the effects on the ecosystem of the decrease in the numbers of inshore cod because of increased offshore fishing. The numbers of capelin upon which the cod feed have greatly increased, and these smaller fish themselves destroy cod and haddock eggs, even baby fish, thus depleting the resource still further. Now, before it is too late, we should consider the possible effects of mining ships slurping up life and habitat together as they harvest mineral nodules from the ocean floor in a gigantic vacuum operation. We know enough now to fear the results of disturbing the ecosystem.

However, we do not yet know how to exercise control to protect and preserve the wealth from the waters. How can we control the depletion of fish stocks through overfishing — which means not only taking too many fish, but taking them at the wrong place or the wrong time and thereby disrupting their capacity to maintain their species? Regulations protecting cod or salmon from inshore fishermen are quite useless unless the fish can also be protected against foreign, deep-sea fishing fleets.

The clue of the little fishboats

Geographically, Canada is in a preferred position to compete for the offshore fishery. Yet, although the world catch has more than doubled since 1950, Canada has slipped from fourth world producer and now no longer ranks among the six leading fishing nations. Why? There are many reasons, but one factor is the little fishboats. Inshore methods using inefficient gear still dominate the Canadian effort.

The mystique that every fisherman has the right to a share in the common resource and the fear that jobs will disappear if fishing becomes too mechanized go far to explain the reluctance to abandon traditional methods. Equity among fishermen sometimes seems to conflict with efficiency in the fishing industry. Fishermen are often restricted to one or two days' work a week. Regulations forbid the use of large, mechanized boats at certain times so that fishermen using less efficient gear can have a chance to operate with more success. Meanwhile, foreign factory ships operating far out to sea are harvesting the same resource, and doing so with awesome efficiency. How do we protect the needs of the small fisherman without hampering large, mechanized operations from competing successfully with other nations for the marine resources of the North Atlantic and Pacific?

The clue of the vanishing fishermen

The use of inefficient gear is not the only reason to question whether Canada is taking full advantage of the marine resource. Fewer young people are taking up fishing as an occupation. What is more, the number of Canadian fishermen is declining at the very time when there are more consumers and higher prices for the catch. Mechanization helps to compensate for declining numbers, but inability to pay for additional equipment forces many fishermen out of business, thus depleting the work force still further. There is concern that the traditional fisheries cannot be maintained unless ways can be found to induce more people to become fishermen.

The ones that got away

Another reason for Canada's decline as a world fish producer is our unwillingness to take advantage of the variety of our marine resources. Vast numbers of fish caught are thrown back because there is no market for them. And even the fish that are kept and processed are not fully utilized. Certain

Clifford Dunphy

Inshore fishermen gutting and cleaning their catch.

127

parts of fish, such as cod roe and perch tail, are discarded as waste because they do not appeal to consumers. Peoples' eating habits determine which species and which parts of species are processed as food. But peoples' eating and buying habits can be changed. Take the case of the Alaska pollock. In 1974, by mincing their product and making it into spiced cakes, the producers found a ready market in Boston for this fish, long ignored as tough and tasteless. Perhaps if we consumed larger quantities and greater varieties of fish, we could again become a leading fish-producing nation.

The search for solutions

The fishery is a **renewable resource**. If we farm our waters wisely, they will yield a rich and recurring harvest. How do we ensure a steady fish crop that will meet the food needs of people not only today but through all the tomorrows? How do we determine the intensity of effort that will meet the nutritional and economic needs of Canada and yet allow the resource to regenerate itself rapidly enough to yield a continuing maximum return?

A **maximum sustainable yield** policy requires conservation measures based on the results of marine research. Various boards and commissions are involved in fisheries studies. Merely by keeping records of the numbers and sizes of fish and fishboats, research organizations obtain clearer and more accurate knowledge of marine resources. The International North Pacific Fisheries Commission (NORPAC) co-ordinated the efforts of thousands of people in a ten-year study of salmon habits. They traced the journeys of all species of salmon back to their spawning streams on both sides of the ocean. The Canadian Fisheries Research Board sends technicians and marine biologists hundreds of kilometres out to sea each spring to check on fish stocks and

Foreign fishing fleets dot the surface of the Grand Banks.

A Tracker aircraft checking a foreign fishing trawler in Canadian waters.

Canadian Forces Photo

forecast the size and timings of different runs. During the fishing season, stations of departments of fisheries resemble wartime command centres as information flows in by shortwave radio from fishery officers and patrol boats.

These detailed and up-to-date data greatly assist the management of the marine resource. Openings and closings of salmon fisheries are revised as information comes in. The analysis of the data over a period of years also assists long-term policies. General trends and habits of species are recorded, maximum sustainable yields are determined, and quotas are set based on scientific observation. A study of the Pacific halibut fishery, prompted by a dangerous decline in stocks, resulted in quotas being imposed by the International Pacific Halibut Commission (IPHC) in 1924. The fishery recovered well — until the alarming current decline due to modern technological know-how that enables fishing vessels to vacuum the ocean floor. High-powered foreign vessels not bound by IPHC quotas scoop up all marine creatures without regard for size or species, the halibut along with the species of groundfish for which these vessels are actually fishing.

Survival of the spawning fish

As pressures on fish stocks mount, it becomes increasingly apparent that conditions in spawning areas are of vital importance. Many species, such as cod and haddock, reproduce at sea, where the sheer magnitude of the environment makes management very difficult. However, a good deal can be done to assist **anadromous** fish (those that ascend rivers and streams to breed in fresh water before returning to the sea.) These, too, are threatened by natural enemies and by environmental changes — perhaps even more so than sea

129

Ten kilometres of artificial spawning channels have been constructed at Babine Lake, British Columbia, as part of a salmon-conservation program.

lives. Some fisheries experts are proposing management of the complete cycle: **aquaculture** or fish farming. This method has been successfully used for lobsters, oysters, clams, and scallops. In 1974, salmon from British Columbia's first fish farm appeared on the market. Only eight to twelve months were required to raise these fish to market size, and only 10 per cent of the eggs hatched failed to mature. Since only 1.5 kilograms of food are required to produce 1 kilogram of salmon — compared to 10 kilograms for beef, 4 kilograms for pork, and 2.5 kilograms for poultry — aquaculture would appear to be an efficient method for the production of protein-rich food. Although the first "crop" of fish was priced slightly higher than salmon fished from the sea, farmed fish stocks can be more easily controlled and can provide fresh fish all year. Perhaps one day fish will be added to the list of other creatures that are now raised "down on the farm" for their flesh, their milk, or their skins.

The need for co-operation and control

Only the most ruthless exploiters dispute that we should try to manage and conserve our resources so that we do not exhaust them utterly and leave nothing for the future (which may well be our own immediate future let alone that of generations to come). But how do we carry out and back up policies of conservation and maximum sustainable yield?

We can pass laws. We can regulate the mesh size of nets, prohibit the use of certain equipment, protect egg-bearing females, set limits on the size of fish landed,

fish because industry and technology often cause disruptions in the freshwater environment. Human beings can compensate for some of the effects of their actions by improving the breeding conditions for anadromous fish. In artificial spawning channels, water flow and depth can be controlled, and hazards of flash flooding or extreme low water are virtually eliminated. Gravel of ideal size for spawning and egg incubation can be provided, and the dangers of heavy silting or of materials smothering the eggs can be avoided. Some channels, such as those of the Big Qualicum and Fulton rivers in British Columbia, are designed to control water temperatures as well.

Artificial spawning channels merely assist the fish at one stage of their natural

Raising salmon on the family farm, Earl's Cove, British Columbia.

Vancouver Sun Photo

and impose quotas. But of what use are such laws unless they are standardized across Canada, indeed around the world? The lobster that at 8.1 centimetres is safe from capture in Gloucester County, New Brunswick, may swim into a trap in Restigouche County, Quebec, and be legally caught. Fish small enough to swim through the large mesh of a regulation British Columbia net may be caught in a smaller-meshed foreign net and end up in the hold of a factory ship. What good will it do if the city of Windsor ceases to dump sewage into the St. Clair River while the much larger city of Detroit continues to poison the waters? How can Newfoundland fisher-

men be expected to observe a quota on haddock unless operators from other nations fishing the Grand Banks do likewise?

Fish are a nutritious, protein-rich food. Canada must be alert and determined to protect and preserve this renewable marine resource. The management of fishery resources involves complex political, economic, technological, and ecological factors that must be weighed and considered in reasoned co-operation between different levels of government, between government and industry, and between Canada and foreign nations.

But the impetus for all this has to come from each and every one of us.

131

Study and Research

1. In 1973, a smaller proportion of the Newfoundland catch was salted than ever before. What does this mean in terms of:
   (a) jobs and working conditions for individual Newfoundlanders?
   (b) changing markets for Newfoundland fish products?
   (c) the future of the Newfoundland fishery?

2. Make a study of the sardine fishery of New Brunswick.

3. A proposal for the co-operative management of a defined lobster district in Prince Edward Island by fishermen who would collectively share the returns of the fishing effort was turned down by the men themselves.
   (a) What would be the advantages of such a scheme?
   (b) Why do you think it was rejected by the lobstermen?

4. Write a report on the decline of the fishing industry on Lake Erie. How can the loss of other freshwater fisheries be prevented?

5. For some years now the topic of a high dam in the Fraser canyon has been hotly debated in British Columbia.
   (a) What would be the purpose of such a dam?
   (b) What interests are supporting it?
   (c) Who is opposed?
   Write a report for or against the motion: "It is resolved that the construction of a high dam on the Fraser River would not be in the best public interest."

6. A group of Micmac Indians at Eskasoni, Cape Breton Island, is raising 70 million oysters on strings of scallop shells suspended from rafts in the Bras d'Or lakes. Evaluate this project from the point of view of:
   — a scallop fisherman in New Brunswick
   — a Micmac teenager in Eskasoni
   — a restauranteur in Montreal
   — a motel owner in the Bras d'Or lakes
   — an oyster fisherman of Malpeque, P.E.I.
   — an official of the federal Department of the Environment
   — an official of the Nova Scotia Department of Fisheries.

7.

British Columbia Herring Catches

	Landings in '000 kg	Value in $'000
1966	139 549	5,107
1969	2003	221
1973	55 377	9,142

   (a) Account for the quantities landed and the value in these three years.

(b) Compare the quantities of herring landed and the value in 1966 and 1973. How do you think these changes will affect the following:
— the activities of the B.C. fishing fleet
— the processing of the herring catch
— the conservation of the resource?

(c) What people besides herring fishermen are likely to be affected by this trend?

(d) Do you think the ban on herring fishing for non-food consumption achieved its purpose? Explain your answer.

8. From the latest statistics available, rank in order the top ten world fish producers. How do you account for the position of Japan? The USSR? Peru?

9. Technology is being used to solve problems created by technology. The construction of fish ladders is only one example of technology's attempts to meet the needs of industry, consumers, and governments.

(a) What are some other examples of the use of technology to solve problems in the fishing industry?

(b) What further problems have these solutions created?

(c) What has been lost and what has been gained?

10. Discuss the changes in the methods and importance of inland fishing from earliest times to the present day. Pay special attention to:

(a) sources and effects of pollution

(b) bilateral agreements between Canada and the United States.

11. If you decided on a career in the Canadian fishing industry:

(a) What role would you choose for yourself?

(b) In which of the three regions would you choose to work?

(c) In what part of the fishing operation would you invest most of your money?

(d) What changes would you make in the method of operation?

(e) What markets would you aim for?

(f) How would government regulations affect your operation?

12. Write a report for the federal Department of the Environment summarizing the evidence presented in this chapter, adding any further "clues" you have uncovered in personal research, and speculating on any further evidence that might yet be forthcoming.

Append to the report your recommendations for (a) short-term measures to meet immediate crises and (b) long-range planning.

Chapter 5 **The forest resource**

A tree, it is said, was first of all food and shelter for birds and mammals — and people. As time passed, it became material for new shelters and fuel to heat them. Then it provided a weapon, a tool, and, at a later point in time, a wheel — transportation. Now the tree serves us from cradle to casket. It's syrup for pancakes and rubber for gaskets. It's floors and doors, tars and spars, chairs and stairs. It's boxes, bureaus, bags, and boats . . . paper, plastics, paints, and posts. It's habitation, transportation, conservation, occupation, recreation, inspiration. To a lumberjack it's a giant to be felled. To a carpenter it's a house, a cupboard, plywood, panelling. To a fisherman it's a boat, a campfire — and sometimes survival. To an athlete it's a baseball bat, a hockey stick, a tennis racket. To a child it's a climbing place, a private world. To an artist it's inspiration for a painting, potential for a sculpture. To a homeowner it's landscape gardening, increased property values. For the lumbering-industry executive, it's big business measured in cubic metres. For the environmentalist, it's protection against flash floods and soil erosion, habitation for wildlife, producer of life-sustaining oxygen. For all of us and for generations of life to come it can be an everlasting resource.

Opening photograph: Roads built for use in harvesting and replanting the timber resource have opened up Vancouver Island forest areas for public use. Courtesy Crown Zellerbach

Over 5,000 different products come from trees, some of which are mentioned in the tree form opposite. Make a list of the products mentioned, classifying them under two headings: those made from lumber, and those made from pulp and paper. Add to the list any other wood products you can think of. Keep this list for use later on in this chapter.

The tree form on page 136 is a graphic presentation of the importance of the forest to the quality of our life and to our standard of living. Forest industries directly employ something like 300,000 Canadians — about 4.5 per cent of the work force. But these industries *indirectly* affect the employment of a large segment of the population: authors, editors, and publishers;

journalists; artists; craftsmen; interior decorators; carpenters and cabinet makers; advertisers and retailers; and so on. In fact, there is probably not a single Canadian who does not benefit from the forest industries, either as a producer of some forest product or as a consumer of many of these products.

From region to region, and from province to province the importance of the forest industries varies. One in thirteen employees engaged in manufacturing of any kind in Ontario is employed directly in the lumber or pulp-and-paper industries. In Quebec, the figure is about one in nine. In New Brunswick, the figure rises to one in three, and in British Columbia it reaches a staggering 44.7 per cent, almost one of

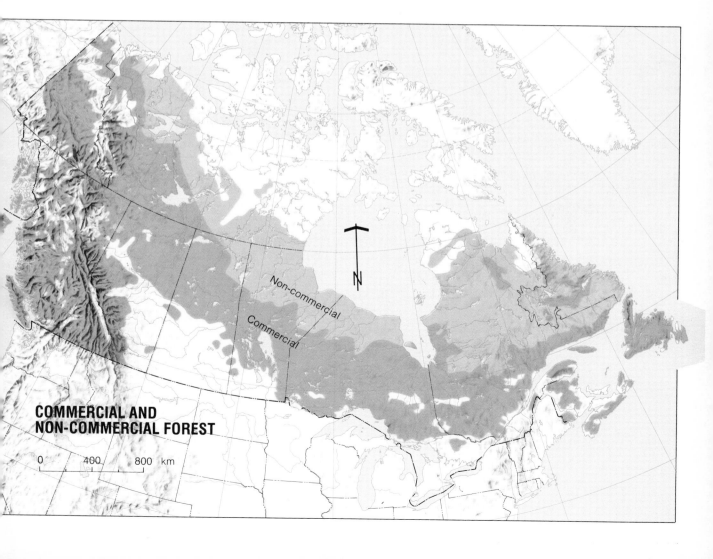

COMMERCIAL AND
NON-COMMERCIAL FOREST

0   400   800 km

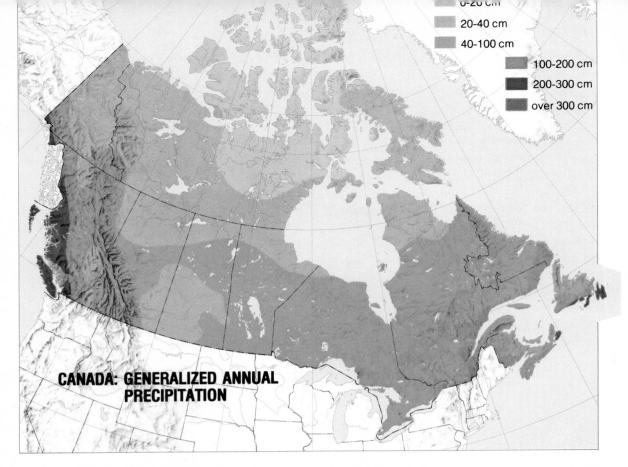

	0-20 cm
	20-40 cm
	40-100 cm
	100-200 cm
	200-300 cm
	over 300 cm

CANADA: GENERALIZED ANNUAL PRECIPITATION

every two workers engaged in manufacturing. The only region with proportions lower than any of these is the Prairie Provinces. The only area of Canada with no significant forest industry of any kind is Prince Edward Island.

However, the value of trees cannot be measured only in the amount of raw materials they provide for manufacturing or in the number of workers employed in the forest industries. Their value in determining the kind and quality of plant and animal life is impossible to measure. They provide humus for the soil and home for wildlife. They help to regulate the flow of water that falls upon the land and reduce soil erosion and flooding. They soften the contours of our concrete jungle and offer a retreat when the world is too much with us. They even infuse the very air we breathe with oxygen.

Study 27

Canada's forests cover roughly one-third of the country — 3.1 million square kilometres of land that stretch in an unbroken belt, 1000 to 2100 kilometres wide, from the Atlantic to the Pacific.

Nearly 2.6 million square kilometres are classified as commercial forest: capable of producing recurring crops of marketable timber. Most of the

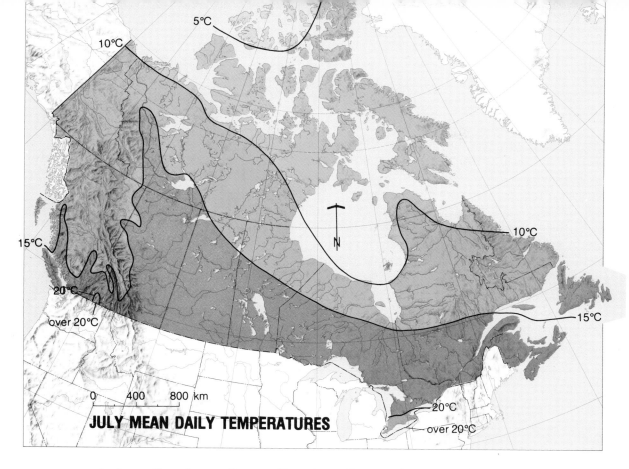

JULY MEAN DAILY TEMPERATURES

remainder suffers from adverse climatic, soil, or moisture conditions. The trees are either too small and slow-growing or the species too poor to be worth logging on a commercial scale. Of the commercial forest itself, 1 860 000 square kilometres are close enough to road, rail, or water to allow profitable logging.

1. Examine these two maps of Canada.
   (a) Which July isotherm approximates the northern limits of the forest?
   (b) What amount of precipitation appears to determine the forest limit in the southern parts of Saskatchewan and Alberta?
   (c) Farther north, less precipitation will still support forest. Explain this curious fact.
2. Account for the non-forested areas of British Columbia.
3. Account for the lack of significant areas of commercial forest in the Atlantic Provinces and in southern Ontario and Quebec.
4. If close to 750 000 square kilometres of commercial forest are not being exploited, why are they classified as commercial?
5. What features in the photographs of the Canadian Shield on page 9 help to explain why it has been left as forest and not cleared for agriculture?
6. Summarize the important factors you have discovered that help to account for the present distribution of forests in Canada.

The forest regions of Canada

Most of Canada's trees are **softwoods** — pine, spruce, fir, hemlock, cedar. These **coniferous** trees, with single main stem, needle-like leaves, and cone-form fruit, are ideally suited to the combination of low temperatures and limited availability of moisture in northern latitudes. **Hardwood** trees — maple, oak, elm, birch, beech, aspen, cottonwood — generally have broad **deciduous** leaves and branching trunks, and flourish in regions with fairly warm temperatures and a moderate supply of moisture. Individual species within these two cate-

gories are sensitive to variations in temperature, precipitation, sunlight, and soil conditions. Consequently they tend to group in communities of a few dominant species. These communities define forest regions.

Warm, moist westerly winds carry the moderating effects of the Pacific Ocean to the **coast forest** region, blessing it with an abundant rainfall and a long growing season. Here tower such forest giants as the Douglas fir, with a trunk diameter of from one to five metres and a height up to 100 metres. The western hemlock, the western

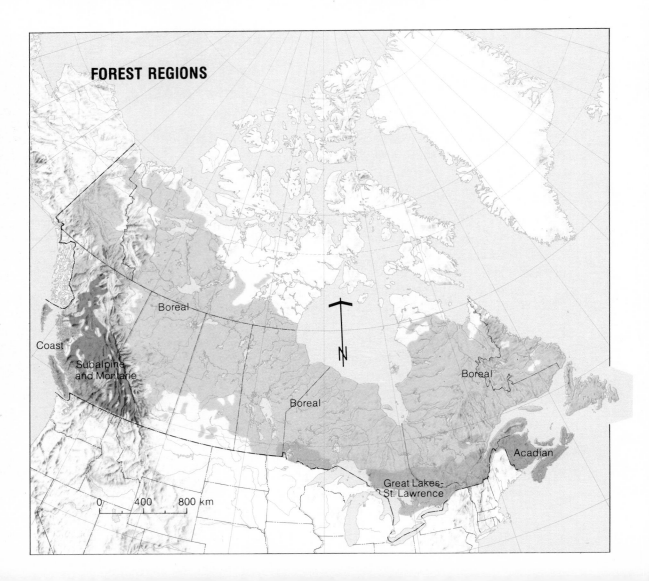

FOREST REGIONS

Boreal

Coast

Subalpine and Montane

Boreal

Boreal

Acadian

Great Lakes–St. Lawrence

0   400   800 km

N

red cedar, and the Sitka spruce soar as high as 60 metres. A Douglas fir, felled in the 1890s by a man called George Carey, was said to have been 127 metres high and 7.6 metres in diameter. If true, then it was the largest living thing ever to have existed on earth.

In the **subalpine, Columbia,** and **montane** forest region in the interior of British Columbia, there is less precipitation and a shorter growing season, because of an inland location. Consequently, there are less majestic versions of the species found in the coast forest, together with smaller Ponderosa and Lodgepole pines.

The **boreal forest** region is dominated by the black spruce. The length and strength of its fibres make it one of the world's leading pulpwood trees. Other important species include the hemlock and balsam fir (sometimes producing a "hembal" forest since they often occur together) and the jack and white pines. The colder, longer winters of a continental climate retard growth. In this region, trees may take seventy-five years to reach a height of 18 metres; during the same period of time, similar species in the coastal forest of British Columbia may well have grown twice as tall.

The largest tree native to Canada is the Douglas Fir. Its extremely strong wood is used to produce large pieces of structural lumber, and siding, interior finishing, and flooring.

Courtesy MacMillan Bloedel Limited

The **Acadian** and **Great Lakes-St. Law-rence** forests are essentially transitional, a mixture of deciduous and coniferous trees. The Acadian forest tends to be slightly more boreal than that of the Great Lakes-St. Lawrence, but in both regions the proportion of broadleaf trees increases with the higher temperatures of warmer climates.

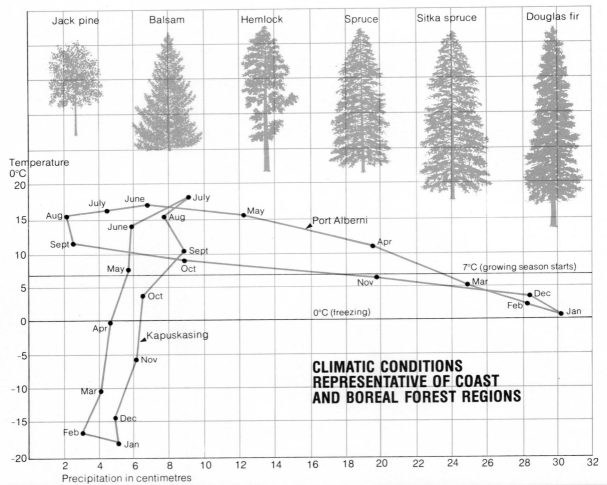

CLIMATIC CONDITIONS
REPRESENTATIVE OF COAST
AND BOREAL FOREST REGIONS

Study 28

1. Explain the term "tree line."
2. Look at the map on page 140. Name eight to ten cities that are located in the Great Lakes-St. Lawrence forest region. With such a concentration of cities, why is it classified as a "forest" region?
3. The original forest of the St. Lawrence Lowlands was felled by settlers and lumbermen. What were the principal species of this forest? How extensive was it? What uses were made of it?
4. Research some of the uses of Canadian hardwoods and softwoods and their suitability for these uses.

...duction areas

...la's forest regions can be divided into two fairly distinct production areas. British Columbia supplies most of our building lumber and plywood, and the boreal and mixed forests produce most of our pulp and paper and newsprint.

British Columbia's forests amount to 8 per cent of the total forest area of Canada. Yet they contain a little over 50 per cent of the nation's commercial timber reserves and have an amazing annual output:

- 50% of all wood cut
- 70% of the shipments (by value) of all sawmill plants
- 80% of all building lumber and *softwood* plywood
- 100% of all cedar shingles
- 26% of all pulp and paper
- 14% of all newsprint.

In fact, the province's forest industries account for approximately 50 per cent of all dollars earned in British Columbia. Why? Species and climate. A Douglas fir provides enough lumber to construct five bungalows; cedar makes naturally waterproof shingles, siding, and fencing. The mild climate does more than provide ideal growth conditions. It permits year-round logging operations: if snow halts work at high elevations, lumbermen move down to log lower elevations.

The boreal and mixed forests produce about the same volume of cut wood as British Columbia — but here all similarity ends. Their production of building lumber is relatively small, although most of Canada's *hardwood* plywood comes from the mixed forests of the east, where deciduous trees are more common. However, the major difference between the two areas is in the production of wood pulp. Nearly 70 per cent of all pulp and paper and 86 per cent of Canada's newsprint are produced by the eastern forests.

The forest industries

Forest industries can be separated into three main divisions: **logging** operations, which fell the trees and provide the raw material; **primary manufacturing**, which makes a relatively simple product directly from a raw material — lumber, plywood, and pulp and paper; and **secondary manufacturing**, which processes a primary product into a finished or semi-finished item — doors, sashes, furniture, prefabricated building structures.

Logging

Differences in tree species and size and differences in climate and landforms determine different methods of extraction. About 80 per cent of the area logged in Canada is **clear cut**: everything usable in a stand is felled, and trees that are rotting or diseased are cut down and burned. What makes clear cutting the most widely used method? It is the increased use of a greater variety of species, and the need to reduce costs by producing more. Used wisely, clear cutting is a good conservation practice. Some species, such as pines and Douglas fir, do not grow well in shade, and so benefit from clear cutting. In addition to being a quick, easy method, clear cutting offers the advantage of a new crop of trees that will be ready for harvesting at the same date. In the coast forest region, **patch logging**, a variation of clear cutting, is commonly used in stands of Douglas fir. The advantage of this method is that it allows natural reforestation of the logged area: the logged patches are reseeded from the surrounding trees.

Most tree species in British Columbia grow to a fairly uniform size within the same number of years. Thus the best method of logging is one that clears the ground and permits the establishment of an entirely new forest. Clear cutting in patches, a widely used method in B.C., aids natural regeneration and also reduces the hazard of fire.

Forests of mixed species or uneven age profit from **selective cutting**: thinning out crowded stands of trees to give younger and stronger specimens more growing space. Leaving the best specimens to mature will actually produce more timber than would have been the case if the forest had not been thinned! Selective cutting is especially suited to such species as cedar and hemlock that prefer heavy shade while growing. In young stands, some of the evergreens are thinned out for the Christmas-tree market. In older stands, thirty- or forty-year trees are cut out for the pulp-and-paper industry. At the end of an 80-year cycle, the mature trees are cut.

Mature trees that have been felled for lumber are bucked (sawn into lengths) and dragged to a loading yard, where grapple-equipped loaders lift the big logs onto trucks. If the logging site is close enough, the timber is usually trucked directly to the mill. To reduce transportation costs, sawmills tend to be located near forested land. However, in some areas of the coast region, the logging area and the mill may be up to 300 kilometres apart. The cost of transportation is not as important here because the fiord-indented coast makes it possible for most forest operations to locate near water. Water is the cheapest form of transporting bulky goods over long distances.

144

Study 29

1. Draw a sketch map of the area located within the circle.
2. Locate and name other inlets on your map.
3. How far from the sea is the farthest inland point?
4. What advantages to the forest industry can you see from this type of coastline?

Hauling timber from Domain Industries' logging operation on mountain slopes overlooking Jervis Inlet, British Columbia. On the horizon is the dim outline of Vancouver Island.

Jervis Inlet, British Columbia

PACIFIC

OCEAN

0   100   200 km

U.S.A.

145

When a tree weighing several tonnes is toppling earthwards, you don't worry much about shouting "Timber!" You just get out of the way of a potential rebound. Felling the enormous specimens of the west-coast forest precisely where required — and without damaging them — demands a lot of experience and considerable skill. The one-man, gasoline-powered chain-saw has replaced the two-man hand saw and the double-bladed axe, and the job of felling is done more quickly and more efficiently.

146

After felling, trees are delimbed and then "bucked" or sawn into lengths. These are dragged as much as 275 metres to the loading area by a portable steel spar (in the background). This is the process called yarding. Then, as shown above, a grapple-equipped loader — operated by one man — stacks the timber on trucks. These loaders, mounted on caterpillar-type tracks, move under their own power to yarding sites, which may be half way up a mountain or deep in some remote valley.

147

Faster and more versatile log barges have replaced many types of timber rafts. However, the flat-boom type shown here is still an important means of transportation through sheltered waters.

Trucks dump the logs into these long, deep, narrow inlets where "boom boats," like cowboys rounding up a herd, dash around sorting logs into booms by species, size, and quality. The booms are then towed to a sawmill. For longer distances over open water, logs are loaded into self-dumping barges capable of carrying up to 18 000 tonnes.

In the boreal and mixed forests east of the Rockies, **strip logging** is practised in addition to the various logging methods of the coast forest. In strip logging, each cutter is allotted a stretch of forest measuring 20 metres in width and penetrating 460 metres into the forest from the logging road. Using a power saw, he systematically clearcuts the trees in his strip and then removes tops and branches. A wheeled or tracked vehicle called a "skidder" drags these tree lengths to the road, where they are mechanically loaded onto trucks and then carried to water, rail line, or mill.

In some small logging operations in parts of eastern Canada, horses and sleighs are still used, but in many areas logging is fully mechanized. Multi-function, diesel-powered machines with enclosed all-weather cabs operate day and night the year round. A "log-all" fells trees and piles them onto a machine that hauls them to the roadside, where a "processor" debranches, debarks, and slashes them into pulpwood lengths. At break-up time, the harvest of wood that has accumulated all winter on frozen rivers begins its journey downstream to a mill. The world's biggest log drive is on the St. Maurice River in Quebec, where something like 3 600 000 cubic metres move downstream each year. But the traditional log drive of eastern Canada is disappearing; trucking reduces handling costs and ensures a steady supply of timber.

In eastern Canada, stands of trees suitable for lumber are limited in number. In pioneer times, much of the region was cleared of its original extensive forests of tall, massive timber. In their place grew the less valuable pulpwood species or second- and third-growth trees that have considerably less volume per tree than the original stands. Hence many lumber operations in the east are on a much smaller scale than their western counterparts — and thus have difficulty in competing. However, lumber is only part of the forest operation. The map of sawmills and major pulp-and-paper mills on pages 158-159 and the table of exports above Study 30 give a more complete picture of the forest industry.

The self-loading, self-dumping log barge is used primarily for open-water, long-distance hauling. Loading is done by means of the two cranes, unloading by flooding the tanks on one side of the barge.

Untouched by human hands: in eastern Canada, a "Log-all" shears, lifts, and piles whole trees.

Principal Domestic Exports, 1972 (in millions)	
Motor vehicles and parts	$3,390
Newsprint	1,157
Lumber	1,128
Wheat	917
Wood pulp	817

Study 30

1. Total these exports. Total the value of wood products shown. What percentage of principal exports do they represent?
2. Compare the value of lumber exports with that of newsprint and wood pulp combined.
3. One of the exports is a raw material, three are primary manufactures, and one is a secondary manufacture. Identify each.

Primary manufacturing

Competition in the lumber industry is intense, and the most efficient and profitable way of processing the tall trees of the coast forest region is by using huge machines. Giant trees have consequently given rise to giant, integrated enterprises that have the necessary large sums of capital to invest in heavy equipment and machinery.

A description of the various manufacturing processes carried on in an integrated complex may give you some idea of the vast amounts of money required to mechanize the forest industry.

Courtesy Crown Zellerbach

Left: Extract from the Quadra Island, British Columbia, sheet (92 K/3 West Half, Edition 1 ASE, Series A 721 of the National Topographic System. Scale 1:50,000. Courtesy Surveys and Mapping Branch, Department of Energy, Mines, and Resources, Ottawa. Above: In the foreground is the rail line leading to and from Crown Zellerbach's Elk Falls Mill at Campbell River.

CROWN ZELLERBACH'S Elk Falls Mill

Introduction and Miscellaneous
Elk Falls Mill is a forest industry complex manufacturing pulp, paper and lumber. The total capital investment is about $130 million. About 1,200 people are employed at the plant, which is located on Duncan Bay near Campbell River, B.C.

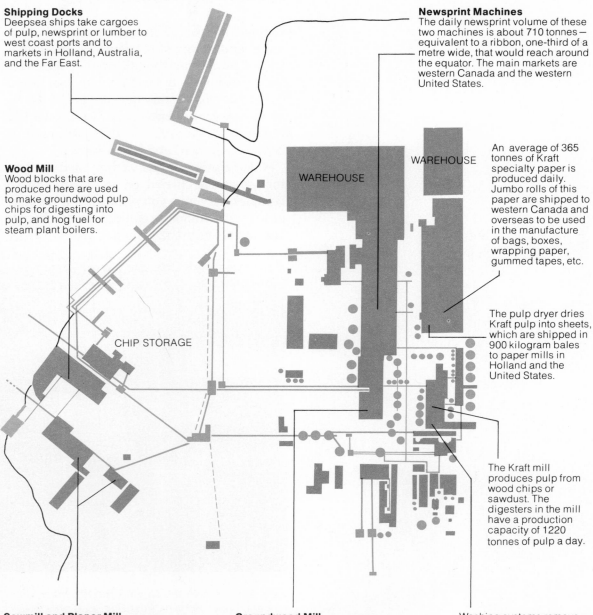

Shipping Docks
Deepsea ships take cargoes of pulp, newsprint or lumber to west coast ports and to markets in Holland, Australia, and the Far East.

Newsprint Machines
The daily newsprint volume of these two machines is about 710 tonnes — equivalent to a ribbon, one-third of a metre wide, that would reach around the equator. The main markets are western Canada and the western United States.

Wood Mill
Wood blocks that are produced here are used to make groundwood pulp chips for digesting into pulp, and hog fuel for steam plant boilers.

WAREHOUSE

WAREHOUSE

An average of 365 tonnes of Kraft specialty paper is produced daily. Jumbo rolls of this paper are shipped to western Canada and overseas to be used in the manufacture of bags, boxes, wrapping paper, gummed tapes, etc.

CHIP STORAGE

The pulp dryer dries Kraft pulp into sheets, which are shipped in 900 kilogram bales to paper mills in Holland and the United States.

The Kraft mill produces pulp from wood chips or sawdust. The digesters in the mill have a production capacity of 1220 tonnes of pulp a day.

Sawmill and Planer Mill
An average of 130,000 board feet of lumber is produced in an eight-hour shift. Lumber is shipped to markets on the Pacific coast and in the eastern United States. Sawdust and chips are recovered for use in the manufacture of pulp.

Groundwood Mill
Blocks of wood from the wood mill are pressed against huge grindstones to produce an average of 560 tonnes of groundwood pulp per day.

Washing systems remove impurities from the pulp. The bleaching process changes the natural brown color of pulp to a bleached or semi-bleached color.

Study 31

1. Describe the coastline shown on the topographic map of Campbell River (Elk Falls) on page 151.
2. Describe fully the relief. What would be the probable land uses of this area?
3. Draw a sketch map from the photograph and label the various mills, using the plant plan as a guide.
4. From the photo and the topographic map, isolate all the physical features that contribute to the advantages of this site for a major forest operation. Mark them on your sketch map.
5. Apart from the physical advantage of *site*, Elk Falls also has the advantage of *location*. Write a paragraph on the advantages of this location as a forest-industries town. (Consider raw materials, sources of power, market access, etc.)

Lumber

Logs enter the sawmill on a conveyor belt. They pass through a hydraulic barker, in which a stream of water under great pressure removes the bark. A head saw squares the larger logs, which are then sized and cut into desired widths by a gang saw, a machine consisting of a series of parallel circular saws. Smaller logs go directly to the gang saws after debarking. After the sloping outside edges have been sliced off, trim saws cut out the defects and square the ends. Graders then inspect and classify each piece of lumber before it is sorted and moved by fork lift to a kiln to be dried, or to a well-exposed yard for seasoning.

Council of Forest Industries of British Columbia

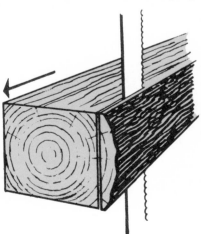

A head saw squaring a log.

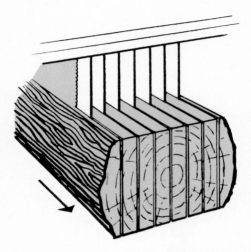

A gang saw cutting a log into boards.

An edger removing "wane" or sloping edges.

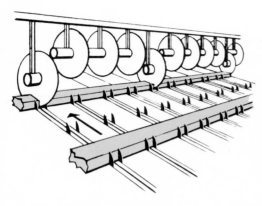

Trim saws removing defects and squaring ends.

Council of Forest Industries of British Columbia

Plywood

Logs used in the manufacture of plywood are known as "peelers." The term comes from the production process, in which a thin layer of wood called a "veneer" is peeled off the log after it has been debarked. High-grade logs used for plywood are selected for straightness, roundness, and freedom from knots and other defects. Douglas firs are considered prime peelers, although high-grade hemlock, balsam, spruce, and pine are also used.

Recipe for Plywood

Unroll a log into a continuous, thin sheet of wood.
Cut the sheet into manageable pieces.
Put the sheets together in a wooden decker "sandwich," with the grain of each layer running at right angles to its neighbor.
Prior to layering the sandwich, "butter" the centre pieces with waterproof glue that is stronger than the wood.
Cook in a hot oven for 12 minutes at 130°C - 150°C, while applying a pressure of 1400 kilopascals.
Trim edges and serve.

155

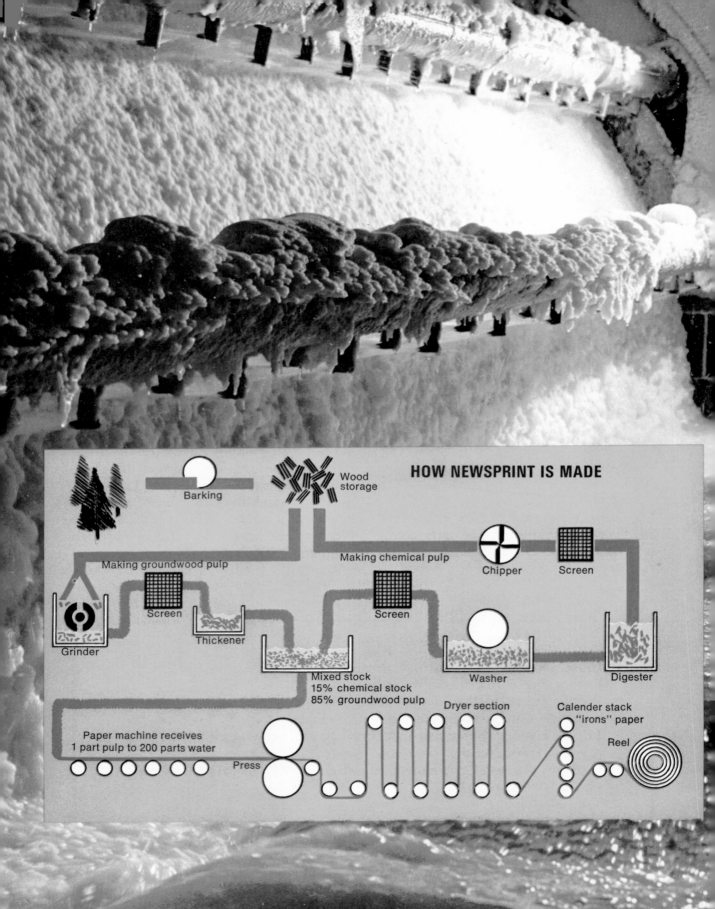

Pulp and paper

Second-growth trees, low-grade logs, and waste wood from plywood mills and saw-mills provide raw materials for pulp-and-paper mills.

There are two methods of making pulp: mechanical and chemical. In the mechanical method, logs are shredded into fibres between huge grinders. The saturated wood fibres are then drained through screens to remove knot particles and foreign substances. This **groundwood pulp** is usually mixed with chemical pulp to provide added strength to the paper produced.

In chemical pulping, the wood is chipped rather than shredded. These chips are pressure cooked along with a sulphate or sulphite acid in huge tanks called "digesters." Under steam pressure the acid dissolves the natural glue (lignin) that holds wood fibres together, and also the resins, mineral salts, and other unwanted constituents. The resulting pulpy mass of cellulose fibres is blown from the digester to tanks, where vacuum washers remove waste products.

In the paper-making process, the slurry of pulp (99 per cent water and 1 per cent fibres) is fed rapidly onto a Fourdrinier machine, a conveyor-belt screen with as many as nine hundred tiny holes per square centimetre. Constant vibration of the rapidly moving screen and powerful air suction from boxes below the screen cause the water to drain and the fibres to interlock, thus producing a thin sheet of pulp. The sheet is dried by being passed through a series of steam-heated rollers, after which it is ironed by polished steel rollers to give it a smooth finish. The paper is then wound onto reels for storage and later rewound and cut into smaller rolls or sheets.

The finished product may be a newspaper or wrapping paper, a paper bag or wallpaper, a birthday card or this book.

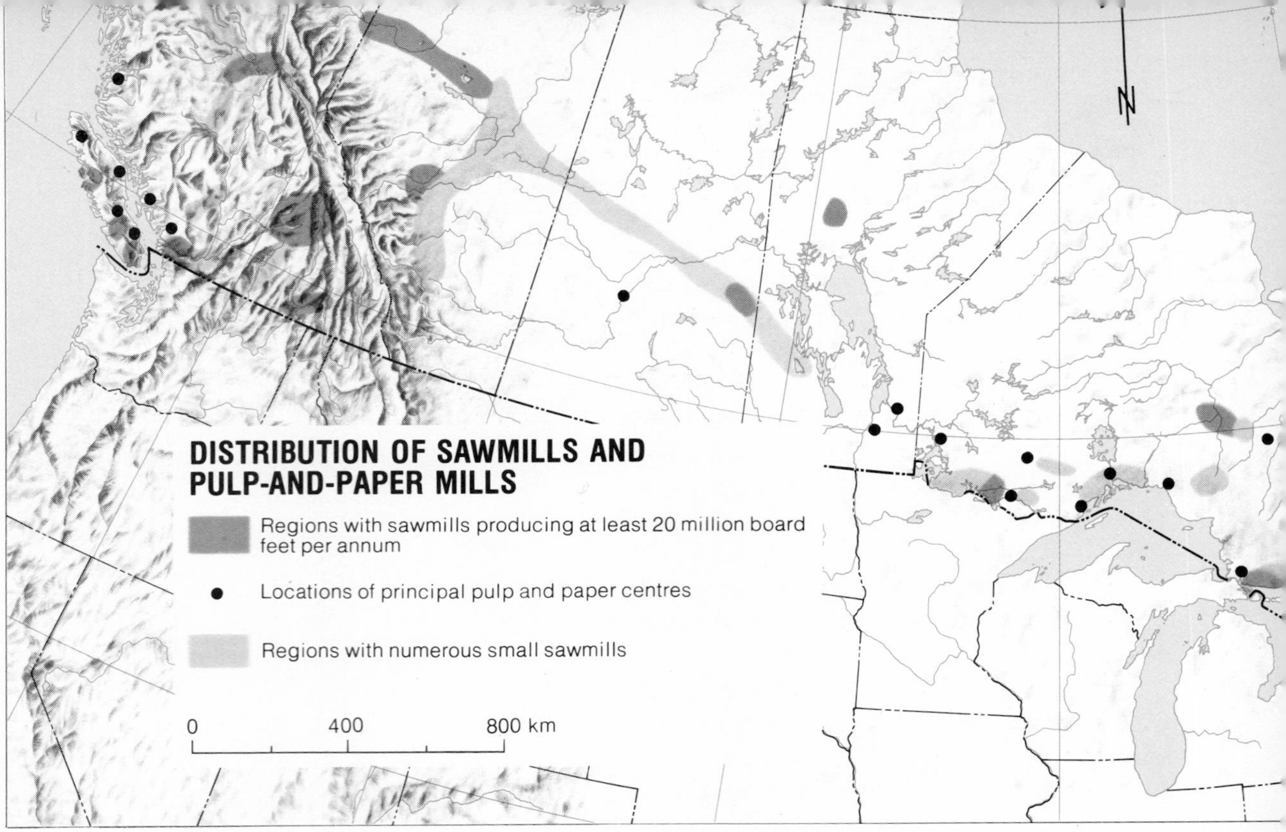
DISTRIBUTION OF SAWMILLS AND PULP-AND-PAPER MILLS
Regions with sawmills producing at least 20 million board feet per annum
Locations of principal pulp and paper centres
Regions with numerous small sawmills
0
400
800 km
N

Study 32

1. Make a sketch of this map and draw a line enclosing the major concentration of pulp-and-paper mills. Circle the next two major concentrations.
2. From all the information you have gained from the chapter, account for the location of each of these concentrations. (Consider forest regions, species, history, transportation, markets, etc.)
3. Account for the "strung-out" nature of sawmilling in the Prairies.
4. Requirements for one tonne of newsprint:
   4.4 cubic metres of wood
   1 690 kilowatts of electrical energy
   6.5 kilograms of salt cake
   45 kilograms of lime rock
   273 700 litres of fresh water

   How would these requirements determine the location of a pulp-and-paper mill?
5. Which requirements would be the overriding factors in location?
6. One tonne of newsprint is required for 1650 copies of the Saturday edition of *The Toronto Star*. (The total Saturday run is about 750,000 copies.) Discuss the implications of these facts in terms of conservation policies, energy priorities, national interests, and trade relations.

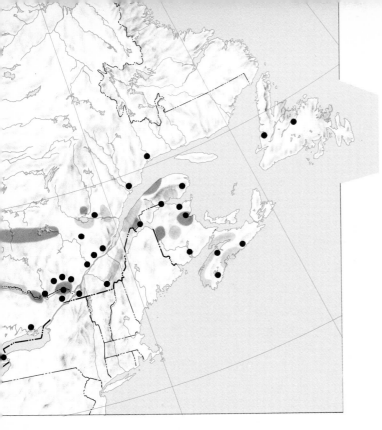

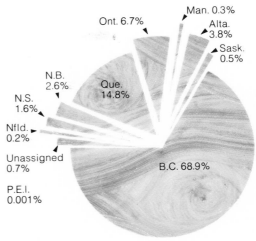

Lumber production by province, in millions of board feet, 1970.
Canada total: 10,671,645 M bd. ft.

Ont. 6.7%

Man. 0.3%

Alta. 3.8%

Sask. 0.5%

N.B. 2.6%

Que. 14.8%

N.S. 1.6%

Nfld. 0.2%

Unassigned 0.7%

B.C. 68.9%

P.E.I. 0.001%

Primary and secondary manufacturing

The very first thing you were asked to do in this chapter was to list wood products under the headings "lumber" and "pulp and paper." Why were you asked to divide the list in this way?

Sawn lumber, plywood, and pulp and paper are *primary manufactures*. In most primary manufacturing, the weight or volume of the raw material is reduced considerably during production. For instance, lengths of wood cut from a tree have a total weight and volume much less than that of the original tree trunk. Freight charges are usually by weight or by volume. Thus it is normally cheaper for the manufacturers of primary wood products — sawmills, pulp-and-paper plants — to locate near the source of the raw material, where excess volume and/or weight is removed.

The reverse is true in the manufacture of *secondary products*, which increase in volume or weight during the production process. Tables and TV sets are much bulkier than the pieces of wood used in their manufacture; books and magazines are much heavier than the paper they are printed on. Freight rates to ship the finished products from factories to markets (population centres) will therefore be higher than those to ship the raw material to the factory. Consequently most secondary manufactures tend to locate close to major markets.

Even so, relative proximity to major markets is an advantage even for primary manufacturing. The largest market in the world for Canadian pulp-and-paper products is the northeastern region of the United States. This helps to explain why Quebec and Ontario production of pulp is so much greater than that of British Columbia.

Hydro-electricity at work — the pulp mill at La Tuque.

Photographic Survey Corporation Limited

◀ *Extract from the La Tuque, Quebec, sheet (31 P/7W, Edition 1 ASE, Series A 761) of the National Topographic System. Scale 1:50,000. Courtesy Surveys and Mapping Branch, Department of Energy, Mines, and Resources, Ottawa.*

Study 33

Use the map and photograph, as well as other research materials, to answer these questions.

1. Why has this area not been cleared for agriculture?
2. What evidences are there of the last ice age?
3. On what river is La Tuque located?
4. What advantages or disadvantages does this area pose for
   (a) a pulp-and-paper industry?
   (b) a lumber industry?
5. What route will the manufactured product probably take to the United States? Include in your report major geographical names and the different modes of transportation.
6. Other important pulp-and-paper mills in Quebec are located at Shawinigan Falls and Trois Rivières. From research on the Laurentide Scarp, explain why so many Quebec mills are located here.

The forest as farm

High in a modern office building in the heart of Vancouver, the manager of a large lumbering company was talking with colleagues in the codified language of specialists. To an outsider, there was little meaning in their casual references to "TFL Number Two in '74." But, to these executives, this phrase meant that a crop of wood the company had tended for twenty-five years was ready for harvesting. The company could begin full-scale logging of the crop of second-growth timber in Tree Farm Licence (TFL) No. 2: 202 000 hectares of forest land on Vancouver Island, alongside Johnstone Strait, and in the Queen Charlotte Islands.

Just over 90 per cent of Canada's forests stand on Crown lands, that is, government-owned property. Logging rights are leased to private companies on provincial government terms. A tree farm licence is a contract by which the Forest Service of the British Columbia government assigns a logging company responsibility for the use and protection of a defined area of forested land. (The area may be Crown land, or it may be a combination of Crown land and property owned by a company.) The purpose of the licence is to provide a logging company with an assured, long-term supply of timber. In return, the company agrees to log in accordance with terms laid down by the Forest Service and to pay stumpage charges on timber removed. The terms of the contract are based on a **sustained-yield** policy: the annual harvest of trees must not exceed the net annual growth, after allowing for all crop loss, including that due to fire, insects, diseases, or wind.

Licences such as the TFLs of British Columbia encourage the management of forest-industries companies to treat the forests as a *co-operative* farm.

- Provincial tree nurseries sow seeds and raise seedlings.
- Reforestation is done by loggers and the Forest Service.
- Selective cutting is practised by the company in order to assist growth.
- Fire protection and fire-fighting are special aspects of crop management and are the joint responsibilities of the companies and the provincial government.
- Logging is the responsibility of private companies.

These measures came too late to save the giants of the Acadian and Great Lakes-St. Lawrence forests. Those trees soared as high as today's Douglas firs on the Pacific Coast. The "cut and get out" operations of early logging companies plundered those forests, treating them as a one-time bonanza, not as a crop to be harvested.

Today's conservation measures are based on the realization that trees are a **renewable resource**. A forest is a farm to be worked, and trees are crops to be tended and harvested. There was a time when only the "choice cuts" of trees were utilized: narrow treetops were discarded, tall stumps were left to rot, defective parts unsuitable for high-grade lumber were simply thrown aside. Now, the timber harvest is more carefully treated. Now, **close-utilization** harvesting methods minimize wasteful logging practices: trees are felled lower down, and the parts of a tree that are not high-grade lumber are used in pulp-and-paper mills. In fact, logging companies in British Columbia that practise close-utilization methods are rewarded by corresponding increases in allowable cuts of timber.

162

Utilization of British Columbia's timber

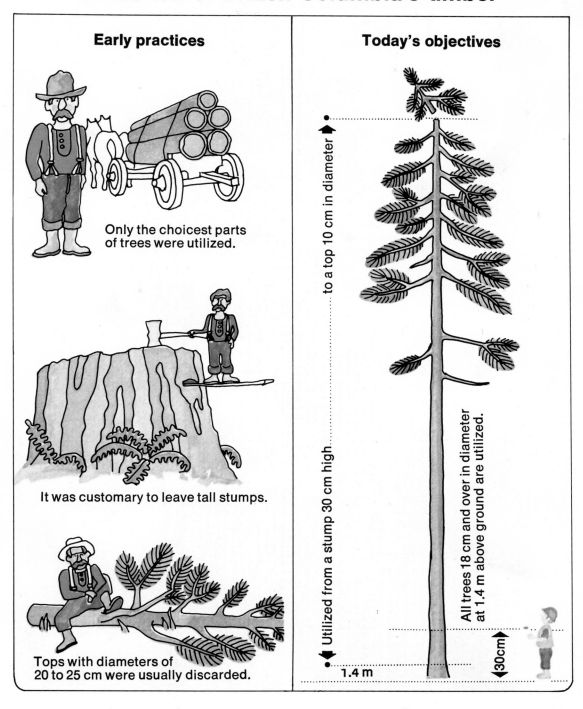

Early practices

Only the choicest parts of trees were utilized.

It was customary to leave tall stumps.

Tops with diameters of 20 to 25 cm were usually discarded.

Today's objectives

to a top 10 cm in diameter

Utilized from a stump 30 cm high.

All trees 18 cm and over in diameter at 1.4 m above ground are utilized.

1.4 m

30cm

Courtesy British Columbia Forest Service

Study 34

1. The conservation practices just described apply particularly to the lumbering industry in British Columbia. Research conservation practices in the pulp-and-paper industry in another part of Canada, preferably in your own province.
2. Account for any variations in practices between British Columbia and the region you chose.
3. What factors led to the introduction of these practices?

Conservation is important for many reasons beyond purely economic ones. Even in agricultural regions, it has been estimated that 20 per cent of the land should be kept as forest in order to regulate the flow of water and reduce soil erosion. Trees trap the snow and shade the drifts, so that the water supply is released slowly instead of in floods. Tree branches break the force of rain, so that soil is not washed away by heavy downpours. Dead leaves can hold 150 - 200 times their weight in water. This soft forest floor acts as a sponge, retaining water for underground storage or releasing it slowly downslope in the form of rivulets and streams. Via rivers and lakes, this water eventually supplies farms, industries, and communities in surrounding areas.

Trees are vital to the life system of this planet. They take in carbon dioxide exhaled by animals and use it in the manufacture of food for themselves. In this process they release oxygen, which is essential to animal life. Thus, the loss of a forest, whether from fire or disease or ruthless overlogging, affects not only the economy of a nation and the quality of human life but the very biology of the earth.

Trees are potential tables, chairs, newspapers, or any one of a hundred and one things, but they are also a future forest. Managed wisely, like fruitful fields, a forest can yield many a rich and recurring harvest. Only through wise conservation and management practices can we have our forest and utilize it, too.

Study and Research

1. What percentage of the labor force in your province derives its income directly from the forest industries?
2. Compare the map on page 140 with that on pages 158-159. The northern parts of Saskatchewan and Alberta are forested land. Why, then, are there so few pulp-and-paper mills?
3. Rank in order the principal exports listed in the table on page 150 for the following regions: the Atlantic Provinces, Quebec, Ontario, the Prairie Provinces, British Columbia.

4. Research export data from the *Canada Year Book* and add up all of the exports directly derived from the forest. What percentage of total exports do they represent?

5. What was life like in lumber camps a hundred years ago? Compare this with life in a lumber camp today. What are the gains and losses?

6. Name half a dozen items that used to be made of wood but are now made more commonly with metal or plastic. Why do you think these substitute materials are being used? Do you think this trend will accelerate? In what products? What are the relative advantages of wood, metal, and plastic?

7. Most of the Acadian forest is second and third growth. What do these terms mean? Trace the development of the forest industries in this region from the original emphasis on timber to the present. Account for the development.

   Would you expect the forest industries of British Columbia to follow the same pattern? Explain your answer.

8.

Province	Pulp-and-Paper Mills		Sawmills and Planing Mills	
	Total Establishments	Total No. of Employees	Total Establishments	Total No. of Employees
New Brunswick	11	5,114	83	2,551
Nova Scotia	5	2,474	121	1,461
Prince Edward Island	—	—	18	18
Newfoundland	2	2,341	56	204
Source: Statistics Canada, 1972				

What is the average number of workers per mill in the pulp-and-paper industry and in sawmilling in each of the Atlantic Provinces? In the Atlantic Provinces as a whole? Account for the differences in average number of workers. Research comparable data for British Columbia and explain any significant differences.

9. Write a report on the three great enemies of the forest: insects, disease, and fire.

10. How have the forest industries made their operations more efficient? (Consider technology and the utilization of former waste materials.)

11. What is the role of government in the operations of the forest industries?

12. To what extent do the interests of the forest industries and society coincide? If there are conflicts of interest, what are some ways of resolving them?

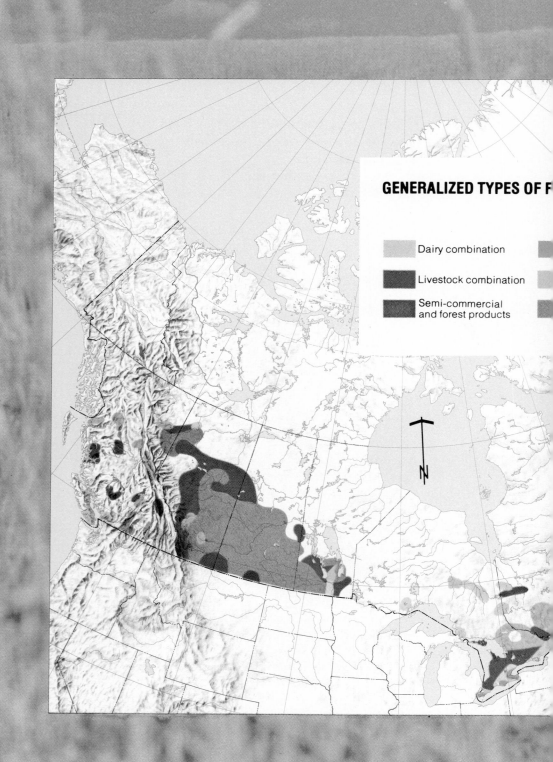

GENERALIZED TYPES OF F

Dairy combination

Livestock combination

Semi-commercial
and forest products

d special crops

arming

Chapter 6 *The good earth*

In pioneer days in Canada, most of the first settlers were farmers. They had to be. There were no supermarkets or corner stores. Every family had to grow its own food, and this was not easy. In most regions, forests had to be cut down using axe and saw (no chain saws in those days). Then the ground had to be cleared of brush and roots, broken up, and seeded.

On the Quebec, Three Rivers, and Montreal plains of the St. Lawrence River and along the Richelieu River, land was steadily cleared. Farms were established from the Shield's edge to the foothills of the Appalachians. Farmers prospered, and the establishment of seigneuries with their "long-lot" pattern is a unique, intriguing part of the Canadian saga.

In the Appalachian region there was little arable land available, especially in Newfoundland. Attracted by the sheltered coves and fisheries, settlement was confined mainly to the coast. Only tiny plots could be cultivated. Exceptions were the Avalon Peninsula, Prince Edward Island, the Annapolis Valley, the Saint John Valley, and some areas in what is now Quebec's Eastern Townships. Where land was cleared elsewhere, the soil was generally too shallow and sour, and farms were often soon abandoned. In fact, the original attraction of the region's interior was lumbering. However, once the great stands of timber were gone, many a lumberman became a farmer.

In the Great Lakes region, trees were usually burned. Stumps were either left in the ground to rot or laboriously hauled out using teams of oxen or horses. The land between the stumps was utilized for crops and stock. Some native grasses were cultivated, but in the main, European grasses had to be sown. So, with toil and sweat, land was brought into production. It took a lifetime for a family to clear and break in a complete farm, particularly in what is now southern Ontario. Here the great stands of hardwood — maple and oak — took many a backbreaking day to clear. But slowly farms spread out from Kingston, the Niagara River, York, and Lake Huron to fill the region from the Great Lakes to the Shield's edge. Before the

The beginning of better things on the Prairies. The sod hut is sturdy and warm, and a fertilizer company will pay good money for buffalo bones. (All this and a roof garden, too!)

Prairies were settled, large acreages in southern Ontario were devoted to wheat for export and for sale to local flour mills. In fact, wheat was Ontario's first really significant cash crop, and flour milling the first industry.

On the Prairies, settlers found the tough, matted sod difficult to break. But here the farmer had two great advantages: underneath lay some of the richest soil in the world; there were almost no trees to clear. With the construction of the Canadian Pacific Railway and a well-organized settlement pattern worked out by army surveyors, it was not long before land-hungry families spread throughout the southern section of the Prairies. They came from the steppes of Russia, from central Europe, from Ontario, Quebec, and the United States; a million of them in the course of twenty years. And they made the Prairies the "breadbasket of Europe."

British Columbia had very little arable land. Around Victoria on Vancouver Island and on either side of the Fraser River delta were the only areas that could be farmed to any extent for a long time. Ranching on the superb rangeland of the interior valleys and fruit growing in the Okanagan Valley came later.

In view of Canada's long, hard winter, finding enough to eat to survive that rigorous period was a first priority. Some vegetables — lettuce, cabbage, celery, tomatoes, and so on — were produced for immediate consumption, and some crops — rye, oats, clover, alfalfa, and hay — were grown for fodder and stored for winter. But food consisted mainly of root crops and preserves, for little else would keep without refrigeration. Imagine a meal table without the varieties of meat we enjoy, without fresh vegetables and fruit all year long, without ice-cream and cold milk.

What a time the fall was for the farm family! Potatoes, carrots, and parsnips were stored in sawdust or sand in the root cellar. Green peas and beans were cooked and sealed in preserving jars. Ears of dried corn and onions were strung up on kitchen walls to dry. Bushels and bushels of apples, pears, plums (and, if you were fortunate enough, peaches) were boiled in a syrup, poured into sterilized jars, and stored in cupboards. Jars and jars of jams soon lined the shelves. And permeating the house was the pungent, delightful aroma of pickles chuckling in the pot. In practically every household, the kitchen was the personal preserve of busy mothers and bustling daughters tending wood or coal stoves, peeling fruit, shelling peas, snapping green beans, slicing cucumbers, sterilizing, pack-

Backyard farming, Toronto-style, around 1900, before going to the office. In addition to the cherry tree seen here, grapevines supported on chicken wire were cultivated, and the vegetable garden produced carrots, beets, lettuce, and radishes.

ing, and sealing glass jars — and then cleaning up the mess.

Even non-farm settlers — the village merchant and schoolteacher, blacksmith and carpenter — had their own vegetable patch and the odd fruit tree. Even the 10 per cent of the population that lived in towns and cities usually raised chickens, fruits, and vegetables.

This way of life has practically disappeared. Settlement patterns have changed the geography of the countryside. Since the end of the nineteenth century there has been a steady interior emigration from farm to city. In the 1920s, the ratio of rural to urban population was about 50:50. With the onset of rapid industrialization, movement from country to city accelerated. Furthermore, immigrants coming to Canada after World War II tended to settle in cities. Now at least 75 per cent of Canadians live in urban centres. However, of the remaining 25 per cent, about 17 per cent are classified as "rural non-farm" (storekeepers, professional people, etc.), leaving only 8 per cent of the total actually living on farms. Yet this small number of farming families produces an abundance for every other Canadian *and* a surplus for export.

To understand Canada's total agricultural output, you have to know your geography. Most of the farmers in Canada live on the Prairies, Saskatchewan being the leading farm province there. By far the least urbanized province is Prince Edward Island, long famed as the "Million-Acre Farm." The most urbanized is Ontario. The Great Lakes-St. Lawrence Lowlands have not only the highest population concentration in the country — 68 per cent of the national total — but also the largest number of people living in cities — 80 per cent. Yet this region is the most agriculturally productive in dollar value *and* in yields per hectare in the country.

Despite the small proportion of farmers in Canada, agricultural production has increased amazingly. Obviously, techniques have changed. Gone is the wooden, horse-drawn plough. Indeed, in the early days of Prairie development, it was not uncommon for a man, too poor to own a horse or ox, to strap the harness over his own broad chest and, with his wife guiding the plough, furrow his fields step by torturous step. Gone are sowing, threshing, stacking hay, milking by hand, and many other laborious, manual tasks. The machine has taken over. Without it, the great productivity we enjoy today would be impossible. Mechanized agriculture whereby a few men reap great quantities of foodstuffs from huge areas of land is called **extensive farming**. (In **intensive farming**, many people work small areas, as, for instance, the rice fields of Asia.) The use of artificial fertilizers, a greater knowledge of soils, the scientific breeding and feeding of stock, and other innovations have led to a higher yield per hectare and more nutritious food. So it is that, although number of farms, total of labor force, and total amount of land cultivated have steadily declined in recent years, agricultural production has steadily risen.

In most cases the size of individual farms has increased. The day of the small farmer has just about gone. To operate economically, there must be a fairly large holding and the expertise to farm it scientifically. Farming is now a business, and only the qualified can survive. Agriculture in Canada is a large, important industry. It is fully one-quarter of the country's economy. Not only does production supply most of our own needs, but there is a large surplus for export.

The value of what one country exports to another is known as **foreign exchange**. Agriculture accounts for 20 per cent of Canada's foreign exchange, and we rank fourth in the world as exporters of agricultural products. And it's mainly because of the wheat.

Study 35

1. How did the habitant farmer work his long, thin strip of farm? What crops did he plant? What are the main agricultural products of Quebec today?
2. The Avalon Peninsula, Prince Edward Island, the Annapolis Valley, and the Saint John Valley are the few areas of arable land in the Appalachian region. What crops are cultivated in each of these areas? What are the main agricultural products of each?
3. What reasons explain the decline of wheat farming in southern Ontario?
4. When was the heaviest twenty-year immigration to the Prairies? What was the average size of farm worked at that time? What is the average size today?
5. What other regions in the world are "breadbaskets"? Rank Canada's production with that of other wheat-producing nations. What facts explain Canada's significance as a "breadbasket"?
6. Rank the provinces by number of farmers and by dollar value of agricultural production.

The staff of life

Wheat field and farm near Grande Prairie, Alberta. The rich, chernozem soil of a region centred on the junction of the Peace and Smoky Rivers produces magnificent crops of wheat.

Wheat was Canada's first really solid economic base. Fish, furs, and lumber each played a part in the country's development, and with the advent of pulp and paper, Canada's forests became enormously significant. But it was wheat that first put Canada on the world's economic map.

Wheat is a grass. Early peoples couldn't help noticing those grasses that grew the largest seed heads. By sowing these particular seeds, they gradually developed various strains of grass, mainly wheat, rye, oats, and barley. Collectively these are known as "cereals" (from *Ceres*, the Roman goddess of the harvest). In England, wheat, the main grain grown, is referred to as "corn" (hence the Corn Laws and the Corn Exchange). The Biblical "Corn of Egypt" refers to wheat. What we in North America call "corn" — sometimes artificially produced on TV — is known in Europe as "maize" or "Indian corn" because the species is native to North America.

Flour can be made from all cereals. The seeds are husked from the stalks by threshing and winnowing; they are then ground, and the bran (the skins of the kernels) is separated from the flour. Of all cereals, wheat is the most nutritious. Bread is the staff of life, and wheat is the best grain for it. For over five thousand years, it has been cultivated throughout the Middle East and the Western world.

There are three kinds of wheat: soft, hard, and **durum.** The last is used to produce pasta to make macaroni, noodles, spaghetti, and vermicelli. **Soft wheat** grows best in wet summers and contains a relatively large amount of moisture. It can be used to make bread, but the product tends to be both coarse and crumbly; it is best for cakes and cookies. Since soft wheat is planted in the fall, germinates, grows a little, and then lies dormant throughout the winter, it is known as **fall wheat** or **winter wheat.** In the spring it revives and grows, maturing and ripening at the end of summer, when it is harvested.

Hard wheat makes the best breads. It is high in protein and gluten content. In the history of wheat, it is just a youngster. It was developed, scientifically, in the late 1800s to ripen quickly enough to avoid the early fall frosts in the great wheatlands of the west. Sown in the early spring as soon as the frost is out of the ground (which is thus ready for ploughing and cultivating), it grows rapidly, maturing and ripening in the fall. Hard wheat is low in moisture content and grows rapidly in the hot, dry summer days of the Prairies.

As mentioned earlier, the first great wheatlands were the rolling hills of southern Ontario. By the Corn Law of 1825, wheat could be imported into Great Britain when the price of domestic wheat became too high for the common people to buy bread. This stimulated wheat production in the Great Lakes region, and this grain became Ontario's first significant export. In fact, it not only revolutionized the landscape, it raised the agriculture of that day from the subsistence level to that of commercial farming. Wheat was grown far and wide in southern Ontario until competition

A chernozemic or grassland soil profile near Olds, Alberta. Glacial lakes drained away very, very slowly, leaving behind plains formed of deep, lake-deposited silt and clay. On this fertile soil developed the famous tall grass of the Prairies.

GLACIAL LAKES

172

from the great wheatlands of the Prairies in the late 1800s practically put wheat growing out of business.

As settlement spread over the Prairies, Canada became one of the world's greatest wheat-producing nations. The region was Nature's perfect farm for the job. Rich, deep soils — black, chestnut and brown, and brown — gave wheat easy birth and nourishment; melting snow, frost, and fresh spring rains quenched its thirst; hot, dry summer days nurtured it and encouraged rapid growth; then warm fall days and cool dry nights ripened it — Number 1 Hard, the best wheat in the world.

The most popular type of wheat grown on the Prairies is Selkirk. It is a rust-resistant, rapidly maturing variety whose leaves and stalks do not fall prey to foliage-destroying fungi.

Study 36

1. Define and explain the following: threshing, winnowing, gluten, protein, Corn Laws.
2. How is wheat processed into flour in Canada?
3. What are the uses of wheat other than flour making?
4. What are the uses of rye, oats, barley?
5. What is the grain production per province? Answer in terms of hectares, kilograms, and dollar value.
6. On an outline map of Canada locate the following: flour-milling companies, cereal manufacturers, bakery-product manufacturers. What factors do you think helped to determine their locations?

Wheat farming

Laid out in 32-hectare units — the amount two combines can harvest in one day — the land is ploughed as early as possible in May, meaning the moment the frost is out of the ground. In fact, the two operations of ploughing and seeding are performed simultaneously. Giant tractors draw several machines that prepare the ground and broadcast grain all in one operation.

When the wheat is growing, during the hot days of June and July, fields are sprayed to reduce weeds, which rob the soil of moisture. Every bit of it is needed by the wheat. In a region that receives only 38-43 centimetres of precipitation a year, the soil, after evaporation and transpiration by plants, will have a moisture "bank" of about 10-13 centimetres in the spring. This amount, plus the precipitation from spring rains, is just sufficient to produce an excellent crop.

In due time the wheat matures and ripens and is then harvested by combine. This self-propelled machine (a Canadian invention) performs the combined operations of cutting, threshing, and winnowing grain. The wheat may be loaded into the combine's storage compartment or directed in a continuous flow into a truck moving alongside. Chaff and stubble, called **trash**, are left strewn over the fields to be ploughed in later. From the farm, grain is trucked to the elevator at the railhead, where the wheat is graded and stored. Harvesting

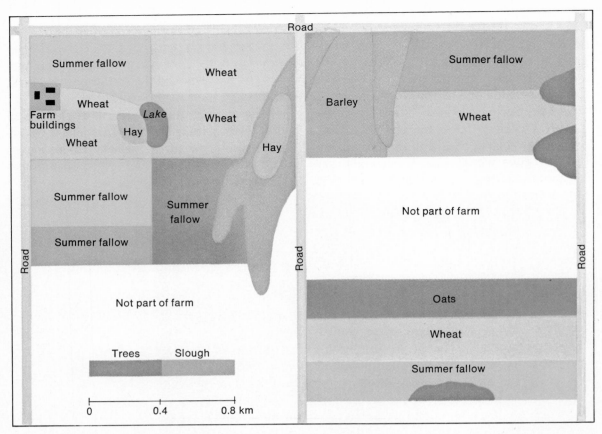

Road

Summer fallow

Wheat

Wheat

Farm
buildings

Lake

Hay

Wheat

Wheat

Hay

Summer fallow

Summer
fallow

Summer fallow

Road

Not part of farm

Trees   Slough

0   0.4   0.8 km

Summer fallow

Barley

Wheat

Not part of farm

Oats

Wheat

Summer fallow

Road

Road

A typical Saskatchewan wheat farm. Note the considerable amount of summer fallow left unseeded. This land is kept weeded all summer, perhaps with the dead weeds left on the surface as a mulch cover.

goes on during August and into September.

Not all the land can be used at one time. Soil must be allowed to recuperate. Usually, a farmer will work two-thirds of his farm and leave one-third fallow. (In drier areas, the proportion will be one to one.) Thus the soil will be able to accumulate sufficient moisture and nutrients for future production. In order to receive and retain as much moisture as possible, fields are lightly ploughed six or seven times during the year, especially after rain showers. The trash holds the moisture, and the light ploughing, properly called cultivating, allows water to sink into the soil and digs up weeds, thus conserving soil moisture.

Of course, the whole process is by no means as neat and tidy as this. Wheat farmers have to tackle problems that can

be heartbreaking. About the only stable item in growing wheat is the soil. The farmer can control its need for regular fertilizing and crop rotation. It is the vagaries of climate, over which he has no control, that can drive the farmer out of his mind. Spring rains may be – and often are – late. Or they are so heavy that fields cannot be ploughed. If the rains are light – especially if there is not much snow left over from the winter – or if there was little rain the previous fall, the crop will be poor. If it is a wet summer or, worse still, a wet fall, the crop will contain too much moisture and its grade will drop alarmingly. Again, too much rain during the fall will prevent full maturing and delay ripening. Late spring frosts can destroy seedlings, and early fall frosts seriously damage the grain.

Even if the weather has co-operated to produce a perfectly matured and ripened field of wheat, the farmer cannot relax until the wheat has been harvested. In the production of wheat there is a precise moment for harvesting. Drawing on his knowledge and experience, the farmer says to himself, "It's time to get this field of wheat in." Ninety-nine times out of a hundred, harvesting is no problem. All the sweat and toil of ploughing, cultivating, and sowing, all the many labors necessary to bring wheat to its final state, all the money spent to buy, replace, and maintain equipment, all the anxious waiting and fearing the weather will do him in is over — once the wheat is in storage. But there is always the possibility of that one chance in a hundred becoming the reality: just half an hour before he begins to harvest, it hails. Great devilish chunks of solid ice smash the grain to the ground. There lies the wheat, broken and bruised, worth a fraction of a cent a kilogram at most. Part, or sometimes all, of a family's crop can be ruined by a freak, solitary hailstorm of a purely local nature. One man's crop may be destroyed, while his neighbor's is left unharmed. It takes a stout heart and strong determination to pick up the pieces and begin all over again next year.

It is not only the weather that affects the prosperity of the wheat farmer. World prices fluctuate according to supply and demand, and so influence the price he gets for his grain. If wheat-growing countries all over the world produce good crops, the demand for Canadian wheat will drop. If, however, Europe has a poor season and Canada a good one, demand will up the price. And if the Prairie farmer has had a number of bumper crops in a row, he has the problem of finding enough places to store his wheat. (It has been piled in farmyards and streets before now.) Just to show the fluctuations that can take place, con-

Harvesting in the Swift Current area of Saskatchewan.

Photographic/Art Division, Government of Saskatchewan

The Prairie landscape: railway, trading centre, elevators, contour-ploughed wheatfields, sloughs, and scattered farmsteads. Pasqua, Saskatchewan.

sider the following figures. In 1961, the average yield per hectare was 740 kilograms of wheat. In 1966, it was 1880 kilograms. In 1969 the yield per hectare was 1810 kilograms, but it was an inferior crop; the price dropped to 4.7 cents a kilogram from the 1967 price of 7.2 cents.

The Prairie farmers' problems with prices and markets have been eased tremendously by the creation of the Canadian Wheat Board. It was born in 1935, at a time when increasing surpluses of wheat, built up in the late 1920s, could not be marketed in the depression years of the 1930s. (In 1932 the price of wheat had collapsed to 1.4 cents a kilogram, an all-time low.) The Board was set up to do two things: establish a reasonably stable price so the farmer would not be at the mercy of world fluctuations in price; handle the mar-

keting of Prairie wheat, oats, and barley, both within and outside Canada.

At the beginning of the crop year the Board establishes the price per kilogram, subtracts the current price of storage plus transportation costs, and thus determines the "floor" price the farmer receives. If the Board does not receive this price in its trading, the farmer still gets his money. The loss is made up by the federal treasury. Only twice in all the years of the Board's operation has this occurred. Money is paid to the farmer in two stages. He receives part-payment prior to the start of the crop year. (Imagine living on two pay days a year!) However, from time to time, the farmer can go to the nearest grain elevator agent and obtain interest-free cash advances.

Marketing is a function that embraces

all the activities involved in getting a product from the producer to the consumer. The Board's marketing function includes grading and storing wheat, finding out how much wheat Canada and foreign countries need, promoting sales, establishing quotas, and transporting the wheat to the purchaser.

The Board controls the actual total of wheat grown on the Prairies in any given year. Its decision is based on its knowledge of the probable requirements for wheat at home and abroad. Sub-totals are controlled by elevator agents on instructions from the Board. Local farmers are informed accordingly on a quota basis, so that large and small farmers are treated equitably.

The transportation of grain is an intricate and fascinating pattern of organization.

Say, for instance, that we have sold 1 350 000 tonnes of wheat to Britain — generally our best customer, certainly our steadiest. Say, we have also sold more or less the same amount to the People's Republic of China, the Soviet Union, and Japan. Other customers are likely to be India, the Federal Republic of Germany, Italy, and Cuba. Wheat goes out from the Prairies in three directions: west to Vancouver, the principal wheat port; east to Thunder Bay, where it continues by rail or freighter to the many storage elevators all along the Great Lakes-St. Lawrence waterway or right out to sea in ocean-going vessels; north (a tiny amount) via Churchill. Now there just are not sufficient rail cars, lines, ships, or docking space in Canada or in other countries to accommodate all of this wheat at once. Obviously, it must be moved over a period of time. How is this done?

The whole process begins not in Canada, but in the country to which we are exporting the wheat. An agent in England, for example, will notify the agent in the Canadian Wheat Board handling sales to Britain that "x" storage space will be available in wheat elevators at Liverpool, England, on a certain date. The Canadian agent then finds available storage and shipping points by consulting a computer. It may indicate Sept-Iles, Montreal, or any of a dozen other wheat ports. He picks the most suitable one. Then he reserves docking space at the port for ships and notifies CP Rail or CN that "x" amount of wheat must be in the elevators at this port by a fixed date. The railway company then feeds all the necessary data into its computer, tying everything in with the transportation system as a whole. Certain elevator agents in the Prairies are notified as to how much wheat will be taken from their particular storage facilities on such and such a date. And so the wheat moves out— from Prairie elevator to rail car, to laker, to port elevator, to ocean-going vessel, to Liverpool, and from there, via rail and truck, to British flour mills.

Wheat being loaded aboard a grain ship in Trois Rivières Harbor, Quebec.

Information Canada Phototèque

Study 37

1. Match the following items and copy the complete definition into your notebook.

    Red Fife is
    a famous Canadian boxer,
    a Maple Leaf hockey player,
    a musical instrument,
    a brand of wheat.

    Marquis is
    a theatre sign,
    a voyageur,
    a type of wheat,
    a maker of boxing rules.

    Saunders was the man
    responsible for the development of early-maturing wheat,
    responsible for introducing the steel plough,
    who introduced turnips into crop rotation,
    who developed elbow grease.

    A combine is
    a co-operative,
    a machine that cuts, threshes, and collects grain,
    a machine that grooms horses,
    a flower.

    A quarter-section is
    the rear end of a steer,
    a district in a Prairie town,
    the amount of land a farmer received during Prairie settlement,
    a corral for cattle.

2. Find out the importance of the following to the wheat farmer: crop insurance, elevator, Co-operative Commonwealth Federation (C.C.F.), steel plough, certified grain, C P R, C N R, co-operative.

3. Where do farmers obtain seed? Write a brief report on the growing of seed wheat in the Prairies.

4. What are the principal strains of wheat grown on the Prairies? Account for these strains in terms of the reasons for their development and the special qualities of each.

5. List the ways in which wheat is important in the economy of Canada. In that of Saskatchewan. In that of the Prairies as a whole.

6. (a) Of the total Canadian wheat production, from 1968 to 1971, what percentage was exported? To what countries?

    (b) What percentage was milled for flour?

    (c) What percentage of the milled flour was exported?

    (d) How would you account for the fact that Canada exports both wheat *and* flour milled from wheat?

Livestock

Early peoples found that certain animals could be domesticated for various purposes. From these have developed the cattle, horses, oxen, hogs, sheep, chickens, and turkeys that we refer to as **stock.** They are raised for two purposes: to be butchered and eaten, as beef, veal, pork, bacon, mutton, lamb, and broilers; or for such by-products as milk, butter, cheese, eggs, and so on.

All in all, Canada has about 13 million beef cattle, most of which are raised in or near the foothills of the Rockies and in the drier areas of Saskatchewan. Since population is relatively sparse on the Prairies and there is not much demand for milk and other dairy products, ranching is the most profitable and economic use of land. This type of farming is done in rough, short-grass country, and huge ranches are neces-

sary to make the enterprise pay. It takes from 10-20 hectares to support one of these animals, hence the need for immense areas of grazing land.

There are, nonetheless, substantial beef herds in Ontario, a response to the increasing demand for meat in this highly urbanized part of Canada. Beef cattle are also raised in Quebec, the Atlantic Provinces, and British Columbia, but this type of farming is not very marked because of a lack of suitable land. (Yet, in remote valleys between mountain ranges in British Columbia, are large areas of rangeland that are not being utilized.)

Raising beef cattle is a specialized, yet diversified, business. Some ranchers simply breed cattle in order to sell the calves at the end of the grazing season. Those who buy the calves from "breeders" are called

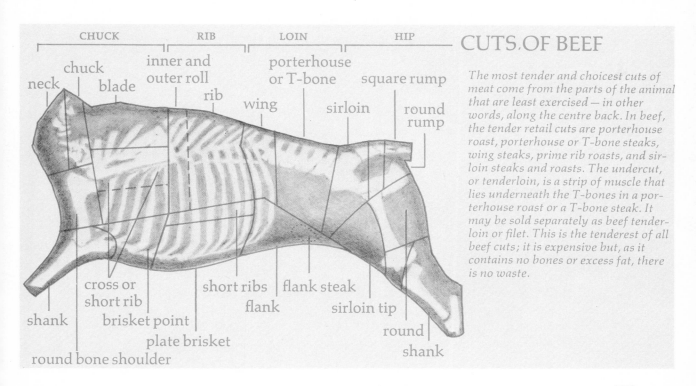

CUTS OF BEEF

The most tender and choicest cuts of meat come from the parts of the animal that are least exercised — in other words, along the centre back. In beef, the tender retail cuts are porterhouse roast, porterhouse or T-bone steaks, wing steaks, prime rib roasts, and sirloin steaks and roasts. The undercut, or tenderloin, is a strip of muscle that lies underneath the T-bones in a porterhouse roast or a T-bone steak. It may be sold separately as beef tenderloin or filet. This is the tenderest of all beef cuts; it is expensive but, as it contains no bones or excess fat, there is no waste.

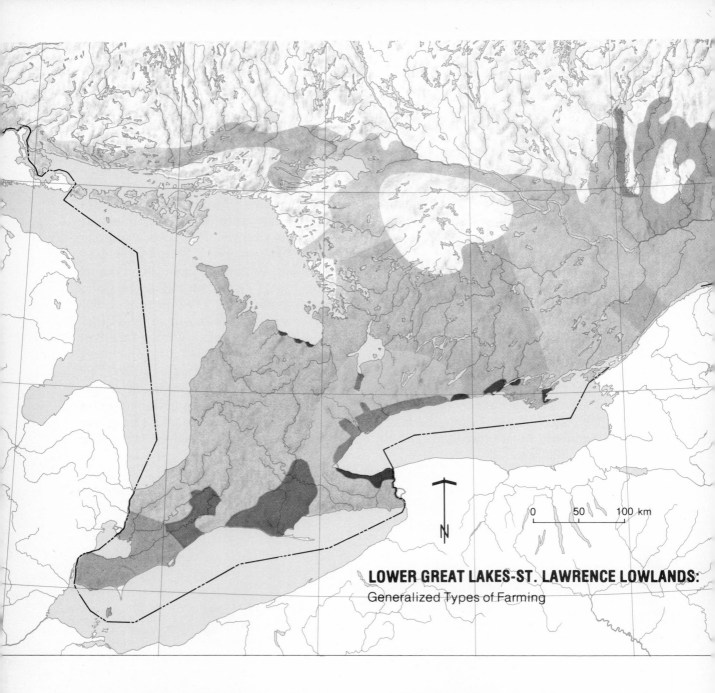

LOWER GREAT LAKES-ST. LAWRENCE LOWLANDS:
Generalized Types of Farming

0   50   100 km

N

"feeders." A great deal of cattle raising in Ontario is done by feeders. They buy the calves, feed them over the winter on such forage as silage, hay, and other grains, and then send them out to pasture for the summer. The cattle are then fattened, mainly on corn and lush grass, before becoming roasts and T-bones. Some farmers are located where conditions allow them both to graze cattle and to grow adequate supplies of winter feed and corn. So they are really in the business of raising beef cattle, to be sold as calves or full-grown steers. Generally a calf is sold when it has reached a weight of about 180 kilograms, and a prime beef steer when it is a little over 450 kg.

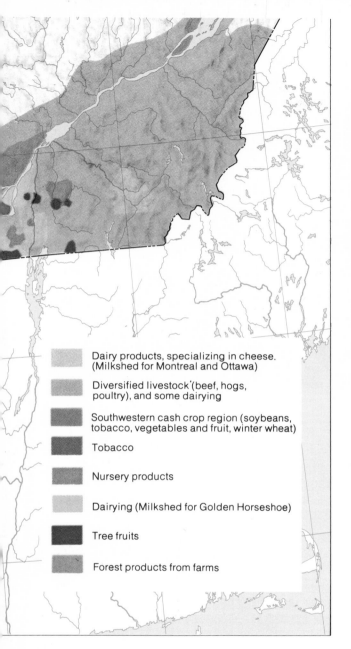

Dairy products, specializing in cheese. (Milkshed for Montreal and Ottawa)

Diversified livestock (beef, hogs, poultry), and some dairying

Southwestern cash crop region (soybeans, tobacco, vegetables and fruit, winter wheat)

Tobacco

Nursery products

Dairying (Milkshed for Golden Horseshoe)

Tree fruits

Forest products from farms

Dairying

Whereas beef cattle are increasing in numbers, dairy cattle are gradually declining. There are roughly about 2.5 million of them. However, total milk production remains just about the same and will prob-

ably increase, thanks to more scientific methods of farming. In other words, output per cow is steadily being increased.

By far the greatest dairying region in Canada is the Great Lakes-St. Lawrence Lowlands. It accounts for about 75 per cent of all production, due to an equable climate, abundant pastures, and the availability of such supplementary feeds as hay and oats. Above all, and by far the most important reason, is the high demand for dairy products from the heavy concentration of urban population in the region.

Dairy cattle were brought into Canada by the French in the 1600s; Louis Hébert, the first settler, established a farm on the Quebec plain. From this small beginning, milk production in Quebec has grown until it now accounts for half the milk produced in Canada.

At first, dairy cattle were owned by both farmers and townspeople. Surplus milk, butter, and cheese were exchanged for other commodities or sold. For 250 years butter was made in the farm dairy; such **dairy butter** is still produced today. However, 90 per cent is now manufactured in creameries, and is thus called **creamery butter.** The first creamery in Canada was established in Athelstan, Quebec, in 1873, and the first cheese factory in Oxford County, Ontario, in 1864.

Of all the milk in Canada shipped to factories, 42 per cent is used to manufacture butter, 30 per cent to produce fresh milk and cream, 14 per cent to manufacture concentrated milk products (milk powder and condensed and evaporated milk), and 9 per cent to make cheese. The remaining 5 per cent of milk production is utilized on farms for feeding calves, making dairy butter, and, of course, for family use. Canadians are drinking less fresh milk and eating less butter, but they are eating more cheese and drinking more processed milk. Most farmers who produced cream used to separate the milk on the farm, ship the

Mealtime at an automated feeding trough.

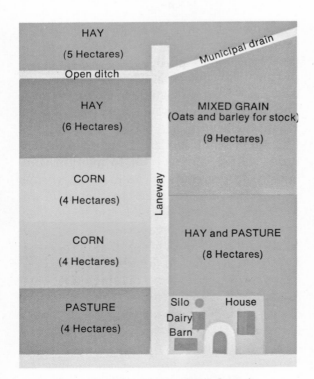

HAY
(5 Hectares)

Municipal drain

Open ditch

HAY
(6 Hectares)

MIXED GRAIN
(Oats and barley for stock)

(9 Hectares)

CORN
(4 Hectares)

Laneway

CORN
(4 Hectares)

HAY and PASTURE

(8 Hectares)

PASTURE
(4 Hectares)

Silo   House

Dairy
Barn

A modern, mixed farm in southern Ontario.

cream to the creamery, and feed the skim milk to calves and pigs. Today, however, they ship their entire milk output in tankers to a creamery, where it is separated. The result is that more skim milk is being converted into commercial products.

By far the most popular breed of dairy cattle is the Holstein-Frisian, followed by the Jersey. The former produces the most milk per cow, the latter that richest in butter fat. Thus, if you are a farmer producing **fluid milk** for drinking, your herd will be Holstein-Frisian; if **solid milk** to be made into butter and cheese, your cows will be Jersey. Some farmers keep a few of each. And then there is the dual-purpose Shorthorn, a breed producing reasonable quantities of milk as well as good beef.

Of all forms of agriculture, dairy farming is unquestionably the most scientific and the most specialized. To be a successful dairy farmer, you need a great deal of

182

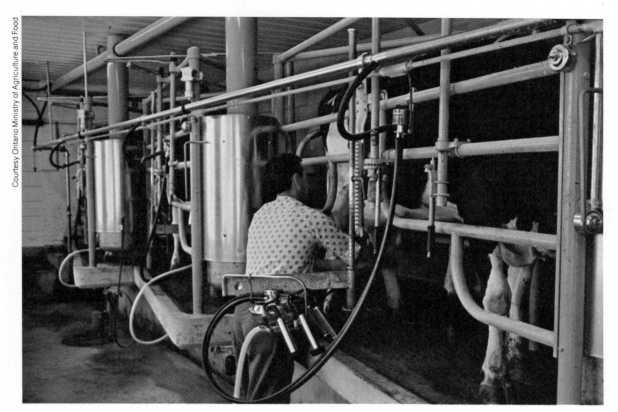

Untouched by human hands: attaching the suction cups of the milking machine.

knowledge and organization (to say nothing of hard work and long hours). You have to select your breed of cattle in light of the milk market available and the location of your farm. Having bought your herd (loans are available for this), you have to know what to feed your cattle.

Cattle require nutrients in their diet just as humans do. The necessary health and energy is obtained only from large amounts of carbohydrates, proteins, and fats. After all, a cow is really a factory "in production" most of the year. Fresh green pasture is the most ideal feed for dairy cows — about 55-65 kilograms per animal per day — together with large amounts of fresh water. (Milk is about 85 per cent water.) Unfortunately our climate does not permit the growth of enough grass in the course of any one year. Consequently, supplementary

feeds must be supplied, even when the cows are out in the pasture. These include corn, oats, barley, wheat, and hay (which is not only fodder, but also produces heat, enabling the animals to resist the cold of winter). These feeds are high in carbohydrates and roughage. Soybeans, soybean meal, linseed meal, cottonseed meal, and brewers' and distillers' grains are also grown or purchased as feed. A properly balanced diet will also contain the necessary vitamins (mainly A and D) and minerals (calcium, phosphorus, salt, iodine, and cobalt). The last three are generally combined into blocks and set out in the fields as "salt licks." The proportion of each nutrient that must be fed to cattle depends on the type of pasture available, the age and size of the cow, the amount of milk the cow is producing, the time of year, and so on.

183

This is only the beginning. Cattle must be properly and comfortably housed; calves must be tended. Since dairy cows vary greatly in their ability to produce milk and butterfat, each good dairyman has to keep a record of each cow's performance. Low-producing cows can then be culled from the herd. Diseases and sickness, from mastitis and dysentry to indigestion and pneumonia, have to be treated. Winter feed must be stored and fed out, fields must be ploughed, cultivated and fertilized, barns cleaned and repaired, fencing attended to, and a hundred and one other chores done. Dairying is very complicated and time-consuming.

So the next time you are out for a drive in the country and see cows grazing in the fields, remember dairying is not quite as simple and idyllic as it looks.

Study 38

1. What are the following: condensed milk, evaporated milk, skim milk powder, buttermilk, yogurt?
2. What is the particular value of the following: soybeans, brewers' and distillers' grain, carbohydrates, protein, calcium, phosphorus?
3. What is Canada's beef population by province? Account for this distribution. Is the population increasing or decreasing? Why?
4. What other uses are made of livestock and their by-products besides those already mentioned?
5. Why is there still undeveloped rangeland in remote valleys between the mountain ranges in British Columbia?
6. What goes on in a milk factory? In a dairy factory? In a cheese factory?

Market gardening

About 56 kilometres north of Toronto, Highway 400 cuts across an area of flat, black soil. West and east it stretches as far as the eye can see. When John Galt of the Canada Company first saw it in 1825, he described it as "a mere ditch swarming with bullfrogs and water snakes." Today this land is valued at from $2,500 to $7,500 per hectare. Producing about $15 million worth of vegetables a year, Holland Marsh is one of the richest market-gardening regions in Canada.

Nothing much was done with the Marsh in the early days except to twist its reeds into cord. Then, in 1912, Professor Day of the Ontario Agricultural College at Guelph suspected it had possibilities as farmland. He tested the soil and found it quite free of acid — remarkable in a marshy soil, containing as it does so much moisture. Little

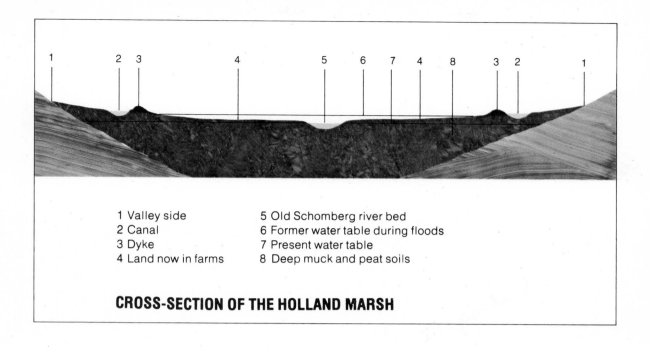

1 Valley side
2 Canal
3 Dyke
4 Land now in farms

5 Old Schomberg river bed
6 Former water table during floods
7 Present water table
8 Deep muck and peat soils

CROSS-SECTION OF THE HOLLAND MARSH

was done at this time, however, because of the outbreak of World War I. It was not until the mid 1920s that the first productive step was taken; drainage of the land was begun.

Around the Marsh a canal 17.5 miles long and 7 feet deep was dredged. In addition to the drainage from the headwaters of the Schomberg River and its tributary, the Holland, all the natural drainage from the surrounding hills flow into this canal and are carried around the Marsh. The earth from the canal was used to form an embankment or dike, which was lined with clay to prevent seepage. The Schomberg River was drained and deepened to form a canal running through the centre of the Marsh. Then four hundred drainage ditches were dug, each 6 feet deep and 2 feet wide, and connected to the old river bed. Working on the principle that water finds its lowest level — and the bed of this canal is below land level — water now drains out of the soil and into the drainage ditches and the central canal.

Across the narrowest portion of the Marsh, connecting the dikes of the canals, a 450-foot dam was built to hold back the waters of Lake Simcoe. Pumps, installed on the dam, remove water from the central canal to the surrounding canal. Thus the level of water is controlled in the wet season. When conditions are dry in summer, water from this canal is pumped back into the ditches in the Marsh. Sprinklers are also used to irrigate the land.

In the first years of operation, the Marsh was worked mainly by Canadian-born farmers. However, they were unaccustomed to the special needs and problems inherent in market gardening. Many of the original inhabitants very soon gave up the struggle, and field after field became deserted. However, some European farmers, mainly Dutch, achieved remarkable success. (Many people believe the area received its name from the number of Dutch farmers there. It is actually named after Major S. Holland, the first Surveyor-General of Upper Canada.) During the Depression years of

1. What would you say most distinguishes the Marsh from the surrounding area?
2. Find:
   (a) The course of the old Schomberg River
   (b) The present Schomberg River
   (c) The dam
   (d) The surrounding canal
   (e) Highways 400 and 11
   (f) Two towns. Name them.
3. Why are the fields in the Marsh long and narrow?
4. Is all of the market gardening carried on inside the canals? If not, where? Give a reason for your answer.
5. What type of farming is carried on in the surrounding area? What would be the main product? Why?

Aerial view (1:50,000) of the Holland Marsh, Ontario

Northway Survey Corporation Limited

the 1930s, a Mr. Snor, Canadian representative of the Netherlands Emigration Foundation, came up with the idea of settling the Marsh with Dutch farmers who had failed elsewhere in Ontario and were on relief. Each family willing to move to the Marsh was promised $600 assistance, to be made up of equal contributions by federal, provincial, and municipal governments. Each family was to pay back $450 of the original amount. However, the municipal government in question reneged on its share, and the government of the Netherlands, in response to an appeal from Mr. Snor, made up the $200. The eighteen families that finally located on the Marsh formed the nucleus of the present village of Ansnorveld.

In 1958, the Province of Ontario helped numerous Netherlands families to settle in the area, and today at least a third of the five hundred growers on the Marsh are of Dutch descent. Others are of Italian, German, East European, and Japanese origin. These people are accustomed to working on farms where soil is measured in centimetres rather than hectares. They are prepared to put in the required long hours, they recognize the need to use mechanized machinery as well as a stooped back, and they know the importance of restorative fertilizers. You see, the soil of the Holland Marsh is something of an oddity: it is black, but not rich. The very nature of a marsh means that it is plumb full of water, so it will be leached of the mineral salts vital to plant growth.

When first drained, this land contained great quantities of nitrogen, essential to crop growth. But the intensive use of the Marsh — three crops per year — used up all the nitrogen long ago. So what makes the land so valuable? First, the soil is flat and of such fine texture that it is easily worked.

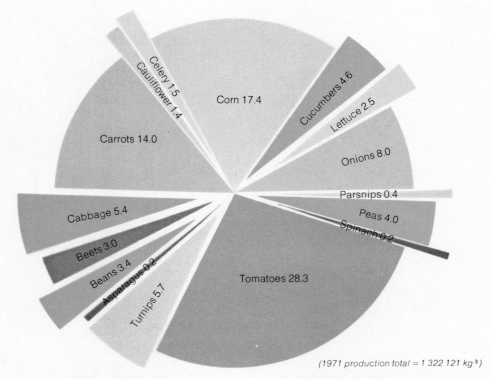

(1971 production total = 1 322 121 kg³)

PERCENTAGES OF CANADIAN COMMERCIAL VEGETABLE PRODUCTION, 1971

It is quite spongy in most parts and readily absorbs fertilizer and moisture. Because the soil is black, it absorbs and retains heat, and is thus a "warm" soil. However, the Marsh's most valuable asset is its location near the largest market in Canada — Toronto and the other towns and cities of the Golden Horseshoe. With such an available market, the Marsh's farmers can afford to pour into the soil the huge amounts of fertilizer necessary to produce three crops a year. Cold-storage plants are a recent innovation, and now marketing is carried on beyond the Toronto district, even as far east and west as Halifax and Saskatoon.

The five major products are onions, lettuce, potatoes, carrots, and celery. The low-lying Marsh is particularly suited to lettuce growing. Cold air settles in its hollow, and lettuce, a "cold crop," thrives particularly in the cool, early-morning air.

The mechanics of market gardening are vastly different from mechanized operations on the Prairies, although both are forms of extensive agriculture. Marsh holdings are quite small, but the amount of machinery used is prodigious. On 80 hectares of land, there might be thirty tractors, fifteen garden tractors, twenty ploughs, fifteen cultivators, and twenty-five discs. This is the result of great competition among the farmers and little co-operation. Very individualistic is the Holland Marsh farmer. He has always marketed his own crops, and even today this habit is hard to break. In fact, it was not until 1946 that onions were marketed co-operatively.

In 1956 the Holland River Gardens Company, organized by three Horling brothers, began operating. Its history is fascinating. These enterprising gentlemen arrived at the

Hand harvesting lettuce on the Holland Marsh.

Marsh in the lean years of the Depression with $600 among them. Working on the adage "to each his own," they divided up the work, each specializing in a particular aspect of the operation. One took complete charge of production and mechanical equipment, another supervised personnel, and the third devoted his time to marketing.

By 1940, they were the biggest landowners on the Marsh. Then they began to look farther afield. George, the marketing expert, was convinced that there were markets other than in Toronto. However, success depended on getting perishable produce to customers "harvest fresh." Thus in 1946 the three brothers put their life savings into the construction of an ice-packing plant. Insulated by powdered ice, vegetables would stay fresh during thousands of kilometres of transit. Within two years, the Horling brothers' ice-packed vegetables were being marketed in every province in Canada, in the eastern United States, and even in far-distant Hawaii. In New York City today, their lettuce earns a premium of fifty cents a case over the best American produce. They have a standing order to supply Detroit with fifteen hundred cases of lettuce a day as available. They could, if they were able to, ship a trainload of vegetables a day to New York City alone, an output equal to the total sold in all Canada. Why? Because the Marsh is only twenty-two hours' trucking distance from New York, whereas California, the Horlings' biggest competitor, is 5000 kilometres away. Lack of sufficient continuous production is the only obstacle.

Today, the Horling brothers' ice plant is worth half a million dollars. "The Marsh," says George Horling, "can grow greater quantity and better quality for lower costs than any other competitive area on the continent."

Study 39

1. What is market gardening? What are truck crops?
2. Account for the locations of market-gardening regions in Canada.
3. Ask the produce manager of your local supermarket where he buys the following fruits and vegetables: lettuce, potatoes, carrots, turnips, celery, onions, cabbage, cucumbers, strawberries, blueberries, raspberries. From the information that he gives you, make a time line that shows where each product is bought throughout a twelve-month period.
   (a) What percentage of each is bought locally?
   (b) What percentage is bought from Canadian market-gardening areas such as Holland Marsh?
   (c) What percentage is imported?
   (d) Account for the importing of agricultural products that are also available from Canadian farmers.

Fruit farming

Some years ago, hundreds of orchards edged the Canadian shores of Lake Ontario. Today, many of them have disappeared beneath urban sprawl. The most significant section of the remaining orchard lands lies in the shadow of the Niagara Escarpment between Hamilton and the Niagara River. The narrow, 65-kilometre-long Niagara Fruit Belt produces on its 8100 hectares well over 75 per cent of all Canada's peaches, cherries, and plums, and 90 per cent of all grapes.

Fruit trees and grape vines like well-drained, light soils. These are provided by the gravelly, sandy, silty, gently sloping shoreline of ancient glacial Lake Iroquois. And stone fruit and grapes thrive in warm, moist climates. The Niagara Fruit Belt, located in the most southerly section of Canada, has a warm, moisture-filled growing season of 154-183 days. Now, as you know, bodies of water have a moderating influence on land temperatures. Thus, the waters of Lake Ontario prevent summers in the Fruit Belt from being too hot for optimum stone-fruit and grape growing.

However, these waters have a much more valuable contribution to make. In spring, Lake Ontario is colder than the surrounding land, which prevents the shores from heating quickly. So frost-free days begin later than they do farther inland, with the result that fruit trees do not blossom until the danger of late spring frosts has passed. An excellent example of this climatic "plus" is the history of peach growing in southern Ontario. Peaches were once grown widely throughout this area. Then, around the turn of the century, a series of intense frosts killed the peach trees — except those in the Niagara Fruit Belt. Here, the coolness of spring had, as usual, retarded new growth. With no buds exposed, these peach trees survived.

Fruit is perishable. It bruises and spoils easily. Thus a readily available market is an important factor in fruit production. The Niagara fruit farmer has Canada's largest market more or less on his own doorstep. In late spring, tens of thousands of people flock to the Niagara Peninsula to view the glorious profusion of the blossom festival. Later in the year, many of these same visitors return to shop in the fruit stands, filled with luscious peaches, plums, and grapes, that line the Queen Elizabeth Way and Highway Number 8. And all summer long, truck load after truck load of fruit — especially pears and peaches — enters the Ontario Food Terminal, Toronto. Although the principal market is Metropolitan Toronto and nearby cities and towns, Niagara fruits are sent to many centres across Canada. In addition, a large proportion of the fruit is processed and canned — and turns up on the shelves of your local supermarket or neighborhood grocery store.

Victor C. Last

"Will that be cash or Chargex?"

191

Extract from the Grimsby, Ontario, sheet (30 M/4E, Edition 4 MCE, Series A 751) of the National Topographic System. Scale 1:50,000. Courtesy Surveys and Mapping Branch, Department of Energy, Mines,
and Resources, Ottawa.

Fifty Mile Pt

DND
Rifle
Res

I

II

III

ESCARPMENT

V

Mile

Buffalo

Grassie

649

656

646

13

20

Kimbo

12

14

16

17

18

19

20

75

76

77

78

79

80

81

82

85

84

Town Lis

Grimsby

Greenhouses

Hosp

C

BM
329

Grimsby Point
Bluff

657

650

650

633

647

Creek

Gas
Pipeline

Grimsby
Centre

NORTH GRIMSBY TP
SOUTH GRIMSBY TP

Treatment
Plant

Grimsby
Harbour

Nelles
Beach

Grimsby Beach

Queen

Elizabeth

Way

C

Hosp

BM
312

Beamers
Falls

Radio
100'

Dam

Mile

Thirty

Dump

PT

Spring

C

625

650

625

600

500

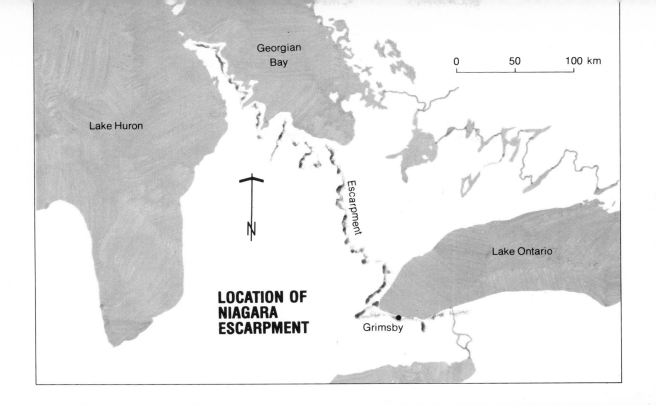

LOCATION OF
NIAGARA
ESCARPMENT

Study 40

1. How can you pick out the Niagara Escarpment?
2. In referring to the escarpment, we sometimes use the terms "above" and "below." On the map, which is north of the escarpment? Which is south?
3. Examine the vegetation below the escarpment. How can you tell that it is not natural?
4. What features — other than your answer to question 3 — indicate that this is a fruit-farming area? Give two possible reasons why fruit farming is carried on mainly below the escarpment, not above it.
5. What is the difference in elevation between the shoreline of Lake Ontario and the foot of the escarpment? What is the approximate gradient from Cherry Beach to the foot of the escarpment? How does this favor the growth of fruit trees?
6. What do you think was the original reason for the location of the town of Grimsby?
7. Highway No. 8 marks the approximate shoreline of the ancient, glacial Lake Iroquois. What does this tell you about the soils between this highway and the shoreline of Lake Ontario?
8. Look at the transportation routes below the escarpment. Considering also that this area is quite close to the industrialized areas of Hamilton and Toronto, discuss the problems of land use that arise.

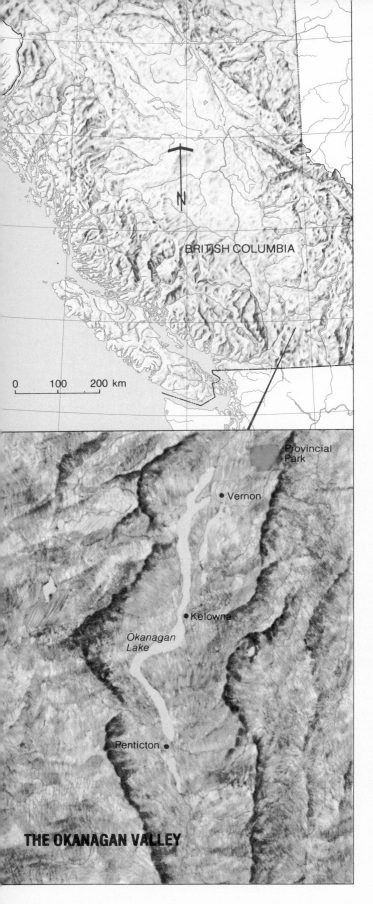

THE OKANAGAN VALLEY

Hemmed in between the Cascade Mountains on the west and the Monashee Mountains on the east lies the Okanagan Valley of south-central British Columbia. Even in ancient times, there was a valley here; but gouging glacial ice deepened and widened it. Eventually, the ice retreated and left a post-glacial lake. As the level of the lake fell in stages, beaches and terraces were left exposed at various heights on either side of a valley about 120 kilometres long.

Trader-explorers stumbled on the Okanagan Valley on their way to the fur-rich Thompson River country. At first, the valley was simply a transport route for trains of pack horses laden with goods or packs of furs. Later, when gold was discovered in the Cariboo Mountains farther north, prospectors in their thousands trudged through the valley seeking their fortunes. Some, attracted by the grasslands, stayed and began cattle raising. They were joined by a few disappointed (or broke) prospectors, and so ranching was the reason for early settlement in the region. It is still important, especially on the lush grasslands of the northern section. Later still, ranching was succeeded by irrigated agriculture, especially fruit raising. This is the dominant land use today.

Orchards established by part-time farmers comprise about 70 per cent of the valley's fruit lands, and the size of each of these orchards is about 4 hectares. Attracted by the valley's climate, quite a number of retired people have settled here. They supplement income by growing fruit. Other residents combine such activities as ranching, logging, and tourism with fruit farming. In fact, tourism brings more dollars into the Okanagan Valley than fruit farming does. To make a living from fruit farming alone, you have to work about 80 hectares of land.

Precipitation in the Okanagan area is sparse. One reason is distance from the

Pacific Ocean. By the time the Westerlies have blown across 400 kilometres of mountain ranges, there is little moisture left for the valley. Another reason is its location. Tucked in behind towering heights, the southern section of the Okanagan receives only about 25-30 centimetres of precipitation, which results in a natural vegetation of scrub and bunch grasses. Soils are mainly brown, and summer average temperatures are about 22-23°C. In the northern section,

which has from 33-48 centimetres of precipitation, the vegetation is rich grasses, with resultant deep, black soils. Summer averages are in the 19-20°C range.

Although the valley's people engage in a number of economic activities, in Canada, the name Okanagan spells fruit. Apples are by far the dominant crop, followed by pears, peaches, cherries, apricots, and plums. In the south, where temperatures are warmer, Delicious apples are grown. How-

A vehicle called a girette comes in very handy when it's grafting time in an Okanagan orchard.

ever, the north is too rigorous for these, and the concentration here is on the hardy McIntosh. Peaches and apricots will only grow with real safety in the south.

It is on the terraces above the valley floor that the Okanagan orchards are situated. Here, the soils are light and somewhat gravelly, suitable for fruit trees. However, the most important reason for this location is climatic.

You will recall that precipitation in the Okanagan Valley is fairly sparse. Thus skies are generally clear, and cloudless air allows a rapid escape of heat. The result is that temperatures can become very cold indeed, and the masses of cold, heavy air that accumulate on the heights above the valley flow downslope. This freezing air drains through and past the orchards on the terraces and settles on the valley floor. (This temperature phenomenon is aptly called "air drainage.") If the orchards were located here, the low temperatures would probably kill the trees; situated as they are high above the valley floor, they are more protected from killing frosts. It is on the valley floor that there is wheat growing, dairying, market gardening, and ranching.

While there is not sufficient precipitation for fruit growing, high above the valley in the plateau country are many lakes and streams fed by melting snows. Orchards are irrigated with water channelled down by means of wooden, metal, or concrete flumes (or pumped up in pipes from Lake Okanagan and the Okanagan River). Water is then led through portable aluminum piping to sprinklers set in the orchards. This irrigation system can provide controlled moisture conditions — the equivalent of 5-6 centimetres of rain within twelve hours — which results in improved yield.

Study 41

1. What sort of work is necessary for a successful orchard operation?
2. How is Okanagan Valley fruit — including grapes — marketed?
3. The Annapolis and Saint John River valleys are areas where farming plays an important role in the region's agricultural economy. How do they compare with the Okanagan Valley?
4. What are the major markets for the fruit produce of the Annapolis and Saint John River valleys?
5. Which provinces are the major producers of the following fruits: apples, peaches, apricots, plums, strawberries, blueberries? Explain your answers.
6. Although over many years there has been a steady decline in the number of orchard trees farmed in Canada, stone-fruit production has doubled in the course of the last forty or so years. Why?

*   *   *

The rains fall upon the land, and the summer sun warms the good earth. We plough it, seed it, and cultivate it. We harvest its riches in abundance. From it, we get food to sustain us; from it, we get textiles to clothe us; from the animals that graze on it we get many other necessities of life. If the climate is too dry, we irrigate the good earth; if too wet, we drain it. Soil plus climate plus sweat equals agriculture.

VALUE OF AGRICULTURAL PRODUCE, IN PERCENTAGES, 1970

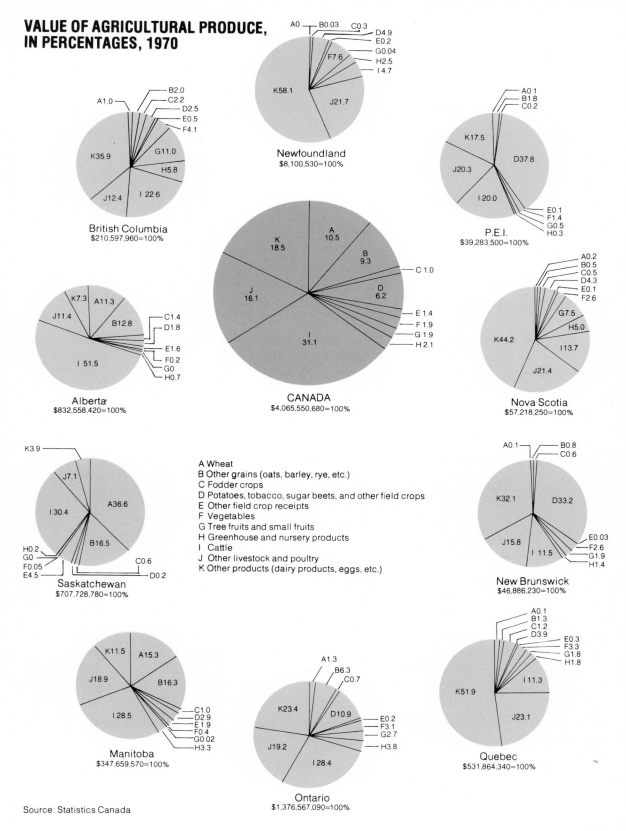

British Columbia
$210,597,960=100%

A1.0
B2.0
C2.2
D2.5
E0.5
F4.1
G11.0
H5.8
I 22.6
J12.4
K35.9

Newfoundland
$8,100,530=100%

A0
B0.03
C0.3
D4.9
E0.2
G0.04
H2.5
I 4.7
F7.6
J21.7
K58.1

P.E.I.
$39,283,500=100%

A0.1
B1.8
C0.2
D37.8
E0.1
F1.4
G0.5
H0.3
I 20.0
J20.3
K17.5

Alberta
$832,558,420=100%

K7.3
A11.3
J11.4
B12.8
C1.4
D1.8
E1.6
F0.2
G0
H0.7
I 51.5

CANADA
$4,065,550,680=100%

A 10.5
B 9.3
C 1.0
D 6.2
E 1.4
F 1.9
G 1.9
H 2.1
I 31.1
J 16.1
K 18.5

Nova Scotia
$57,218,250=100%

A0.2
B0.5
C0.5
D4.3
E0.1
F2.6
G7.5
H5.0
I13.7
J21.4
K44.2

Saskatchewan
$707,728,780=100%

K3.9
J7.1
I 30.4
A36.6
B16.5
H0.2
G0
F0.05
E4.5
D0.2
C0.6

A Wheat
B Other grains (oats, barley, rye, etc.)
C Fodder crops
D Potatoes, tobacco, sugar beets, and other field crops
E Other field crop receipts
F Vegetables
G Tree fruits and small fruits
H Greenhouse and nursery products
I Cattle
J Other livestock and poultry
K Other products (dairy products, eggs, etc.)

New Brunswick
$46,886,230=100%

A0.1
B0.8
C0.6
K32.1
D33.2
E0.03
F2.6
G1.9
H1.4
I 11.5
J15.8

Manitoba
$347,659,570=100%

K11.5
A15.3
J18.9
B16.3
C1.0
D2.9
E1.9
F0.4
G0.02
H3.3
I 28.5

Ontario
$1,376,567,090=100%

A1.3
B6.3
C0.7
K23.4
D10.9
E0.2
F3.1
G2.7
H3.8
J19.2
I 28.4

Quebec
$531,864,340=100%

A0.1
B1.3
C1.2
D3.9
E0.3
F3.3
G1.8
H1.8
I 11.3
J23.1
K51.9

Source: Statistics Canada

197

Study and Research

1. What are the main physical factors that affect the nature and extent of agriculture in each region of Canada?

2. The three main agricultural "regions" of eastern Canada are Prince Edward Island, the Annapolis Valley, and the Saint John River Valley. Investigate and report on *one* of these regions, applying to it all the relevant factors mentioned in this chapter.

3. Ninety per cent of Canada's grapes are grown in the Niagara Fruit Belt. What are the major uses of these grapes?

4. Evaluate the different kinds of farming — wheat growing, ranching, dairying, market gardening, fruit growing — in terms of crop yield and cash return per hectare. What factors other than the physical determine what kind of farming is practised?

5. Account for the location in Canada of the following agricultural activities: poultry raising, hog raising, tobacco growing. Describe the operation of one of these.

6. Why do we import many agricultural products that we also produce right here in Canada? Which products do we import and where do they come from? Why do we import and export the same kinds of products?

7. What is "subsistence farming"? Where is it practised in Canada? Why is it practised there?

8. What is meant by the term "rural poverty"? Why might farms in such areas be uneconomical? Why, then, does this land continue to be farmed?
    What has been done by governments and farm organizations over the last decade to help solve rural-poverty problems? What will probably be the results over the next decade?

9. What is the role of government in agriculture? (Consider: crop control, marketing, price support, etc.)

10. The role of science is becoming increasingly important in agriculture. Evaluate this statement in terms of:
    (a) improved strains
    (b) improved yields
    (c) control of plant disease
    (d) irrigation
    (e) soils.

11. Trace the development of mechanized agriculture in Canada. How has mechanization affected farm size, operating costs, crop yield, crop variety, farm employment, cultivable land?

12. Prepare a study of agriculture in Canada from 1960-1970, in terms of production, land reclamation, farm management, land use, improved yields, new products, reduced variety (e.g., ten strains of apples instead of a hundred), etc. What trends do you see developing? What effects will these have on Canadian agriculture by 1985?

13. The earth is good but many of its products are processed into "junk food." Discuss this statement with reference to the concern of many nutritionists that a large percentage of Canadians, living in a land of plenty, are malnourished.

14. In the mid 1970s, Canada was one of the very few countries of the world to enjoy surplus harvests. Name some of the other countries.
    Develop arguments for and against "giving" this surplus to people in countries less fortunate than our own.

Western Cordillera

Great Plain

0   400   800 Km

Arctic
Lowlands

Canadian
Shield

Hudson Bay
Lowlands

Appalachian
Region

Great Lakes – St. Lawrence
Lowlands

Minerals: The Canadian Shield

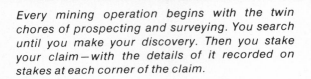

Every mining operation begins with the twin chores of prospecting and surveying. You search until you make your discovery. Then you stake your claim — with the details of it recorded on stakes at each corner of the claim.

The huge horseshoe shape of the Shield sprawls over the face of Canada. It extends from the rugged coasts of Labrador, across the central and northern parts of Quebec and Ontario, on through northern Manitoba and Saskatchewan and the northeastern tip of Alberta, and up into the central section of the Northwest Territories. Indeed, it might be said that the Shield is the inescapable physical fact of Canada; it covers almost half the mainland surface of the country.

What picture comes to mind when you think of the Shield? The refuge of a cottage on a quiet lake, the mystery of trails through shady woodland dressed in the cool green of summer or the shining red-and-gold of fall, the crisp excitement of sparkling snow slopes? These are the scenes and seasons of the Shield that are most immediately familiar. But they represent only a small part of the Shield — the southern edges that border on the densely settled Great Lakes-St. Lawrence Lowlands.

The landscape of most of the Shield is far fiercer, almost hostile. There are many parts where no settlers live, many places where no visitors ever come — kilometre after kilometre of bare rock, dark water, flyridden bogs, and brooding forests, relieved only by scatterings of settlements and patches of barely cultivable land. Awesome, moody is its beauty for the rare and rugged few, but hardly a landscape to invite visitor or settler, especially with the added deterrent of a harsh and bitter cli-mate. Think of the physical and psychological hardships; think of the size and remoteness; think of the transportation and communications problems.

And yet, and yet, this vast unyielding landscape contains some of Canada's greatest assets: millions upon millions of trees for pulp-and-paper mills; swift rapids and tumbling waterfalls for hydro-electric power; innumerable lakes and streams for enormous supplies of fresh water, a vital and disappearing commodity in today's industrialized, urbanized world; and, deep within the rock, great mineral riches for the mines of the Shield and the mills of industry.

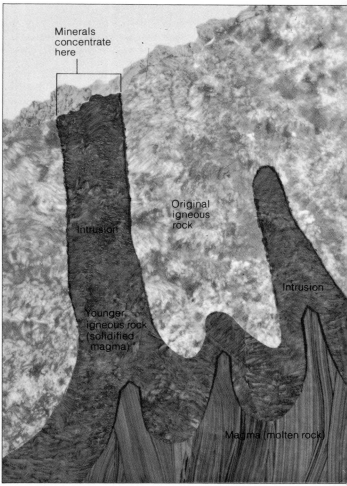

An igneous intrusion, from the outside and the inside. Why do mining companies pay particular attention to such intrusions?

How the minerals got there

The Shield is defined as a distinct region on the basis of its exposed rocks. These are the oldest rocks known to geologists; they belong to the Precambrian Era, a period so far back in time that Shield rocks contain no fossil remains, for they predate any form of life on earth.

Billions of by-gone years ago, after the earth's crust had cooled and hardened, masses of red-hot magma seethed and bubbled deep beneath the surface of the Shield. When pressures became too great, cracks formed in the crust above, and the mineral-bearing magma burst into them to form intrusions. Sometimes it spilled out over the surface as extrusions of lava. Over millions of years of relentless activity, a mountainous mass was formed. Just as relentlessly, erosive winds and waters beat against the rocks, until these ancient mountains were worn down to the "roots," which thus became exposed at or near the surface. Then bouldered glaciers scraped and scoured the rocks and littered the landscape with glacial debris.

Only some of the Shield rock is mineralized. It is the igneous "greenstone" or volcanic formations that contain most of the minerals. These metallic **ores** * are so rich in variety, so large in quantity, and so exploitable because of their surface or near-surface locations that the Shield can justifiably be called "a storehouse of minerals." The region produces most of Canada's nickel, platinum, titanium, gold, and iron, and much of its copper, lead, zinc, silver, and molybdenum.

Roads and railways, airlines and waterways penetrate far northward into the Shield. They bring in food, supplies, manufactured articles, and workers to the towns and settlements scattered far across the region. These same transportation systems carry out the rich mineral resources that have "transformed the Shield from a mighty obstacle to Canadian development to a national asset."

Only very grudgingly did the Shield yield its mineral riches. It remained a "mighty obstacle" to large-scale mining until construction of railways gave the developer — the successor to the voyageur, lumberjack, and prospector — access to the region.

The very name "prospector" summons up the stuff of legend — "strike it rich" and "lucky find." Many of the early finds were indeed lucky. Although many of the mineralized rocks were exposed at the surface, finding them in thick forest cover often depended on luck rather than expertise. More scientific prospecting methods had to await the development of geology and technology — geological maps, the airplane, the magnetometer, the geiger counter, the gravimeter. Today, aerial photographs and recordings from airborne magnetometers narrow exploration to promising areas. Then geologists are sent in to obtain rock samples and drill test holes. Mining engineers and geologists may not evoke the excitement and drama of prospectors and sourdoughs, but it was their knowledge and experience that transformed mining in the Shield from individual discovery to industrial development.

---

*Ore is rock containing mineral deposits, which are distributed unevenly through the rock. High-grade ore refers to rock with a high mineral content.

Study 42

1. Metallic minerals are rarely used in their pure state. In fact, some of them are mainly used to make alloys. (An **alloy** is a metal made by mixing or fusing two or more metals.) Research the minerals mentioned on the preceding page in terms of:
    (a) the properties of each metal,
    (b) the properties of the metal(s) mixed with it to make an alloy,
    (c) the properties of the alloy,
    (d) the uses of the alloy.
2. Compounds of cobalt, lead, molybdenum, titanium, and zinc are used to make a wide variety of products, from rubber to gasoline additives. Research some of the uses of these compounds.

As exploration for minerals intensifies, more sophisticated devices are being employed. This turboprop aircraft is equipped with both electro-magnetic and magnetic survey equipment.

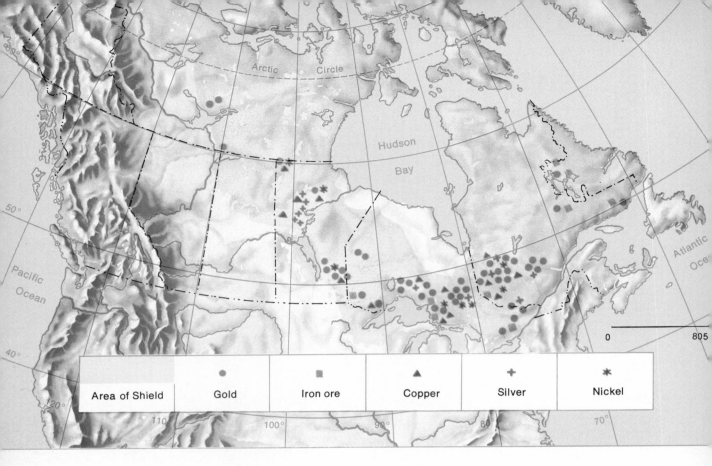

Area of Shield	Gold	Iron ore	Copper	Silver	Nickel
•	•	■	▲	+	*

Mining regions

Mines and mining towns in the Shield appear on maps as clusters. The opening of a mine may be an individual enterprise, but it often leads to the discovery of other mines. The original mining operation thus tends to act as a take-off point from which personnel and equipment penetrate into surrounding areas. These clusters of mining activity form a mining region. Mining does not occur everywhere within the area, only in particular small places, and mines may even open and close at different places; but within the region mining is a major activity.

Rocks of the southern edges of the Shield contain "industrial" minerals — feldspar, graphite, mica, talc, dolomite, some iron ore, and other minerals used in the indus-

tries of the nearby Lowlands. Deposits discovered in the nineteenth century were small and scattered, so no major towns developed. However, steady small-scale mining has continued as an activity in this region for two reasons: the location of the ore bodies near the cities and industries of the Lowlands, which means low transportation costs for the bulky, low-grade ore; industries need these particular minerals.

The Sudbury basin: Nickel-copper-iron

The first major mining town to develop in the Canadian Shield was Sudbury, Ontario. In 1883, construction crews struggling to blast out a right-of-way for the Canadian Pacific Railway uncovered a large deposit of mineralized rock — nickel-copper ore. Who knows how long the rich resources of the Sudbury basin might have lain undiscovered had not the railway's location engineer mistakenly run the line north instead of south of Lake Ramsey!

Copper was the first attraction but, because it contained nickel, was useless. The whole problem was to separate the nickel from the copper. Then a method was discovered. World War I revealed the value of nickel as a steel-hardening alloy for guns and ammunition. Today the ores of the Sudbury basin are the sources of about three-quarters of Canada's nickel output (nearly half the world's total output of nickel) and almost one-third of Canada's total copper production. Platinum, silver, rhodium, and iron ore are important by-products. Actually, iron ore has become so important that it is no longer treated as a by-product of nickel and copper production. New processes have been developed and expensive new machinery installed to recover the iron from nickel-copper ores. In fact, the value of the iron contained in the ore has made it feasible to mine marginal-grade nickel-copper ores that might otherwise have been left in the ground.

International Nickel Company of Canada Limited

Pure nickel cathodes produced in a refinery. Nickel is a "joiner" or "good mixer" that gives strength, toughness, and a corrosion-resistance quality to thousands of different alloys. It is used in a wide variety of materials from household items to space-exploration equipment.

The Ontario-Quebec region: Many metals, many mines

It was another stroke of luck — again during railway construction — that revealed the rich cobalt and silver ores at Cobalt, Ontario. Fred La Rose, a blacksmith employed by the Timiskaming and Northern Ontario Railway in 1903, threw his hammer at an inquisitive fox. He missed the fox but struck a mine, for the hammer broke off a chunk of rock to reveal a vein of glittering silver. From the "boom" town that arose near the mine, prospectors fanned out into the surrounding area. Westward, more silver mines were opened; northward, rich gold deposits were discovered at Kirkland Lake and Timmins-Porcupine; and eastward, gold and copper

The presence of zinc in combination with lead, copper, gold, and silver is quite a common occurrence. Copper is mined mainly in Ontario and Quebec, and lead chiefly in the Northwest Territories. Canada is the world's largest producer of zinc and silver.

ores were found at Noranda-Rouyn and Val d'Or. After World War II, exploration with airborne magnetometers permitted extensive "prospecting" in untracked, inaccessible areas. Copper-zinc-gold deposits were discovered in the Chibougamau-Matagami area. New railways were built northward into the Shield to bring these bulky ores out to smelters at Noranda or Montreal.

The existence of settlements, transportation lines, and an established labor force helps promote the development of new mines and products. Thus from the original core at Cobalt, mining expanded outward until this became the largest mining region of the Shield, extending from Elliot Lake to Chibougamau. At the same time, the region also developed intensively as the number of productive mines and the vari-

ety of metals produced within the region increased. Some of the old gold mines at Timmins and Kirkland Lake closed down, but new mines opened nearby producing molybdenum, copper, zinc, lead, silver, and iron, so mining remained a major activity.

New mining towns were created to provide accommodation and services for the miners, but old centres did not necessarily die. Although some did indeed become ghost towns, others grew and are continuing to thrive on mining development in the region. Old business districts have been modernized, and new suburban communities have been created. And throughout the region a network of roads and railways has been built to transport people and products. The isolation of the old mining frontier is breaking down.

The Labrador-Quebec region: Iron

Victor C. Last

An iron-ore mine at Schefferville, Quebec. The pit is cut downward in "benches" or steps until, at a certain depth, further open-pit mining often becomes uneconomic. If the mineral vein can then be mined profitably by underground methods, a shaft is sunk and ore hauled to the surface.

Our demand for iron is inexhaustible. Just think of all the things we use that are made from iron, or the more refined product, steel: everything from automobiles to zippers — and the machines that make them. We live in, sleep on, eat from, travel in, relax with, and generally make use of all kinds of products manufactured from iron and steel.

As far back as the turn of the century it was known that there were large deposits of iron ore in the Labrador-Quebec region, but they were so inaccessible that it was unprofitable to mine them. The costs of constructing transportation systems and opening up mines to exploit the deposits would have priced the ore too high. It would not have been able to compete with

iron ore from the established and more accessible Mesabi range in Minnesota. But by the 1940s this high-grade ore was nearly exhausted. New sources of iron ore were desperately needed to feed the inexhaustible demands of North America's war machine and, later, its postwar technology. Fortunately, the construction of the St. Lawrence Seaway helped reduce the cost of the long haul from Labrador-Quebec to steelmaking centres on the Great Lakes; enormous lake freighters could be used to transport the bulky ore most of the way. What was unprofitable at the turn of the century had now become economically feasible.

A railroad was pushed into the wilderness northward from Sept-Iles, and open-pit iron mines came into production at

Schefferville in 1954. Once the mines had begun producing the high-grade ore and the initial heavy **capital costs** of railway construction and mining equipment had been met, smaller and lower-grade ore bodies could be developed.

To reduce the costs of transporting the bulky, low-grade ore to iron-and-steel mills hundreds of kilometres away, **beneficiation or pelletization** plants were established at the mine site. In these plants, low-grade ore containing 30-35 per cent iron is crushed, the waste rock containing little or no iron is discarded, and the residue is processed into pellets containing 65-70 per cent iron. In effect, raw low-grade ore is processed into pellets of high-grade ore. This new technology helped to open up a new mining region.

By the 1970s Canada had become the world's fourth-largest iron producer. The mines in the Labrador-Quebec region provide the bulk of the output. The deposits now being exploited are expected to produce for several decades. Farther north, enormous low-grade ore bodies still await full development. Perhaps some day it will

be profitable to extend the railway from Schefferville all the way to Ungava Bay to get plain, ordinary, but vital iron.

The development of iron ore in the Labrador-Quebec region transformed the settlement pattern and economy of the north shore of the estuary and gulf of the St. Lawrence. Jobs in mining and transportation provided a higher-paying alternative to those in fishing and forestry. New towns like Wabush and Labrador City were created, complete with commercial, service, and recreational facilities to supply the needs of workers in the mining and transport industries. As new centres like Gagnon and Fermont opened up, transportation systems expanded to link the centres. Now rail and water transport moves iron ore and pellets to markets in the Great Lakes, roads connect the new communities of the North Shore to each other, and air service connects them to the Lowlands cities of southwestern Quebec. The isolation of this eastern frontier of mining is breaking down, and the Labrador-Quebec region is being linked into the economy of the Quebec heartland.

Iron-ore pellets, brought from Schefferville by train, are loaded aboard a freighter at the St. Lawrence port of Sept-Iles, Quebec.

Victor C. Last

The Lake Superior region: Scattered metals, scattered mines

The concept of a mining region is less applicable to this area than to other regions of the Shield. Mines are scattered all over the place. Each has been developed individually. This distribution is related to the geology of the region; the areas of volcanic rocks are generally small and scattered, and there is no large area of greenstones within which mining activities could be connected. Fortunately, transport lines east, north, and west of Lake Superior had already been established to connect the people and industries of the Great Lakes-St. Lawrence Lowlands with the lands and economy of the Prairie Provinces. Thus when minerals were discovered, there was the great advantage of transport close by.

It is difficult to generalize about mining in this region. Perhaps it can be best described as one where mines have been short-lived, where the closing of old mines and the opening of new ones has not followed the more typical pattern of development from a core. Within this large, loosely-defined region, new mining towns have been created, as in other parts of the Shield. Manitouwadge is as compact, comfortable, and well serviced as new communities in Labrador-Quebec. But in the Lake Superior region the pattern of mining towns is rather one of isolated "boom-bust" development. Michipicoten is an example. Early in the century, the iron-ore mine near Michipicoten supplied ore to the steel mill at Sault Ste. Marie, but it proved to be an isolated mine in an area of granites that did not appear to have any other mineralization. It did not become a core that generated further mining activity. When high-grade iron ore was found in the Mesabi range, the Michipicoten mine closed down. After World War II, when beneficiation plants made feasible the mining of low-grade ores, the ore body was reopened at a site nearby. But this was not an expansion outward from a core at Michipicoten. A new town was built for the miners, and Wawa appeared on the map of Canada.

The northwestern mining region: Faraway minerals

In the sparsely occupied area between Lake Superior and the Province of Manitoba, only scattered gold and iron-ore mines have developed. Steep Rock Mines at Atikokan, Ontario, are on good east-west transport lines that move ore and pellets to loading facilities at Thunder Bay. But many gold-mining communities such as Red Lake and Pickle Crow are isolated north of the east-west routes.

However, a distinct mining area has evolved near the Manitoba-Saskatchewan border. The old original core was at Flin Flon, Manitoba, where copper-zinc-gold

Headframe

Crusher

Mill

Hoist

Conveyor

30 metres

Ore-bearing vei

69 metres

Backfill

Sto

ore

91 metres

Ore cars

Crusher

Skip or cage

Loading

122 metres
212

ores were produced in the 1930s. (The political situation of Flin Flon is similar to that of Schefferville; both are border communities, their centres straddling provincial boundaries.) As in the Ontario-Quebec metals region, mining expanded outward (from Flin Flon) and intensified internally in the core area. Intensification occurred with the opening of new mines, east of Flin Flon at Snow Lake and Chisel Lake, and westward as far as La Ronge. Expansion took place after World War II with the opening of nickel mines at Lynn Lake and Thompson. The role of transportation and its effect on mining production followed the same pattern here as in Labrador-Quebec. New rail lines had to be built to take out the ores and bring in goods and supplies. Once railways had been built and capital costs of development (plant, equipment, railway construction) reduced, mining companies could consider producing lower-grade ores.

Feasibility

The factors that help to determine the feasibility — profitability — of exploiting a mineral resource are:
1. demand for certain metals
2. supply of these metals, within the region and elsewhere
3. production costs
4. transportation costs
5. technology.

Let's take a look at these factors and their application to the northwestern mining region. Here, the disadvantage of location adds extra importance to the transpor-

tation factor in determining the feasibility of mining development.

The ore bodies in this region are far removed — in distance, time, and costs — from industrial markets in eastern Canada and the United States. Distance between producer and markets is measured by transportation costs rather than kilometres. (A thousand kilometres by sea may cost less than 300 kilometres by rail, which may cost less than 100 kilometres by road.) Because of the northern and interior location of this region, cheap water transportation is not available. So the high capital costs of constructing roads and railway lines and setting up heavy equipment, plus the transportation costs of moving bulky ores over great distances, play a large part in determining whether or not it is feasible to develop the region's metallic resources. These high costs have to be offset by other factors for a mining operation to be feasible. In order for northwestern mines to compete with more accessible ore bodies in the eastern Shield, production costs must be lower, or quality and value per tonne of ore significantly higher, or the product economically transportable. It was for such reasons that gold production at Yellowknife, in the Northwest Territories, proved to be feasible — despite the very considerable disadvantage of location. The ore body was rich in terms of kilograms of gold per tonne of ore, and the product — gold bricks — could be shipped out by air. Similarly, it was at one time feasible to exploit the pitchblende deposits at Port Radium and Uranium City, N.W.T., because the demand for radium and uranium was high, and supplies were scarce elsewhere. But with the discovery of large deposits of uranium at Elliot Lake, Ontario, a location much closer

Most mining projects involve underground work, either from the start or as a continuation of what was at first an open-pit operation. Usually, ore is initially processed at an underground crusher, where large chunks are reduced to a more manageable size before being stored in the head frame building or shafthouse. Secondary crushing and grinding on the surface is followed by mill treatment, in which filters, flotation cells, and tanks of chemicals are used to separate the useful mineral from the waste rock.

to markets, the supply picture changed. The further development of these mines, therefore, was no longer feasible.

* * *

Mining regions in the Shield have developed at different times, at different places, and at different rates. But *patterns* of development have been *similar* in time and space: expansion outward from a core, and intensification within the core area. Factors of demand, supply, costs, and technology, however, are elastic in time and space. Yesterday's "vital" metal may not be in demand today; today's inaccessible region may be made accessible by tomorrow's technology. *Feasibility* of development *varies* at different times and in different regions.

Ontario Ministry of Natural Resources

International Nickel Company of Canada Limited

Mining old style: you needed a strong back, a sturdy pair of legs, and well-calloused hands.

Mining new style: with a flick of the fingers, a miner controls a diesel-powered drilling rig.

Study 43

1. Copy into your notebook the generalized mining map on page 206. Mark on your map the mining regions mentioned in the chapter and the centres that played a role in the evolution of these regions.
2. Select one mining centre in each region and answer the following questions for each centre you have chosen.
   (a) What is the population?
   (b) What mining activity goes on there?
   (c) When did production begin?
   (d) How far is the settlement from the nearest large concentration of manufacturing activities?
   (e) What conditions made production feasible?
3. What does this information indicate about the problems of developing mining centres in the Shield?
4. "Economic boundaries rarely coincide with provincial borders." Explain this statement with reference to the map.

Elliot Lake: Uranium supply and demand

The story of Elliot Lake is an excellent example of how a shift in feasibility factors affects mining development.

After World War II, the stockpiling of uranium for the production of atomic weapons was considered a matter of utmost urgency. Until then, the sources in Canada had been Port Radium and Uranium City in the northwestern Shield, 1300 kilometres from a railhead at Waterways, Alberta, and 5800 kilometres from the refinery at Port Hope, Ontario. Imagine then the excitement of two prospectors, Carl Gunterman and Aimé Breton, when one of their rock samples labelled "Long Township" set geiger counters clicking in the office of the Department of Mines in Sault Ste. Marie, Ontario. Long Township covers 93 square kilometres of heavily wooded country on the north shore of Lake Huron, near the town of Blind River. Where, precisely, in that dense cover had the radioactive sample come from? There was only one way to find out — track through the bush to identify the rock outcrop in question.

Gunterman and Breton eventually found the location of the mystery sample, eagerly staked claims, and immediately contacted potential buyers. Here, however, was another mystery. Field men explored the area, geiger counters clicking wildly, but analyses of surface rock samples revealed only a trace of radio-active materials. The prospectors couldn't explain the mystery, the mining companies backed off, and the claims were allowed to lapse.

215

Ontario Ministry of Natural Resources

Geology of Ontario

LEGEND

PALEOZOIC AND MESOZOIC

Sedimentary rocks.

PRECAMBRIAN

Mainly granitic and hybrid rocks.

Mainly volcanic, sedimentary and intrusive rocks.

SMC 12713

But one prospector-geologist, Franc Joubin, had a theory to explain why geiger counters reacted sharply, although sample analyses failed to indicate radio-active materials. Uranium values at the surface had been leached during centuries of exposure to the elements, but deep below they remained intact. He persuaded his company to risk $30,000 in drilling. Sure enough, drill cores from deep beneath the surface indicated a worthwhile uranium content. The company staked claims and began studying geological surveys. A 1925 map showed a distinct break between old rocks and younger sedimentary deposits, and the drill cores had come from a layer between the two. The shape of the contact zone appeared to form a rough, 130-kilometre "Z" running northwest from Lake Huron. If mineralization occurred along the length of the zone of contact . . . ! The company set out to stake every foot of land along "The Big Z."

This was no ordinary project; routine claim-staking methods were out. "Operation Backdoor Staking Bee" was carefully

Prospecting equipment. The essential tool is the pick-cum-hammer, either short- or long-handled. (Not shown but next in importance is an axe for camping and staking.) Hammer, chisels, and goggles are helpful aids. But, you do need a mortar and pestle to crush rock, and pans in which to wash rock debris and thus isolate heavier mineral grains.

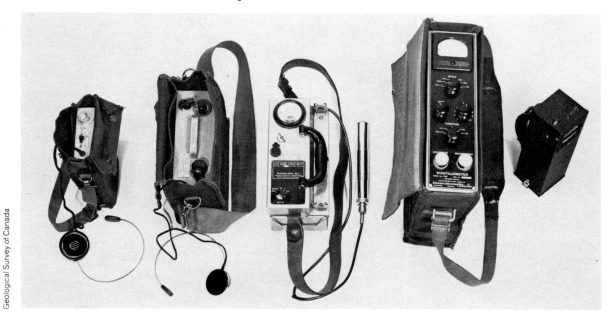

Uranium-prospecting equipment. Almost all important discoveries of uranium in recent years have been made using small to large Geiger or scintillation counters. The item on the far right is a "mineral light" or ultraviolet lamp, a handy aid which indicates whether a rock sample contains mainly uranium or thorium (another radioactive, metallic element).

217

planned and carried out in strictest secrecy. The company recruited prospectors who were experienced in staking procedures — and in keeping their mouths shut. The men obtained the necessary miners' licences from different recorders' offices all across the province, so that no one would suspect an organized operation. Then planeload after planeload of prospectors — and a team of lawyers to check that the claims were completed correctly — was secretly flown into the bush. The secrecy paid off. On July 9, 1953, the prospectors emerged from the bush holding title to more than 1,400 claims covering 23 000 hectares.

When the news broke, a rush of prospectors invaded the area to stake claims in the remaining parts. The boom had begun. Drilling crews were flown in, drill cores bored and analysed — and the uranium value of "The Big Z" was confirmed.

Once the immensity of the ore supply was established, there was no problem of markets. The Canadian government negotiated contracts with the Atomic Energy Commission of the United States for more than a billion dollars' worth of uranium oxide, to be delivered by 1963.

The size, cost, and urgency of the project were stupendous: eleven mines to be established, the smallest of which would dwarf most uranium-mining enterprises anywhere in the world; housing to be constructed for workmen; roads to be built to bring in

How many characteristics of the Canadian Shield can you see in this photograph? Information Canada Photothèque

At Elliot Lake, the processing and service facilities required by mining companies have been set up in an industrial area quite separate from the residential sections of the town.

machinery and equipment — and all this in thickly wooded, rocky, swampy terrain.

The most immediate need was a road, any kind of a road, just as long as it was built with all possible speed. In three short months a tortuous trail was laid through the swamps and over rocky outcrops, and traffic began to flow northward from Highway 17. Under the best weather conditions the 50-kilometre trip was considered a full day's work for any driver. Yet one traffic count over a 24-hour period showed an average flow of fifty trucks an hour — one every 72 seconds. Some of the trucks carried men and supplies, but most hauled heavy loads like 20-metre steel girders. Mine shafts were sunk, gigantic mills were constructed on the bedrock, and temporary accommodation was set up for thousands of workmen.

A mining empire was in the making.

But mines and mills and machinery do not run themselves. Workers operate the machines. In the end, the most important element in any industrial empire is the human resource, and the needs of workers and their families have to be met. So government and industry got together to plan and build a pleasant and permanent community. Too many ugly shanty developments had blighted too many mining towns in the past. Elliot Lake would be planned to serve the needs of its residents and to preserve the beauty of its setting.

The town was laid out in the form of a number of neighborhoods, each surrounded by a green belt of parkland but inter-connected by a network of roads. Schools, churches, and recreational facilities served the needs of each neighborhood. A large community centre, a hospital, a central high school, and a complex of stores, offices,

219

and hotels served the needs of the entire community.

The new houses were scarcely occupied, the fine public buildings barely opened, when the town was hit by the shattering fallout of a sudden change in United States' defence policy. There would be no further build-up of uranium stockpiles; domestic sources in the United States would be sufficient to meet reduced demands. This abrupt removal of one factor – demand – drastically affected the feasibility of uranium production. Elliot Lake had only one product to sell – uranium – and no markets. Mine after mine closed. Uranium production fell from a value of 268.5 million dollars in 1959 to 40.5 million dollars in 1966. Hundreds of miners were forced to leave their homes and seek jobs elsewhere; many stores and small businesses had to close. More mines stopped production.

But Elliot Lake did not die and become a ghost town. Governments and industry had co-operated to build the community; now they worked together to keep it alive. Research and educational centres were established; tourist attractions were promoted and developed; and the Canadian government agreed to accept for stockpiling over a five-year period the uranium production of the three mines still in operation. But this was only a stay of execution. What Elliot Lake needed to survive was markets for its only product.

The demand for uranium was revived by a change in two factors: technology and energy supply. Scientists found ways to control atomic reaction. Nuclear-generated electric power and nuclear-powered ships and submarines moved off the pages of science fiction and into the world of reality. Canada, the United Kingdom, and Japan placed long-term contracts for Elliot Lake uranium. So what had become unfeasible with the loss of markets became feasible again with renewed demand.

Demand should continue to grow. The Elliot Lake area contains the largest known reserve of uranium. As industrial development around the world draws increasingly on supplies of traditional, non-renewable sources of energy, the possibility of uranium as an alternative source of energy becomes even more feasible. Furthermore, technology is finding new uses for uranium by-products: yttrium, used in the manufacture of color television tubes, and thorium, used as a fuel in some types of nuclear reactors. Elliot Lake may once again thrive as "The Uranium Capital of the World."

Steep Rock Mines

The factors of demand, supply, and technology, which played such an important part in the production of uranium at Elliot Lake, are even more dramatically represented in the development of the Steep Rock Mines at Atikokan, Ontario. Imagine demand for iron so high, supplies so low, and technology so advanced as to make feasible the draining of a whole lake to get at iron ore!

Iron – or to be precise, the more refined product, steel – is indispensable to our industrialized society. The overwhelming demands for iron to make weapons for two world wars had severely diminished high-grade ore reserves all over the world. And an anticipated increase in the postwar production of consumer goods would place further demands on dwindling resources. The reserves of the Mesabi Range would soon be unable to meet the needs of industry in Canada and the United States. Clearly, alternative sources had to be found. So it became feasible to invest the tremendous amounts of money, manpower, and exper-

This is the whole point of any iron-ore mining operation — the production of steel, steel, and more steel.

tise necessary to develop other iron resources of the Canadian Shield — even underwater sources of iron ore.

At Atikokan, the valuable ores lay at the bottom of Steep Rock Lake, 18 square kilometres in extent and 20 to 90 metres deep. The first step was the diversion of the Seine River, which necessitated the construction of several dams and 24 kilometres of roadway over rugged terrain. Then, with the main inflow diverted, came the monumental task of pumping out 450 billion litres of water from the lake. For six months, fourteen pumps spewed out 136 000 litres per minute, day and night. At last the bottom of the lake was exposed. But there were still millions upon millions of cubic

metres of silt to be removed. Two barges equipped with suction pumps and water nozzles dredged up the lake bottom. (About $15 million was spent on this pumping task alone.) Meanwhile a giant ore dock was being built at Port Arthur (now Thunder Bay), and a new highway was under construction from Atikokan to the Lakehead. Full-scale production began in May 1945.

These mines now produce about 3.6 million tonnes of ore and pellets each year, and an estimate of reserves shows that they could produce 7.7 million tonnes of ore each year for the next hundred years. The ore is taken first from open pits. After the pits have been mined to maximum capacity, they are filled in, and underground operations are started. The ores at Steep Rock Lake are exceptionally rich — about 70 per cent metallic iron — and therefore highly profitable to exploit. A beneficiation plant has been installed to pelletize lower-grade ores.

Steep Rock Lake, once indistinguishable from thousands of other expanses of quiet water in the lonely wilderness, is now a gigantic hole in the ground. Its site is scarred by open-pit excavation, its bed churned up by heavy vehicles, and its peace shattered by the grinding and whining of machinery. For what? For the production of iron, without which none of us could function for a single day.

Study 44

1. Is Elliot Lake in fact thriving as "The Uranium Capital of the World"? Bring the story of Elliot Lake up to date. How would you write the next chapter?
2. Compare the production of iron ore at Steep Rock and Schefferville in terms of supply, reserves, size of operation, transportation, markets, etc.
3. Elliot Lake and Steep Rock are just two examples of mining enterprises in the Shield. Select one other enterprise and write its story.

The Shield: Cornerstone of industry

The development of the Shield's storehouse of minerals has benefited Canadians in so many ways that enumerating them would result in a list comprising most of our industries, most of our consumer goods, and most of our exports. In fact, it would cover most of our daily activities, from popping a slice of bread into a toaster to snuggling down into a spring-filled mattress at night.

Thousands of Canadians work in industries that are directly related to mining development in the Shield. Prospectors, geologists, and mining engineers research promising locations for mineral exploration. Construction crews lay roads, erect mines, and build houses for the miners, using material and equipment made from Shield metals. In the wake of miners, clerks, and technicians who come to work for the mining companies, a host of people follow to service their needs — teachers, nurses, storekeepers, plumbers, electricians, mechanics, and so on. The list is long. And then there are all the workers all across Canada who handle the products of the mines, from dockworkers loading ore onto a freighter to salesmen visiting a buyer in a distant city — or country. For Canada exports much of its mineral production from the Shield to markets all over the world.

All these occupations are more or less directly related to the establishment of a mining centre or to the handling of its products. But there are also countless jobs in industries that are *indirectly* related to mining activity. The development of the mineral resources of the Shield is just the cornerstone of a complex, national and worldwide, industrial structure. Nickel from the Sudbury basin is added to iron from Labrador-Quebec to make steel in Hamilton to be shipped to Oakville to make cars. Or to Toronto to make refriger-ators. Or to Vancouver to make rail cars. Or to Montreal to make snowmobiles. Or to Saint John to make trawlers. Or to Argentina to make cans for corned beef. Or to France to make steel-belted radial tires. And the export dollars Canada earns from selling steel to Argentina and France — and the United Kingdom, and Brazil, and the United States, and a lot of other countries — enable us to buy French wines and British motorbikes and Brazilian coffee and any number of other imported goods. Add to the nickel and iron the copper, gold, lead, zinc, silver, and all the other metals of the Shield, and you can begin to comprehend the overwhelming importance of the Shield's mineral resources.

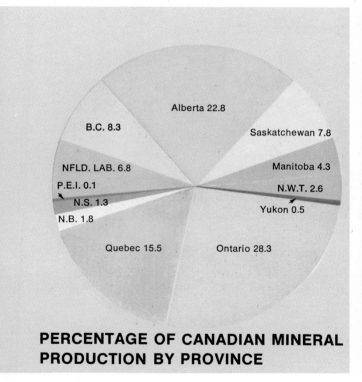

PERCENTAGE OF CANADIAN MINERAL PRODUCTION BY PROVINCE

CANADIAN MINERAL PRODUCTION (EXCLUDING PETROLEUM), 1971 *

Metallic minerals	Value (in millions of dollars)
Copper	$798
Iron Ore	754
Nickel	559
Zinc	410
Non-metallic minerals	
Asbestos	210
Potash	128
Structural materials	
Cement	194
Sand and gravel	134

*Only those minerals whose value exceeds one hundred million dollars have been listed.

Study and Research

1. Refer back to the map on page 10.
   (a) How does this map indicate that the area is part of the "used" southeastern edge of the Shield?
   (b) In what ways would you expect the Shield landscape of northern Saskatchewan and of northern Keewatin to differ from the area shown in the map?
   (c) Why then do geographers consider these different terrains to be part of a single geographical region — the Canadian Shield?

2. Compile a list of gear, provisions, and other items you would need for a prospecting trip into the bush of northern Quebec or Ontario. Explain your selection.

3. If you were to move to a mining town in the Shield, how would the work and leisure activities of you and your family be affected?

4. How has modern technology helped in making the Shield a major world producer of iron ore?

5. Write a report on the development of mining in the Shield outlining the sometimes conflicting interests of trappers, conservationists, governments, industry, and camping and recreational services. How do you evaluate the needs of each group?
   "Although governments have an interest in mining development, they should also have an overriding role." Debate this motion.

6. How has the federal government's "Roads to Resources" policy affected the economic development of the Shield? What other resources are to be found in this region? Why then has mining been the principal form of economic development so far?

7. Write a report on the development of safety standards in the mining industry. (The Department of Energy, Mines and Resources, the United Steelworkers Union, and individual mining companies will supply free information.) What effect have changes in safety standards had upon the development of mining activity in the Shield?

8. Manitouwadge was the first planned mining community in the Shield. What steps were taken to prevent its becoming another ghost town?

   Whose responsibility is it to keep one-industry towns alive when the ore runs out or when the wells run dry? What steps can be taken to prevent boom towns from going bust?

9. "It is resolved that royalties on minerals extracted from the Shield should be greatly increased." Debate this motion.

10. Mining in Canada is by no means restricted to the Shield. Write a brief report on the mining of metals in other parts of Canada. How do these operations resemble those of the Shield? Why is production in these areas overshadowed by that from the Shield?

11. "If there is one geographical region that has determined the development of Canada, it is the Shield."
    (a) Draw a map of Canada and on it draw the limits of the Shield.
    (b) Mark the centres that have a population over 35,000.
    (c) Mark the major transportation routes.
    (d) Mark the major industries.
    Relate your map to the above statement. Does the statement hold? What qualifications, if any, would you make?

12. Make a study of Knob Lake (Schefferville), Quebec, in 1935, in 1965, and as you think it might be in 1995. Account for the following feasibility factors: demand, supply, production costs, transportation costs, technology.

Net production by Industry, 1972, in billions of dollars

22
20
18
16
14
12
10
8
6
4
2

Fishing and Trapping

Forests

Electric power, gas, and water utilities

Agriculture

Mines, quarries, and oil wells

Construction

Public administration and defence

Transportation, storage, and communication

Finance, insurance, and real estate

Trade

Community, business, and personal service

Manufacturing

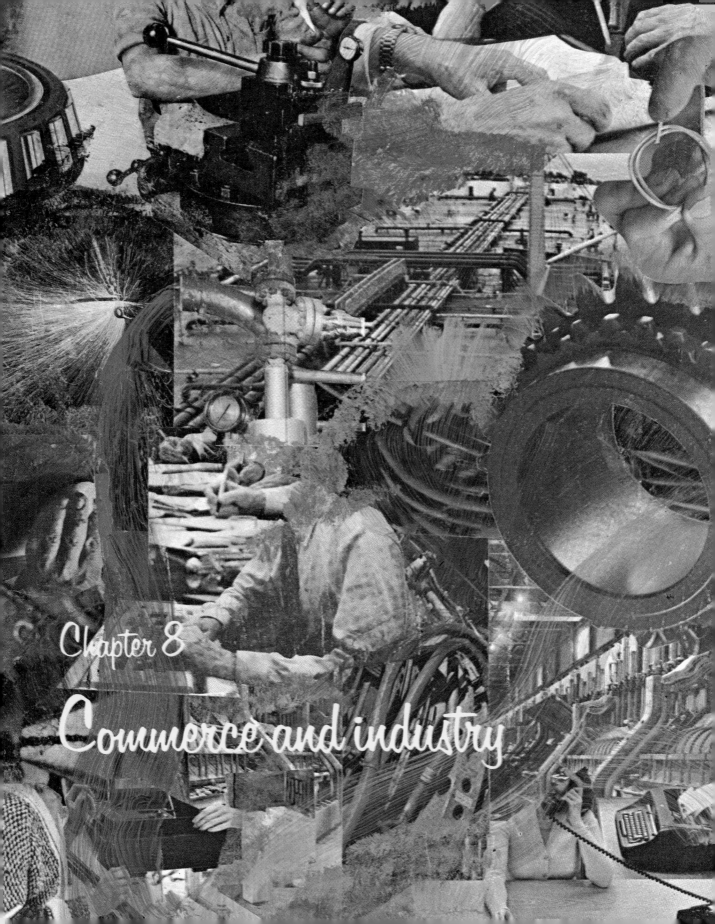

Chapter 8

Commerce and industry

EMPLOYED LABOR FORCE, 15 YEARS OF AGE AND OVER, BY PERCENTAGES, 1971

N.W.T. and Yukon
19,105 persons = 100%

A0.1
B15.2
C2.6
D5.2
E11.9
F9.4
G22.9
H18.4
I 14.3

Newfoundland
147,990 persons = 100%

A0.8
B9.6
C12.0
D10.5
E11.1
F15.6
G23.6
H8.0
I 8.8

P.E.I.
42,995 persons = 100%

A13.6
B5.3
C9.8
D6.5
E7.0
F13.9
G24.0
H11.0
I 9.0

British Columbia
910,085 persons = 100%

A2.5
B5.1
C16.1
D7.0
E9.5
F16.2
G29.4
H6.3
I 7.9

CANADA
8,626,925 persons = 100%

A5.6
B2.8
C19.8
D6.2
E7.8
F14.7
G27.8
H7.4
I 7.9

Nova Scotia
286,444 persons = 100%

A2.5
B5.2
C14.4
D7.5
E8.3
F15.2
G26.3
H13.4
I 7.2

Alberta
688,290 persons = 100%

A12.7
B4.2
C9.1
D7.6
E8.0
F15.1
G28.0
H7.9
I 7.4

A Agriculture
B Fishing, Trapping, Forestry, Mines, Quarries, Oil Wells
C Manufacturing
D Construction
E Transportation, Communication, Utilities
F Trade
G Finance, Insurance, Real Estate, Community, Business, and Personal Services
H Public Administration and Finance
I Unspecified and undefined

New Brunswick
223,525 persons = 100%

A3.0
B5.5
C16.3
D6.9
E10.1
F15.4
G25.1
H9.8
I 7.9

Quebec
2,169,150 persons = 100%

A3.4
B2.3
C23.1
D5.5
E7.9
F13.6
G28.2
H6.4
I 9.6

Saskatchewan
371,065 persons = 100%

A27.1
B2.3
C5.4
D4.8
E7.5
F13.9
G24.9
H7.1
I 7.0

Manitoba
413,920 persons = 100%

A11.4
B2.1
C13.8
D5.4
E9.7
F15.8
G26.6
H8.2
I 7.0

Ontario
3,354,360 persons = 100%

A3.9
B1.5
C24.4
D6.1
E6.6
F14.8
G28.1
H7.5
I 7.1

Source: Statistics Canada

Industry and commerce make and sell goods and offer services. Most **goods**—furniture, clothes, automobiles, processed foods, and so on — are produced by workers in manufacturing industries and bought by consumers. Between the time a product is manufactured in a factory and the time it is purchased by a customer, a lot of **services** go on — transportation, advertising, and sales. These services involve the handling of a product, but some services — medical, dental, legal, etc.— have little or nothing to do with goods. Although the value and definition of some goods and services may sometimes be debatable, one thing is beyond dispute. We are dependent on others to make or provide almost everything we need or want. Try to imagine one day without the goods and services provided by others. What would you have for breakfast? What clothes would you wear? How would you get to school? What would you do in school? (Seriously!) In today's complex society, it is virtually impossible to be a totally self-sufficient individual. Each of us contributes to and benefits from the goods and services provided by the other members of our society.

Study 45

1. Some communities produce almost everything they need. They are said to be **self-sufficient**. Their economy is a **subsistence economy**. To what degree would these terms apply to the following:
   (a) an agricultural community
   (b) a suburb near a large city
   (c) a developing nation
   (d) your community?
2. Our specialized way of life is very much the result of the Industrial Revolution. What do we mean by this term? When and how did it all begin?
3. What are some inventions that got this Revolution going?
4. How have some modern inventions affected our way of life today?
5. Where are your groceries produced? Take a good look at the labels on packages and cans of food in the local supermarket. Name a dozen sources inside and outside Canada. How many countries are represented in the total class sample? How many provinces? Which goods are produced both inside and outside Canada?

Retailing: Selling goods and services

One of the best ways of checking your dependence on commerce and industry is to take a trip to your local **plaza**. Find out the what, where, how, and why of the goods and services it provides.

• What is the approximate size of each store and what type of goods does it sell?
• Do any of the stores have more than one floor? If so, are there differences between the floors in the kinds of goods sold?

- How many stores are owned by companies that have retail outlets in other neighborhoods or in other towns and cities?
- Are there stores only? Are there offices for lawyers, doctors, and dentists? Are there offices that provide other services?
- Are there service outlets — beauty salons, laundromats, repair shops?
- Is there a restaurant, a bank, a cinema, a gas station?
- How many hours a day are the stores and offices open? How many days a week?

In any neighborhood, there are usually a number of different types of small stores. Some specialize in a narrow range of goods: men's or women's clothing, shoes, books, baked goods. Others are general-purpose "mom and pop" stores — corner groceries, variety stores — which offer a wider range of items in fairly constant demand: foodstuffs, tobacco, candy, toys, magazines, etc. In large cities, there are scatterings of small specialty stores, catering often to ethnic tastes, that tempt the adventurous shopper with items such as baklava, breadfruit, and blintzes. At the other extreme are large, multi-level **department stores.** They get their name from the fact that they sell so many different types of goods that these have to be handled by various departments—furniture, appliances, sportswear, and so on — each of which sells a certain kind of merchandise. In large metropolitan centres, department stores usually have a main store downtown and branch stores in suburban plazas.

In between these two are **supermarkets** and **discount stores.** Both are large, retail outlets that stock a limited range of inexpensive basic goods. Supermarkets usually concentrate on non-specialty foodstuffs, and discount stores on low-quality clothing and household goods. A combination of large discounts allowed on volume buying and a quick turnover of items enables these stores to offer goods at prices lower than

Shopping for groceries used to be an almost daily activity. There are still regular market days in many small towns. In Kingston, Ontario, this market is a thrice-weekly event.

Yorkdale Shopping Plaza, Toronto, a typical suburban shopping centre. Note that easy access to the Plaza is provided by two highways and a four-lane city street.

those of retail outlets selling similar goods.

Some large companies operate several supermarkets, discount stores, or other retail outlets. These **chain stores** — food, drugs, appliances, etc. — are located across a province, sometimes even across Canada.

In addition to different kinds of stores, there are various types of **shopping centres** located in different areas and serving different needs. The size and variety of plazas vary from clusters of small stores serving the needs of an immediate neighborhood to sprawling complexes that contain stores, offices, cinemas, restaurants, and recreational facilities serving an entire community. But a common factor is that their location is auto-based. Plazas tend to be located in open, suburban areas where there is easy access by automobile and where there is lots of parking space. The diagrams of a plaza in Scarborough, Ontario, illustrate a large, modern shopping centre that draws a mobile clientele not

only from Scarborough, but from communities all around Toronto.

The automobile has also affected the location of many service facilities — motels and gas stations, for example. Although some motor inns have been built in downtown areas, most motels are in suburban districts near highways and expressways. Gasoline stations are also positioned for convenience of automotive service: beside highways, at the edge of plazas, and usually on street corners.

In fact, transportation generally is an important factor in the location of services. Large hotels were located downtown near railway stations to provide accommodation for train travellers during the golden age of the locomotive. The greater use of air travel by business people has resulted in the development of "airport strips" where hotels offer accommodation, convention rooms, restaurants, entertainment, and even shopping facilities.

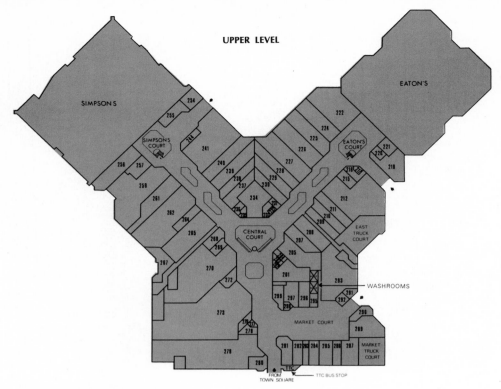

UPPER LEVEL

SIMPSONS

EATON'S

SIMPSON'S COURT

EATON'S COURT

CENTRAL COURT

EAST TRUCK COURT

WASHROOMS

MARKET COURT

MARKET TRUCK COURT

FROM TOWN SQUARE

TTC BUS STOP

Courtesy Scarborough Town Centre Management and Leasing

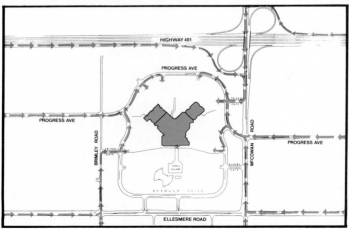

HIGHWAY 401

PROGRESS AVE

PROGRESS AVE

PROGRESS AVE

BRIMLEY ROAD

McCOWAN ROAD

ELLESMERE ROAD

Directory by type of service

232

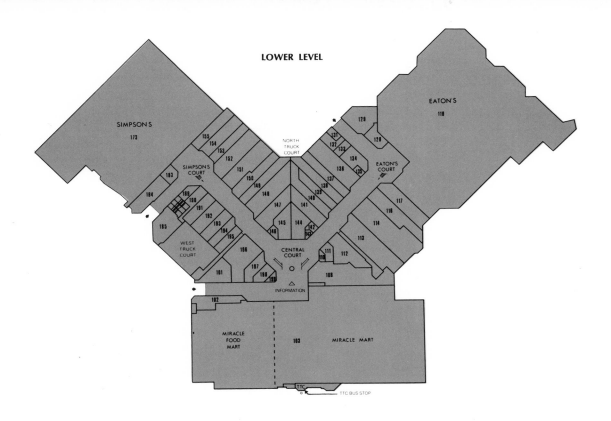

LOWER LEVEL

The growth of suburban plazas and airport strips has by no means reduced the number and variety of retail outlets in downtown shopping districts. These were well-established long before the arrival of the automobile, long before the sprawling growth of cities.

Surprisingly, heavy traffic and congested streets have not discouraged the motorized shopper. Downtown retailing is still relatively strong and healthy because of the following developments that take into account transportation, sprawling growth, consumer needs, and use of space.

- Public transportation services have expanded to offer easier access to and from the city centre.
- Since horizontal (surface) space is limited, both under- and above-ground multi-level parking garages have been built.
- Large department stores, which offer a greater variety of goods and services, are expanding and rebuilding downtown.
- Underground shopping malls, such as Place Ville-Marie in Montreal, are being built into downtown office and residential complexes.
- Multi-level complexes, for example, the ManuLife Centre in Toronto, utilize vertical space to offer shopping, office, and residential facilities.
- Attractive shopping squares and streets full of boutiques offer specialty goods and services.

Study 46

1. Why do people shop at some plazas and not at others? Where do they come from and what do they buy?

   To get some answers to these questions, prepare a generalized map of the area around a shopping plaza. Obtain permission from the plaza's general manager to ask shoppers the questions in the survey below. (At the same time, ask him if there's any particular question he would like answered and add it to the questionnaire.) As you approach each shopper, introduce yourself and explain the purpose of the survey before asking any questions. REMEMBER TO CARRY YOUR ID CARD.
   (a) How often do you shop at this plaza?
   (b) What do you generally buy here?
   (c) What are your particular reasons for shopping at this plaza?
       Probe here for such reasons as location, specific stores, convenience of transportation, particular services and facilities such as dentist, hairdresser, movies, etc.
   (d) What means of transportation did you use to get here?
   (e) Would you mind telling me where you live?
       Mark the location on the generalized map.
   (f) If the person's answer indicates that home is more than 10 kilometres from the plaza, ask:
       Why do you come here to shop when you live so far away?

In the classroom, under the direction of your teacher, create one large map of the area around the shopping plaza. Mark on it all the locations where the people came from.

- What pattern(s) do these results form?
- What is the farthest distance anyone came from?
- Rank in order of popularity the reasons why people shop at the plaza.
- Which store was most popular?
- What was the most popular means of transportation?
- What results came from the manager's question? (A report of the results of the survey would be a courteous and useful way of thanking the manager for his co-operation.)

2. In light of the results of your survey, would you reorganize the plaza? If so, how?

3. The competition from large supermarkets and discount stores is forcing many small "mom and pop" stores to close. What services do these provide? Which of these services are now provided by supermarkets? Which, if any, can supermarkets not offer? Have any other stores come along to fill the gap?

   If these services are important to you, what concessions would you allow these small stores (e.g., later closing hours, licences to sell certain goods or services not allowed to larger stores, etc.)?

4. The distinction between goods and services is sometimes blurred. Is the manufacturer of prepared foods (TV dinners and other "heat and serve" items) selling a product or servicing a life style? How do the following "goods" provide a "service": automobiles, refrigerators, snowmobiles, bulldozers, instant breakfasts, synthetic furs, automatic washers?

5. How have the above affected our way of life?

   How are "needs" determined? What are your "needs"? What goods service these needs?

6. The large department stores have branch outlets in many suburban plazas, but the original main stores were built, and are still located, downtown. Why were they built there in the first place? Why have they not closed their downtown operations and relocated?

7. What other services (recreational, governmental, informational, etc.) are located downtown?

8. Why do many city planners set aside a larger percentage of space in downtown buildings for apartments than for offices?

You begin to get some idea of the huge volume of Canada's exports when you see just one small section of the Exhibition Hall in the Place Bonaventure complex, Montreal, Quebec. Used for trade shows, the Hall has 185,000 square metres of display space!

Wholesaling: The "middleman"

Retailing is the business of selling finished goods to the final customer – you and me. But where do the retailers buy the goods they sell?

Most retailers buy either from a middleman called a **wholesaler** or directly from the manufacturer. The wholesaler obtains large "job lots" of goods from several manufacturers and divides them into smaller lots for retailers. This saves the manufacturer the handling and distribution costs involved in dealing with many small accounts. For the retailer, the advantage is a centralized source of purchase.

Actually, this is a somewhat simplified explanation of the process. Some products are handled by several wholesalers, especially if these items are being traded between countries. To understand what happens in international marketing, let's trace a fairly common product – a can of peaches – from a shelf in an Ottawa grocery store back to Australia.

Cans of Australian peaches are carried by most grocery stores, large or small. In Ottawa, each store owner buys them from the Ottawa division of M. Loeb, a wholesaling firm that handles a great variety of packaged foodstuffs. Now many governments throughout the world make arrangements for their products to be handled by **brokers** (agents or representatives) in foreign countries. In this case, M. Loeb, the wholesaler, has obtained the peaches through a Montreal broker, the House of De Grandpré, which imports them on consignment from the Australian government. (Like similar brokers in the Province of Quebec, the House of De Grandpré must hold a licence from Provincial Food Brokers in Montreal in order to do business.) More than likely, the brokerage house never sees the foodstuffs it handles; it simply sets up the machinery for bringing merchandise into Canada. A similar chain of wholesalers and brokers handled the can of peaches in Australia before it could be exported.

The distribution of Canadian-produced goods is generally not as complicated. For instance, women's dresses made in Ontario or Quebec and sold all across Canada are usually ordered directly from the manufacturers. However, the link between manufacturer (or wholesaler) and retailer is not always so simple. Take most products made of steel. Before the different parts are finally put together in the assembly plant, an automobile or a refrigerator passes through several manufacturing firms — and possibly even some steel brokers.

Manufacturing: Making goods

We have traced the movement of a product from the manufacturer or wholesaler to the retailer, and finally to the consumer in a plaza, shopping centre, or store. Now, let's back up all the way to the plant or factory where the product is made.

Manufacturing is the process by which raw materials are turned into finished or semi-finished goods for sale at a profit. A list of all the articles that are manufactured today would fill the pages of — well, just think of all the items listed in the yellow pages of a telephone directory for a start. There is every form of vehicle from a motorcycle to an airplane, and the fuel to run them; every type of accommodation from a tent to a hotel, and the furnishings that go with them; every kind of clothing from shirts to shoes, and the chemical substances to clean them with; every variety of processed food from canned soup to packaged pudding, and the utensils to eat them with; every kind of synthetic product from imitation turf to artificial eyelashes, and the numerous plastics and nylons to make them with. Pick any item — even the paper these words are printed on — and it is probably manufactured.

The plants that manufacture these hundreds of thousands of items vary enormously in size. Some are literally one-man operations. Others employ several thousand people. The ideal way to get a clear understanding of manufacturing would be to visit several plants and factories. Short of that, perhaps a brief look at three different operations — steelmaking, clothing, and electronics — will give you some idea of the complexity of manufacturing.

Steelmaking

Of all the many minerals basic to our society, none can compare in importance with iron. From iron comes steel. Steel is transportation — airplanes, railways, ships, automobiles; steel is work — machines, desks, typewriters; steel is pleasure — skis, TV sets, pianos; steel is appliances — stoves, automatic washers, vacuum cleaners; steel is construction — factories, bridges, skyscrapers. Think what life would be like without it. No rapid transportation. No weekends at the cottage. No great variety of processed goods. No mass construction of giant structures. In fact, no mass production of almost anything. Just about everything would have to be handmade.

Anyone visiting an iron-and-steel mill is stunned by size, sight, and sound. Gigantic machines emit thunderous noises. Rivers of

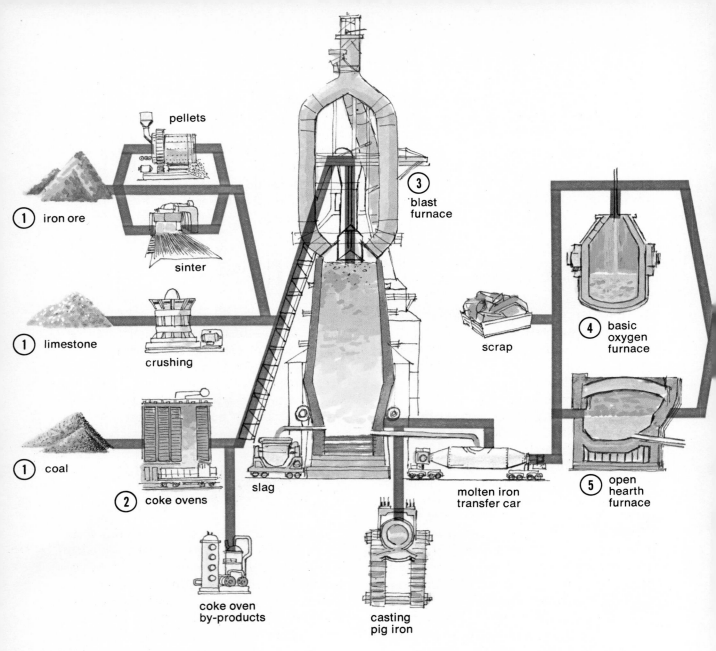

pellets

① iron ore

sinter

① limestone

crushing

① coal

② coke ovens

slag

coke oven
by-products

casting
pig iron

③ blast
furnace

scrap

④ basic
oxygen
furnace

molten iron
transfer car

⑤ open
hearth
furnace

molten metal pour forth. Red-hot ribbons of steel roll out at 300 metres a minute. A typical example is Dofasco's plant in Hamilton, Ontario. It is a fully **integrated operation** (iron and steel) comprising coke ovens, blast furnaces, foundry, and mills.

To produce iron, four ingredients are necessary: iron ore, limestone, coke, and superheated air.

Ninety-five per cent of the ore arriving at Dofasco is in the form of pellets. Limestone serves two functions: it makes the ore's impurities melt more readily and then combines with them to float to the surface of the molten metal. Coke is produced from coal by baking it in ovens to drive off gases and other impurities. The resulting porous fuel will burn at the tremendous heat

238

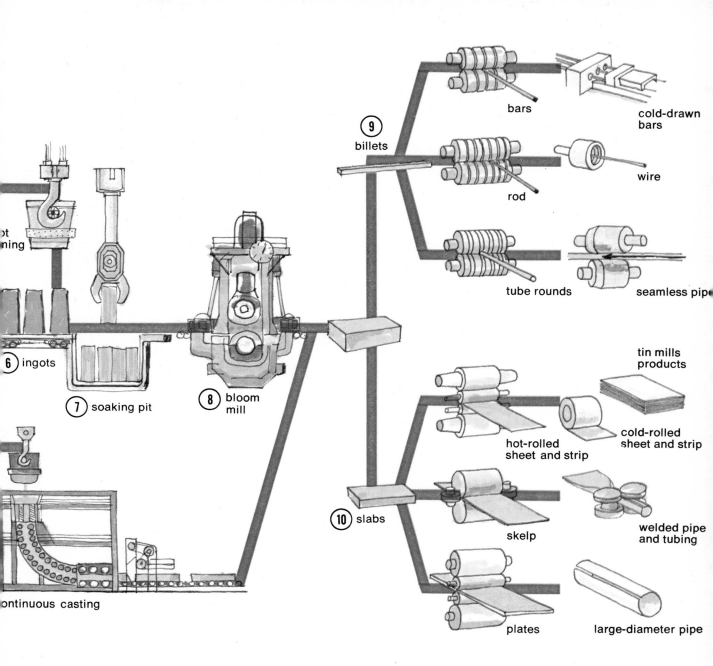

bars

cold-drawn bars

9 billets

rod

wire

tube rounds

seamless pipe

tin mills products

hot-rolled sheet and strip

cold-rolled sheet and strip

10 slabs

skelp

welded pipe and tubing

plates

large-diameter pipe

6 ingots

7 soaking pit

8 bloom mill

ontinuous casting

necessary to melt iron ore. Heated air steadily blasted into the furnace makes the coke burn at a temperature high enough to melt the ore. Carbon monoxide released by the coke combines with oxygen given off by the molten iron. These ingredients and these processes produce iron.

And there is one very important additive: water, in immense quantities, to cool the outsides of the blast furnaces. A furnace turning out 1000 tonnes of iron daily requires about 55 million litres of water to avoid overheating.

In the blast furnace, which can be up to twenty-three storeys high, the pellets are combined with coke and limestone in a "baking" recipe of about seven parts iron ore, three parts coke, one part limestone,

United States Steel Corporation, Fairless Works

Molten pig iron being poured from a ladle into the top level of an open hearth furnace. The furnace is so named because the metal is exposed to the sweep of flames blown across the hearth. At the height of the refining process, the pool of molten steel and slag in the furnace becomes turbulent, like a violently boiling liquid in a pot hanging above an old-fashioned kitchen hearth.

and sixteen parts air. The solid ingredients are steadily poured in at the top of the furnace by self-emptying cars, and a steady blast of preheated air is forced through the mixture to raise the temperature to about 1650°C. The limestone floats to the top of the heavier molten iron, attracting impurities and forming **slag** (used in making road-building and insulating materials). Thus, iron and slag can be tapped from the furnace separately. The **pig iron** produced at this stage has limited uses. A high carbon content, produced by the coke in the blast furnace, makes pig iron rather brittle.

It requires refining to give it toughness and durability.

The refining process — steelmaking — also involves furnaces and high temperatures. But the difference between the two "cooking" processes is like the difference between making an ordinary sauce and making that same sauce, straining it free of unwanted bits of onion and tomato seed, and then flavoring it with herbs and spices to add "refinement." Steelmaking is essentially a matter of removing excess carbon and other impurities from the pig iron and then adding very carefully measured

240

Rolling mills convert ingots into finished products. Nowadays, most mill operations are directed and regulated by computer. Here, one man oversees the conversion of white-hot slab steel into plate steel, which is then shaped into products as varied as a bank-vault door or the curved plates of a ship's hull.

amounts of manganese, nickel, chromium, tungsten, or vanadium. Steel is an alloy of iron and small, definite amounts of these minerals. The mixture depends upon what type of steel is wanted; there are thousands of different kinds of steel alloys.

Dofasco uses the Basic Oxygen Process to make steel. Pig iron, some scrap steel, and a little limestone are poured into giant, pear-shaped furnaces. An oxygen lance (a large hollow tube) is lowered into the furnace to within 2 metres of the molten mass. Then pure, high-pressure oxygen is blown into the molten mixture at supersonic speed. This burns off the excess carbon, and the remaining impurities rise to the surface as slag. After twenty minutes or so, the lance is removed. The total process takes less than an hour, in which time several hundred tonnes of steel have been produced.

When the steel is ready for pouring, the furnace is tilted one way to remove the top layer of slag and then another to pour off the steel into a massive ladle. A crane carries the ladle over a number of hollow **ingot** molds, a cover opens the pouring holes in the bottom of the ladle, and steel flows into the molds. (Liquid steel is also **cast** in molds of other shapes, suitable for specific uses, but most steel is poured into ingots.) When the ingots have solidified sufficiently on the outside (the centres still red-hot), they can be stripped of their molds. They are then carried to various mills to be rolled into various shapes.

But before steel can be rolled, the ingots must again be heated to bring them to a uniform temperature. They are therefore placed for several hours in a soaking pit and then are squeezed on a roughing mill into a thick slab ready for hot rolling. The slab is then rolled under tremendous pressure into steel stripping or sheets.

At this point, Dofasco steel may be coiled and shipped as a finished product called "hot rolled plain." Or it may undergo still further processing to produce cold rolled steel (for automobiles, appliances, office furniture, and other fine-finish products), tin plate (tin-coated steel for cans), galvanized steel (zinc-coated to protect against corrosion), and painted steel (baked-on for decorative purposes and corrosion resistance).

241

Study 47

1. About 90 per cent of all pig iron made in North America is used to make steel. The remaining 10 per cent is shipped to foundries to be made into cast iron. What use is made of this type of iron?
2. How is wrought iron made? What use do we make of it?
3. List the advantages of a waterside location to an iron-and-steel plant.
4. The Basic Oxygen Process is only one means of making steel. There are also the Bessemer and open-hearth methods, and some plants use electric furnaces. Using flow charts (easily obtainable from any steel company) describe each of these methods, explaining their advantages and disadvantages.
5. Less than half of the steel produced is rolled into sheets and strips. What uses are made of the rest of the steel?
6. An integrated operation is one producing both iron and steel products. Locate the three integrated centres of Canada.
   (a) What companies operate these centres?
   (b) Where do they obtain their iron ore?
   (c) What factor is common to the location of all three integrated centres?
   (d) Why is this factor so important?

Clothing

The manufacture of clothing is one of the largest industries in the world. People wear clothes for all activities and for all seasons.

Clothes come in a variety of materials, from natural furs and fibres to synthetic plastics and polyesters. Some are still custom-made by dressmakers and tailors, but most are ready-to-wear items, mass produced by the "needle trade." Factories that manufacture clothes usually specialize in certain products (suits, dresses, hats, shirts) and in certain "lines" — expensive frocks, sportswear, housedresses. The clothing industry tends to concentrate its manufacturing in one section of a city, which is called the "garment district." The name of a certain street in that district is often used to refer to needle-trade activity: Seventh Avenue in New York, Spadina Avenue in Toronto. Ruby-Lou is part of a five-company firm located in the heart of Montreal's garment district. Each company produces a different clothing line; Ruby-Lou manufactures inexpensive dresses.

The manufacture of clothing is subject to the whims of changing fashions in styles, fabrics, and social customs. Today's "new look" is tomorrow's "old hat"; a new miracle fabric is outmoded by a still newer synthetic marvel; what was once "compulsory attire" is now "dress optional." Thus a sharp sense of timing is needed to keep up with — and anticipate — changing trends. This develops through long years in the needle trade. And it is this experience that helps dress manufacturers to select popular styles, choose suitable fabrics, decide color and size quantities, and estimate production runs.

The first step in the manufacture of ready-to-wear dresses is the design. The managers of Ruby-Lou and the designer visit fashion centres in New York City and Boston to see the latest styles and get ideas for new models. The designer then draws sketches for new styles and makes sample dresses, from which the managers select the lines that will be made in various colors, sizes, and fabrics. He then makes patterns from the samples.

It is at this point that cutters, sewing-machine operators, and finishers take over, and the mass production of dresses begins. Pattern pieces are placed on top of hundreds of layers of fabric and outlined in chalk on the top piece of material. Using electric machines or hand tools, cutters slice through the thick layers of fabric following the out-

Spinning frames in a modern textile mill. The word "textile" comes from the Latin texere, *"to weave," but the term is now used for all manufactured fabrics, from woven cloth and knitted goods to complex terry and jacquard weaves.* American Textile Manufacturing Institute

line of the different parts of the garment — front, back, sleeves, collar. Since hundreds of dress parts are cut out at once and all the pieces must fit together, these workers need a steady hand and a sure eye. (Perhaps cutting errors explain certain "less" styles — sleeveless, backless, etc.?)

The various pieces are then bundled and taken to the sewing room, to be stitched together by an "assembly line" of sewing-machine operators. Each section of operators handles only one or two parts of a garment. One group may sew only shoulder seams or side seams; another may attach sleeves or collars. When all the pieces have been machine-stitched together, finishers add the last touches — buttons, hooks, hems, etc.

Ruby-Lou sells its dresses direct to retailers, mainly to chain outlets and department stores.

Study 48

1. How have synthetic materials influenced our way of life? Consider a range of activities, from skidooing to ironing, and also the effect of synthetic materials on services and industries related to clothing.
2. Take examples of a fashion change — pantihose, jeans, miniskirts, pantsuits, turtlenecks — and explain how they have affected the clothing industry in Canada.
3. Why and how do fashions change?
4. Why does a bikini cost as much as a grannie gown?
5. Some workers in the needle trade are paid by "piece work." What does this term mean? What are the advantages and disadvantages of this kind of wage system?
6. Where are most clothing manufacturers located in Canada? What factors might explain their location?
7. The textile industry supplies most of the material used in clothing manufacture. Research the Canadian textile industry and write a report on location, number of workers, markets, exports, etc.
8. The clothing industry has been "protected" by tariffs. What does this statement mean?

Electronics

Developments in the electronics industry have revolutionized transportation and communications. The world has been reduced to a "global village." If a major problem arises in a British subsidiary of a multi-national corporation, a business executive hops on the next jet to London. If an election is held in Canada or France or Japan, the outcome is flashed around the globe, and the mass media in Ottawa, Paris, and Tokyo all feature the results of the polls.

Raytheon Canada Limited (RayCan) in Waterloo, Ontario, produces electronic equipment for air-traffic control and tele-communications systems. Airport-surveillance radar devices manufactured by Ray-

This remote-television station is one of seventeen built by RayCan to receive TV signals beamed to northern communities (mainly in the Northwest Territories) via Canada's satellites Anik I *and* Anik II. *Completely automatic in operation, these stations amplify the signals and feed them to local transmitting stations for rebroadcast.*

Can provide air-traffic controllers with an electronic scan of aircraft location and movement within 80-100 kilometres of an airport. (Imagine trying to juggle arrivals and departures at an international airport without such aids!) Remote television stations produced by RayCan for the Telesat System feed live network television signals from Canada's communications satellite to far-distant northern communities. RayCan also produces missile systems for Canadian Armed Forces' destroyers and operational support ships.

Apart from its Canadian markets, RayCan has a substantial export business that includes markets in India, Indonesia, Japan, Malaysia, New Zealand, Lebanon, Israel, Greece, and Germany. A microwave radio-relay system, designed and developed for India, consists of ninety-eight stations connecting Delhi, Bombay, Calcutta, and Lucknow (and intermediate points) with 1,800 telephone circuits, a total of 5.6 million channel-kilometres.

About 35 per cent of RayCan's employees are highly skilled engineers and technicians. The manufacturing operation is carried out by assembly workers and inspectors. From design to manufacture, products are quality-tested to meet rigid standards of accuracy and reliability. With increasing air travel, quick-succession take-offs and "happy landings" depend on air-traffic control systems.

Study 49

1. What are the principal products of the electronics industry? How have they affected our way of life?
2. Would you rather work in an iron-and-steel mill, a clothing factory, or an electronics plant? What factors determined your choice?
3. "The simple transistor has revolutionized the communications industry." Explain this statement with examples.
4. Is the Canadian electronics industry protected by tariffs? If it is, do you approve or disapprove? If it isn't, should it be? Give reasons.

Location factors

We have examined some aspects of the manufacturing and service industries. Now let's take a look at what sometimes seems a bit of a puzzle. Why are plants and factories located where they are? Some manufacturing establishments are next door to each other. Others are isolated, well away from the nearest town. Why?

Most plants and factories are not located in a haphazard way. A great deal of thought and planning went into their location, and a lot of factors were considered long before a single brick was laid. Was the land cheap enough to be a good buy? Were local taxes low enough to be attractive? Were there enough people living locally to work in the factory? Was it reasonably easy for these people to get to work? Were there transportation routes — rail and road — to bring raw materials to the factory and ship out the finished articles? Was there an available market in which to sell the goods?

Some small manufacturing companies are concerned only with the selection of a site within a particular city, usually the one in which the owner already resides. However, most locations are the result of a management decision reached only after detailed studies of several communities within a region. In some cases, especially when a large corporation is involved, several regions — or even countries — may be considered.

Primary manufacturing industries (ore smelting, pulp and paper) use the products of mine or forest as **raw materials.** The weight or volume of these materials is greatly reduced during the production process. Not all of the tree or the rock is used, and the resulting primary product (lumber, ore pellets) is less heavy and bulky than the raw material from which it was made. Therefore, to reduce transportation costs, primary industries tend to locate near the source of their raw materials and close to cheap transportation routes. When these industries use imported raw materials (for example, sugar), they tend to locate at ports for the same reason. Many primary manufacturing industries (oil refineries, iron-and-steel mills, pulp-and-paper mills) require huge quantities of water in the production process, so they also try to locate close to a water supply. Furthermore, water transport is a cheap form of transportation, so where possible they locate where there is easy access to river systems or lake shipping.

In **secondary manufacturing** the volume or weight of the finished products

Petroleum refining involves the use of enormous quantities of water, and the industry also needs water routes for cheap transportation of oil products to market. This explains refining operations at Sarnia, Ont., a processing centre for major Canadian oilfields.

(clothes, furniture, cars) usually increases during the production process. The cost of shipping products is almost always greater than that of bringing in materials. Therefore, to reduce transportation costs, secondary manufacturers tend to locate near major markets. Accessibility to major markets was the most important factor in the relocation of Ford's assembly operation from Windsor, Ontario, to Oakville, near Toronto. But, **size and accessibility of markets** are not an absolute rule in determining the location of secondary manufacturers. Transportation costs of small-volume products — electronic components — are not as high as those of finished assembled products — TV sets — which are much increased in volume and weight. Therefore, in the electronics industry, easy access to major markets is not as important a location factor to component producers.

Another factor in the location of secondary manufacturing is **labor force**. In secondary industry, labor costs make up a high percentage of total production costs, so manufacturers try to locate near a plentiful supply of cheap labor. Thus textile manufacturing in Quebec tends to locate in the Eastern Townships, where there is a large labor pool to draw from and where the average wage of workers is low. However, a cheap and plentiful supply of workers is only one aspect of the labor factor. Variety of labor force is also an impor-

247

tant consideration. Some plants require unskilled labor, others need highly specialized workers. Size and variety of labor force are, of course, closely related to centres of population. Large centres attract certain industries because they have a large labor pool with a wide range of skills, from assembly-line operators to executives.

Many manufacturers are attracted to medium-sized or large cities (more than 50,000 population) for reasons other than labor and market. Large population centres often have **specialized services**: market research companies, information centres, data-processing facilities, varied transportation services, financial institutions, advertising and public relations agencies. In addition, there is greater opportunity for direct contact with a variety of business people in these centres, which promotes an exchange of ideas. When all these are com-

bined with cultural opportunities (CFL football, theatre, concerts, several TV channels, museums, hockey arenas, etc.) and a wide variety of educational institutions, it is not difficult to see why larger centres continue to be a magnet for manufacturing.

The factors already mentioned do not explain the location of all industry. A century or more ago, most manufacturers tried to locate close to sources of power. Many of the world's major industries are still located on top of, or next to, coalfields, even though these industries no longer use coal for power. Why? Large industrial complexes are almost impossible to move, mainly because relocation would cost too much. Some power-hungry industries — aluminum smelting, wood pulp — must still locate near a power source, though today this power is hydro-electricity.

A train hauls a load of automobiles westward around Lake Superior. If you buy a Canadian-made car and you don't live in Ontario, you'll quickly appreciate the cost of location factors!

Factors of Location

Capital costs	Land, plant construction, machinery
	Road and rail construction
Production costs (other than Labor and Transportation)	Power
	Water
	Materials
Labor	Wages
	Productivity
	Labor/management relations
	Size and variety of labor force
Transportation	Cheap supply routes
	Low freight cost of raw materials
	Low freight cost of finished product
Market	Access to major markets
	Market potential
	Competitive advantage
Social and political	Political stability
	Government incentives, tax benefits
	Cultural amenities — schools, day-care centres, religious institutions, theatres, galleries, libraries, recreational areas, etc.
Convenience	Availability of land and existing buildings
	Location near existing plants or head office
	Location near related industries

Study 50

1. Although Ford's assembly operation was relocated to Oakville, engines are still produced in the Windsor plant. What factors explain this division? Why did Ford originally locate in Windsor?
2. What is the head office location of each company mentioned in this chapter? What factors influence the location of head offices?
3. Write a brief report on the pros and cons of the proposed location of a major manufacturer in your community.
4. Compare the advantages and disadvantages to a community of the establishment of a heavy industry (steelmaking, for example) versus the establishment of a light manufacture (electronics).
5. The table on this page lists the major factors that help to determine the location of a manufacturer. Which factors tend to maintain population patterns? Which help to change them? Which ones affected the location of such manufacturers as General Electric, Goodyear Tire, Abitibi Pulp and Paper, Canada Concrete, and Johns-Manville?

Manufacturing tends to attract population. Industry needs people. People need jobs. If necessary, people, especially in economically depressed regions, will follow industry almost anywhere. Large plants, therefore, can and do attract workers to wherever they locate, even to new communities carved out of the wilderness. Several northern Canadian towns were established by companies that had to locate near raw materials and/or hydro-electric power: Kapuskasing, with its pulp-and-paper mills; Kitimat and Arvida, with their aluminum smelters; Thompson, with its nickel mines.

In contrast to manufacturing, one location factor dominates retailing: market. Retailing follows population. The success of a store is entirely dependent on customers. It is a rare customer, indeed, who goes far out of his or her way for anything other than a really special product or service. Thus the location of retail outlets is heavily dependent on market needs. Goods and services are very closely related to population patterns: numbers, income levels, social classes, cultural tastes.

Wholesalers supply retailers and so tend to locate near them, and therefore near population centres. However, certain wholesale brokers, particularly in international or inter-regional trade, do not have to depend on accessibility of markets. Some places, ports in particular, become a focus of commercial activity because of their key role as links between trading areas.

Study 51

1. What is the most important retail and service centre?
2. How much more important is it than Class 3 centres?
3. London and Brantford are both Class 2 centres. Notice the difference in the size of areas they serve. What is an umland? How does the nature of the umland explain the difference in size necessary to make each a Class 2 centre?

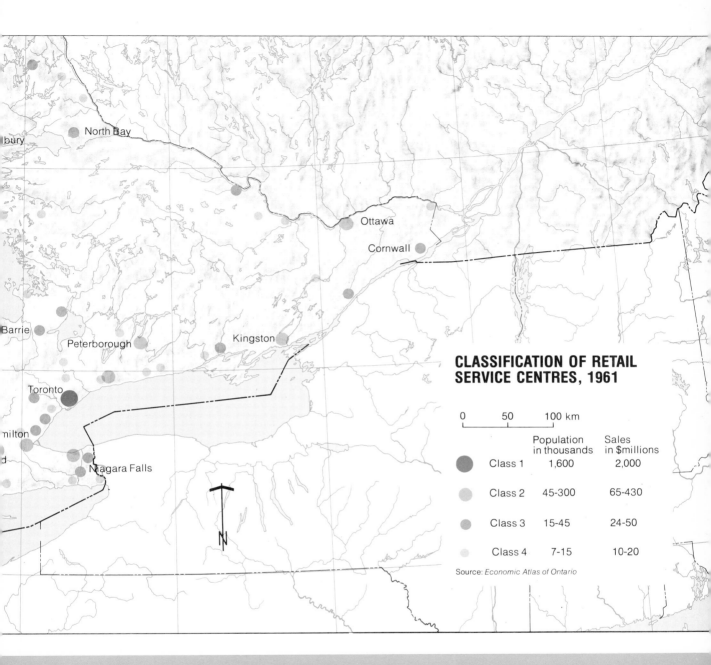

CLASSIFICATION OF RETAIL SERVICE CENTRES, 1961

| 0 | 50 | 100 km |

		Population in thousands	Sales in $millions
	Class 1	1,600	2,000
	Class 2	45-300	65-430
	Class 3	15-45	24-50
	Class 4	7-15	10-20

Source: *Economic Atlas of Ontario*

4. Draw a line encompassing Oshawa, Barrie, Brampton, Guelph, Kitchener-Waterloo, Brantford, Hamilton, and Niagara Falls. What name has been given to this region? Consult the *Canada Year Book* to find out what percentage of the population of Ontario lives here. Is there any relation between the population figures and the importance of Toronto?

5. Why have the following become important: Sarnia, Windsor, Oshawa, Peterborough, Hamilton, London, Brantford, Kitchener-Waterloo, St. Catharines?

Because manufacturing tends to attract population and commerce tends to follow population, planners try to attract manufacturing in order to encourage economic development in an area. Manufacturing stimulates economic growth by providing jobs for workers, which sets the stage for more industries and services in a community. Wages paid to workers are spent in local retail outlets – stores, restaurants, recreational facilities, etc. – and thus generate further local income and provide employment for workers in the service industries. A major manufacture (automobiles) often attracts related industries (automotive parts and accessories). These industries attract more workers, who spend more money for goods and services in the community. Increases in population and business create a bigger tax base and so provide increased revenue for roads, schools, and other government services. These, in turn, provide employment for more construction workers, more civil servants, etc. – and so on and so on, in a spiral of economic growth that benefits the entire community.

Or does it? What price growth? Are there any unfortunate side effects from industrial growth and urban development?

What price growth?

So far, location of manufacturing, retailing, and wholesaling has been looked at on a regional or national scale, and only in concrete measurable terms – freight rates, material supply, market size, etc. But what about more intangible considerations – quality of life, environmental factors, impact on residential neighborhoods, etc.? How does the location of commercial and industrial activities in a town affect the way people work, shop – and live?

"A man's home is his castle," so runs an old proverb. But if communities do not plan urban development and commercial growth carefully, his home may well become his fortress. He may have to protect his home and his neighborhood against encroaching business interests that create revenue through taxes but destroy the quality of life in the community. The total living environment must be considered, not just the commercial domain; human growth, not just economic development. If we do not consider the effects of commercial development on the total urban picture (land use, traffic flow, social needs, cultural interests) then we could end up strangled in traffic, choking on noxious fumes, deafened by machines, and alienated from one another and from the community.

Life today is a far cry from what it was when physical survival was all – kill a beast, use its skin for clothing, cook its flesh for food. Even after the invention of skill tools and instruments and the development of small communities, life was fairly simple and people were relatively self-sufficient. They worked at home in cottage crafts and industries or in the fields around the farmhouse; they lived behind their shop or next door to their smithy. Then came machinery and new sources of energy and giant industries and large settlements. Now our industrialized society is so complex that it is virtually impossible for individuals to be self-sufficient. We contribute our specialized service to the total structure and depend in turn on the specialized services of others in the community. Every service affects other services; every change in the structure affects the rest of the community. We must so plan any changes in the urban landscape that the quality of life in towns and cities remains healthy, pleasant, and safe.

One of the features that distinguish Canadian towns and cities from American urban centres is residential neighborhoods

Above: the junction of Eglinton Avenue East and Danforth Road in Toronto, 1954. Below: the same junction in 1969. What price growth? Good or bad?

in the downtown area. Millions of Americans flock downtown to work in stores and offices and then go home to suburban communities, leaving a deserted city core at night. Although commerce and industry are encroaching on the downtown residential areas of Canadian cities, they have not yet destroyed the possibility of a home in the core of a city. With careful urban planning and controlled commercial development, people and business may continue to co-exist downtown.

Let's examine the effects of the location of a new shopping or office complex in a downtown community. The population density increases immediately; more people come into the area as workers and shoppers. Some, in order to live near their work, move in as residents. This increases the strain on existing services: transportation, libraries, restaurants, shops, cinemas, etc.

How do the workers get to the office or store? If they use public transit, then buses, streetcars, and subways become overcrowded so that transportation services must be expanded. If they drive, the increased traffic congests city streets and results in a clamor to widen streets or build an expressway to accommodate the extra cars. In either case, the character of residential areas — quiet, safety, gardens, neighborhood — is ruined.

In fact, as we zero in on urban development, we realize that traffic is a major problem and the automobile the prime offender. It threatens the safety of residential streets and pollutes the air with noise and gases. Roads are also used by trucks, of course, but it is easier to re-route trucks away from residential streets. Most heavy

Habitat '67 in Montreal, Quebec. With more and more people settling in cities all the time, is this the self-contained, moveable housing of the future?

Row housing in Saint John, New Brunswick. All over Canada, architects and builders are being forced to economize on land use in order to accommodate the increasing number of people seeking homes in cities.

trucks are delivery vehicles between manufacturers and wholesale or distribution centres. So if we can control the location of manufacturing and distribution points by restricting them to areas close to expressways at the outside limits of communities, then large trucks will not need to drive through residential neighborhoods. Automobiles are a more complicated problem. There are so many of them, and they are generally used for private convenience, as often as not one person per automobile. What an inefficient means of transportation! Industrial expansion and urban growth have made it necessary for most people to travel to work, but do they have to do so by automobile? Concentrations of commercial and recreational facilities attract a lot of people downtown, but do they have to get there by car? Alternative modes of transportation – subways, buses, commuter trains, streetcars – may be more efficient.

The automobile increases traffic congestion, uses a diminishing, non-renewable resource most inefficiently, and pollutes the air with fumes and noise. We all know this. The problems is – how do we persuade people to give up private convenience for public benefit?

255

Study 52

1. If people were persuaded to use public transportation, what industries, besides automobile manufacture, would be affected? What would be the trade-off between environmental benefit and cost to the economy?

2. Draw up a series of six or seven questions that you would include in a survey of the traffic patterns in your community. Make up a class survey incorporating the commonest individual questions. Do a survey of residents in your community, asking the questions of every tenth household in order to obtain a random sample. REMEMBER TO CARRY YOUR ID CARD.

   Tabulate the results, separate the problems into different categories (e.g., parking, too many one-way streets, not enough stop signs, downtown congestion, etc.), and separate the solutions into different categories (expand public transportation, build more expressways, ban cars from downtown areas, stagger work hours, organize car pools, etc.). After a class analysis of the results, write a report summarizing your findings and recommendations.

Breathing space

If people cannot be persuaded to switch, then perhaps municipal councils could lessen the need for automobiles by integrated land-use plans. Urban development could be planned to meet residential *and* commercial requirements: living, office, and service facilities could be located in the same development project. Such complexes would lessen the transportation load to and from work, shopping, and recreation, and, especially downtown, would help to keep the core alive after shops and offices close.

Automobiles are the prime, but not the only, air polluters. Manufacturing also fouls the air — and the water. Industry and pollution are often lumped together as cause and effect. True, water pollution is often the result of industrial effluent — chemicals, acids, detergents — but it is most often caused by untreated domestic sew-age. (Does your community have a sewage plant?) Furthermore, not all industrial plants pollute, and many that do are working hard to "come clean." Indeed, some manufacturers take special care not to pollute the attractiveness of a setting. Light-manufacturing plants are often designed to blend in with the surrounding neighborhood, and the grounds around them are attractively landscaped with trees and shrubs. Such plants could be located near residential areas, creating more revenue for the community and providing convenient employment for nearby residents without ruining the neighborhood environment.

Heavy industry is another matter. No one wants to live near belching smokestacks or fouled waters. Should industries that so pollute the environment be located away from residential neighborhoods and community activities? Look at the land-use map of Edmonton. Why do you suppose certain industries are located where they are?

When it comes to locating heavy industry, we have to ask ourselves some pretty awkward questions — and find answers to them. What steps could be taken to prevent land developers from putting up housing projects near heavy industry? Should such steps be taken? What measures could be taken to reduce industrial pollution? Who should be responsible for such actions?

The needs of commerce and industry represent one-half of the equation. The other half is represented by the needs of workers, consumers, and residents. The equation can only be solved if both groups take into account the quality of life as well as the standard of living. We must all work to preserve the measureless benefits of a "green and pleasant land."

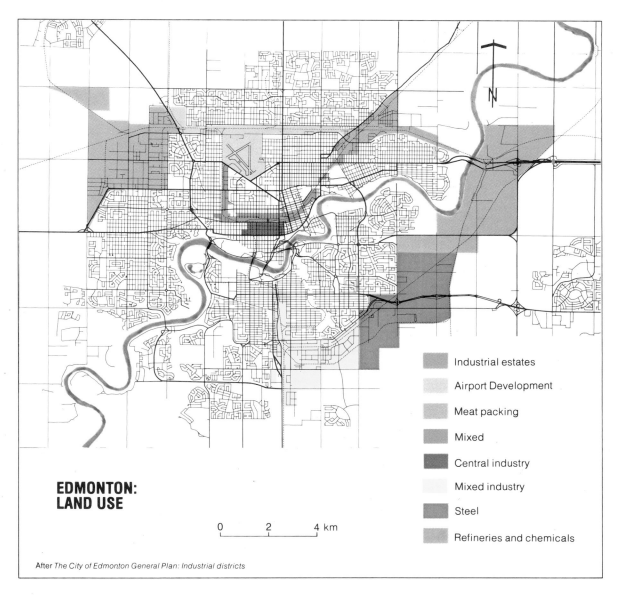

EDMONTON: LAND USE

0   2   4 km

Industrial estates

Airport Development

Meat packing

Mixed

Central industry

Mixed industry

Steel

Refineries and chemicals

After *The City of Edmonton General Plan: Industrial districts*

Study and Research

1. Examine the *Summary Statistics of Manufactures, by Province, 1968 and 1969* on page 342. Use the 1969 figures to answer questions 1 and 2. Express your calculations to the nearest hundred thousand.
   (a) What are the three major manufacturing provinces in Canada according to value of shipments of goods of own manufacture?
   (b) How many employees contributed to the manufacture of these goods?
   (c) What was the total cost of materials and supplies used?
   (d) How much value was added by manufacturing?
   (e) What salaries and wages were paid?
   (f) How much fuel and electricity were used?
   (g) How many establishments (factories) are there in each of the three provinces?
   (h) Total each of the above. Total those for the rest of the provinces in Canada. In percentage terms, assess the importance of the three major manufacturing provinces to Canada as a whole.
2. Refer to the column marked "Value of Shipments of Goods of Own Manufacture" in the provincial breakdowns on pages 342-345.
   (a) What are the top six manufactures in each province?
   (b) What differences do you note?
   (c) What manufactures occur in every province?
   (d) What are the six most important manufactures in Canada?
   (e) How many billion-dollar industries are there in Canada? In which province are most of these located?
   (f) Which province has the most establishments?
   (g) Rank each manufacture in order of importance.
   (h) Which province used the most fuel and electricity?
3. Dofasco is a non-union operation; Stelco, another Hamilton steel firm, is unionized. What are some differences between working in a unionized plant and a non-unionized one?
4. RayCan Limited is a subsidiary of a United States company, Raytheon. What are some advantages and disadvantages to the Canadian economy of foreign-owned subsidiaries?
5. From all the information you have obtained in this chapter, what factors would apply to the location of the following: a food-catering service, a publishing company, a hobby or handicrafts shop, a meat-packing plant, a direct-mail advertising service, a food-canning factory, a second-hand clothing store, a garden centre, a bowling alley?
6. What are some advantages and disadvantages of living in a small town near a large centre? In a small town remote from any large concentration of population? In a large metropolitan centre?

7. Apply the factors of location you have learned about to account for the goods that are manufactured and the services that are provided in each of the following centres: Montreal, Vancouver, Sudbury, Halifax, Winnipeg.

8. The Ford Motor Company relocated its assembly plant to Oakville; Thompson was a planned community from the beginning. Investigate the pattern of growth of manufacturing, commerce, and population in these two centres. Which manufacturers and which services were established, and in what order? How did the population growth relate to the establishment of these?
   (a) Develop a chart for Oakville and Thompson showing the growth and interweaving of those three strands: manufacturing, commerce, population.
   (b) Apply this pattern of location to a third centre in Canada to see if the pattern holds.

9. The conflict between business and residential interests has resulted in the formation of community organizations and the establishment of municipal planning boards. Write a brief report, based on the situation in your own community, on one of the following:
   (a) a specific local issue, such as community opposition to an expressway, council debate on a proposed development project, etc.,
   (b) the issues in a municipal election,
   (c) the functioning of the planning board. (Consider the land-use recommendations made by the board, the way these recommendations were arrived at, their implementation through legislation, and the effects of the legislation on the community.)

10. Write a report on assembly-line production in a particular industry. In your report trace the changes that have taken place and the reasons for them, including changes in plant operations and workers' roles.

11. What role does government (federal, provincial, municipal) play in industry?

12. Amsterdam, Tokyo, Brasilia, New York City, Pittsburgh, Los Angeles, and San Francisco are examples of cities that are in various stages of growth, degeneration, and rebirth. Research the experience of these cities in their attempts to cope with the problems of urban settlement.

    How can metropolitan centres in Canada benefit from the experience of these cities, avoiding their mistakes and applying, with necessary modifications, their solutions?

Chapter 9 The bonds of transportation

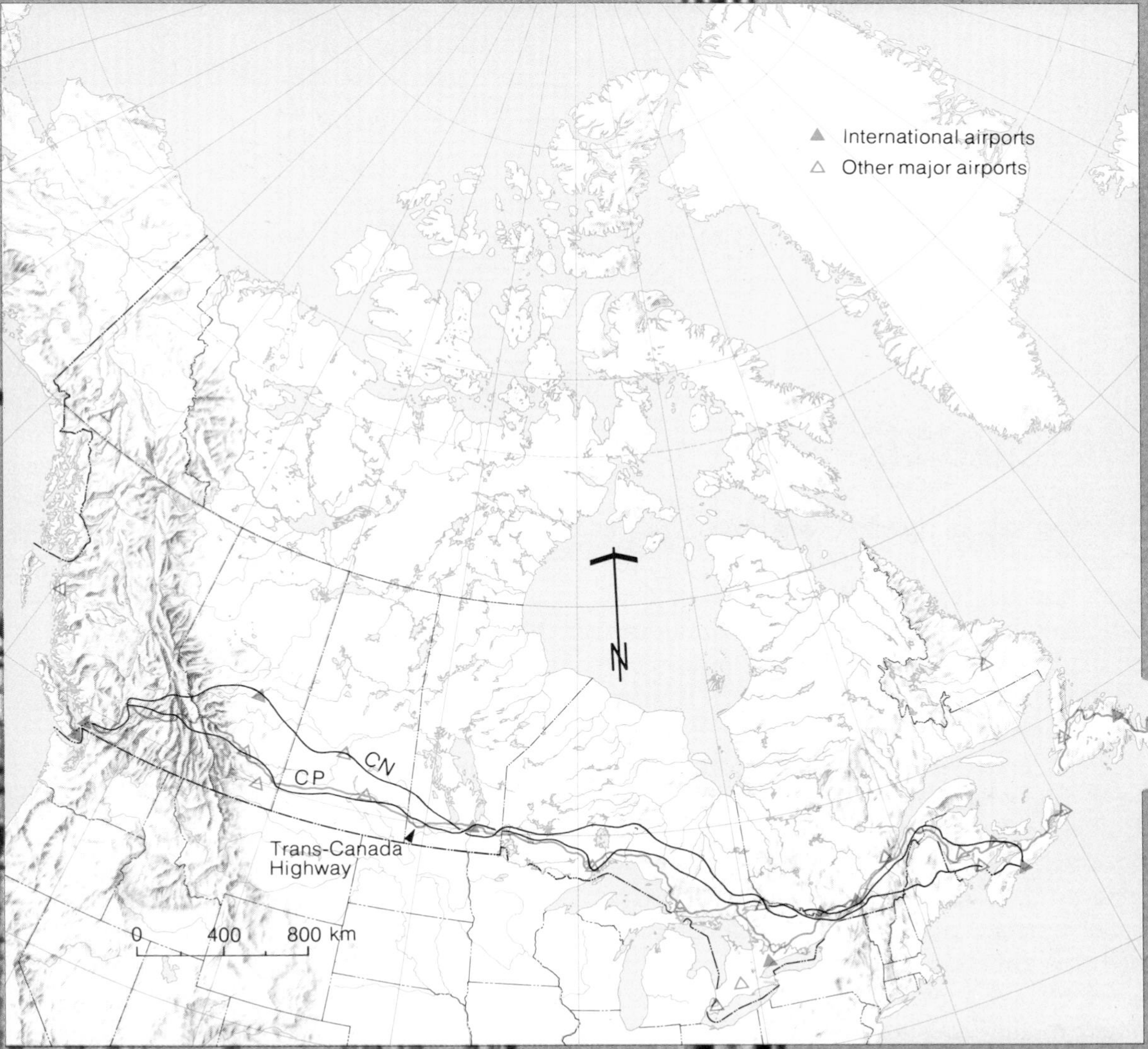

International airports
Other major airports

CP
CN

Trans-Canada
Highway

0   400   800 km

N

The action never stops. Every minute of every hour of every day, week after week, month after month, and year after year, it goes on. Canada's waterways, railways, highways, and airways are never entirely empty.

These links are vital to our economic and social life. Of all the factors that make up this country of ours, transportation is one of the most essential. Without it, we could not survive as a nation. Iron would remain in the ground, and steel would never be smelted. No raw materials would ever be delivered to plants and factories; no manufactured articles would ever reach our homes. And these homes would be little more than log cabins or mud huts. There would be few fine houses, and no high-rise apartments or office buildings. Trade and commerce would be practically non-existent. Our lives would be spent more or less in the area where we were born. Life, as we know it, would slow to a snail's pace.

Historic waterways

The first link in the chain of transportation was water. Frozen or free-running, it has been the historic means of travel in Canada. And with so many rivers running into so many lakes, what more ideal watercraft than the birchbark canoe? It could be navigated upstream as well as down. It could be portaged readily past falls and rapids or from one lake or river to another. When Europeans came to Canada, they quickly adopted the Indians' canoe — and their long-established river routes. Cheap and reliable, the canoe was a marvellous means of transportation.

Of all the many people who helped to open up the vast land of Canada, few can

A Portage *by John Innes.*

Courtesy of the Glenbow-Alberta Institute

compare with the tough, hardy, adventuresome voyageur. He was the workhorse of the Montreal fur merchant. Close to sixty strokes a minutes the voyageur paddled, and rested but ten minutes of each hour. Twelve to fourteen hours a day he and his fellows drove their birchbark craft. When falls and rapids hindered progress, the men got out of their canoes and "lined" them with ropes through shallow rapids or portaged everything around violent ones. And what a test of strength portages were! Trade goods were done up in standard 90-pound packs, kegs, or cases. No voyageur worth his salt carried less than two packs at a time; some hoisted three.

Some fur traders — men such as Alexander Mackenzie, David Thompson, and Simon Fraser — recorded the land and charted its lake-and-river highways. From Montreal to the Pacific, they maintained a 3,000-mile route. Trader and voyageur conquered the wilderness using the birchbark canoe. In creating a far-flung trading empire, they founded a nation.

Study 53

1. On an outline map of Canada, mark:
   (a) the voyageur route from Montreal to Georgian Bay, to Lake Winnipeg, to the Rocky Mountains
   (b) the routes Simon Fraser and David Thompson pioneered through and beyond the Rocky Mountains
   (c) the main trans-Canada railway and highway routes.
2. Explain the coincidences.
3. How many fur-trade posts were the origin of modern Canadian communities?

The Great Lakes–St. Lawrence waterway

Streams by the thousand tumble through the Shield into the immense catchment basin of the Great Lakes. Strange to say, none of these becomes a river of any note. Mighty tributaries such as the Ottawa, St. Maurice, Saguenay, Manicouagan and Outardes are only to be found far downstream. With a water surface of 246 000 square kilometres, the five Great Lakes form the most extensive collection of fresh water in the world.

From Lake Superior, the waters of the St. Mary's River pour along at something like 2000 cubic metres per second and fall into Lakes Michigan and Huron. Rushing down the 2.4 metre drop from Huron to Erie by way of the St. Clair River, Lake St. Clair, and the Detroit River, waters flood into Lake Erie at an average rate of 5000 cubic metres per second. North from Erie this torrent hurries and scrambles along the Niagara River to the Falls; here, the river hurtles over two awesome cataracts and plunges into the Niagara Gorge. Once past a swirling whirlpool, the river is swift but more peaceful and widens out to join the calmer waters of Lake Ontario. At the eastern end of the lake, the St. Lawrence River begins its long journey to the sea. By the time it flows past Montreal at the Lachine Rapids, all this water has reached an incredible velocity of 7500 cubic metres per second. Stand by the river's edge and say "One thousand and one" and, in the time it takes to say these words, this enormous volume of water has swept past you — a tremendous source of energy!

The mouth of the St. Lawrence River is so wide that the first explorers thought it an inland sea. Instead, it proved to be an enormous gateway to a highway that leads 3700 kilometres into the very heart of the continent.

Like a great magnet, the waterway draws resources from nearby and faraway regions. Wheat comes from the Prairies to the mills of Ontario and Quebec, and then out to Great Britain and Europe. Iron ore from Labrador, Quebec, and Ontario feeds many hungry furnaces along the waterway's shores. Coal from Pennsylvania and West Virginia fuels these furnaces. Bauxite from Guyana and Jamaica is shipped to the aluminum smelters of Arvida and Shawinigan. Petroleum, chemicals, building materials — in fact, an amazing profusion of raw

Begun in 1779, this was the first major lock canal in North America — all of 40 feet long and 2½ feet deep.

materials and manufactured goods — flow back and forth on the waterway of the Great Lakes-St. Lawrence.

Yet this was not always so. For hundreds of years the rapids at Lachine, the Long Sault, and the St. Mary's River (to say nothing of Niagara Falls) prevented the optimum use of the waterway. Canoes and ships had to be content to sail only lakes and navigable portions of the St. Lawrence. A 2-foot ditch was dug around the Lachine Rapids in the early 1700s, but little use was ever made of it. By 1825, a 5-foot canal by-passed these same rapids. But this was only playing around with the problem.

Then, as so often happens, at the right time and in the right place, a man arrived to change the whole scene. If evidence is needed that the basis of geography is the interaction of human and natural environments, the development of the St. Lawrence Seaway is proof positive. Its

creation is a tribute to the vision and determination of many Canadians — and of one in particular.

In 1812, Captain William Hamilton Merritt left his farm at St. Catharines, Upper Canada, to defend his country against the American invasion. Three years later, the war over and won, he came home. But his ambitions went beyond the farm and general store to which he returned. At first, he was absorbed in the task of constructing a canal to increase the water power to his new sawmill. A little later, with the vision that elevates ambition beyond personal gain, Merritt conceived the idea of a canal that would allow vessels to pass to and from Lakes Erie and Ontario. His enthusiasm for the project excited several other businessmen, and the Welland Canal Company was founded.

What a gigantic task it all turned out to be! Ton after ton of earth had to be laboriously removed by hand shovels and horse-drawn scoops. At first, the line of the canal followed Twelve-Mile Creek from Lake Ontario to Allenburg. From here, an 8-foot-deep cut was dug *clear through the Niagara Escarpment* to Port Robinson! At this stage, forty wooden locks were constructed, each 110 feet long, which could handle ships up to 165 tons. It was a Herculean task; nothing like it had ever been done before in North America. However, the engineers hit an unexpected snag: there was just not enough water to operate the locks. So a feeder canal was dug from Dunnville through the marshes, carried over the Welland River by a specially constructed viaduct, and so led to Port Robinson. Where the viaduct crossed the Welland River, the town of Welland grew.

At Chippewa, where the Welland River joins the Niagara River just above the Falls, there were treacherous currents and eddies. Thus the engineers decided to continue the canal south to Gravelly Bay on Lake Erie. The city of Port Colborne grew up here, at the southern terminus. Even though a serious cholera epidemic broke out, the work was completed by 1833.

Merritt's energy and ambition were far-ranging. He became involved in reorganizing the Ontario public school system, building libraries, and constructing railways. It was due to his efforts that a suspension bridge was built over the Niagara Gorge, first for carriage travel and, later, as a railway bridge. Above all, he spent much of his time urging the construction of a navigable waterway, a *seaway*, from Montreal to the Great Lakes. He did not see the realization of this in his lifetime, but other men followed his lead.

By 1850, a system of 9-foot canals had been completed around the Lachine Rapids at Montreal. As time passed and larger ships were built to handle ever-increasing cargoes of Canada's bulk resources, these canals and channels had to be continually deepened. Midway in this century, the 41 miles of canals were only 14 feet deep (with the exception of the Welland, which was 25 feet). Yet the shipping channels in the St. Lawrence below Montreal were 20 feet deep. Obviously ships could proceed only so far, then their goods had to be off-loaded and transported around bottlenecks.

In November, 1829, five years after the first sod had been turned, two ships, the Ann and Jane *of Toronto, and the* R.H. Broughton *of Youngstown, N.Y., "climbed down" the escarpment through the locks to Port Robinson.*

A modern vessel using the Welland Canal makes the Ann and Jane *of Toronto look like a lifeboat.*

Ontario Ministry of Industry and Tourism

Study 54

1. Define and explain the following terms: catchment basin, drainage basin, escarpment, viaduct, feeder canal.
2. What were the bottlenecks that existed along the route of the waterway?
3. What activities in Port Colborne and Welland would not be carried on if the Welland Canal had not been built?
4. A special technology developed to handle shipping in the Great Lakes-St. Lawrence waterway, including ship design and operation, navigational aids, port facilities, etc. Write a report on the development of Great Lakes technology.

The St. Lawrence Seaway

For the first fifty years of this century, groups of Canadians tried again and again to develop a continuous navigable waterway from the Atlantic Ocean to the head of the Great Lakes. Time after time, something occurred to block this plan — two World Wars, opposition from the United States, or just a plain lack of money. Then two circumstances combined to "make an offer that was impossible to refuse." Shortly after World War II, the major iron-ore reserves of the United States in Minnesota were running low, and the richest available replacements were deposits in Labrador-Quebec. At the same time, due to demands generated by a population explosion and an almost miraculous industrial growth, much of the State of New York was short of hydro-electric power. Differences between Canada and the United States were forgotten, and fifty years of dilly-dallying came to an end.

In 1954, Prime Minister Louis St. Laurent of Canada, Premier Leslie Frost of Ontario, and Governor Thomas Dewey of New York State each turned a shovelful of sod, symbolically starting what was to be one of the most stupendous ditch-digging events in the history of the world. The project took five years to complete. When it was all over, seven new locks had been built along the International Rapids section of the St. Lawrence River — five by Canada and two by the United States. Each lock is 232 metres by 24 metres and 9 metres deep, and each requires 109 million litres of water to fill. (Each can be either filled or emptied in less than ten minutes.) New channels had been created, and old ones reshaped and deepened to 8 metres. The Welland Canal became a system of eight locks, three of which are twin locks in flight. A total of sixteen locks permits a continued lift of about 180 metres

Thanks to twin locks in flight, there are few traffic line-ups on the Welland Canal. Ships can move in both directions simultaneously.

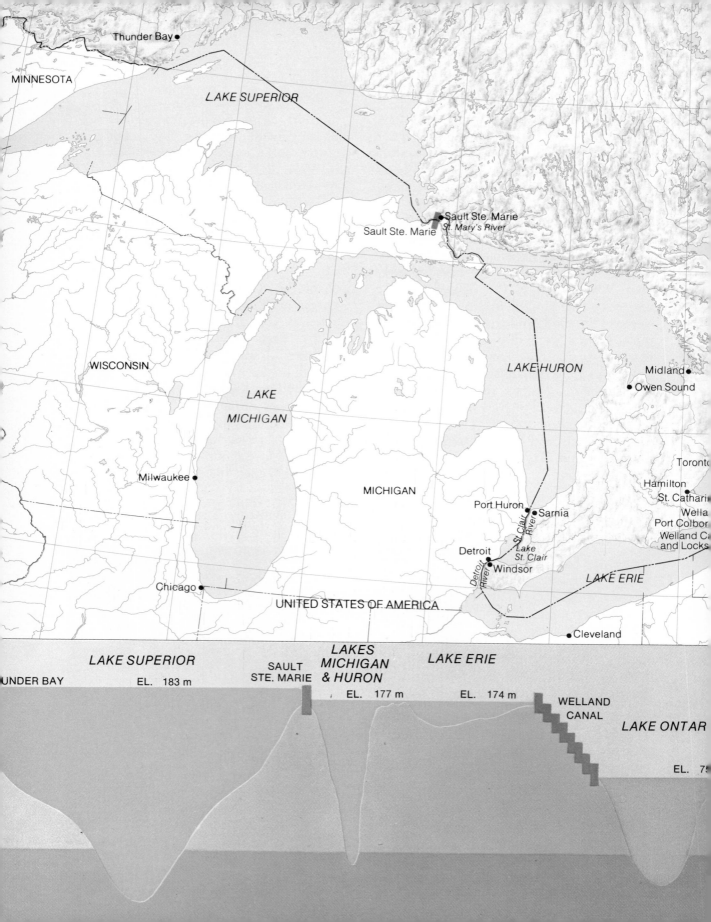

Thunder Bay •

MINNESOTA

LAKE SUPERIOR

Sault Ste. Marie •
Sault Ste. Marie
St. Mary's River

WISCONSIN

LAKE MICHIGAN

LAKE HURON

Midland •
• Owen Sound

Milwaukee •

MICHIGAN

Toronto

Hamilton •
St. Cathari

Port Huron •
• Sarnia

Wella
Port Colbor
Welland Ca
and Locks

Detroit •
Windsor •

Lake St. Clair

St. Clair River

Detroit River

LAKE ERIE

Chicago •

UNITED STATES OF AMERICA

• Cleveland

LAKE SUPERIOR	SAULT STE. MARIE	**LAKES MICHIGAN & HURON**	**LAKE ERIE**
UNDER BAY	EL. 183 m		EL. 177 m	EL. 174 m

WELLAND CANAL

LAKE ONTAR

EL. 7

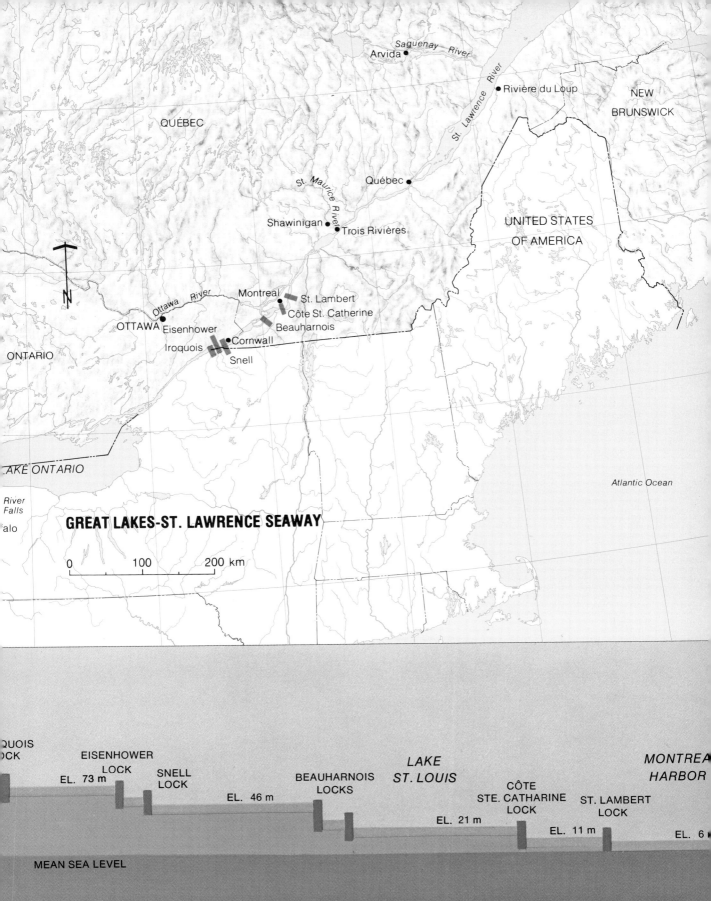

Arvida

Saguenay River

Rivière du Loup

St. Lawrence River

NEW BRUNSWICK

QUÉBEC

St. Maurice River

Québec

Shawinigan
Trois Rivières

UNITED STATES
OF AMERICA

Ottawa River

Montreal

St. Lambert
Côte St. Catherine
Beauharnois

OTTAWA
Eisenhower
Iroquois
Snell
Cornwall

ONTARIO

LAKE ONTARIO

River
Falls

Atlantic Ocean

alo

GREAT LAKES-ST. LAWRENCE SEAWAY

0   100   200 km

QUOIS
OCK

EISENHOWER
LOCK

EL. 73 m

SNELL
LOCK

EL. 46 m

BEAUHARNOIS
LOCKS

LAKE
ST. LOUIS

CÔTE
STE. CATHARINE
LOCK

EL. 21 m

ST. LAMBERT
LOCK

EL. 11 m

MONTREA
HARBOR

EL. 6

MEAN SEA LEVEL

between Montreal and the Upper Lakes. Ships up to 223 metres in length and carrying cargoes of over 27 000 tonnes can be handled. At first, vessels were allowed a draught of up to 7.6 metres, but in 1974 this was increased to 7.9 metres. (The term "draught" refers to the depth of water a vessel displaces, so obviously ships could now increase the tonnage they carried.)

The total cost of this new work was $460,000,000, of which $330,000,000 was raised in Canada. What has been the result of building the Seaway?

First of all, the amount of bulk tonnage carried has increased fivefold. Ocean-going vessels that previously could not pass Montreal can now proceed to Great Lakes ports, thus connecting western Europe and the centre of the North American continent. Once it was realized that increased numbers as well as different types of ships would be using the Seaway, older ports were modernized and new port facilities came into being. For example, at Port Cartier and Sept-Iles, brand-new ports were constructed to handle the iron ore of Labrador-Quebec. Baie Comeau received new grain elevators, and those at Quebec City were enlarged. All the major lake ports enjoyed a substantial growth in trade.

However, the Seaway has not fully realized the smooth success its planners expected. During the first three years of its operation, the Great Lakes region experienced serious summer droughts, and there was just not enough water in the Seaway to provide sufficient depth. Ships were forced to carry lesser cargo tonnages, losing millions of dollars in the process. There have been other disappointments. Fewer ocean-going vessels are using the Seaway than expected. Their size and shape make it difficult for them to navigate the Seaway's locks and canals. Secondly, the specialized equipment developed to load and unload lakers is not as suitable for use with ocean-going vessels and makes the handling of their cargo a slower, more involved operation. (When you are handling cargo at $1,000 an hour, costs rise sharply!)

One cheerful note to end on. The Seaway is a wonderful tourist attraction. A campsite has been opened beside the channel at the foot of the Lachine Rapids. In the Thousand Islands' area, 1200 hectares of land have been turned into the St. Lawrence River State Park. There are beautiful scenic drives along the Long Sault Parkway and the road from Barnhart Island to Waddington. Observation areas have been set up at both the Canadian and U.S. powerhouses. Spread all along the Seaway are information booths, sandy beaches, marinas, camping areas, and viewing sites. So go and take part in that new Canadian sport — ship-watching.

Study 55

1. Why did Canada contribute $330,000,000 toward the cost of the Seaway while the United States paid only $130,000,000?
2. List the five principal import commodities and the five principal export commodities transported along the Seaway. What *type* of goods are they, mainly?
3. What percentage of principal import and export commodities are raw materials? What percentage are manufactured articles?
4. Rank the three major Canadian ports in terms of tonnage handled.

5. Of the total tonnage handled by all Canadian ports, what percentage is handled by Seaway ports? How much tonnage goes through the Canadian Sault Ste. Marie lock? How much through the American?
6. Account for the fluctuations in tonnage statistics since the Seaway opened.
7. Write a short report describing the degree of success of the Seaway. Your report should take into account original intentions, operation and management, and alterations and improvements. Has it truly become a *sea*way?
8. In what ways has the Seaway changed the geography of transportation in Canada?

The "Iron horse"

Canada is a tough country in which to construct railways. In the east, the Appalachians are a rugged series of twisting, turning ranges without a single continuous pass from east to west. Occupying much of the centre is the huge, wrinkled mass of the Canadian Shield, a seemingly endless wilderness of muskeg, rock, and forest. In the west, the Cordillera is a formidable barrier to navigation. Everywhere, swift rivers tumble down numberless rapids. Most of the year, most of Canada is frozen hard. And, to add insult to injury, our northern summer breeds black flies and mosquitoes that can drive both man and beast out of their minds.

Settlers arriving at the Station in Manitoba. *An anonymous engraving.*

It is safe to say that, had not men been determined to build transcontinental railways, Canada would have remained an untamed land for a long, long time. More than any other country in the world, Canada has depended, for settlement and development, on the iron horse.

Before the first transcontinental line was built, Canada hardly existed. Patches of settlement had been established, but the Appalachians isolated the Atlantic settlements from those of the St. Lawrence. From here, there was a 1000-mile stretch of rocky desolation to the Red River, where a small band of men and women struggled to raise crops and cattle. Then there was a yawning stretch of emptiness all the way to and beyond the Rockies before you came to two small settlements,

one at the mouth of the Fraser River, the other at the south end of Vancouver Island. This was the Canada of the late 1800s.

In an amazingly short space of time, railways changed all this. They brought millions of people to dig for the mineral treasure of the Canadian Shield, to break the sod of the Prairies, and to build thousands of settlements. Without railways, the Canadian West and Pacific coast might well have been gobbled up by an expanding United States. Without railways, there would have been no nation of Canada as we know it today. Only the "iron horse" could overcome the physical obstacles and bond the country's separate parts into a nation.

Canada has some forty railway companies, but almost 90 per cent of all rail freight is carried by two of them: CP Rail

Unit trains like the one here bring Rocky Mountain coal to the superport of Roberts Bank, British Columbia, just south of Vancouver. In the shed behind the ship, mechanical jaws gently grasp each hopper car, turn it over, and empty out its 100 tonnes in 90 seconds. Coal then rattles away along a conveyor belt to storage heaps or directly to a waiting ship. Vancouver Sun Photo

and CN. These are transcontinental lines. CN operates in ten provinces, and CP in all but Newfoundland and Prince Edward Island.

These two giant railways do more than run trains. They operate what is known as an **intermodal transport** system: that is, they also operate ships, trucks, planes (and hotels), and are even involved in pipeline transportation. In this way they reduce or eliminate competition. For example, shortly after World War II, with a better and expanded highway system, railways lost a great deal of freight traffic to more efficient truck transport. By setting up their own trucking organizations, CN and CP make profits that would otherwise have been lost to them.

The intermodal method of transport is efficient and economic. A company so organized does not have to deal with any other company, and the routing of goods can be planned and carried out from the one office. For instance, bicycles from a Dutch firm can be sent to Rotterdam and packed in CP containers. These can then be loaded onto a CP ship, landed at a port, and transferred to a CP train for distribution to major cities in Canada. At these centres, the containers can be offloaded into CP trucks, which take them to various warehouses. There, the containers are unpacked, and CP vans deliver the bicycle parts for assembly by the merchant who purchased them. Similarly, a Canadian exporter can ship goods to Asia or Europe.

Study 56

1. Write a brief report on the scattered settlements in Canada in the late 1800s with particular emphasis on transportation routes and links.
2. Evaluate the statement that only rail lines could overcome the physical obstacles and bond the country's separate parts into a nation.
3. Write a brief report on the construction of one transcontinental railway in one region of Canada.
4. Select either CP Rail or CN and explain how it came to be.
5. If CP Rail and CN handle 90 per cent of all rail freight in Canada, what is the function of the other thirty-eight railway companies?
   What is their relationship to the two major companies?

Frontier links

A unique feature of Canadian railway construction is that we are forever tearing up old lines that are little used or unprofitable while laying thousands of kilometres of new ones. No other country in the Western world builds as many kilometres of rail.

Why? Canada is one of the few countries in the world with vast regions still undeveloped. New tracks are being laid to exploit the riches of the wilderness. Most of these connect Canadian frontiers with main routes, the St. Lawrence shipping artery, or the sea.

An excellent example of a frontier link is the White Pass and Yukon Railway (W.P.

In order to lay certain stretches of track on the W.P. & Y.R., men hung suspended on ropes from cliff tops while they placed dynamite charges in rock clefts.

& Y.R.), begun during the famous gold rush of the 1890s. Thanks to some of the most awesome topography in the world, its route through the mountains was not finished until the gold rush was over. Thus the 110-mile track from Whitehorse to Skagway, although the only link between Dawson City and the outside world, remained comparatively idle. Then came World War II. The northern part of the continent became strategically important.

Thousands of men and tons of equipment and supplies were carried by the W.P. & Y.R. to build airport bases and to construct the Alaska Highway. Since 1945, with the discovery of minerals in the area, particularly silver, the line has more than paid its way.

In order to move ores more economically, the W.P. & Y.R. invented **containerization.** This process begins with the loading of freight into specially built containers,

274

On a 24-hectare site located beside ice-free, deep water at the southern end of the harbor at Halifax, Nova Scotia, is the largest container port of its type in the country. The port's operations link central and western Canada and the large metropolitan markets of the eastern United States with the United Kingdom, continental Europe, the Mediterranean, Australia, New Zealand, Japan, Taiwan, and Korea.

which will fit train, truck, or ship. Freight is loaded into containers at the source of origin and easily transferred to whatever type of transportation is necessary. Thus the old method of dumping freight onto trucks in bulk, unloading it bit by bit onto railway rolling stock, repeating the process from train to ship at a dock, and so on — and then reversing the process at the other end — is eliminated. Now, you simply load a container that fits train, truck, or ship. Such a simple, time-saving, money-saving method has been copied by freight companies in Canada and in other countries.

However, the real importance of the White Pass and Yukon Railway is more than the achievement of having built an impossible roadbed or having revolutionized the handling of freight. The line was constructed to bring out mineral resources from the northern interior. Once built, the W.P. & Y.R. made possible the expansion of mining development in the region and spun off settlement along its route. It is now

the very lifeline of a regional economy.

Another link in our transportation system is the Quebec, North Shore, and Labrador Railway (Q.N.S.L.R.) from Schefferville, in northern Quebec, to Sept-Iles, thus connecting the frontier with the St. Lawrence shipping artery. The Q.N.S.L.R. runs a mere 576 kilometres, but carries more tonnes per kilometre than any other railway in Canada: this line was built to carry nothing but iron ore. Airplanes and helicopters flew in machinery, men, and supplies to build the line — and also the town, the dam, and the hydro-electric installations at Schefferville.

The Q.N.S.L.R. was the first line in Canada to use diesels only, and its daily operation is a miracle of technology. The whole organization is masterminded by a computer. At Sept-Iles, a controller sits at an electric control panel. In response to data produced instantaneously by the computer, the controller manipulates buttons on the panel. At a loading depot, 115 rail-

cars are gently rolled along, one after another, to a chute-opening and each is filled
with 82 tonnes of ore. Then the cars are
guided by the computer to a specially
designated track in the marshalling yards
and coupled together. The computer then
co-ordinates the movement of four diesels,
which are attached automatically to the
assembled line of ore cars. When all is
ready, the train sets off south along the
single track to Sept-Iles. Seven trains per
day make the 15-hour trip from mine-site
to port. All along the train's route, the
computer controls the switches that divert
one train into a siding to allow another,
empty, northbound train to pass, decides
the speed of each train, and controls the
braking. At times a train may be stopped
by a crewman to pick up passengers along
the line. The computer takes account of
this and makes the necessary adjustments
throughout the whole organization. In
time, these trains will be completely devoid
of crews and will run entirely automatically, as does the Quebec-Cartier Mining
Railway from Gagnon to Port-Cartier.

Other lines connect northern frontier
regions with the sea. The Hudson Bay Railway (H.B.R.) was built to link southern
Manitoba with Hudson Bay. The hope was
that a thriving trade would result from
shipping Prairie wheat via this route rather
than by the much longer haul east via rail
to the port of Montreal. Unfortunately,
this scheme turned out to be a dismal fail-
ure, mainly because of navigation hazards
caused by the long ice season in the Bay.
Even today, very few ships ever call, and
only a very small proportion of wheat is
exported by this route.

However, every cloud has a silver lining.
Vast deposits of minerals – particularly
nickel, copper, and gold – were discovered
on either side of the railway. Mine sites
were established at Lynn Lake, Sheridan,
Flin Flon, and, later, Thompson. Branch
lines bringing out ores and taking in supplies to all these mining centres have made
the construction of the main line worth-
while. Furthermore, International Nickel
Company of Canada has built a model
town at Thompson and, 48 kilometres

A train, loaded with iron-ore concentrates, makes the daily 443-km run from the Scully mine in Labrador to the St. Lawrence port of Pointe Noire, Quebec.

away, a huge dam and power site. The H.B.R. played a vital transportation role in the creation of these facilities.

If you have the pioneer instinct, take a trip on the Hudson Bay Railway. Go on the "Muskeg Special" to Churchill and see polar bears roaming the streets and being driven away by helicopters. Visit Fort Prince of Wales, built as an impregnable fortress against the French, but which they captured without firing a shot.

The British Columbia Railway (B.C.R.), initially known as the Pacific Great Eastern,* is another provincial link that helps to bond this country of ours into a national whole. The line passes through fearsome mountain ranges between Vancouver and the valley of the upper Peace River. It does much more than carry lumber, minerals,

stock and agricultural products, and passengers. The B.C.R. has helped develop the northern section of the province around the oil and natural gas region in the vicinity of Fort Nelson. Since it meets the Alaska Highway at Dawson Creek, it gives the Peace River district a connection with the Pacific Ocean.

What began as the Timiskaming and Northern Ontario Railway, now the Onta-

*The P.G.E., which linked the hamlet of Squamish near Vancouver with the little community of Quesnel on the Fraser River, was 547 kilometres of rail that was described for over thirty years as "beginning nowhere and ending nowhere." Critics said PGE stood for "Prince George Eventually," "Please Go Easy," and "Past God's Endurance."

HOW INTERCITY FREIGHT IS CARRIED IN CANADA

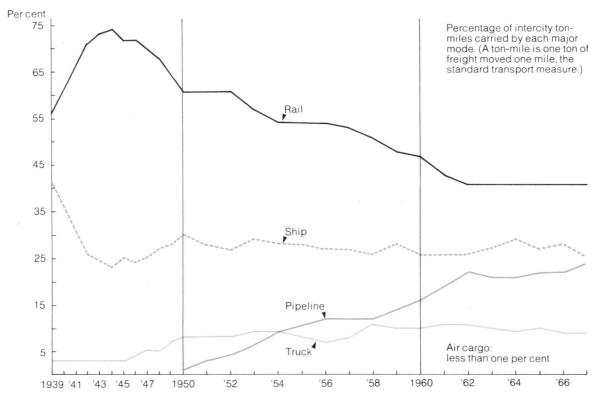

Per cent

Percentage of intercity ton-miles carried by each major mode. (A ton-mile is one ton of freight moved one mile, the standard transport measure.)

Rail

Ship

Pipeline

Truck

Air cargo: less than one per cent

Source: Statistics Canada

277

rio Northland Railway (O.N.R.), had as glorious a beginning as any rail line anywhere. Built to open up the Clay Belt to agricultural settlement, what it actually accomplished was something far more dramatic. The construction of the railway was the prime cause of the discovery of silver at Cobalt and also aided the development of gold-mining areas in such places as Noranda, Timmins, and Kirkland Lake.

The O.N.R. passes through spectacular scenery and is a fascinating tourist attraction. In summer, the "Polar Bear Express" runs from Cochrane to Moosonee on James Bay, a land of luck and legends, fortunes and folly. Officially, the train makes only eight stops; actually, it halts anywhere any time to pick up hunters, fishermen, trappers, and tourists. (Occasionally, the crew has to stop the train to coax a moose off the line.) A thrilling part of the trip is getting off at Moose River Crossing and taking the canoe trip guided by the Moose River band of Indians. And if you are at all fascinated by the voyageur's place in history, stay at the French River Reserve overnight and then continue "down north" by a 300-year-old fur trade route to Moose Factory.

No account of rail transportation in Canada would be complete without at least a mention of the Newfoundland Railway's "Bullet." Alas, it is no more. In its day, the "Bullet" was more than just a train; it was an institution. It has become a legend.

The line wound its way from Port aux Basques on the southwest, across Newfoundland, to St. John's, passing through places with such unlikely names as Foxtrap, Kitty's Brook, and Tickle Harbor. The "Bullet" never ran on a rigid schedule; it travelled at a leisurely pace. The dining car had impeccable white damask tablecloths, gleaming silver, and crystal goblets. Even Canadians who never rode the "Bullet" repeat yarns about it with affectionate exaggeration. Gales that threatened to blow the "Bullet" off the rails and moose battling each other on the track are all part of its story.

Study 57

1. What industries have developed because of frontier links?
2. "Railways precede roads." Apply this statement to the development of Canada.
   What will the pattern of development be in the future?
3. What has been the role of government in forging frontier links?
4. Five frontier railways have been mentioned in this chapter. Mark these on an outline map of Canada. For each line, indicate by symbols the product or products carried by the railway.
   (a) Why do these lines run north and south?
   (b) Why are there no east-west links?
   (c) What do you think this railway pattern will be in 2000 A.D.?
       What are the reasons for your answer?

Where the rubber meets the road

With the invention of the internal-combustion engine came the automobile and the truck. Between them, they have completely revolutionized our travel habits and the transportation of bulk goods. Of all travel done by Canadians, 75 per cent is in the family car. Add to this the thousands of buses, taxis, trucks, vans, and motorcycles, and you will understand why the demand for road construction and maintenance is an increasing problem for all levels of government.

In recent years, the average person's standard of living has increased dramatically. To take just one example, we are eating a better and more varied diet of fresh vegetables, meat, milk, and fruit. Since these are perishable items, they must be delivered rapidly from producer to market to prevent spoilage and preserve freshness. Today, even in the crowded, built-up Metropolitan Toronto region, vegetables picked and packed 56 kilometres away at Holland Marsh can be at a food terminal in Toronto within an hour of pick-up. The same is true of apples, peaches, and pears from the Niagara Fruit Belt. What makes this possible is the combination of a network of highways and roads, and fleets of trucks and vans.

Roads and highways thread the well-populated areas of Canada. All in all, there are about 724 000 kilometres of highway, 10 per cent of which are paved. Saskatchewan leads all provinces with 204 000 kilometres of road, although all but 8450 of these are either gravel or dirt. Ontario, on the other hand, has only 122 000 kilometres of road, but by far the largest paved road surface of any province—about 32 000 kilometres. These figures illustrate the difference in road demands between a sparsely populated, predominantly rural region with large farming areas, and a densely populated one where industry dominates the economy. Further proof of this is figures for automobile ownership: about two million in Ontario compared with something like 270,000 in Saskatchewan. In fact, if you were to add up all the automobiles, trucks, buses, and motorcycles in use between Quebec City and Windsor, you would find that this amounted to a far greater number than the total for the rest of Canada. No wonder this section of the country — Ontario in particular — has one of the best highway networks in the world.

The Trans-Canada Highway was completed in 1962. Since then, many a Canadian family has driven its 7768 kilometres clear across the country. And many a trucking company has realized its great commercial value. It may cost more to transport goods over long hauls by truck rather than by rail. However, to send a large trailer long distances is often more convenient and less time-consuming than to transfer its contents to a rail car.

Special types of trucks have been designed for specific transport purposes. Most familiar of all is the tractor-trailer. This consists of two units: the tractor, which is the engine with the cab; and the trailer, which can be a flat-top or a tank. The flat-top rests on a bogie and can be transferred on or off the bogie in one to two minutes. Flat-tops are used for carrying lumber, raw steel, aluminum, and other such products. Tankers carry gasoline to gas stations or fuel oil to homes.

An obvious cost factor is that, once a

You will not meet the diesel-electric TEREX 33-15 on the highway. However, it's a good example of a lot of "rubber meeting the road" that we don't see or hear about. Thanks to such new breeds of hauling equipment, the mining industry is able to lower transportation costs, and thus the price of products.

General Motors of Canada's Diesel Division is the sole GM source for large, Diesel-electric TEREX haulers. This model can transport a payload of 152 tonnes at speeds of up to 47.5 k/h. For the technically minded, its engine provides 1200 kW of power at 1900 r/m, and is turbocharged and intercooled. The vehicle has three independent braking systems.

load has been delivered, the tractor-trailer generally has to return empty. Thus, some unusual types of road transport have been designed to get around this problem. One such trailer consists of a huge tank divided into three compartments. The front and rear ones contain liquids, the middle compartment holds solid goods, such as mineral concentrates. In this manner, fuel can be taken to a mine site and concentrates hauled away. This is a tremendous convenience for mines that are too small to be served economically by a railway.

So important is the function of highways that we cannot afford to have rain, snow, hail, or sleet stop the smooth flow of traffic. Because of our climate, maintaining an "open road" program is not easy. Snow and ice are present for three to four months every year in most regions and longer still farther north. Thousands of snowploughs and trucks are used to keep highways and streets clear. (The snowplough is a Canadian invention, proof of the old adage that necessity is the mother of invention.) In addition to making driving hazardous, Canadian winters make road repair and maintenance a never-ending job. Frost

heaves, buckles, and cracks surfaces, necessitating perennial pothole plugging and road resurfacing.

Apart from such problems as weather, potholes, and congested highways, truckers have to face different government controls. Since each province has its own licensing and operating laws, interprovincial trucking companies have to contend with eleven sets of controls. A company hauling goods from Alberta to Quebec, for example, has to obtain licences valid in Alberta, Saskatchewan, Manitoba, Ontario, and Quebec. A licence costs between $1,200 and $1,700 per tractor-trailer. And each province insists that fuel be bought in the province in which the truck is travelling, otherwise a tax must be paid. Furthermore, Quebec will not allow any but domestic trucks to convey goods north of Montreal. For years, truckers have tried to get the federal government to set up regulations to stabilize laws affecting interprovincial trucking. Ottawa passed the National Transport Act in 1967, but so far little has been done to set up control machinery.

Known for its deep snows and frequent avalanches, British Columbia's Rogers Pass forced the CPR to build the 5-mile-long Connaught Tunnel. When the Trans-Canada Highway was constructed through the Pass, it seemed more economical to build a few snowsheds and buy a lot of snow-clearing equipment.

Study 58

1. Rank the provinces in terms of car ownership and number of paved-road kilometres.
2. The tractor-trailer is only one type of truck. What other special types of trucks have been designed and for what specific purposes?
3. Study a road atlas and a railway map of Canada. Account for differences in the rail and road networks in the following terms: number of kilometres, concentration, passenger/freight traffic.
4. What factors determine whether goods are transported by ship, rail, or truck?
5. What are the relative costs per kilometre of rail vs. truck vs. ship transport? What factors determine these costs?
6. Draw a map of the road network of your community and the surrounding area.
   (a) Mark on it the different road classifications (truck route, bus route, streetcar route, highway, expressway, by-pass, concession road, county road, etc.) and road surfaces (paved, gravel, dirt).
   (b) Trace the development of this road system, accounting for changes in the following: population densities, local industrial development, settlement patterns, external influences from other communities, government, etc.
7. Road construction and maintenance can be the joint or separate responsibilities of different levels of government.
   (a) How is the responsibility divided among the different levels?
   (b) Which responsibilities are shared by two or more levels of government?

Urban transit

Urban transportation is a headache in itself. Take Toronto, for example. Each day of the work week, roughly 700,000 cars pour into the downtown core and stream out again. Multi-lane expressways and parkways designed for high-speed travel can become choked by a single accident, which slows up traffic for hours. In 1961, the Toronto Transit Commission carried about 267 million people by streetcar, bus, and subway; by 1973 this figure had risen to about 360 million — close to one million passengers per day. Then there are trucks and vans on pick-up and delivery errands, not to mention all the vehicles moving around in suburban areas. Anyone who can possibly do so gets off the roads by 4 p.m. — especially in downtown Toronto.

There are other, related problems. In the 1960s, the cost of parking in downtown Toronto was ten cents for the first half-hour. In the seventies, it had risen to fifty cents — and is still going up. More high-rise office and apartment buildings are being built, and their numerous car-driving ten-

Here's the essence of the motor traffic problem. How many cars are carrying one person?

ants only add to the congestion. Yet, if the heart of any city is to live, it must continue to grow and develop.

What is the answer?

Canadians love their cars. Most of us prefer to drive in relative comfort and at our own convenience rather than hang onto a strap while stuffed in a crowded subway or catch a bus at a specific time. Missing the bus and waiting for the next one in the wet or cold of a winter's morning is no joke. Furthermore, with the amount of groceries a modern family consumes, it is just about impossible to lug them home in the arms of one person or even in a pushcart. So, despite the fact that the automobile is a costly, polluting, landgrabbing monster, we prefer to live with it.

Is the answer more roads? Consider the following.

In 1947, the Ontario Department of High-ways recognized the need for a highway to by-pass Toronto to the north. The southern through route along the Lakeshore Boulevard, the Queen Elizabeth Way, and No. 2 Highway was thick with traffic. The new route selected was well north of any urban development. Although a two-lane highway was thought to be sufficient, the planners decided on a four-lane by-pass — just in case. So a limited access, 91.4-metre, four-lane right-of-way was carved out.

When Highway 401 opened in 1952, it was ten years out of date. At peak hours, it looked like an open-ended sardine tin. Twenty years and twelve lanes later, this 27-kilometre stretch of what is now called the Macdonald-Cartier Freeway is still packed in the rush hours and pretty well filled up twelve hours a day. Attracted by this transport artery, subdivisions and shopping plazas grew like fungi. The result is that

283

Again, how many of these are single-passenger vehicles?

Toronto now stretches almost as far north of the Freeway as it does south. Suburban traffic problems have only increased. In fact, for optimum efficiency, the Macdonald-Cartier Freeway would need at least twenty-six freeway lanes and about fifty feeder lanes. This, of course, is impossible within the allotted 91.4-metre right-of-way.

Now planners are thinking of *another* freeway in the vicinity of Steeles Avenue, the northern boundary of Metropolitan Toronto. Do you have an answer?

One answer to vehicle congestion is a technological one. Toronto was the first city in the world to handle traffic flow by means of a computer. Electric sensors, buried at 100 intersections, feed the rate of flow into the computer, which changes the lights accordingly. The average delay per motorist has been reduced from about three minutes per light to roughly twenty seconds.

Another solution may be subway transportation. Toronto has 40 kilometres of it. Any one line can carry about 36,000 people per hour, three times the capacity of street cars running on the surface system. Average speed is 32 kilometres per hour (including stops), which is better than that of an automobile using the same route, especially at rush hours. Furthermore, a subway does not take up valuable land: streets, houses, and shops can be built along most of the way.

There is no doubt that subway transportation is a most efficient way of moving

The Macdonald-Cartier Freeway cuts a wide swath through Metropolitan Toronto.

people. The problem, of course, is cost of construction and maintenance. Toronto's 40 kilometres of subway cost in excess of $400,000,000. However, anywhere a subway is built, land values just about quadruple and business increases by leaps and bounds. Thus, the city acquires additional taxes with which to subsidize the subway.

In Ontario, the provincial government is also in the business of transportation subsidies. About four million people live in a semicircle of about a 100-kilometre radius that takes in Oshawa, Barrie, Kitchener-Waterloo, Brantford, and the north shore of Lake Erie to the Niagara River. By 1980, this Golden Horseshoe, or Mississauga Conurbation, will contain at least five million people. Subtract three million as residents of Metropolitan Toronto, and this leaves two million. Most of these will have to find a way to and from Metropolitan Toronto. It is Canada's most extensive industrial, financial, commercial, and educational concentration, as well as being one of its biggest cultural and social centres. Now, the busiest section of the Mississauga Conurbation lies within a corridor 8 kilo-

metres wide and 100 kilometres long extending from Oshawa to Hamilton. Even as far back as the 1960s, 15,000 people living along the corridor travelled to work in Toronto every day, 14,000 of them by car!

On May 19th, 1965, the Province of Ontario decided to attack this problem and made plans for a subsidized commuter-train service. Canadian National Railways agreed to handle the operation for the government. CN had completed its northern by-pass, and freight marshalling yards had been moved north from downtown Toronto to Markham-and-Vaughan Township. Thus CN lakeshore lines were sufficiently relieved of traffic to handle commuter trains. The Ontario government would buy passenger trains at a cost of $7.5 million and subsidize the commuter-train operation by $2 million annually. So GO (Government of Ontario) Transit came into being. Spending $2 million annually in subsidies made much more sense than building highways at a cost of $3.7 million per kilometre — or $10 million per kilometre on elevated expressways.

On May 23rd, 1967, GO Transit carried its first passengers, using twenty-one trains

The McGill Station of Montreal's subway system. In a climate like ours, it makes a lot of sense to put as many facilities as possible underground, including public transit.

285

per day. By November of the same year, the number of trains had jumped to fifty-two — two years ahead of anticipated capacity. GO service has now been extended all the way to Hamilton in the west and Bowmanville in the east. In 1973, twenty thousand passengers were being carried daily.

The GO train is a fast, economical, and efficient rapid-transit service — and you don't have to park your car when you get downtown. (It has been estimated that a motorist can save $700 a year in gas and parking by using this rapid transit.) Plans are on the drawing board to extend GO services north of Toronto, using existing CN lines.

Will such rapid transit work in Winnipeg or Vancouver? What about the increasing chokehold the automobile has on other Canadian centres — St. John's and Saint John, Quebec City and Hamilton, Edmonton and Calgary? What will be their answer in an era of mushrooming metropolises?

Some bonds don't link. They strangle.

Study 59

1. What have been the transit problems in your community over the past ten years? What actions have community groups and governments taken to solve these problems? What have been the results?
2. A few answers to the problems of urban transit have been suggested in this chapter. What other solutions might work?

A new dimension in transportation

In the story of transportation, no chapter is more romantic or fascinating than that of the airplane. Since time began, the dream to fly has obsessed humans. The Greeks told the tale of Icarus, who attached wings to his body with wax. However, he flew too close to the sun, the wax melted, his wings fell off, and Icarus dropped completely out of sight! Leonardo da Vinci built a model airplane five hundred years ago and experimented with it on a hill outside Florence, Italy. The machine was aerodynamically perfect, but da Vinci could not get it off the ground — he had no effective propellant. Then came balloons and gliders. But it was not until December 17, 1903, that the first heavier-than-air machine took off and flew. The Wright brothers had realized the age-old dream to fly. On February 23, 1909, John McCurdy took off in the *Silver Dart* and flew over the frozen surface of Bras d'Or Lake in Cape Breton Island. The first plane had been flown in Canada.

Then came World War I, and airplane design improved almost miraculously. In the 1920s and early 1930s the enormous timber and mineral wealth of Canada's northern wilderness was beginning to be exploited commercially. After World War I, many Canadian pilots had returned home with no other skill or ambition than that of flying a plane. They were a breed of their

A generation ago, few Canadians would have even thought of travelling by air. Today, you only have to mention "jumbo jet" and you're immediately asked if you've been on the Boeing 747.

own, these men — independent, fearless, reckless to a certain degree. Many of them were caught and held by the enchantment of being alone and flying free between heaven and earth. So was born the bush pilot.

In the northern wilderness, these bush pilots earned their special niche in aviation history. They flew "by the seat of their pants," for the land was uncharted; there were no maps, no navigational aids, no air-ports. They took their ski- or pontoon-equipped planes into the farthest corners of Canada, bringing with them supplies, medicines, drilling tools, general cargo, mail, and the odd passenger. They brought regular communication to lonely outposts, aided explorers and prospectors, and flew geologists and surveyors in and out. Above all, these pilots created a lifeline with civilization. Today, there is no centre of any size in Canada's north without a sizable airstrip.

Scheduled services

In 1937, the federal government established Trans-Canada Airlines (TCA), which we today call Air Canada. Its first aircraft were 10-passenger Lockheeds, which in the post-war period were exchanged for 20-passenger D.C.3s. Within six years of establishing transcontinental service, TCA began to fly internationally. Five years after the establishment of TCA, the privately-owned company of Canadian Pacific Airlines entered the field. At first it served outlying areas in the north and northwest. Today, CP Air is both a transcontinental and an international airline.

Speed and convenience attract people to air travel. In 1937, it took seventeen hours to fly from Montreal to Vancouver. Today, a jet makes the journey in one-third the time. Capacity has increased from ten passengers in a Lockheed to 383 in a Boeing 747. Increased capacity has enabled airlines to move into the freight-carrying business; quantities of goods carried and total kilometres flown are increasing rapidly. In 1966, Canadian airlines carried about 163 000 tonnes of goods about 2 200 000 "tonne kilometres." Only four years later, this had nearly doubled. A Boeing 747, besides its full complement of passengers and baggage, can carry 23 tonnes of freight; the cargo version of this aircraft can transport 90 tonnes.

Of all airlines in Canada, few are more versatile, inventive, and hustling than

THE CANADIAN PACIFIC RAILWAY
DINING CARS
Excel in Elegance of Design and Furniture
AND IN THE
Quality of Food and Attendance
ANYTHING HITHERTO OFFERED TO
TRANSCONTINENTAL TRAVELLERS.

The fare provided is the best procurable, and the cooking has a wide reputation for excellence. Local delicacies, such as trout, prairie hens, antelope steaks, Fraser River salmon, succeed one another as the train moves westward.

The wines are of the Company's special importation, and are of the finest quality.

These cars accompany all transcontinental trains, and are managed directly by the Railway Company, which seeks, as with its hotels and sleeping cars, to provide every comfort and luxury without regard to cost—looking to the general profit of the Railway rather than to the immediate returns from these branches of its service

Air Canada

For the few who could afford it, the first transcontinental trains provided luxury dining cars and fine cuisine. For the many who travel by air, there are meals, music, and movies. (An American airline is even entertaining passengers by televising takeoffs and landings.)

288

DECREASING TRAVEL TIME VANCOUVER TO HALIFAX

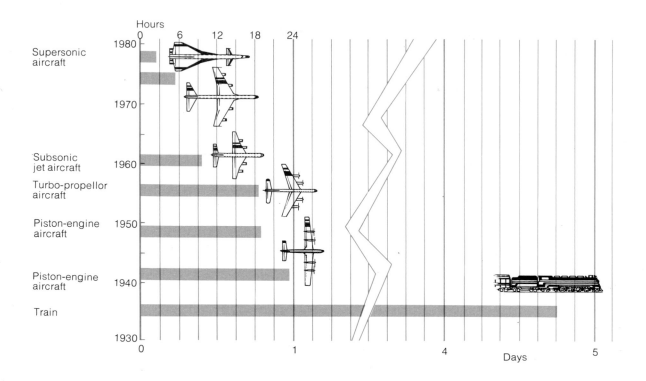

Transair-Midwest, formed in 1969. It carries anything from watches to mobile homes. Transair-Midwest's flight routes cover the Prairie Provinces, and scheduled flights are made into Ontario and the Arctic. The company also offers charter flights to anywhere in Canada, the United States, Mexico, and the Caribbean. Transair-Midwest is opening up new routes and services and assisting in the exploration and development of mining and oil resources in the north.

The company's varied fleet consists of everything from single-engine aircraft equipped with wheels, skis, or floats, to Boeing 737 jets, whose cargo can be all-passenger, all-freight, or passenger and freight. In 1970, Transair flew something like a quarter of a million passengers about 7.2 million kilometres and hauled 9100 tonnes of freight.

*   *   *

It is a far cry indeed from the day of the ox, the horse, and the mule. Changes in methods of transportation have taken place at a breathless pace. In years to come, in what sorts of machines will you or your children travel?

Study and Research

1. Write a brief report on the expanding freight services provided by airlines from the time when mail was the only cargo.

2. (a) What percentage of earnings of CP Air and Air Canada is derived from freight traffic? From passenger traffic?
   (b) How have these percentages changed over the past decade?

3. (a) How many commercial airlines are there in Canada?
   (b) Group them under the following categories: those that serve national needs; those that serve regional needs; those that serve an industry or a group of industries; those that offer specialized services, such as charter flights, rental aircraft, etc.
   (c) Indicate for each category the specific services provided.

4. (a) What role has technology played in aviation? Consider airplane design, navigational aids, passenger comfort, fuel, air-traffic control, airport function.
   (b) In what ways has technology created problems in air transportation?
   (c) What steps have the railways taken in an effort to compete with increasing air travel?
   (d) Project over the next decade any transportation trends you see from your answers to these questions.

5. (a) What was the role of the CPR in the settlement and development of Canada in the nineteenth century?
   (b) How were the main terms of agreement worked out between the federal government and the CPR?
   (c) How do the results of these terms continue to affect the CPR even today?

6. CP Rail is now a publicly-owned company; CN is government owned. Compare the operations of each. What differences in their operations are due to the difference in ownership?

7. Why is there increasing community opposition to the building of expressways? Which community groups tend to favor expressways? How can these conflicts be resolved?

8. Transportation bonds help to link us together in nationhood. Communications bonds are also a unifying force.
   (a) What different media are included under the broad term "communications"?
   (b) Why are there so many different means of communication?
   (c) What are the special functions of each of these different media?
   (d) Which media are most important to you?
   (e) Rank the different means of communication in order of national importance. Give reasons for your order.

9.

Time Period	Transportation	Communication	Reasons for Ranking
1600-1700	1. 2. 3.	1. 2. 3.	
1700-1800	1. 2. 3.	1. 2. 3.	
1800-1900	1. 2. 3.	1. 2. 3.	
1900-	1. 2. 3.	1. 2. 3.	

Make a chart in your notebook similar to the above. Fill in the three most important means of transportation and communication for each time period. In the far right-hand column, give reasons for your choices and for the order of their importance. Write a summary paragraph explaining any changes in the rankings from 1600 to the present.

10. "Canada is a multicultural country." Support this statement with evidence from communications media.

11. What is the role of the federal government in transportation and communication?

THE CANADIAN ECUMEN

Sporadic

Pioneer fringe

Broken

Bloc

0   400   800 km

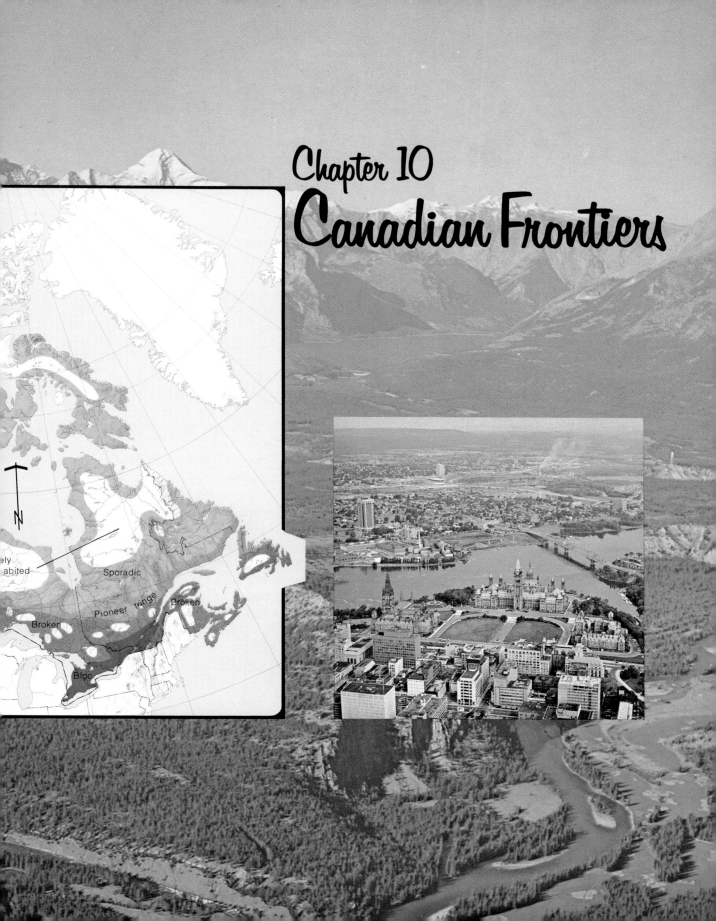

Chapter 10
Canadian Frontiers

It would be fascinating to be able to take today's technology back into the past. If we could launch a camera-equipped satellite into the sky of tens of thousands of years ago and keep the camera rolling to the present, what would it record? How would the face of Canada change through time?

For thousands of years the film would record only the changing physical landscape. Then a slow trickle of tiny dots would appear and move down the edges of the Rocky Mountains. Some dots carry on southward over the Great Plains. Others wander eastward into the belt of forest land that sprawls across Canada from the Atlantic almost to Arctic shores. Still other dots show up at isolated points on the Arctic coast of North America and remain more or less in these same locations. The Indian and Eskimo peoples have discovered North America.

Hundreds of years pass, during which the only signs of human life are further Indian migrations over the face of the continent. Then, in the period 1608-1700 A.D., dots suddenly appear along the south coast of the island of Newfoundland, while others begin to creep along the banks of the St. Lawrence and a couple of its tributaries. Some clusters of dots thicken to form circles. By 1800, there is a rapid movement of dots into Nova Scotia and the Saint John River Valley, and also into the lower Great Lakes region — especially into the peninsula formed by Lakes Ontario and Erie. The westward advance of dots stalls for a while along the edges of the Shield. For the first time lines appear and begin to spread, linking the larger circles and some of the smaller ones.

Far to the west, a cluster of dots shows up around the junction of the Assiniboine and Red rivers. The dots converge, and, in 1882, a line suddenly emerges from the small circle. As this line inches across the prairie, isolated dots appear on either side. The line slowly winds through the Western Cordillera and ultimately joins up with a few isolated dots and a short line that has made its way up the lower valley of the Fraser River. After 1890, other lines spread more rapidly over the prairie, north and south, and east and west.

The settled land thickens with dots and circles. Meanwhile, in some formerly blank areas, dots begin to accumulate in small blocs, in long ribbons, or in isolated clusters.

The last piece of film would clearly show three large, separate blocs of settled land: a southeastern one consisting of the Ontario and Quebec Lowlands; an interior one in southern "Alsama" (Alberta, Saskatchewan, and Manitoba); and a smaller, western bloc in the Fraser delta and the southeastern portion of Vancouver Island. These are the main cores or heartlands of settlement in Canada today.

Study 60

Use an atlas, together with the map on pages 292-293, to answer the following questions.
1. What landforms are characteristic of these three main blocs of settlement?
2. What is a common feature of their location?
3. What advantages do these locations possess over other less settled areas of Canada? (Think in terms of climate, soil, food supply, natural routes, etc.)

The ecumene

If we could enlarge the last frame of this film into a gigantic aerial photograph, we would find a study in contrasts. The pattern of blocs of dots and circles connected by a criss-cross of road and railway lines would stand out from blank areas devoid of settlement and any signs of communication. The ancient Greeks called land strongly stamped with the human imprint the **ecumene.** This is the term geographers use to describe the inhabited or settled parts of the world.

A closer examination of our giant photograph would show a less continuously settled band of territory immediately to the north of and between the three bloc ecumenes. This continent-wide band is a **broken ecumene**: scattered smaller blocs of settlement separated by considerable areas of uninhabited land. Narrow road and rail lines link these settlements with the bloc ecumenes and with the Atlantic and Pacific shorelines. The broken ecumene can be traced along the river valleys and coasts of the Atlantic Provinces and the St. Lawrence estuary, over north-central Ontario, across northern Alsama, and, in British Columbia, in the interior valleys, the plateaus, and parts of the coastline.

The tracts of settled land range from old-established small settlement cores in the Annapolis Valley, to isolated mining centres in the Shield, to widely dispersed ranches on the Fraser plateau. Although much of the broken ecumene is rocky, wooded highlands and uplands, much of its forest and rock is being utilized, and much of its most productive land has been effectively occupied. Further filling in of the blank areas may occur from these small, isolated cores of settlement.

Farther north of the ecumene and broken ecumene lies the vast northland of Canada, dotted by sporadic settlement. Here, in this zone, individual pioneers and ambitious corporations are pushing into a fringe area occupied mainly by Indians and Inuit. Science and technology are changing the land and life style of these first settlers. At present, the situation is a fluid one. The zone is in the process of developing; the dominant use of its lands and waters has not yet been resolved. In this transition period, these groups co-exist — there is an overlapping of settlement types and land uses. Such a zone of change is called a **frontier.**

Frontiers exist in both time and space — in time, because they are a stage in the evolution of societies; in space, because the changes take place in definite locations. In frontier zones, conflicts are almost inevitable until the question of which group is to occupy the land effectively and determine its use is decided; until "what was" has become "what is." At that point in time and in that place, the frontier disappears.

The development of the north has not been planned or co-ordinated as a whole. The direction and rate of northward advance have largely been determined by size of profits. Some of the important factors

When you see a sign like this, you're in a frontier zone. The warning is posted near the southern terminus of the Robert Campbell Highway, a resource road that runs through the southern Yukon Territory from Watson Lake to Carmacks.

Richard Harrington

International Nickel Company of Canada Limited

The thrust of mining in northern Manitoba. In order to develop the vast nickel deposits at what is now Thompson, the "Snowball Express" brought in equipment and supplies 24 hours a day, 7 days a week.

that reduce the profitability of many enterprises are a limited operating season, a difficult terrain, distance from major national and international markets, and the high wages necessary to attract skilled labor to remote areas. However, as this chapter will show, slowly but surely movement goes on, sometimes forward, on occasion backward. Still, in the long run, it will be ever northward. New strains of crops (quick-maturing varieties of grain), new inventions and techniques (the snow-cat and the airborne magnetometer), and decreasing world supplies of food and resources at a time of rapidly growing national and international demands for raw materials help increase the feasibility of such high-cost ventures.

"Go north, young man!"

In the United States, the movement of the frontier westward has been immortalized in many a novel, movie, and television program. "Go west, young man!" was a powerful slogan of the nineteenth century. Thousands pushed into lands occupied by Indians of the Midwest and Great Plains, creating a zone of change. The overlapping of the newcomers' culture and settlement patterns with the Indians' life styles and land uses created a frontier, with inevitable conflicts. Explorers and traders were followed by wave after wave of cattlemen, farmers, and miners. In time, the land was effectively occupied by growing numbers of service and manufacturing centres tied together by a network of communications. The frontier had disappeared.

Today's Canadian frontier movement is essentially a series of different thrusts advancing northward from widely separated cores. In one place there is an agricultural thrust, in another a mining one, in yet another an industrial or a hydro-electric one. Each affects the advance of the others. All of them change the land and its uses.

Scientific research, too, has pushed northward. A federal government laboratory at Igloolik, Northwest Territories.

The frontier movement in the United States created conflicts between original inhabitants and later settlers who wanted to occupy the land and use its resources in a different way. The effects on the environment were not realized until the frontier had disappeared — and with it the large herds of buffalo, the tall stands of virgin timber, the abundant sources of clean water. In the Canadian frontier there are also conflicts between original inhabitants and new arrivals who have different goals and values. And there are also dangers that threaten the physical environment. But our frontier is in another time and another place. The conflicts between overlapping societies are more complex, and the effects of changes on the environment are more dangerous.

Modern technology has produced powerful machines that can drastically affect the extremely fragile ecosystem of the north. Here, land recovery is extremely slow. Bulldozer tracks made in the Arctic twenty-five years ago are still clearly imprinted on the landscape. In fact, effective land recovery may be impossible in higher lati- tudes. Technology poses dangers to the environment because massive machinery can make bigger, faster changes whose effects can therefore be more immediate and far-reaching. But technology has also given us scientific instruments and techniques to study environments more fully and exactly. We know now, for example, that any change in a part of an ecosystem affects the whole system. We must use our increased scientific knowledge of the physical environment in a wise and careful application of technology in the northward advance of the frontier.

Machines alone will not determine the rate of advance, however. Movement in the frontier is two-edged. Industrialized settlement is changing the life style of native peoples, but their reaction to these changes is also affecting the advance of the frontier.

This chapter outlines some of the thrusts in the northward advance of the frontier and indicates the unique challenges presented. These challenges must be faced in order to prevent irreparable harm to the environment and to the way of life of native peoples.

Extract from the Dawson Creek, Peace River Land District, British Columbia, sheet (93/P 16, Edition 2 MCE, Series A721) of the National Topographic System. Scale 1:50,000. Courtesy Surveys and Mapping Branch, Department of Energy, Mines, and Resources, Ottawa.

Study 61

1. Is the land represented on the map flat or gently rolling? Explain your answer.
2. Glacial deposits cover the sedimentary rocks of the district and provide the parent material for rich soils; however, these same deposits have interrupted the drainage pattern. What landform has resulted?
3. Estimate the percentage of land that has been cleared.
4. How far is this area — Dawson Creek — from a major direct east-west rail line? (Use an atlas to answer this question.) How will this affect a farmer's profits?

Grande Prairie, Alberta

	J	F	M	A	M	J	J	A	S	O.	N	D	Annual
Temp.	−14	−14	−7	3	10	13	16	14	10	4	−6	−13	1.3°C
Precip.	3.6	3.6	1.8	2.0	3.8	5.1	6.4	4.1	3.3	2.5	3.0	3.6	42.8 cm

Average date of last spring frost: May 23
Average date of first fall frost: Sept. 4

5. Examine the climate data for Grande Prairie, which is just east of the map area shown. What is the average length of the frost-free period? Why are *averages* not very useful to a farmer?
6. Spring wheat requires ninety frost-free days. If you were a farmer in this area, what would you do after a two-year period of (a) high prices for wheat, (b) low prices for wheat but high prices for beef? Be specific and state the steps you would have to take and the time it would take to make any changes.
7. There are still large areas of land available for settlement in the Peace River district. For what reasons might you hesitate to move to the area shown on the map?
8. Assume you are a member of the Dawson Creek Chamber of Commerce. Prepare a full-page advertisement to attract pioneer farmers to this region. Include in your advertisement the local services that are available to the farmer and his family.

The thrust of agriculture

The Indians in Canada's northern frontier were — and many still are — a hunting, fishing, and food-gathering people. They lived off the land; they did not work it. They hunted wildlife, fished streams and lakes, and gathered the fruits of plants. When the agricultural thrust pushed northward, there was an overlapping of settlement types and land uses, and a frontier was created. The amount of cultivable land in these northern latitudes is relatively small, so that farming activities do not seriously threaten the Indians' way of life. So far, the agricultural and hunting societies co-exist in this frontier, and there is little conflict between pioneer farmers and Indians.

What changes in the agricultural thrust might increase the possibility of conflicts?

In 1947 a World War II army veteran received a homestead lease on 130 hectares of land near Grande Prairie, Alberta. His first task was to clear land. He rented a caterpillar diesel equipped with a V-shaped cutter at the front, which removed all but the largest trees on a 16-hectare lot. The remainder he felled with a chain saw. He then rented a bulldozer and heavy-duty plough to break the sod, after which he disced and harrowed the land a number of times in order to break up roots. By machine and by hand he gathered up root clumps and removed stones. The soil was ready for sowing. In this way, bit by bit, year by year, the pioneer farmer cleared land until, after ten years, his entire holding (except for a few small woodlots) was farmland.

The virgin soils of this area, developed over thick glacial deposits, are unusually fertile, and precipitation is adequate for most temperate-climate crops. However, the limited frost-free period restricts choice of operations. Consequently, like most farmers in the district, he had specialized in quick-maturing small grains. He sowed Garnet and Reward, two of the new varieties of spring wheat that require less than ninety frost-free days. (This district is known for its prize-winning wheat, which is shipped out by rail to national and international markets.) He also sowed some barley, which matures even more quickly.

Some of his neighbors raise beef and grow alfalfa, oats, and hay for cattle feed. Others practise **mixed farming**, raising some animals and producing some crops for cash. The growth of the oil and gas industry in the area has provided farmers with an expanding local market.

The thrust of agriculture in the frontier of the Peace River district advanced with the completion of the Great Slave Lake

Alberta Government Photographic Services, Bureau of Public Affairs

The focus of agricultural settlement in the Peace River country is the "islands" of black soils around the junction of the Peace and Smoky rivers. These islands are hemmed in by the grey soils of the boreal forest.

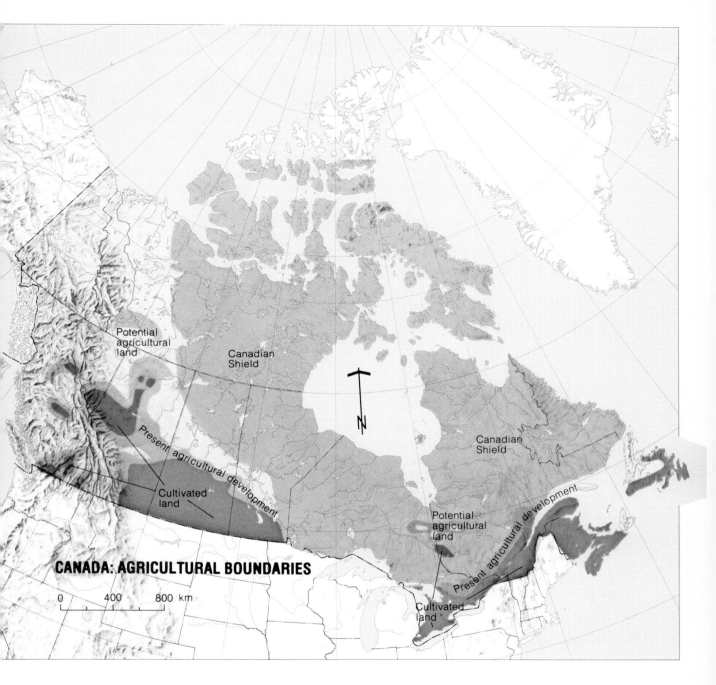

CANADA: AGRICULTURAL BOUNDARIES

Potential agricultural land

Canadian Shield

Present agricultural development

Cultivated land

Canadian Shield

Potential agricultural land

Present agricultural development

Cultivated land

0   400   800 km

Railway in the 1960s. Built to carry lead and zinc ores out of the Northwest Territories, this line also served to bring in materials for the construction of the most northerly grain elevators on the continent, at High Level, Alberta.

Outside of the Peace River district, the most active agricultural thrust is in the Great Clay Belt of Ontario and Quebec. Here, in the heart of the Canadian Shield, the bed of a long-vanished glacial lake offers an extensive area of deep silt deposits, on which fertile soils have developed. The discovery of mineral deposits all around the Belt and the consequent development of road and rail systems have helped pioneer farmers sell to such nearby markets as Rouyn, Timmins, and Kirkland Lake. Their products, for example, milk, eggs, pork, and potatoes, compete successfully in the local market with the same items produced in the south. However, farmers have difficulty selling outside the region. Long winters, which increase production costs, and distance from major markets make it difficult for them to compete with the much more productive and better located agricultural areas in the Lowlands. Thus, in the Ontario portion of the Belt, some farmers have left the frontier for higher-paying, more secure jobs in cities.

In these places, the wilderness has taken over again, and the frontier is retreating. In the Quebec portion, on the other hand, the frontier is still advancing, partly because the provincial government has assisted settlers by a system of grants.

If demand for world food supplies continues to increase and prices continue their upward trend, further advances can be expected in the Peace River district and perhaps also in the Clay Belt. The Canada Land Inventory has estimated that the entire country has 16 000 000 hectares of virgin land available for arable crops, and another 22-24 000 000 for wild pasture.

Study 62

1. Why has the agricultural thrust not advanced as far north in the Canadian Shield as in the Peace River district? Use relevant factors of climate, topography, soils, and markets in your explanation.
2. List with examples the factors that have led to agricultural thrusts in
   (a) the Peace River district
   (b) the Great Clay Belt.
3. Why is distance from major markets a greater disadvantage in the Clay Belt than in the Peace River district? Give at least three reasons.

The thrust of industry

Modern technology and increasing demand for metals, fuels, and hydro-electric power have advanced industrial development in the north. The Inco mine at Thompson, Manitoba, is an example of an industrial thrust in the Canadian frontier.

Minerals are a **non-renewable resource.** The International Nickel Company of Canada (Inco) knew that its nickel mines at Sudbury would not last forever. Even before World War II, industry's ever-growing

demand for nickel as a steel-hardening metal spurred Inco to start searching for new ore bodies. The wilderness of northern Manitoba made exploration on the ground too difficult and hazardous. Inco geologists explored the vast areas of forest and muskeg by plane, using airborne magnetometers. In 1955, they made their strike: 640 air kilometres north of Winnipeg and 420 air kilometres south-west of Churchill.

But discovery does not necessarily lead

International Nickel Company of Canada Limited

The bomb-shaped magnetometer trailing below the aircraft records variations in the earth's magnetic field that might be caused by ore bodies. This was how the Thompson nickel deposits were discovered.

to exploitation. How rich was the deposit? Extensive diamond-drilling established the size and high mineral content of the ore body. What would the transportation costs be? There were no roads, no trails. The nearest point on CN's Hudson Bay Railway was 60 kilometres away, at Sipiwesk. So was the mining operation feasible? In December, 1955, Inco decided to go ahead with development.

Every single piece of equipment, from nails to bulldozers, was brought in over the frozen ground by tractor trains. The "Snowball Express" ran twenty-four hours a day, seven days a week, until the railway spur from Sipiwesk to the new mining development was completed in October, 1957. Then men and materials began to pour in.

Inco had to build more than a mine; it had to create a fully serviced town as well, to fulfil the terms of agreement worked out

In 1955, all this was forest and muskeg. By 1970, Thompson had achieved the status of a city.

with the Government of Manitoba. This was to be no ramshackle shanty town; it was to be a planned community that would serve the needs of workers and their families. The new town was named Thompson in honor of Dr. J. F. Thompson, Chairman of the Board of International Nickel.

Commercial production of nickel began in 1961. Not only is the ore mined and the nickel concentrate extracted and smelted at the Thompson mine, but it is also refined there instead of being sent to the company's Port Colborne refinery. The finished product is shipped directly from Thompson to markets all over the world.

Along the transportation lines that are cutting through wilderness to develop the resources of the north, other industrial thrusts are advancing into the frontier, especially pulp-and-paper. Kapuskasing, Iroquois Falls, and Smooth Rock Falls, Ontario, are typical of a new generation of forest-industry towns. Formerly such centres hugged the *eastward-* and *southward-flowing* waterways of the Laurentide Scarp, the Great Lakes, and the Maritimes. These newer centres, like many recent mining centres, are taking advantage of the untapped hydro-electric potential of the *northward-flowing* rivers of the Shield.

Study 63

Frontier Towns in Canada

Atikokan, Ontario	Lynn Lake, Manitoba
Chapais, Quebec	Manitouwadge, Ontario
Chibougamau, Quebec	Marathon, Ontario
Devon, Alberta	Matagami, Quebec
Elliot Lake, Ontario	Murdochville, Quebec
Gagnon, Quebec	Pine Point, N.W.T.
Hay River, N.W.T.	Redwater, Alberta
Hinton, Alberta	Schefferville, Quebec
Iroquois Falls, Ontario	Sept-Iles, Quebec
Kapuskasing, Ontario	Smooth Rock Falls, Ontario
Kemano, British Columbia	Snow Lake, Manitoba
Kitimat, British Columbia	Terrace Bay, Ontario
Labrador City, Quebec	Thompson, Manitoba
La Ronge, Saskatchewan	Uranium City, Saskatchewan
Lively, Ontario	Wawa, Ontario

Refer to the appropriate maps in *The National Atlas of Canada* to answer the following questions on frontier settlements.
1. Why are these centres called "frontier towns"?
2. Draw a map of Canada, marking on it:
   (a) the major bodies of water
   (b) the provincial boundaries
   (c) the frontier towns in the above list.

3. Using red circles for metallic minerals, green ones for fossil fuels, yellow ones for pulp and paper, and blue ones for hydro-electric power, indicate beside each town the major industry or basis for the town.
4. Draw a line to connect the southernmost settlements and another line to connect the northernmost. Compare your map with that of the ecumene on pages 292-293. What area in that map corresponds with the area bounded by the lines you have drawn on your map? What name is given to this east-west corridor in which these mining and industrial thrusts are taking place?
5. From everything you have learned about the industries marked on your map, what similarities are there in the location and development of these towns? What further information would you mark on your map?

Frontier conflicts

In August, 1969, a conference was held to consider the planned development of what was called the "Mid-Canada Corridor." From the various proposals presented, it was clear that there were two opposing points of view: those who wished to develop the corridor rapidly, and those who claimed that extensive development would seriously threaten the fragile Arctic environment and the way of life of the native people who depend upon it for their existence. The Mid-Canada Corridor remains a zone of controversy; conflicts arising from the settlement of the frontier, the use of its land and resources, are still not resolved.

* * *

Each spring, the land of northern Quebec and Ontario shakes off the icy grasp of winter. The meltwater of snow mingles with that of thawing ice in the rivers leading to James Bay. Raging torrents of water thunder to the sea. Trees put out new leaves, flowers bloom, insects buzz, birds arrive in their hundreds of thousands from the south, fish spawn in the oxygen-rich waters, and animals give birth to their young. The brief warmth of summer is soon replaced by the chill of autumn and, with the onset of winter again, the annual cycle is complete.

In this harsh land Cree and Ojibway Indians make their home. They live off the natural bounty of the land (sometimes plentiful, sometimes poor) — hunting, trapping, fishing. Their life is in tune with the cycle of nature and the rhythm of the seasons. How will this way of life be affected when the machines of industry — which are geared to a different rhythm — come to these lakes and rivers for new sources of energy to keep the wheels turning?

The machines of the bustling cities to the south consume energy in ever-increasing quantities. As existing supplies of energy are tapped, plans are made to find and develop others. Most of the best southern locations for hydro-electric power have already been developed, or are earmarked for development. Still the need for energy increases. Thus the search for new sources in the north has intensified. These same rivers that now plunge through the Shield on their way to James Bay have all the attributes necessary for hydro-electric development — a *reliable flow* of water, a

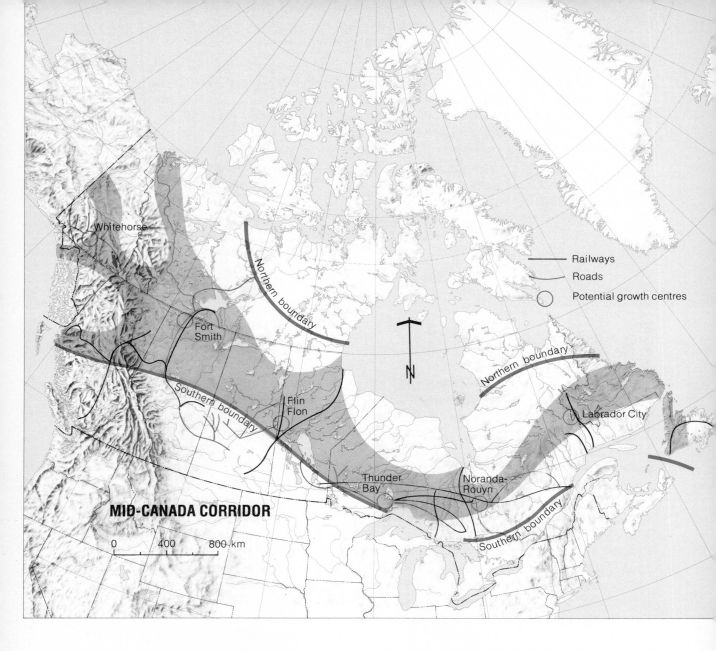

Railways

Roads

Potential growth centres

MID-CANADA CORRIDOR

0   400   800 km

large volume of water, *falling* water, and a *valley* location. As an example, even the Broadback, a relatively small river, is 480 kilometres long, drains 22 000 square kilometres, drops 210 metres in its final 120 kilometres, and flows at a rate of from 70 to 850 cubic metres per second.

There is another important consideration. Many Shield rivers flowing into James Bay are within effective hydroelectric transmission range of Montreal.

The Nottaway, Broadback, Rupert, Eastmain, and La Grande rivers drain one-quarter of the Province of Quebec. Harnessing their energy will provide millions of kilowatts of electricity. But hydro-electric development has other, less desirable, results, as has been shown elsewhere in Canada. Far to the west, for instance, British Columbia's giant W. A. C. Bennett Dam supplies power to the mills and factories of the province's northern interior.

On Eldorado Creek near Dawson, Yukon Territory, hydraulic dredges extracted gold from the creek bed, leaving behind this ugly devastation of windrows. Nature, in the form of willows and alders, is beginning to cover over the man-made scars.

The dam also regulates the flow of the Peace River and prevents the annual spring flooding of its delta, 1100 kilometres downstream at the western end of Lake Athabasca. As a result the waterfowl habitat has been severely reduced, the muskrat population has declined, and commercial fishing is collapsing as the shallower waters of the delta now freeze to the bottom. Since the delta is on one of the great North American flyways, bird migration patterns may well be affected. As a consequence, the basic food supply, main source of income, and whole way of life of several hundred Indians are being threatened.

Cree and Ojibway Indians in northern Ontario and Quebec fear the same fate will be theirs. They recognize only too clearly that water, vegetation, and animal life are all closely interlinked with their own way of life. To sever one strand in the weaving

of these threads will disrupt the whole pattern. These hunters and trappers want their old pattern preserved — and yet the energy demands of pulp-and-paper mills and metal smelters and refineries keep rising. Hydro-electric power is an important thread in the pattern of industrial development. Here is a clear-cut set of frontier conflicts arising from overlapping patterns of land-use needs.

Actually, a frontier zone cannot be divided by so simple a line of conflicting needs and interests. Not all native peoples of northern Canada are opposed to the changes taking place. Many Indians recognize that old hunting and fishing ways are disappearing, but they have not yet decided what things to take from a technological culture and how to adapt these for their own use. They want to stay on their land and make the reserves commercially productive — but they also want to keep the values of their own society. Other Indians want to be educated for employment outside the reserve — but they want to be instructed near their homes and families. In either instance, native peoples want the freedom to choose and work out their life style. Still other Indians are struggling for a broader policy resolution of frontier conflicts. Rather than fight for specific claims — as in the case of the multi-million-dollar agreement between the Province of Quebec and James Bay Indians — they want a general political settlement of all aboriginal and treaty rights in terms of land, money, development programs, etc.

So the frontier has created conflicts not only between the needs of original inhabitants and those of new settlers, but among the Indians themselves. These are just a few of the human problems in the northward advance of the frontier.

Environmentalists point out another set of problems associated with vast hydro-electric developments. They claim that the tremendous reduction in spring flow could delay the break-up of ice in Hudson Bay and thus make the climate of Quebec and Ontario colder and wetter — perhaps eventually speeding up the advance of another ice age. More immediately, the effects on sea life are unknown.

And yet those energy demands of industry keep rising. Although hydro-electric plants are expensive to construct, their operating costs are low. Since other forms of energy are rapidly rising in price, the use of cheap hydro-electric power could help maintain the competitive position many of Canada's manufactured goods have in world markets.

Industrial needs for the immediate future and environmental concerns about possible long-term effects represent a conflict typical of the Canadian frontier.

In the Yukon community of Old Crow, a Loucheaux Indian mother shows her daughter how to operate a gas-powered washing machine. Hung out to dry are muskrat pelts (the main source of income) and caribou skins. Oil exploration at nearby Old Crow Flats is disturbing water levels and, therefore, muskrat nests and breeding conditions.

HYDRO-ELECTRIC GENERATING CAPACITY IN CANADA, 1950-71

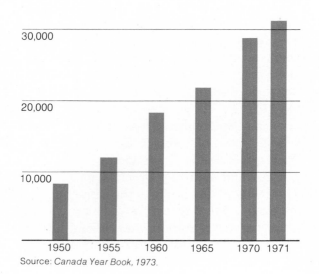

Source: *Canada Year Book, 1973.*

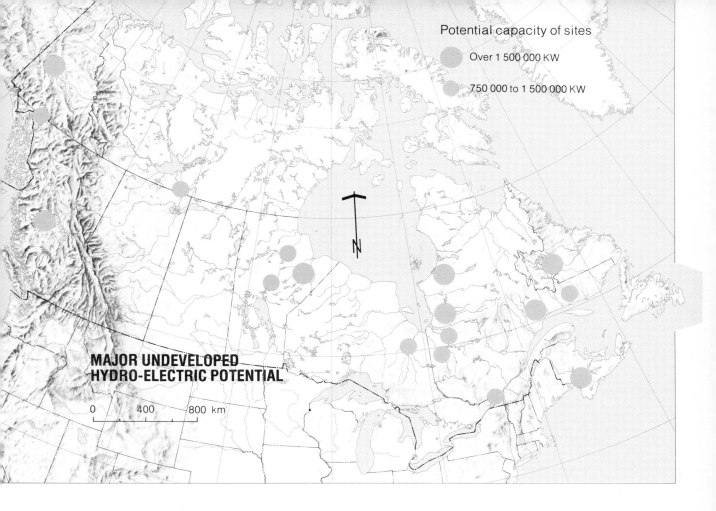

Potential capacity of sites

Over 1 500 000 KW

750 000 to 1 500 000 KW

**MAJOR UNDEVELOPED
HYDRO-ELECTRIC POTENTIAL**

0   400   800 km

Study 64

1. Locate the Nottaway, Broadback, Eastmain. and La Grande rivers.
2. Refer to the map on the opening pages of Chapter 3. Compare and account for provincial hydro- and thermal-electric capacity.
3. Where in the provinces would demands be greatest? Why?
4. Using *Canada Year Book* statistics, calculate the percentage increase in the electric energy consumption in Canada between 1950 and 1971. Assuming the same rate of increase, what will Canada's needs be in the year 2000?
5. Compare the map you drew for question 3, Study 14, with the map of Major Undeveloped Hydro Potential above. Explain any differences between the two maps.

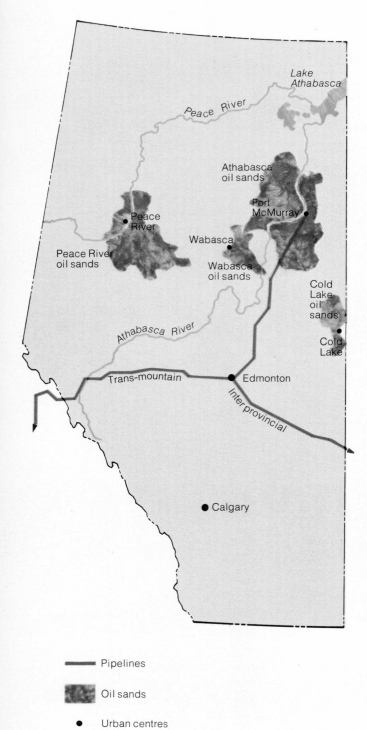

Pipelines

Oil sands

● Urban centres

**LOCATION OF ALBERTA
OIL SANDS DEPOSITS**

Hydro-electric development is closely linked with the northward thrust of the mining and forest industries. Like hydro-electric development, these are also creating frontier conflicts. The pulp-and-paper industry, for example, has used up the choice locations of the Laurentide scarp — those near southern markets and ports, close to large supplies of water and ample power, and next the enormous timber supply of the Shield. More recently, mills have been established along road and rail routes in the Shield, especially in the Great Clay Belt. Here, they have been able to utilize the northward-flowing rivers for power and water. But this industrial advance in the frontier has caused considerable concern about the pollution produced by many pulp-and-paper mills. One effect of the pollution has been a dangerously high level of mercury in fish, the staple food of local Indians. Once again, there is conflict.

How can these frontier conflicts best be resolved? How can the cultural needs of one group of people be reconciled with the high-energy needs of another group? Must the physical environment be sacrificed to maintain a standard of living based on spiralling economic growth? Indeed, how long can this standard of living be maintained if the physical environment is damaged? What role will government, native peoples, industry, and environmental groups play in the resolution of these frontier conflicts?

The thrust of oil exploration is yet another example of conflicts arising from the advance of the frontier.

For hundreds of square kilometres around Fort McMurray, Alberta, lie great strata of sedimentary rock consisting of black, sulphurous-smelling dirt — the famed Athabasca tar sands. These molasses-like sands are said to hold about 45 billion kilolitres of crude petroleum.

The existence of oil in the tar-soaked sands had been known since the eighteenth century, but nothing was done to exploit the oil. Coal was the common source of energy to power the machines of the Industrial Revolution, drive the engines of ships and locomotives, and heat factories and homes. In the 1920s, Dr. Karl Adolf Clark of the Alberta Research Council developed a method of extracting the oil from the sands by a steam-cooking process. Still nothing was done to exploit the deposits. Although oil was becoming more important as a source of energy, world supplies were more than sufficient to meet demands. Development of the tar sands was not a feasible proposition. Production costs and the low percentage of crude recovered from the sands would make this oil far too expensive. Much cheaper supplies were available elsewhere in Canada and the world.

In the late 1960s the Athabasca tar sands suddenly became very important. The tiny frontier settlement of Fort McMurray was transformed into a bustling boom town that boasted the third-busiest airport in Alberta. Giant trucks rumbled over the frozen muskeg carrying away 140-tonne loads of materials that had been stripped off the surface to expose the sands beneath. A monstrous digging machine clawed up 4500 tonnes of tar sands an hour and loaded them onto a conveyor belt leading to a refinery.

What had happened to produce this dramatic change? Oil had become the common source of energy for the machines of mass production, the engines of modern transportation, and the furnaces of factories, skyscrapers, and homes. Petroleum by-products had created a whole new industry — petrochemicals — which produce chemicals, fertilizers, detergents, and a whole range of synthetics, including plastic, rubber, nylon, etc. Without oil, twentieth-century technology would grind to a halt, resulting in an economic strangulation of industrialized societies.

Let's look at the oil-supply situation to understand the significance of the tar sands.

The world's known reserves are estimated at 100 billion kilolitres; Canada's known reserves from proven oil fields are estimated at 1.4 billion kilolitres. The tar sands of northeastern Alberta — including those of Athabasca — are estimated to contain 135 billion kilolitres. With increasing demand for oil to keep wheels and machines moving, known world supplies are rapidly being used up. These two factors have influenced the feasibility of developing the tar sands. As the technology of extraction improves, the percentage of oil recovered from the tar sands should increase, production costs should be lowered, and further development should become even more feasible.

However, the oil thrust, like other mining thrusts in the frontier, has created social and ecological conflicts. What are the rights of native peoples in this area? How will extensive development of the tar sands and increased settlement in the area affect their life style? What are the effects on the physical environment of oil mining? How will they affect both the Indians' use of land and water and the plant and animal ecosystems of the region?

Strip mining of surface and near-surface deposits poses few problems in land replacement and restoration and creates little impact on the environment. But two-thirds of the 135 billion kilolitres of oil lie buried in sands 460 metres below the surface. What happens to the environment with technological advances that may make possible the excavation of millions of tonnes of tar sands from the earth? Will erosion of the land be hastened with removal of the vegetation? Will silt and soil wash down into rivers and affect fishing downstream? Can a disrupted landscape of about 78 000 square kilometres ever be completely restored?

Elsewhere in the frontier, oil exploration has advanced as far north as the delta of

Imagine a gigantic sandbox into which several buckets of oil have been emptied and then stirred into a gooey mess: that's what tar sands look like. So the best time to excavate is in the depths of winter, when heavy machinery doesn't bog down and its moving parts don't quickly become clogged.

the Mackenzie River and the shallow continental shelf off Arctic coasts. Deposits of oil (and gas) have been discovered, and if they are exploited, transportation methods may endanger the fragile environment of the north. If an underground pipeline is built down the Mackenzie Valley, the oil (heated to 82°C in order to flow through the pipe) might melt the permafrost, causing the line to buckle and break. If a pipeline is built above ground, it is more exposed to external damage, with the same danger of oil spillage. The effects of millions of litres of oil seeping into the tundra, with its long and slow recovery period, might never be repaired. If no pipeline is built, oil will have to be shipped out through the Arctic Ocean, with the danger of oil spills in the equally fragile environment of the ocean.

Technology made possible the advance of the oil thrust in this frontier. However, it is not technology alone that will decide the future development of this thrust. Federal and provincial governments, world prices for oil, and capital investment will all have a role to play in the advance or retreat of the frontier. The outcome is still unknown, for this is a frontier, a zone of change.

Surface extraction using strip-mining techniques is relatively easy. But the technology needed to get at the 90 per cent of petroleum-soaked sands deep underground has yet to be developed.

Canada's external frontier

The discovery of Arctic oil and gas deposits under the continental shelf has created a new type of frontier with more complex conflicts. In this external frontier, conflicts over territorial rights and claims of ownership — provincial, federal, and international — are still unresolved.

In September 1969, a black monster of a ship, the *S.S. Manhattan*, tried to force a way through the Arctic ice of the Northwest Passage to find out whether a sea route could be established to the Prudhoe Bay oil deposits on the north shore of Alaska. Churning its way through Davis Strait, the *Manhattan* hoped to clear McClure Strait and thus stay outside the 5-kilometre territorial limit of Canadian waters. But in McClure Strait the supertanker stuck fast in an ice floe 8 kilometres across. A watchdog ship, the Canadian icebreaker *John A. Macdonald*, had to come to the rescue and free the giant from its icy prison. The *Manhattan* continued on to Prudhoe Bay via the alternative but easier route past Banks Island and down Prince of Wales Strait.

The Canadian government immediately realized that this extension of the frontier presented conflicts — ecological, social, and political. Since oil does not decompose in frigid climates, a spill from a damaged tanker could seriously threaten the marine ecosystem, from plankton to whales. The way of life in coastal Eskimo settlements would be endangered. So Ottawa decided to extend Canadian territorial waters to a *20-kilometre* limit (which would take in McClure Strait). Canada further claimed the right to confiscate or fine ships and seize the cargo of vessels polluting waters within 160 kilometres of the Arctic archipelago. All these claims demonstrate Canada's concern about the fragile Arctic environment and the people dependent on it.

This extension of the external frontier has not gone unchallenged, nor is it restricted to the Arctic. Mineral deposits have also been discovered under the continental shelf off Canada's eastern and western shores. In places, this shelf extends at least 160 kilometres out to sea before dropping steeply to the ocean floor. The question of ownership of continental shelves is still undecided, and so this remains an external frontier zone. The United Nations Geneva Conference on the Law of the Sea in 1958 specified that a coastal nation has the right to exploit the resources of the continental shelf adjacent to its coast to a depth of 200 metres – and to a greater depth if exploitation proves feasible. In addition, the same conference adopted a base-line system by which the territorial waters of a country extend seaward from a series of long straight lines following the general shape of the coast and connecting

When the world's first ice-breaking tanker reached Point Barrow, Alaska, on September 20, 1969, it became the first commercial vessel to navigate the Northwest Passage. Despite a displacement of 155 448 tonnes and 32 000 kW engines, the Manhattan was only able to sail the Passage in the summer months.

Charles Swithinbank

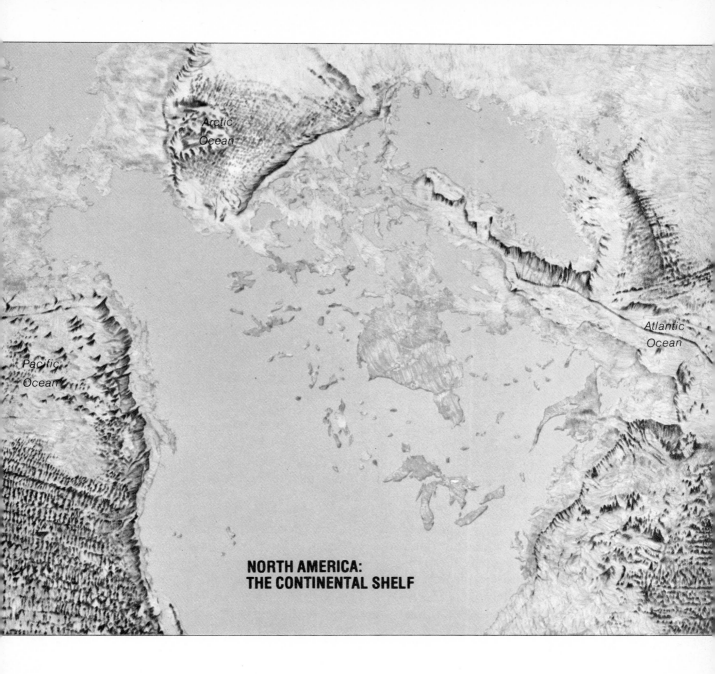

**NORTH AMERICA:
THE CONTINENTAL SHELF**

Arctic
Ocean

Pacific
Ocean

Atlantic
Ocean

protruding points on the mainland with offshore islands and rocks. These specifications have not been accepted by all UN members, but they are a start toward an internationally accepted definition.

*   *   *

In our handling of internal and external frontiers, Canadians have a rich opportunity to demonstrate responsible attitudes toward one another, toward the rest of the world, and toward the environment, on which everyone depends. Success in this aim can be, for each of us, our contribution to history.

Study and Research

1. Research the development in Canada of (a) reindeer herding and (b) musk-ox raising. Assess the different employment possibilities these offer to northern peoples.

2. What other employment opportunities are there for native peoples living in a frontier zone? Research such possibilities as:
   (a) native crafts
   (b) fishing co-operatives
   (c) mining and industry
   (d) government employment
   (e) hunting, trapping, and guiding enterprises.

3. What scientific and technological advances have made possible the development of the Canadian north?

4. From the material you have collected for Question 2 on page 78, write a report on how the reaction of native peoples has affected the type, rate, degree, and extent of changes in the frontier.

5. Compare Canada's northern frontier with the western frontier in the United States. What evidence is there that resolution of conflicts in today's frontier, compared with that of the United States in the nineteenth century, is more complex because more factors are being taken into account?

6. Write a report on the rise and decline of Dawson City, Yukon, with reference to the definition of frontier as outlined in this chapter. Is Dawson City still in the frontier? Was it ever in the frontier?

7. Can frontiers be compared or is each frontier a unique phenomenon? Debate this question.

8. For this chapter, and for each of the preceding nine chapters, make a list of the most important points (at least three per chapter). From this information, write a projection of future frontier development in Canada in the next quarter century.

9. The Arctic environment is often described as "fragile." What does this mean? Research the delicate balance of the Arctic environment with reference to plant and animal life, soil, water, and climatic conditions.

10. "Economic survival of the industrialized ecumene must override possible destructon of the physical environment of the northern frontier." Discuss.
11. What is the role of governments in the frontier?
12. Research and report on a non-North American frontier experience. The USSR experience, because of similarities of climate, terrain, latitude, resources, and technologies with those of the Canadian frontier, should provide interesting comparisons. In your report include:
    (a) development of resources
    (b) conflicts between cultures — political, social, linguistic
    (c) communication and transportation
    (d) development of settlements
    (e) role of government
    (f) role of research and technology.
13. Since this chapter defines "frontier" as a zone of change, which is in the process of evolving, perhaps the definition should also be a fluid one.
    Assess the validity of the definition of frontier in this chapter by
    (a) listing five or six examples in time and space, within and outside North America, that are completely explained by the definition;
    (b) finding five or six examples that do not seem to fit exactly within the definition;
    (c) re-examining the definition and modifying it to account for any "exceptions."
14. How does each of the following fit the definition of frontier?
    (a) the Roman Conquest of Britain
    (b) the New World (do not forget Latin America)
    (c) the British Empire
    (d) the Province of Quebec
    (e) Vietnam, from 1850 to 1970
    (f) Brazil, from 1960 to the present
    (g) the Third World
    Which of the above are still frontiers? For those that no longer are, at what point in time did the frontier disappear?

Chapter II
A land of change:
Resources and resourcefulness

The Canadian ecumene stretches for some 6500 kilometres across the continent. But there are only a few places where the *effectively occupied* part of Canada extends more than about 200 kilometres north of the international boundary. Is it any wonder that Canada is often described as "a country in defiance of geography"? Is it surprising that distinct regional identities have developed? These are the "five Canadas" — British Columbia, the Prairies, Ontario, Quebec, and the Atlantic Provinces. (With the development of the north, yet another identity is coming into being.)

Regionalism: A basic fact of Canadian life

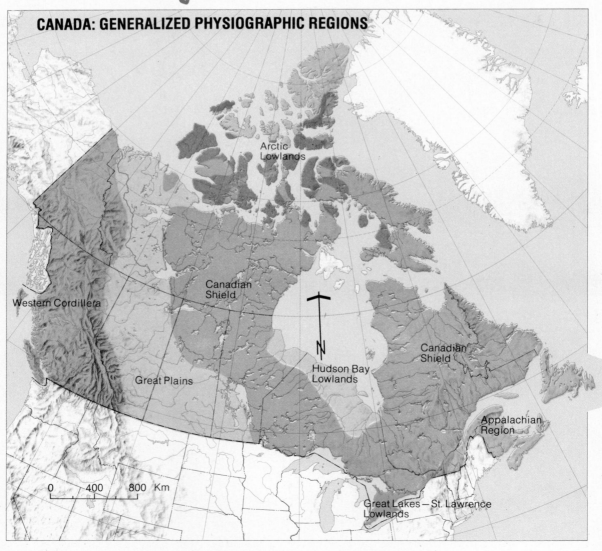

CANADA: GENERALIZED PHYSIOGRAPHIC REGIONS

Arctic Lowlands

Western Cordillera

Canadian Shield

Canadian Shield

Great Plains

Hudson Bay Lowlands

Appalachian Region

0   400   800 Km

Great Lakes — St. Lawrence Lowlands

Where you grow up or live in Canada often decides the kind of life you will lead. A girl born in Prince Edward Island can expect to live for 69.9 years, a boy born in the Northwest Territories, for only 25.2 years. Students in British Columbia or Alberta can expect to have twice as much money spent on their education as is spent on that of students in most other parts of the country. A Canadian who lives in the Atlantic Provinces, Quebec, or British Columbia is twice as likely to be unemployed as a resident of Ontario.

Regional disparity is most graphically expressed in economic terms. Only two provinces — Ontario and British Columbia — record incomes above the Canadian average. At the other end of the scale, at least one-third of the population in the Atlantic Provinces lives below what has been called the "poverty line."* (Wealthy provinces also have disadvantaged areas. In fact, Ontario has 13 per cent of its population living below this line.) Furthermore, in

*Defined by the Economic Council of Canada as "when people have insufficient access to certain goods, services, and conditions of life which are available to everyone else and have come to be accepted as basic to a decent, minimum standard of living."

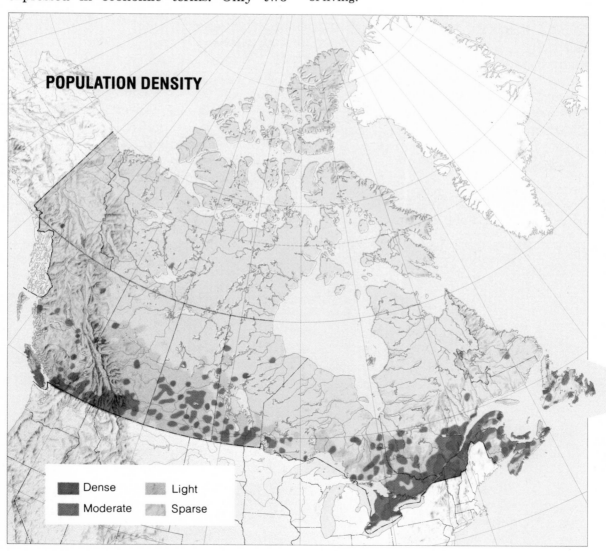

POPULATION DENSITY

Dense   Light
Moderate Sparse

low-income provinces many costs are as high as or even higher than those in wealthier ones. In the eastern and western provinces, the price of manufactured goods is higher than in central Canada because of added transportation costs. It would probably be cheaper for the Atlantic Provinces to import manufactured goods from New England, or for western Canada to buy from Japan. However, the entry of foreign goods is discouraged by tariffs designed to protect Canadian industry. And in sparsely settled, low-income regions, taxes are generally higher: there are fewer people, thus less money, to support essential services. Small wonder that Canadian leaders consider regional disparity to be one of the nation's more pressing problems.

Personal Income *per capita** by Province as Percentage of Canadian Average, 1970	
Canada	100
Ontario	116
British Columbia	107
Alberta	100
Manitoba	98
Quebec	90
Saskatchewan	86
Nova Scotia	79
New Brunswick	72
Prince Edward Island	62
Newfoundland	55

*for every man, woman, and child

Wages and Salaries, by Industry, 1971	
	$'000,000
Agriculture	383
Forestry	519
Mining	1,234
Manufacturing	12,641
Construction	3,910
Transportation, Communication and other Utilities	5,336
Trade	6,566
Finance, Insurance, and Real Estate	2,589
Service	11,477
Public Administration and Defence	3,908
Total Wages and Salaries[1]	48,615

[1]includes fishing and trapping

Study 65

1. Take a look at the maps on pages 320 and 321. How justified is the description of Canada as "a country in defiance of geography"?
2. For each of the "five Canadas" find out:
   (a) when the first European settlers arrived,
   (b) where they came from,
   (c) what kind of society and economy they developed.
   Explain how all these facts influence the outlook of these regions today.
3. According to the statistics above, in how many provinces is the personal income per capita below the Canadian average of 100?
4. Relate your knowledge of the nature and distribution of Canadian industry (Unit II) to the two tables above. What explanation can you give for the differences among the provinces in per capita income?

Regional disparity can be partly explained by differences in incomes by industry. The industries of any region are strongly influenced by its natural resources. In Canada, such natural resources as good farmland, timber reserves, valuable minerals, and supplies of energy are very unevenly distributed. Similarly, transportation facilities — an especially important factor in such a large country — are necessarily unequal. Some provinces lack access to ocean shipping; some regions have particularly difficult terrain; others, sparsely inhabited, are far removed from major markets. There are even disparities in climate, which compel some Canadians to spend more money on such items as fuel, clothing, snow removal, and irrigation equipment.

Obviously, regions that have a lot of valuable raw materials are at an advantage. So are those with large population centres, which provide both a labor force and major markets. Thus industry is naturally attracted to the Great Lakes-St. Lawrence Lowlands. Once such potential for growth is developed, a trend sets in and gathers momentum. Industry and individuals alike are drawn to the place where the action is. In order to attract industries to areas that are less well-favored, governments offer tax benefits and subsidies. Yet, how much money can taxpayers be expected to pay in order to subsidize the development of industry in depressed areas?

The nature of the industry plays a part, too. Take, for example, such secondary industries as the manufacture of furniture, electrical appliances, and plastic products. The costs necessary to turn raw materials into finished products are described as **value added.** The value added to all these goods at various stages of production is much higher than is the case in primary and partial-processing industries. The significance of secondary industry to a region's economy is that the value is added

locally. Thus local jobs are provided in all of the stages of production, and the workers' incomes give them money with which to buy goods and services (providing more local jobs and therefore attracting more workers). Furthermore, the finished goods that are produced can be sold locally (which reduces the amount of goods that need to be imported) and also exported (which brings money back into the region). In contrast, primary industries not only have a lower value added, but they are also far more subject to seasonal fluctuations and changing international demand. Thus jobs in these particular industries are generally less secure and less well-paid. In provinces that depend heavily on primary production, there is often severe unemployment, and personal incomes vary greatly from year to year, or even from month to month. Quebec, although physically similar to Ontario, depends more heavily on primary production, and its unemployment rate is historically 50-100 per cent above that in Ontario.

If you look at regional disparity from the viewpoint of transportation, the story is still dismal. The federal government has invested enormous sums in improving transportation to assist all regions to share in an expanded economy. Freight rates for certain goods have been lowered in the Prairie and Atlantic provinces; a grain port has been built at Churchill; pipelines have been laid; the Trans-Canada Highway has been built. But there has been no substantial improvement in the relative position of the regions thus subsidized. Prosperous regions seem to have benefited far more than slow-growth ones. A good example is the Intercolonial Railway. When it was built in 1876, it was thought that this line would give Atlantic products access to markets in central Canada. What actually happened, however, was that manufactured goods from central Canada found markets in the Atlantic region, thus

Victor C. Last

The oil refinery at Come By Chance, Placentia Bay, Newfoundland. This is one example of recent industrialization in the Atlantic Provinces that will help strengthen the economy of the region.

curbing, and in some cases even destroying, the growth of local industries. Furthermore, central Canada did not send its exports out via the ice-free ports of the Maritimes as had been hoped; freight rates on U.S. railroads were cheaper. So the rich got richer, and the poor got poorer.

Industries that are sensitive to price fluctuations — farming, mining, forestry, and fishing — are supported during lean periods by government subsidies. People living in areas that depend on these industries are thus helped to survive. But it often seems as if such subsidies merely prolong the agony of a doomed industry. A case in point is that of Nova Scotia's coal mines. Towns such as Glace Bay on Cape Breton Island desperately need new industries to replace mining. Ottawa tries to assist development in such slow-growth regions by providing incentives in the form of tax write-offs and tax-deductible costs. Yet new industries are not easily attracted to the Maritimes. How many businesses want to invest money in an area long plagued by economic problems?

Countless development agencies — federal, provincial, and local — have tried to grapple with these problems. In 1969, many of the existing regional development programs were consolidated into one Department of Regional Economic Expansion (DREE). The following are the main elements of DREE strategy, which tries to profit from the experience of other agencies in this field:
- integration of regional development programs,
- co-ordination of all programs of various federal government departments (for example, public works, transportation, manpower) in the context of specific regional-development needs,
- joint federal-provincial plans for economic expansion and social adjustment of special areas,
- incentives to attract industry to slow-growth areas,
- financial contributions to help implement such services as transportation, utilities, housing, hospitals and clinics, schools, etc.

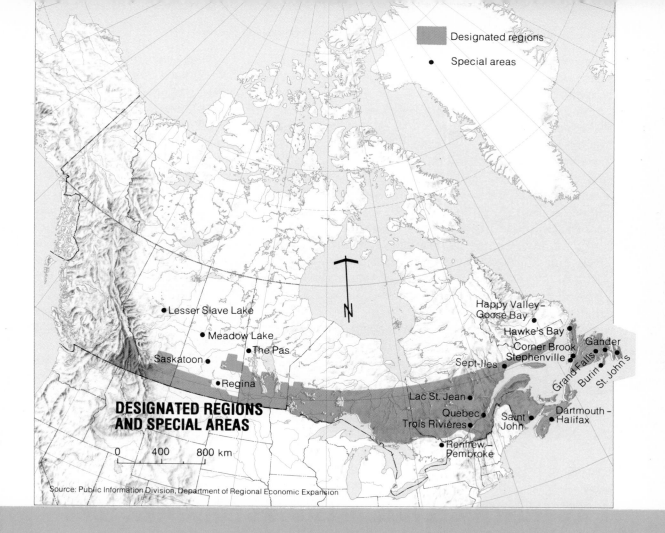

Designated regions

Special areas

Lesser Slave Lake

Meadow Lake

The Pas

Saskatoon

Regina

Happy Valley–Goose Bay

Hawke's Bay

Corner Brook

Stephenville

Sept-Iles

Gander

Grand Falls

Burin

St. John's

Lac St. Jean

Quebec

Trois Rivières

Saint John

Dartmouth – Halifax

Renfrew–Pembroke

DESIGNATED REGIONS AND SPECIAL AREAS

0   400   800 km

N

Source: Public Information Division, Department of Regional Economic Expansion

Study 66

1. Which provinces consist entirely of designated regions?
2. What is the proportion of "designated-regions" land in the other provinces?
3. What percentage of Ontario is eligible for assistance from DREE?
4. Select one special area. What are the major problems there? Discuss possible solutions.

Since there has been so little progress in the past, questions are being raised about the wisdom of continued attempts to ease disparities. A business executive, Robert Bonner, in his address to the 1974 Canadian Conference of Bankers, emphasized the "50-year history of striking and unrelieved regional disparity among the five economic regions of Canada despite heavy federal government programs to subsidize development in the backward areas." He asked: "Should we continue to attempt to

325

move opportunity to people, or should we be thinking instead of doing the opposite, moving people to opportunity?"

People need little encouragement to move out of disadvantaged areas and seek better opportunities elsewhere. Despite all the efforts to provide more local opportunities within the Atlantic Provinces, for example, there has been a steadily increasing emigration from the region. An average of 7,400 people left each year between 1951 and 1956, 11,800 annually between 1956 and 1961, and 20,800 between 1961 and 1966. Most of these emigrants are resettling in cities all across Canada. In Toronto, Maritimers are so numerous that there is a special reception centre to assist them in adjusting to their new surroundings.

Yet, if people continue to move to cities in search of better opportunities, they will aggravate existing urban problems of transportation, housing, pollution, etc. Money might be better spent on direct aid to depressed areas, rather than in trying to solve the multitudinous problems created by the influx of thousands of people into urban centres. In fact, some residents of metropolitan areas, where smog blots out the stars, sewage pollutes the beaches, and crowds invade the recreation areas so that "wilderness hikes" must be booked weeks in advance, might question the definition of "depressed" area. President M. O. Morgan of Memorial University, Newfoundland, observed that the existing life style in places like Newfoundland is "more to be envied than deplored." He criticized Newfoundlanders for using central Canada as a model in their aspirations to catch up with the rest of Canada. Improving the standard of living might end up destroying what he called the "standard of life."

The international scene: A complex web

Competing claims and conflicting interests are not only inter-regional; they extend beyond as well as across Canada. People in many countries rely on Canadian raw materials — wheat, lumber, newsprint, and metallic minerals. These primary materials are shipped out of Canada at low prices and processed into finished goods that we import at high prices. Should we sell such resources — particularly our non-renewable resources — quite so readily? But if exports were drastically reduced, how would we earn the foreign exchange to buy the tea, coffee, cotton, wool, rubber, and so forth that are not produced here? How would other nations produce the goods to sell to us in order to earn the foreign exchange they need to buy Canadian products? And how would all this affect jobs in Canada? On the other hand, if exports of non-renewable resources continue to accelerate, what materials will we use to manufacture products when our natural resources are used up? The web of international trade is extremely complex.

In terms of population and capital, Canada is a small country. Foreign investment has been essential for the development of our resources. But some Canadians are alarmed lest we lose control of these resources — and of our destiny. Estimates of foreign ownership are as high as 91 per cent for petroleum products, 97 per cent for the automobile industry, 92 per cent for

Canada's mining industry, too, is largely foreign-owned. But, it does generate direct employment for almost one million Canadians, and wages are among the highest of any section of industry.

the aircraft industry, 93 per cent for rubber products, 93 per cent for the computer industry, and 90 per cent for the tobacco industry.

The problem of foreign capital and ownership has been hotly debated during the last two decades — and during that time foreign investment has tripled. Various measures to control foreign firms and stimulate Canadian investment have been proposed:

- screening the entry of new foreign firms or the expansion of existing ones,
- toughening up the interpretation of "significant benefit" for Canadians in existing legislation,
- the mandatory appointment of Canadian directors to the boards of all major foreign firms,
- reduced federal income-tax rates for Canadian companies and increased rates for foreign firms,
- legislation requiring that Canadian banks and other managers of large pools of investment capital shift part of their loans and investments to Canadian companies,
- elimination of government grants and loans to foreign corporations and a transfer of this funding to Canadian companies.

Study 67

1. Evaluate the measures proposed to control foreign firms and stimulate Canadian investment.
2. How do Canadians benefit from foreign companies? What do they lose?
3. Should foreign ownership be prohibited in certain industries? Which ones? Why?

Sovereignty over the seabed

National governments may be able to exercise some control over ownership of land resources. But who owns the resources of the seabed? How is control exerted? Oilmen now have the technology to drill wells at underwater depths of 2000 metres or more. Mining companies have the machinery to scoop up minerals from 6000 metres down. Factory ships stay at sea for months on end harvesting and processing cargoes of fish with frightening efficiency. But who is entitled to what? It was to formulate a Law of the Sea that delegates from 149 countries — 29 of them landlocked nations — gathered in Caracas, Venezuela, in June 1974.

The conference quickly lined up into two camps. On one side were countries anxious to stake their claim to a share in the exploitation of the seas, even though they lacked the technology to develop marine resources. Most of these 120 nations want an international seabed authority to protect their rights to the mineral resources of the sea — including their claim to a 100 per cent return of the profits. On the other side were modern industrial nations willing to allow an international authority to control licensing, set rules, and collect a royalty to be shared among the have-not nations. However, after making the investment, providing the technology, and taking the risks, the industrial nations feel entitled to keep most of the profits.

The clash of interests was not only between rich and poor nations. Switzerland, Afghanistan, Bolivia, and Singapore found common cause because they either are landlocked or have extremely narrow continental shelves. Nations with broad shelves, among them India, Argentina, and Canada, pressed for as wide a territorial limit as possible. (United Nations conferences in 1958 and 1960 tried unsuccessfully to clarify questions of territorial limits — which vary from 5 to 300 kilometres out to sea — and continental-shelf claims — rights to mineral resources, fishing, etc.) These matters remain unresolved. Even if everyone were agreed that a nation owns rights in its continental shelf, there would remain the problem of defining the shelf to the satisfaction of all concerned. Canada and the United States claim a 20-kilometre territorial limit and a 300-kilometre "economic zone for the exploitation of minerals and fish." These claims have yet to be accepted internationally.

Meanwhile, our marine resources are being steadily depleted. Foreign fleets not bound by international treaties do not observe fishing bans and quotas. In 1971, the International Commission of the Northwest Atlantic (ICNAF) reported that, of 2,040 vessels of over 50 tonnes fishing the northwest Atlantic, only 504 were Canadian. The fishery resource could be dangerously depleted before agreement is negotiated among the nations involved. Even then the problem may not be solved. After protests from Canada that the coastal catch of Atlantic salmon had declined alarmingly as a result of increased fishing in Davis Strait, ICNAF banned deep-sea salmon fishing. Denmark, however, defied the ban, and stocks have continued to decline.

It is not surprising that fishing grounds are hotly disputed and, wherever possible, jealously guarded. Coast-guard cutters and fishery patrol boats police the seas, arresting crews and impounding vessels when regulations are not observed. Since 1970, Canadian tracker planes have patrolled

Sometimes, we are the bad guys. Here, a U.S. Coast Guard vessel escorts a Canadian fishing vessel out of American waters near Bellingham, Washington.

territorial waters, watching for pollution and enforcing fishing regulations. Originally built for anti-submarine use, these aircraft now pursue a new kind of foe. The enemy is the ship that casually dumps oil or garbage, or the plant whose industrial waste stains waters brown for miles off-shore, or the foreign fishing vessel that has strayed beyond its legal limits.

How many conferences will be necessary to resolve the question of sovereignty of the seabed? Can we conserve our marine resources without international agreements and controls?

Diminishing resources

These concerns have become acute and intense because of the unarguable evidence that land and water resources are being depleted at an alarming rate.

The "oil crisis" of 1973-1974 came as a severe shock to the industrialized world. Oil shortages, long predicted but comfortably ignored as a remote future concern, were suddenly an uncomfortable reality. In the United States, "No Gas" signs appeared at many service stations. There were long line-ups at others. Air fares increased as the price of jet fuel soared, and many flights were cancelled. Thermostats were turned down in homes all across the country. In Western Europe, the price of petroleum skyrocketed. Chilly rooms, luke-warm water, and dimly lit corridors greeted many visitors as hotels and other public buildings tried to economize on fuel. But these inconveniences were nothing compared with the economic effects of the crisis. The sudden, sharp rise in world oil prices was a serious blow to the economy of the European Common Market. And the economy of Japan, the second-largest consumer of oil in the world, was affected even more severely. People everywhere were shocked to realize that an era had ended — the days of oil as a cheap and plentiful source of energy were over.

The oil crisis forced Canada to take a cold, hard look at petroleum supply and distribution. The Canadian government began to consider extension of the pipeline from western oil fields to Montreal, in order to reduce imports and assure a reliable supply of domestic oil to the eastern provinces. As a conservation measure, Ottawa started reducing exports of Canadian crude to U.S. refineries. But these were only short-term measures reflecting the immediate crisis. What is more urgently required is a comprehensive policy of conservation and development that will meet and anticipate Canada's energy needs. Oil is being consumed at such a lavish rate that domestic reserves, although extensive, are dwindling. Serious shortages are anticipated by the early 1980s. Will we then have to compete with other consumers for rapidly and steadily diminishing world supplies? What will we do when all these are exhausted?

The shock of depleted supplies becomes even more frightening when we realize that oil is only *one* of many vital, vanishing resources. We are having to explore farther and farther afield for our supplies of coal and iron. We are pushing agricultural frontiers farther and farther out from the more productive areas, and also wringing more and more out of each hectare of farmland. How far and for how long can technology push food production to keep pace with increases in population? Logged-over areas can be reseeded, but the quality of much of our second-growth forest cannot compare with the original fine stands of virgin timber. Even hydro-electric power supplies, once considered inexhaustible sources of energy, seem endangered as reservoirs are slowly but surely silting up. Are we frightened enough to pay attention to the *rate* at which we are using up our natural resources?

Most alarming of all is the carelessness with which we treat the most valuable of all our resources: fresh water. In Canada, the average household use is about 230 litres of water per person per day — 3-3½ litres for individual physical survival; about 140 litres for a bath; 45 to wash dishes; 20 or 30 to flush a toilet. Then there are industrial uses — 55 000 litres to make a tonne of steel, 301 700 litres to make a tonne of newsprint, 2 000 000 litres to produce a tonne of synthetic rubber. And that is not all. Water turns the turbines that produce hydro-electric power, dilutes and carries away wastes, serves as a means of transportation, provides a home for marine life, and offers recreation for skin divers, surfers, and skiers.

Canada is one of the world's most favored countries in terms of fresh-water supplies. About 90 per cent of the world's surface and atmospheric water is stored in lakes, which Canada has in such abundance that they have never been counted, let alone measured. So how can Canada have water problems? Abundance often breeds carelessness. Forty times as much water is used (and left polluted) to produce a tonne of steel in Canada as is used in California, where water is scarce and expensive (and therefore is recycled). Again, with so much water around, it is all too easy to exploit it as a waste dispose-all. Urban centres have turned many rivers into open sewers. Thus is created a new kind of water problem — a

A twin reminder to Canadians bound for the United States: gasoline is not only scarce but will be even scarcer — and more expensive — in future years.

shortage of *clean* water in a land that contains about one-seventh of all the world's fresh water.

Most North Americans find it difficult to grasp the idea of shortage. Goods have always been so plentiful that the old and the broken are rejected and replaced rather than repaired and re-used. High productivity has generated enormous wealth for North America. It has also used up raw materials at an alarming rate. Many people are worried about what will happen to their jobs, their incomes, and their way of life if these resources should no longer be available. Thus the words "repair" and "recycle," "control" and "conserve" appeared more and more frequently in the vocabulary of the 1970s.

Conservation of resources

The unpleasant but unavoidable fact is that many resources are *non-renewable*. It takes millions of years for metallic minerals and fossil fuels to form, so sustained yield just is not possible. Once these resources are gone, they are gone forever. Increasingly high demand for these raw materials is using up known supplies. Exploration for new deposits and development of new mines and wells is becoming more difficult, forcing companies to go far into the Arctic and deep under the surface of the sea. But one day there may be no such deposits to discover and develop.

Non-renewable resources cannot be replaced, but proven reserves can be controlled by careful conservation policies. We can certainly avoid wasteful and inefficient practices in both production and consumption. Eighteenth-century European coal miners often left behind fully a quarter of the mineral in the form of pillars to support the tunnels. On this continent, early blast furnaces were so inefficient that the slag they cast aside was still rich in iron. In some parts of the world where resources have run out, such wastes are now being mined all over again.

Conservation methods can be used to control rates of production in oil fields. If too much oil is produced too fast, the pressure in the reservoir drops. This reduces the volume of oil that can be withdrawn economically. But even after all the oil that can be withdrawn cheaply has been obtained, there are ways to get maximum production from a well. One secondary-recovery method pumps hot water or steam into the rock strata. This makes the thick crude flow more freely so that more oil can be recovered. Improved technology and new methods assist greatly in making more efficient use of mineral ores. In the past, it was customary to extract the most attractive element, perhaps copper, and discard ore that contained sizable quantities of other metals, notably lead, zinc, nickel, and iron. But the mine that opened at Manitouwadge, Ontario, in 1957 produces significant quantities of silver, lead, and gold in addition to copper and zinc, which are its major products. Think how much metal would probably have been wasted if the deposits had been discovered a century earlier! Think how much iron ore was cast aside in the Sudbury area in the years before the beneficiation process was invented!

Technology has found uses for many former "waste" products. Before the invention of the internal-combustion engine, gasoline was a relatively useless by-product from the production of kerosene for oil lamps. Before nickel was found to be a hardening alloy in steelmaking, it was only a by-product in copper mining. What uses might we find someday for the gases being burned off as waste at oil refineries today? What uses might we find for the mountains of sulphur produced in the mining of the Athabasca tar sands?

Making sure that we extract every possible ounce of usable material from a resource and researching uses for "waste" products are not enough. We must try to conserve the products made from non-renewable resources. Buses, trains, street-cars, and subways are more efficient in their use of energy than automobiles are. Expansion of public-transit services would result in a greater conservation of fuels than would construction of expressways. Kerosene jet fuels could be conserved by reducing multiple overlapping air services and providing fewer but fuller flights.

Non-renewable resources can also be conserved by substituting materials made from renewable resources for those made from non-renewable ones. We could use paper labels on jars and bottles instead of foil ones, cotton thread to attach buttons to cards rather than metal staples, and so on. And do we really need to use so many resources in packaging – a foil envelope packed inside a cardboard carton that is then carried home in a plastic bag? This overpackaging is only going to end up in the garbage can. Disposal of mountains of garbage is a problem in itself, but when the junk includes items made from non-renewable resources, the waste is compounded.

Finally, there is recycling. Tin cans and aluminum foil, plastic containers and cello wrap, glass jars and bottles – these are only a few of the items that can be re-used.

It takes a garbage strike to begin *to show us how much waste we produce.*

In fact, when cans and bottles are taken to a recycling depot, when plastic containers and glass jars are washed and sterilized, when fruit and vegetable peelings, coffee grounds, and unused leftovers are composted and used as fertilizer, and when broken items are repaired instead of replaced, there is a two-way benefit. The problem of garbage disposal is greatly reduced; the conservation of natural resources is greatly increased.

Recycling is not restricted to materials made from non-renewable resources. Nor is it limited to individual consumers or households. Many businesses and factories are recycling. One example is Pacific Press in Vancouver, which publishes British Columbia's two major newspapers. From the time a reporter scribbles something in a notebook to the time when the gigantic presses are rolling out 60,000 copies of that news item per hour, Pacific Press is using enormous quantities of paper, much of which goes in the wastebasket. However, none of the paper ends up as waste. All scrap paper, all the residue from the presses, and all unsold newspapers are shredded, baled, and sold for use in roofing, in insulation, or in protective packaging for fragile articles. Even the lead type that is used to print the two newspapers is recycled. Thirty-six to 45 kilograms of metal are needed to make up a page, and another 18 kilograms to mold a plate for the printing presses. The metal is melted and reused over and over again.

That is not all. Pacific Press's enormous plant uses no heating fuel whatsoever. Heat generated by the machinery, by the lights, and by the hundreds of employees is extracted from the air in the building and stored in water, to be released as needed.

333

Think how much heat, paper, and metal is saved! Think how many natural resources are conserved!

It is good to know that many of our natural resources are self-renewing. We can farm the land, forests, and waters to produce recurring crops of grain, vegetables, animals, trees, fish, etc. But if we take too much too fast, the resource may be ruined or destroyed. The buffalo (often slaughtered by Europeans only for their tongues or hides), the beaver and its cousin, the sea otter (destroyed by the thousands to satisfy the dictates of European fashion), only narrowly escaped extinction. Gone forever is the passenger pigeon, once a valuable source of food. Only through old paintings and pioneer writings do we know that eastern Canada once produced trees comparable in size to those now standing — but rapidly disappearing — in west-coast forests. Many streams and lakes have become so polluted that they can no longer provide a habitat for various species of fish. It is disturbing to reflect that we have been using — in many cases abusing — these resources for only a few hundred years. Prior to European settlement, native peoples had used these resources for thousands of years, without damaging effect. True, their numbers were far fewer, but more important, perhaps, their cultures were not mechanized. They lived with plants and animals, land and water, as part of Nature. Perhaps, even in industrialized cultures, people will yet heed the warning signals and realize

Land is often "mined" for crops or overgrazed. Unless it is conserved by leaving portions fallow, or mulched, or protected by shelter belts of drought-resistant trees and shrubs, fertile topsoil is blown away.

that they themselves are part of the environment and will suffer if other parts are greedily exploited.

That early settlers took what they needed from the environment without much thought for the consequences is understandable. For one thing, they had such a struggle merely to survive; for another, there seemed to be a limitless supply of resources. Forests were so thick that the value of the resource was hidden at first by the sheer numbers of trees that covered most of the land. The settlers' main concern was to get rid of the trees, clear land, and raise crops and animals. But the pioneers soon realized that timber was in demand by countries that had long since depleted their own reserves. Thus began Canada's lumber trade, first with Great Britain, then with the United States, and finally with much of the world. Throughout the nineteenth century, loggers moved like locusts through the woodlands. Thus perished the forest giants of eastern Canada. Left behind was a ravished wasteland that was reclaimed only slowly and by poor quality, second-growth forest. Logged-over land is always an ugly sight. But today governments and forest industries are practising conservation methods that give the forest a chance to restore itself — sustained yield, close utilization, reseeding, fertilizing, disease control, fire prevention, and so on. Long-range planning and intelligent management policy can help conserve the forest resource.

Personal preferences that create heavy demands for certain products often intensify the problems of management and conservation. Take, for instance, the food resource. North Americans like meat, particularly beef. But raising steaks and roasts is a very uneconomical way of using the land. First the feed crops must be raised, then the animal stock. The yield in terms of food value produced per hectare is relatively low. Fish, on the other hand, are an economical source of protein. But Canadians are picky fish-eaters. How long will we continue to throw back varieties of the fish that are caught, simply because they do not appeal to the national palate? Canadians consume a lot of food — and also throw out a lot. How long will we continue to fill our garbage cans with "waste" food? Stale bread can be made into bread crumbs. Vegetable peels and parings can go onto a compost heap. Leftovers can be reheated or mixed together to make a unique casserole concoction. Bones can go into the soup pot. With world food shortages pressing upon us, we may not be able to be quite so choosy and quite so wasteful in future!

If it is hard for most Canadians to imagine a scarcity of food, the idea of a water shortage is even more difficult to grasp. Water has always been so cheaply and easily available that most people think of it as "free." An occasional sprinkling restriction in a period of local drought is the only water deprivation most of us have ever known. But increasing world populations, rising living standards, and continuing industrialization are placing greater and greater demands on the world's supplies of fresh water.

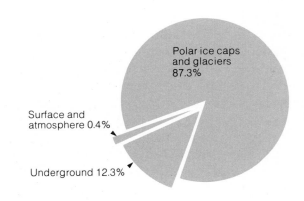

WORLD'S FRESH WATER SUPPLY: 33 000 000 km³

Since only a tiny amount of the world's water is actually used to sustain earth's total population, there is obviously a great deal of unused water in the world. Why then are people concerned about supplies?

To begin with, almost all of the world's supply of water is contained in the oceans. Of an estimated 1360 million cubic kilometres of water on earth, about 97.5 per cent is salt. It is great for fishing, transportation, and recreation, but not much use for drinking, agriculture, or most industrial processes. Salt water can be desalinated at a price. In 1952, the cost of producing 4500 litres of "sweet" water was close to $5.00. By 1968 it had dropped to $1.25. Improved techniques keep reducing the cost of desalinated water, and increased demands are boosting the price of fresh water.

The commercial feasibility of desalinating salt water was once considered utterly fantastic. That such an idea is now receiving serious attention emphasizes the need to conserve the fresh-water supplies now available.

Only 2.5 per cent of the world's total supply of water is fresh. And about 90 per cent of that is locked up in the frozen ice caps of Greenland and Antarctica, beyond the reach of even the most advanced technology. Some fresh water is buried underground and can be brought to the surface by drilling and pumping. **Groundwater** — underground water — has been used for centuries, ever since people first learned to dig wells and draw water. (About 10 per cent of Canada's fresh water is derived from groundwater.)

Earth's total population is sustained by only about 0.4 per cent of the world's fresh-water supply. But this supply of fresh water — in the world's lakes, rivers, and atmosphere — is significant because it maintains and renews itself by constant movement. It falls from the atmosphere as precipitation, it soaks into the earth, it travels through lakes and rivers and eventually reaches the ocean, and it returns to the atmosphere by evaporation and transpiration. At every point in this movement, some water is evaporating into the atmosphere, moving over the earth, and falling again as precipitation. This natural circulation system that maintains and renews the world's fresh-water supply is called the **hydrologic cycle.**

Thus water is constantly being restored and kept on the move. This makes it an efficient and economical carrier of waste materials. But there is a limit to the type and quantity of polluting materials that water can absorb and still renew itself. Indeed, conditions can reach the point where natural forces work to accelerate rather than resist pollution. In Lake Erie, plant nutrients from sewage and industrial wastes have promoted the growth of aquatic vegetation to such an extent that the decay of this vegetation itself releases more such nutrients into the water. At a certain point, the process of decay becomes self-supporting and continues — even if the supply of pollutants from outside is cut off. Many people fear that Lake Erie may already be poisoned beyond hope of recovery.

Domestic wastes from sanitary sewage — water from bathtubs, sinks, toilets, washing machines — can be treated by sewage plants. But these have to compete for the taxpayer's dollar with hospitals, roads, schools, social services, and police and fire protection. Still, many municipalities have invested in water-purification plants. The operating cost of about 2½ cents per person per day is a bargain. Installing a treatment plant now is cheaper than trying to solve the problem of polluted water from untreated domestic sewage at a later date. Industrial wastes, which contain acids, oil, grease, and animal and vegetable matter, present a much larger, more complex problem. Ordinary municipal treatment plants often have no effect on them, and they are returned, still polluted, to lakes and rivers.

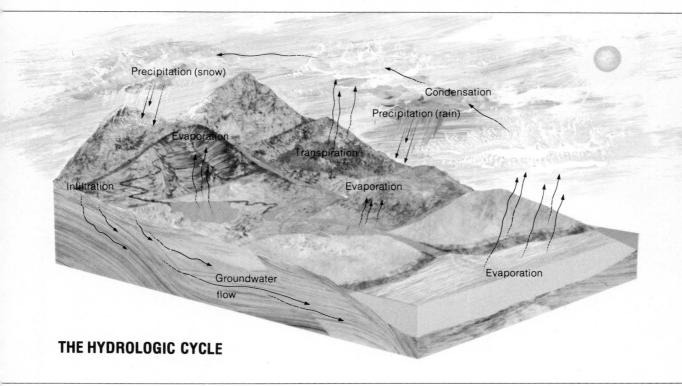

Precipitation (snow)

Condensation

Precipitation (rain)

Evaporation

Transpiration

Evaporation

Infiltration

Evaporation

Groundwater
flow

THE HYDROLOGIC CYCLE

It is easy to say that factories and mills should not be allowed to discharge polluted water untreated. It is not so easy to assign responsibility for treatment and control of industrial pollution. Should the costs of installing anti-pollution systems for industrial wastes be absorbed by the company via reduced profits? Should they be passed on to the consumer via higher prices? Or should these costs be subsidized by the government via corporate-tax deductions? If a plant is forced to shut down because it cannot afford the necessary improvements, who is responsible for finding new jobs for the workers? The company? The community? The union? The government? Each individual worker?

Conservation of resources is clearly vital to survival. However, it is not enough to consider only the economic and ecological aspects of the problem. The human resource is important, too. Sometimes conservation proposals deal with the issue only in the abstract, ignoring the needs of individual people.

It is easy to deplore the opening of an unsightly mine or mill. Yet unemployed workers in a depressed area will gladly accept pollution if it means more jobs. It is easy to argue for underground rather than strip mining, in order to preserve the natural beauty of a landscape. But what if the price for an unscarred landscape is scarred and blackened lungs for underground miners? It is easy to demand strict pollution controls. But if the cost of installing anti-pollution devices were to force the factory you work in to close down, you might settle for less stringent controls.

A general program to conserve natural resources must also meet the needs of individual *people* in various parts of Canada.

Eutrophication: The process by which waste materials add nutrients to water and change the balance of life there.

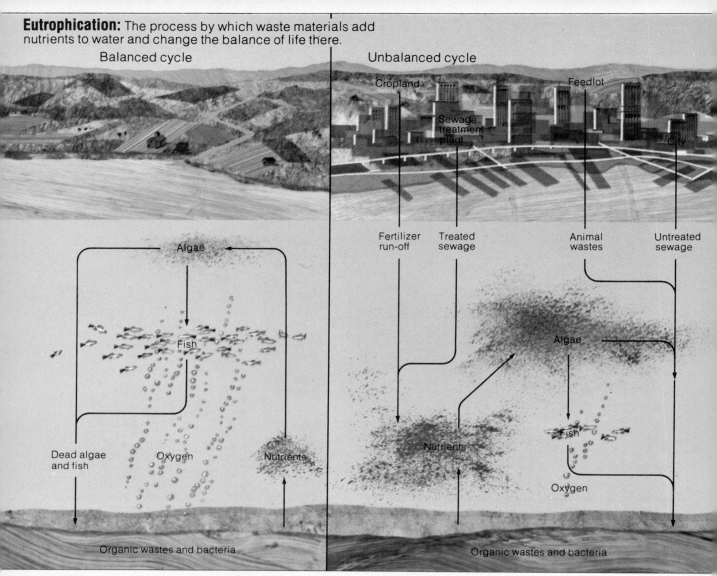

Balanced cycle

Unbalanced cycle

Cropland Feedlot
Sewage treatment plant
City

Fertilizer run-off | Treated sewage | Animal wastes | Untreated sewage

Algae

Fish

Algae

Fish

Dead algae and fish | Oxygen | Nutrients

Nutrients

Oxygen

Organic wastes and bacteria

Organic wastes and bacteria

Increasing demands, *decreasing resources*

Imagine a piece of land close to a large city. It is good agricultural land. The farmer (and various government agencies) wants it maintained for food production. However, the land is underlain by fine-quality gravel, of which there is a shortage. A building contractor (and various other government agencies) wants to develop a gravel pit. As it happens, the land is near a major highway development. A highway contractor (and still other government departments) wants it for a cloverleaf. But

the land is green parkland on the edge of a heavily populated area. A nearby resort hotel (and government agencies at three levels) wants it for recreational land. Who has the best claim?

Conflicting claims and interests are increasing as more and more groups compete for the use of fewer and fewer resources. What criteria will be used to determine priority in agricultural, industrial, and hydro-electric demands for water? What measures will reconcile the needs of inshore

This is congestion? What if each of these persons also drove a car?

and offshore fishermen, conserve the fishery resource, support economic interests, and protect the marine environment?

Furthermore, we are beginning to realize that apparently isolated actions can have far-reaching effects. A paper mill opens in a northern forest — and the fur-bearing animals on a distant delta disappear. A new dam is built — and a salmon run is wiped out. A strip mine opens — and there is a plague of flies and mosquitoes nearby. A forest area is logged over — and the water supply in distant cities drops. It is necessary to consider *all* the effects of any action we take, the effects on the *total* environment.

We know that strip mining can result in scarred hillsides, obstructed valleys filled with stagnant water, and breeding grounds for insect pests. It can also produce coal, cheaply and with far less danger to miners from underground mine accidents or black lung. And strip-mined land can be reclaimed and used for industrial, residential, recreational, and even agricultural purposes. But such reclamation is costly. Are we willing to pay? Can we afford not to pay?

We know that forest land can be devastated by "cut and get out" operations. It can also provide sustained yields of fine lumber and wood pulp, a habitat for wildlife, a refuge for rest and relaxation, and a catchment and storage area for precious water. But it is easier in the short run simply to take what lumber is needed as cheaply as possible. Are we willing to pay for good forest management? In the long run, can we afford not to pay?

We know that a land rich in resources can be spoiled by private indulgence and public neglect — backyard pools and polluted beaches, ornamental fountains and untreated sewage, green golf courses and concrete jungles. It is more comfortable and convenient to drive one's car rather than stand in an overcrowded bus or subway. What a convenience for the individual! What a cost to society in terms of traffic congestion, air and noise pollution, and the selfish use of diminishing resources! Are we willing to give up private convenience for public benefit?

We cannot stop using resources. But we can conserve our non-renewable resources by mining them efficiently and using their products wisely. And we can conserve our renewable resources by managing the lands and waters and harvesting their crops to maintain a sustained yield. We cannot undo all the mistakes of the past. But we can try to avoid future mistakes by planning carefully and acting intelligently — all of us — to conserve the land for its people.

A country that can afford to defy geography can afford to pay the price.

Study and Research

1. Write a report on whichever of the "Canadas" you live in, outlining the factors that make it a distinctive region.
2. The British geographer Wreford Watson said that the Canadian scene was dominated by "separation rather than togetherness."
   (a) To what extent do you agree with his statement?
   (b) What are the relative advantages and disadvantages of separation and togetherness in a nation?
3. Here are some commonly expressed statements by Canadians about Canadians.
   "Quebeckers are all a bunch of separatists."
   "Ontario thinks that Canada stops at the Manitoba and Quebec borders."
   "We have to foot the bill for the rest of Canada."
   "The Maritimes couldn't survive without federal handouts."
   (a) Identify the region(s) of the speakers of each of the above statements.
   (b) Why do you think such opinions are widely held?
   (c) How do you think better "Canadian" understanding can be achieved?
4. Research some of the results of human interference with the hydrologic cycle, with particular emphasis on such practices in your own region.
5. Make a study of the problems of conservation and pollution in your home community and in your region.
   What special problems are involved in cleaning up interprovincial (for example, the Ottawa River) and international (for example, the Great Lakes) areas? What measures have been taken to clean up pollution in these particular areas?
6. Review your answers to the following Study and Research questions.
   Chapter 3 — Questions 7, 8, 9
   Chapter 4 — Question 12
   Chapter 5 — Question 12
   Chapter 6 — Question 10
   Chapter 7 — Questions 5, 9
   Chapter 8 — Questions 4, 6, 9
   Chapter 9 — Questions 7, 8, 9, 11
   In light of what you have learned in this year's study of Canada, how would you modify your answers to these questions? Make any changes you think appropriate.

7. The salmon that spawn in the streams of Atlantic Canada spend their adult lives in the waters off Greenland. The Canadian catch of Atlantic salmon has declined drastically because of overfishing by Danish fleets off the coast of Greenland and because of pollution in the spawning streams. We can do something about cleaning up the polluted streams, but what can we do about overfishing in Davis Strait? The problem is: Whose salmon are they, Canada's or Denmark's?

   (a) Write a report on what Canada has done to help the Atlantic salmon industry — anti-pollution measures, fish-ladder construction, research, etc. (Information can be obtained from the federal Department of the Environment and from the departments of fisheries of the Atlantic Provinces.)

   (b) What has Canada done about the problem of Danish deep-sea salmon fishing?

   (c) What other measures can be taken to protect the Canadian catch of salmon?

8. There will be conferences on the Law of the Sea until "sovereignty over the seabed" is decided.

   (a) Write a brief report on the conferences that have been held thus far. Assess progress and achievements.

   (b) Keep a file of newspaper reports, magazine articles, and other relevant material on the subject of territorial waters, fishing and mineral rights, and other related issues. Periodically, assess the development of international agreements.

9. Canada has been described, physically, as "a country in defiance of geography." Perhaps it can be described, politically, as "a confederation in defiance of economics."

   (a) How are these statements reflected in the British North America Act?

   (b) What is the price of confederation today?

   (c) Why do the high-income provinces feel that they are losers in confederation?

   (d) What criteria would you use to evaluate the claims of and benefits to the "have-not" provinces?

   (e) What are the advantages of confederation, politically, geographically and economically, for both "have" and "have-not" provinces?

10. As a summary of your year's study, discuss what Canada (all six identities) is today. Use the knowledge you have gained to project what Canada will be in 2000 A.D.

...s of Manufactures, by Province, 1968 and 1969ᴾ

...dustrial classification and new establishment and total activity concepts.

Industry	Year	Estab. No.	Production and Related Workers Number	Man-Hours Paid '000	Wages $'000	Cost of Fuel and Electricity $'000	Cost of Materials and Supplies Used $'000	Value of Shipments of Goods of Own Manufacture $'000	Value Added $'000	Total Employees Number	Salaries and Wages $'000	Total Value Added $'000
	1968	254	9,609	21,009	42,964	9,520	99,169	197,464	88,386	11,908	57,582	92,583
	1969	259	9,941	21,461	48,895	11,582	116,351	242,378	112,518	12,302	65,326	120,531
	1968	138	1,730	3,517	5,727	977	34,162	51,657	16,569	2,255	8,219	17,534
	1969	148	2,070	4,246	7,073	1,019	37,885	56,860	18,471	2,605	9,745	19,729
	1968	852	25,187	52,198	103,254	16,590	385,378	663,335	261,044	32,894	148,811	272,288
	1969	846	25,743	53,500	116,166	18,347	419,165	731,476	298,534	33,235	165,660	315,703
	1968	620	21,521	46,103	93,856	24,461	374,338	633,577	240,753	28,139	133,380	249,012
	1969	628	22,046	47,000	104,246	26,490	414,000	708,933	269,848	28,966	148,061	283,786
	1968	10,513	370,537	790,757	1,817,303	236,395	6,341,337	11,742,911	5,215,464	521,250	2,923,728	5,445,448
	1969	10,467	379,907	806,546	1,991,208	255,428	6,975,568	12,808,993	5,672,740	529,154	3,166,501	5,962,686
	1968	12,932	563,777	1,197,631	3,238,023	372,847	11,932,954	21,942,620	9,714,889	810,724	5,171,178	10,516,406
	1969	12,976	574,680	1,220,208	3,549,699	387,197	13,098,606	23,851,499	10,635,970	823,344	5,644,207	11,524,299
	1968	1,393	34,153	71,571	161,942	23,860	657,609	1,118,813	443,002	48,100	251,869	463,577
	1969	1,381	35,803	74,936	182,761	25,340	725,407	1,230,014	486,057	49,435	277,378	507,050
	1968	756	10,348	21,807	56,447	11,000	311,760	489,210	170,002	15,654	89,955	179,420
	1969	748	9,889	20,915	58,687	12,162	332,720	530,442	186,893	15,267	95,081	194,953
	1968	1,822	33,962	71,432	183,747	26,490	1,041,058	1,667,034	604,529	49,759	292,983	629,197
	1969	1,862	36,224	76,381	214,916	29,312	1,133,986	1,849,268	702,810	52,364	335,102	731,864
	1968	3,331	89,268	182,486	574,288	86,547	1,910,838	3,550,399	1,575,436	121,490	826,671	1,615,580
	1969	3,329	93,379	190,417	646,570	93,512	2,124,998	3,917,820	1,745,128	126,434	922,822	1,788,857
	1968	18	62	132	330	45	327	1,194	834	86	438	898
	1969	20	70	146	381	52	653	1,720	1,098	97	538	1,160
	1968	14	72	148	549	31	2,040	3,341	1,296	93	689	1,670
	1969	12	83	173	655	39	2,075	3,504	1,369	116	885	1,995
	1968	**32,643**	**1,160,226**	**2,458,791**	**6,278,429**	**808,764**	**23,090,970**	**42,061,555**	**18,332,204**	**1,642,352**	**9,905,504**	**19,483,614**
	1969	**32,676**	**1,189,835**	**2,515,929**	**6,921,257**	**860,480**	**5,381,414**	**45,932,907**	**20,131,436**	**1,673,319**	**10,831,306**	**21,452,613**

10.—Summary Statistics of Manufactures, by Province and Industry Group, 1969ᴾ

Province and Industry Group	Establishments	Manufacturing Activity							Total Activity		
		Production and Related Workers			Cost of Fuel and Electricity	Cost of Materials and Supplies Used	Value of Shipments of Goods of Own Manufacture	Value Added	Total Employees		Total Value Added
	No.	Number	Man-Hours Paid	Wages					Number	Salaries and Wages	
			'000	$'000	$'000	$'000	$'000	$'000		$'000	$'000
Newfoundland											
...everage industries	97	5,361	11,479	16,822	2,739	51,270	100,726	45,784	6,392	22,762	52,975
...ducts industries	...	...	...	...	...	...	...	...	1	1	1
...tries	3	1	1	1	1	1	...	...	1	1	1
	2	1	1	1	1	1	...	1	1	1	1
...tries	—	—	—	—	—	—	—	—	—	—	—
	2	1	1	1	1	1	1	1	1	1	1
...ure industries	74	304	640	1,065	218	3,017	5,692	2,484	346	1,334	2,615
...dustries	4	1	1	1	1	1	1	1	1	1	1
...and allied industries	4	266	576	1,369	113	1,326	5,917	4,505	530	2,701	4,459
...stries (except machinery	26	1	1	1	1	1	1	1	1	1	1
...quipment industries)	2										
...except electrical	10	355	770	1,823	84	3,758	7,310	3,528	439	2,387	3,660
...nt industries	...	...	...	...	...	...	...	...	1	1	1
...ries	7	1	1	1	1	1	1	1	1	1	1
...ucts industries	1										
...s industries	15	284	648	1,518	506	2,596	7,144	4,146	393	2,266	4,348
...ucts industries	1										
...industries	5	411	841	2,871	1,582	7,001	19,210	10,590	547	4,039	9,832
	6	51	107	187	21	313	836	492	65	288	512
...d	259	9,941	21,461	48,895	11,582	116,351	242,378	112,518	12,302	65,326	120,531
...d											
	79	1,634	3,344	5,298	873	31,658	44,758	12,789	1,980	7,052	13,874
	1	1	1	1	1	1	1	1	1	1	1
	4	52	102	179	21	260	560	292	58	213	298
	28	1	1	1	1	1	1	1	1	1	1
	1	1	1	1	1	1	1	1	1	1	1
	1	1	1	1	1	1	1	1	1	1	1
	7	1	—	1	—	1	1	1			
...inery	6	1		1		1	1	1	1		1

Industry	(1)	(2)	(3)	(4)	(5)	(6)	(7)	(8)	(9)	(10)	(11)
Machinery industries (except electrical machinery)	2	—	—	—	—	—	—	—	—	—	—
Transportation equipment industries	6	—	—	—	—	—	—	—	—	—	—
Non-metallic mineral products industries	5	—	—	—	—	—	—	—	—	—	—
Chemical and chemical products industries	4	—	—	—	—	—	—	—	—	—	—
Miscellaneous manufacturing industries	4	—	—	—	—	—	—	—	—	—	—
Totals, Prince Edward Island	**148**	**2,070**	**4,246**	**7,073**	**1,019**	**37,885**	**56,860**	**18,471**	**2,605**	**9,745**	**19,729**
Nova Scotia											
Food and beverage industries	274	8,114	17,025	28,016	4,428	148,354	229,831	78,381	11,080	44,100	88,796
Tobacco products industries	...	...	...	...	...	...	...	...	...	...	...
Rubber industries	[1]	[1]	[1]	[1]	[1]	[1]	[1]	[1]	[1]	[1]	[1]
Leather industries	12	640	1,356	2,662	312	9,292	14,489	5,666	729	3,231	6,011
Textile industries	6	1,168	2,258	3,392	170	7,292	15,038	8,086	1,299	4,219	8,065
Knitting mills	4	115	233	243	9	610	1,240	566	123	287	566
Clothing industries	209	2,165	4,762	7,115	953	12,811	28,673	16,057	2,408	8,702	16,601
Wood industries	40	216	452	749	58	1,537	2,851	1,254	253	1,008	1,304
Furniture and fixture industries	13	1,986	4,469	13,095	4,528	40,034	89,697	45,429	2,737	19,350	45,566
Paper and allied industries	74	800	1,631	4,131	218	4,035	18,230	14,016	1,402	7,577	14,141
Printing, publishing and allied industries	6	1,017	2,119	5,437	383	11,043	20,560	8,957	1,376	7,635	11,036
Primary metal industries	[1]	[1]	[1]	[1]	[1]	[1]	[1]	[1]	[1]	[1]	[1]
Metal fabricating industries (except machinery and transportation equipment industries)	50	233	513	963	33	1,717	3,242	1,620	420	2,483	1,805
Machinery industries (except electrical machinery)	7	[1]	[1]	[1]	[1]	[1]	[1]	[1]	[1]	[1]	[1]
Transportation equipment industries	58	3,674	7,739	20,957	1,239	45,460	83,126	36,755	4,501	27,181	36,788
Electrical products industries	5	1,216	2,499	4,022	162	11,879	19,304	9,070	1,594	6,988	9,011
Non-metallic mineral products industries	38	674	1,476	3,496	1,225	7,660	19,082	10,484	876	5,029	10,717
Petroleum and coal products industries	2	[1]	[1]	[1]	[1]	[1]	[1]	[1]	[1]	[1]	[1]
Chemical and chemical products industries	10	77	176	387	253	2,567	5,386	2,470	181	1,067	2,491
Miscellaneous manufacturing industries	37	244	520	943	96	1,791	4,422	2,596	332	1,499	2,811
Totals, Nova Scotia	**846**	**25,743**	**53,500**	**116,166**	**18,347**	**419,165**	**731,476**	**298,534**	**33,235**	**165,660**	**315,703**
New Brunswick											
Food and beverage industries	208	6,458	13,379	22,778	3,936	138,292	224,367	83,072	9,227	37,256	89,999
Tobacco products industries	...	...	...	...	...	...	...	...	...	...	...
Rubber industries	[1]	[1]	[1]	[1]	[1]	[1]	[1]	[1]	[1]	[1]	[1]
Leather industries	4	415	823	1,233	129	2,139	4,648	2,319	496	1,544	2,325
Textile industries	8	259	597	738	13	400	1,379	965	287	853	996
Knitting mills	2	[1]	[1]	[1]	[1]	[1]	[1]	[1]	[1]	[1]	[1]
Clothing industries	5	[1]	[1]	[1]	[1]	[1]	[1]	[1]	[1]	[1]	[1]
Wood industries	150	3,096	6,810	11,760	1,490	33,465	60,700	26,049	3,616	14,415	27,269
Furniture and fixture industries	25	197	394	675	30	1,394	3,083	1,723	223	824	1,744
Paper and allied industries	18	4,353	9,939	31,319	16,074	106,022	189,068	67,200	5,313	39,640	70,793
Printing, publishing and allied industries	48	539	1,152	3,088	137	2,818	12,424	9,458	963	5,462	9,411
Primary metal industries	7	[1]	[1]	[1]	[1]	[1]	[1]	[1]	[1]	[1]	[1]
Metal fabricating industries (except machinery and transportation equipment industries)	40	1,110	2,307	5,576	310	12,624	25,598	12,824	1,442	7,795	14,105

[1] Confidential.

10.—Summary Statistics of Manufactures, by Province and Industry Group, 1969ᵖ—continued

Province and Industry Group	Establishments	Manufacturing Activity							Total Activity		
		Production and Related Workers			Cost of Fuel and Electricity	Cost of Materials and Supplies Used	Value of Shipments of Goods of Own Manufacture	Value Added	Total Employees		Total Value Added
	No.	Number	Man-Hours Paid '000	Wages $'000	$'000	$'000	$'000	$'000	Number	Salaries and Wages $'000	$'000
New Brunswick—concluded											
Machinery industries (except electrical machinery)	7	1	1	1	1	1	1	1	1	1	1
Transportation equipment industries	12	1,882	3,771	10,238	235	20,857	36,939	15,997	2,466	14,736	16,473
Electrical products industries	5	1,524	3,123	5,375	244	16,978	32,267	15,023	1,831	7,328	15,122
Non-metallic mineral products industries	37	567	1,234	2,827	1,092	5,055	15,287	9,038	690	3,680	9,139
Petroleum and coal products industries	1	1	1		1		1	1	1	1	1
Chemical and chemical products industries	14	247	523	1,559	1,293	11,277	20,551	7,914	340	2,185	7,910
Miscellaneous manufacturing industries	37	449	901	1,885	117	3,617	9,310	5,376	586	2,943	5,441
Totals, New Brunswick	628	22,046	47,000	104,246	26,490	414,000	708,933	269,848	23,966	148,061	263,786
Quebec											
Food and beverage industries	1,798	37,454	81,436	190,696	28,559	1,493,844	2,286,054	773,841	61,491	351,129	811,106
Tobacco products industries	17	4,857	9,382	30,617	932	116,777	218,270	103,628	6,435	44,361	104,229
Rubber industries	36	4,727	9,882	23,593	2,188	67,110	150,585	80,557	6,761	38,872	83,267
Leather industries	268	13,366	27,224	49,448	969	94,725	196,083	101,844	15,559	64,765	103,688
Textile industries	435	31,698	68,111	143,004	12,338	505,597	874,681	376,793	40,712	209,765	382,292
Knitting mills	203	13,158	28,564	50,821	1,670	156,293	266,615	113,605	14,909	64,300	114,045
Clothing industries	1,552	56,573	112,596	207,933	2,605	478,456	885,609	410,084	63,698	263,380	412,496
Wood industries	1,090	18,227	41,537	75,833	7,578	195,183	363,029	168,556	21,276	96,150	172,340
Furniture and fixture industries	782	14,005	30,276	62,414	2,858	124,287	268,716	144,339	16,981	84,494	145,649
Paper and allied industries	208	32,996	72,939	231,374	80,668	666,024	1,317,366	574,836	43,986	327,246	586,133
Printing, publishing and allied industries	1,054	13,295	27,502	84,299	2,421	153,098	426,916	272,672	22,676	154,140	275,029
Primary metal industries	104	17,985	37,565	122,651	45,480	548,730	1,004,351	411,246	26,065	195,176	438,866
Metal fabricating industries (except machinery and transportation equipment industries)	959	26,661	57,302	160,660	7,690	340,709	728,389	383,190	35,522	232,949	401,177
Machinery industries (except electrical machinery)	133	7,867	17,171	46,597	1,899	108,432	229,251	127,285	14,945	103,948	146,585
Transportation equipment industries	162	24,382	51,522	158,012	6,914	600,403	1,035,074	437,056	36,258	262,712	445,554
Electrical products industries	164	21,440	44,883	124,722	5,072	358,612	719,997	358,380	35,948	238,954	443,728
Non-metallic mineral products industries	334	9,882	21,632	59,586	18,169	105,307	295,709	174,480	13,758	89,244	181,118
Petroleum and coal products industries	19	1,814	4,028	16,678	3,663	389,025	467,319	73,841	3,025	28,017	75,940
Chemical and chemical products industries	335	13,474	28,537	82,009	20,410	320,902	732,655	399,361	28,453	212,181	438,606
Miscellaneous manufacturing industries	814	16,046	34,457	70,261	3,345	152,054	342,324	187,146	20,696	104,718	200,838
Totals, Quebec	10,467	379,907	806,546	1,991,208	255,428	6,975,568	12,808,993	5,672,740	529,154	3,166,501	5,962,686

Ontario

Industry											
Food and beverage industries	2,049	52,151	110,805	288,545	41,084	2,056,770	3,319,692	1,243,342	86,161	542,025	1,307,280
Tobacco products industries	13	2,504	4,903	13,200	900	212,880	269,636	98,372	3,405	20,983	98,733
Rubber industries	55	11,702	25,005	77,027	6,185	220,982	459,920	239,945	17,262	123,379	255,206
Leather industries	201	11,880	24,287	49,997	1,873	99,876	196,050	95,892	14,080	66,257	97,624
Textile industries	391	24,872	53,398	126,030	10,574	402,692	745,779	341,722	30,884	172,878	346,728
Knitting mills	108	6,676	13,849	24,616	1,084	59,054	111,404	53,649	7,824	33,500	53,577
Clothing industries	526	20,728	41,574	78,950	1,070	145,607	303,846	157,417	24,127	104,704	160,350
Wood industries	775	15,143	32,375	73,559	6,092	177,856	341,279	158,514	18,159	96,740	164,211
Furniture and fixture industries	944	17,289	36,392	86,308	3,540	170,334	365,278	195,966	21,387	118,000	199,317
Paper and allied industries	291	34,335	74,944	229,818	54,282	657,221	1,298,696	593,656	45,772	331,863	614,082
Printing, publishing and allied industries	1,584	24,192	49,103	161,198	5,153	255,884	775,296	517,684	43,569	308,544	528,341
Primary metal industries	216	50,536	105,665	358,306	70,712	950,929	1,958,245	938,959	65,532	502,487	952,825
Metal fabricating industries (except machinery and transportation equipment industries)	2,066	60,613	129,881	385,117	21,920	928,119	1,915,200	985,500	81,600	562,596	1,019,592
Machinery industries (except electrical machinery)	498	34,323	72,374	234,630	9,088	665,448	1,295,371	649,403	55,722	419,046	907,246
Transportation equipment industries	357	75,216	164,636	583,278	29,009	3,318,480	5,030,718	1,700,090	100,034	827,844	1,955,600
Electrical products industries	456	53,396	111,218	294,843	13,000	933,485	1,707,662	831,437	80,143	508,794	902,378
Non-metallic mineral products industries	519	19,763	44,020	133,699	38,520	262,925	673,561	380,858	26,679	192,745	393,505
Petroleum and coal products industries	29	2,145	5,122	21,636	6,352	482,193	587,233	102,462	8,726	88,282	101,742
Chemical and chemical products industries	578	21,724	46,836	145,395	57,364	669,538	1,533,789	816,258	42,189	323,568	881,741
Miscellaneous manufacturing industries	1,320	35,492	73,821	182,647	9,395	428,333	962,844	534,844	50,089	299,972	584,221
Totals, Ontario	**12,976**	**574,680**	**1,220,208**	**3,549,699**	**387,197**	**13,098,606**	**23,851,499**	**10,635,970**	**823,344**	**5,644,207**	**11,524,299**

Manitoba

Industry											
Food and beverage industries	337	7,290	14,953	39,100	5,125	332,490	453,462	120,046	11,200	65,384	126,312
Tobacco products industries	...	...	[1]	[1]	...	[1]	[1]	[1]	[1]	[1]	[1]
Rubber industries	1	[1]	[1]	[1]	[1]	[1]	[1]	[1]	[1]	[1]	[1]
Leather industries	17	632	1,223	2,423	78	6,011	10,517	4,479	736	3,111	4,516
Textile industries	43	554	1,123	2,050	108	8,097	12,775	4,453	723	3,057	4,681
Knitting mills	5	[1]	[1]	[1]	[1]	[1]	[1]	[1]	[1]	[1]	[1]
Clothing industries	121	5,740	11,856	19,173	269	47,342	83,665	35,950	6,395	23,785	35,809
Wood industries	91	1,058	2,268	4,816	383	9,491	20,068	10,416	1,236	6,100	10,664
Furniture and fixture industries	109	1,631	3,371	7,227	298	16,169	31,268	15,128	1,946	9,283	15,231
Paper and allied industries	24	1,444	3,058	8,464	2,208	29,441	60,682	29,510	1,869	11,694	29,737
Printing, publishing and allied industries	187	2,397	4,925	14,006	458	19,357	63,423	43,713	4,125	23,927	43,577
Primary metal industries	16	2,214	4,664	14,863	9,336	22,929	64,922	32,520	2,684	19,174	33,123
Metal fabricating industries (except machinery and transportation equipment industries)	132	3,681	7,800	22,465	913	47,565	95,572	47,043	4,860	30,755	52,925
Machinery industries (except electrical machinery)	46	2,055	4,427	10,828	494	42,454	69,602	26,325	3,076	19,115	28,331
Transportation equipment industries	42	3,142	6,914	15,923	752	34,273	72,780	37,388	4,488	25,230	37,400
Electrical products industries	24	1,046	2,158	4,989	271	19,811	33,720	15,316	1,600	8,905	15,475
Non-metallic mineral products industries	45	1,043	2,334	6,266	2,320	14,931	40,883	23,424	1,461	9,425	24,574
Petroleum and coal products industries	6	[1]	[1]	[1]	[1]	[1]	[1]	[1]	[1]	[1]	[1]
Chemical and chemical products industries	32	540	1,135	3,264	1,433	18,629	34,717	15,509	975	6,175	16,815
Miscellaneous manufacturing industries	103	890	1,798	4,016	252	5,216	14,714	9,425	1,206	6,289	11,958
Totals, Manitoba	**1,381**	**35,803**	**74,936**	**182,761**	**25,340**	**725,407**	**1,230,014**	**456,057**	**49,435**	**277,378**	**507,050**

[1] Confidential.

10.—Summary Statistics of Manufactures, by Province and Industry Group, 1969ᴾ—concluded

Province or Territory and Industry Group	Establishments No.	MANUFACTURING ACTIVITY							TOTAL ACTIVITY		
		Production and Related Workers			Cost of Fuel and Electricity $'000	Cost of Materials and Supplies Used $'000	Value of Shipments of Goods of Own Manufacture $'000	Value Added $'000	Total Employees		Total Value Added $'000
		Number	Man-Hours Paid '000	Wages $'000					Number	Salaries and Wages $'000	
Saskatchewan											
Food and beverage industries	227	3,399	7,129	19,690	3,181	155,915	225,490	67,807	5,737	33,742	73,015
Rubber industries	...	...	...	...	...	...	...	...	...	1	—
Textile industries	8	77	153	297	30	642	1,263	766	115	539	800
Clothing industries	3	1	1				1		1		
Wood industries	99	785	1,709	4,205	526	13,215	23,564	10,943	966	5,433	11,218
Furniture and fixture industries	33	66	139	263	15	666	1,347	672	78	322	676
Paper and allied industries	7	1	1				1		1		1
Printing, publishing and allied industries	121	990	2,001	5,325	228	5,518	21,407	15,689	1,641	8,882	15,851
Primary metal industries	3	1	1	1	1	1	1	1	1	1	1
Metal fabricating industries (except machinery and transportation equipment industries)	81	827	1,703	4,484	235	9,861	20,554	10,305	1,232	7,229	12,311
Machinery industries (except electrical machinery)	29	350	728	1,817	136	4,237	10,898	6,605	719	5,062	6,668
Transportation equipment industries	7	76	166	377	14	1,580	2,819	1,241	260	2,062	1,251
Electrical products industries	4	1	1	1	1	1	1	1	1	1	1
Non-metallic mineral products industries	50	698	1,501	3,876	1,402	12,342	28,351	14,592	958	5,681	14,771
Petroleum and coal products industries	10	544	1,143	4,365	939	76,248	97,077	21,112	738	6,136	21,332
Chemical and chemical products industries	11	115	259	815	694	5,225	9,285	3,878	209	1,481	4,362
Miscellaneous manufacturing industries	55	262	535	1,189	74	2,066	4,942	2,774	341	1,749	2,996
Totals, Saskatchewan	**748**	**9,889**	**29,915**	**58,657**	**12,162**	**332,720**	**530,442**	**186,893**	**15,267**	**95,081**	**194,953**
Alberta											
Food and beverage industries	461	8,333	17,467	49,020	5,941	534,781	708,486	172,374	13,436	82,205	179,541
Tobacco products industries	...	...	...	...	...	...	...	...	...	1	1
Rubber industries	4								1	1	1
Leather industries	10	130	260	575	24	1,557	2,831	1,256	188	911	1,350
Textile industries	22	483	1,054	2,506	204	8,086	16,398	8,260	626	3,556	8,460
Knitting mills	3	1	1	1	1	1	1	1	1	1	1
Clothing industries	23	1,661	3,477	6,032	81	12,662	26,266	15,406	2,021	9,254	16,013
Wood industries	250	4,240	8,949	21,562	2,104	62,739	110,578	50,501	5,145	29,109	52,085
Furniture and fixture industries	120	898	1,821	4,289	207	7,984	17,308	9,068	1,109	5,548	9,608
Paper and allied industries	20	1,045	2,282	6,784	1,901	27,227	54,597	24,439	1,482	10,410	25,303
Printing, publishing and allied industries	225	2,124	4,376	13,350	414	15,875	58,544	42,335	3,508	21,871	42,271
Primary metal industries	24	2,191	4,533	14,983	3,173	98,529	152,990	52,346	3,143	23,446	53,044
Metal fabricating industries (except machinery and transportation equipment industries)	229	4,380	9,388	28,542	1,077	65,775	134,228	67,917	5,865	39,930	72,776

Industry	(1)	(2)	(3)	(4)	(5)	(6)	(7)	(8)	(9)	(10)	(11)
Machinery industries (except electrical machinery)	43	1,063	2,250	6,807	316	15,232	32,311	17,155	2,127	15,841	20,355
Transportation equipment industries	69	2,509	5,045	13,971	387	39,365	64,583	26,378	3,293	20,332	29,503
Electrical products industries	17	516	1,077	2,485	185	16,242	28,064	12,132	909	5,301	12,215
Non-metallic mineral products industries	105	2,891	6,358	18,035	3,904	39,034	111,865	68,378	3,784	24,996	68,991
Petroleum and coal products industries	16	755	1,560	6,215	2,048	128,254	177,026	46,587	1,099	9,533	47,029
Chemical and chemical products industries	42	1,532	3,395	11,891	6,859	40,134	110,776	66,221	2,424	19,588	68,375
Miscellaneous manufacturing industries	175	[1]	[1]	[1]	[1]	[1]	[1]	[1]	[1]	[1]	[1]
Totals, Alberta	**1,862**	**36,224**	**76,381**	**214,916**	**29,312**	**1,133,986**	**1,849,268**	**702,810**	**52,364**	**335,102**	**731,864**
British Columbia											
Food and beverage industries	548	10,261	20,569	58,739	6,988	391,957	630,450	237,219	17,352	107,736	247,812
Tobacco products industries	...	...	...	...	...	...	...	...	...	...	...
Rubber industries	8	[1]	[1]	[1]	[1]	[1]	[1]	[1]	[1]	[1]	[1]
Leather industries	16	250	475	1,002	23	1,767	3,871	2,134	296	1,320	2,289
Textile industries	48	780	1,537	3,196	171	8,633	15,972	7,258	964	4,680	7,602
Knitting mills	6	[1]	[1]	[1]	[1]	[1]	[1]	[1]	[1]	[1]	[1]
Clothing industries	52	1,874	3,701	7,057	107	11,025	25,007	13,893	2,117	8,997	14,122
Wood industries	724	34,552	69,266	238,732	18,009	701,082	1,193,787	503,949	39,283	282,602	505,510
Furniture and fixture industries	254	1,786	3,656	9,825	387	17,969	38,987	20,874	2,260	13,315	21,431
Paper and allied industries	54	12,646	26,132	105,805	41,064	347,219	719,556	329,609	17,312	155,419	328,571
Printing, publishing and allied industries	321	3,096	6,159	22,715	753	29,139	104,383	74,704	6,037	43,014	75,859
Primary metal industries	39	6,020	12,608	44,870	6,199	115,500	251,605	130,995	8,134	64,352	134,627
Metal fabricating industries (except machinery and transportation equipment industries)	415	6,715	14,080	48,090	2,010	100,986	213,563	112,310	9,023	67,210	117,254
Machinery industries (except electrical machinery)	65	2,688	5,575	19,930	758	43,682	90,556	48,093	4,335	34,422	49,806
Transportation equipment industries	161	4,566	9,699	33,049	823	86,630	154,313	68,908	6,088	46,022	72,945
Electrical products industries	50	1,354	2,762	8,115	376	31,632	57,690	28,241	2,626	17,721	28,688
Non-metallic mineral products industries	136	2,281	4,946	16,800	4,684	36,704	94,463	53,195	3,253	24,529	57,724
Petroleum and coal products industries	14	571	1,247	5,652	3,549	135,120	167,309	28,020	896	9,271	29,303
Chemical and chemical products industries	102	1,595	3,270	10,683	7,026	48,747	111,983	58,294	3,045	21,933	61,286
Miscellaneous manufacturing industries	316	1,944	3,968	10,806	536	14,740	37,917	23,521	2,703	16,109	29,986
Totals, British Columbia	**3,329**	**93,379**	**190,417**	**646,570**	**93,512**	**2,124,998**	**3,917,820**	**1,745,128**	**126,434**	**922,822**	**1,788,857**
Yukon and Northwest Territories											
Food and beverage industries	5	12	26	58	16	183	446	241	27	135	271
Clothing industries	1	[1]	[1]	[1]	[1]	[1]	[1]	[1]	[1]	[1]	[1]
Wood industries	11	45	94	238	35	182	715	584	53	296	592
Furniture and fixture industries	1	[1]	[1]	[1]	[1]	[1]	[1]	[1]	[1]	[1]	[1]
Printing, publishing and allied industries	5	[1]	[1]	[1]	[1]	[1]	[1]	[1]	[1]	[1]	[1]
Metal fabricating industries (except machinery and transportation equipment industries)	3	[1]	[1]	[1]	[1]	[1]	[1]	[1]	[1]	[1]	[1]
Non-metallic mineral products industries	2	[1]	[1]	[1]	[1]	[1]	[1]	[1]	[1]	[1]	[1]
Petroleum and coal products industries	1	[1]	[1]	[1]	[1]	[1]	[1]	[1]	[1]	[1]	[1]
Chemical and chemical products industries	3	[1]	[1]	[1]	[1]	[1]	[1]	[1]	[1]	[1]	[1]
Totals, Yukon and Northwest Territories	**32**	**153**	**319**	**1,036**	**91**	**2,728**	**5,224**	**2,467**	**213**	**1,423**	**3,155**

[1] Confidential.

TABLE OF URBAN POPULATIONS IN CANADA OF 35,000 OR MORE, 1971

Exactly what is included within a metropolitan area varies from country to country. In Canada, the word "metropolitan" is used to mean a city and its surrounding municipalities.

Belleville, Ontario	35,135	North York, Ontario	503,745
Brampton, Ontario	41,200	Oakville, Ontario	61,490
Brantford, Ontario	64,440	Oshawa, Ontario	91,590
Burlington, Ontario	87,015	Ottawa, Ontario: City	302,435
Calgary, Alberta	403,330	Metropolitan	602,555
Chatham, Ontario	35,325	Peterborough, Ontario	58,150
Chicoutimi-Jonquière, Quebec	133,815	Pointe-aux-Trembles, Quebec	35,550
Cornwall, Ontario	47,225	Quebec City, Quebec:	
Dartmouth, Nova Scotia	64,785	City	186,025
East York, Ontario	104,645	Metropolitan	480,410
Edmonton, Alberta: City	438,425	Regina, Saskatchewan:	
Metropolitan	495,915	City	139,435
Etobicoke, Ontario	282,735	Metropolitan	140,675
Galt, Ontario*	38,910	St. Boniface, Manitoba	46,750
Guelph, Ontario	60,210	St. Catharines-Niagara Falls, Ontario:	
Halifax, Nova Scotia:		City of St. Catharines	109,780
City	122,030	City of Niagara Falls	67,160
Metropolitan	222,650	Metropolitan	303,440
Hamilton, Ontario: City	309,180	St. James-Assiniboia, Manitoba	71,385
Metropolitan	498,505	Saint John, New Brunswick:	
Hull, Quebec	63,565	City	89,115
Kingston, Ontario	59,070	Metropolitan	106,695
Kitchener, Ontario: City	111,810	St. John's, Newfoundland:	
Metropolitan	226,800	City	88,105
Lachine, Quebec	44,435	Metropolitan	132,005
Lasalle, Quebec	72,905	St. Laurent, Quebec	62,945
Laval, Quebec	227,985	St. Léonard, Quebec	52,035
Lethbridge, Alberta	41,200	Ste. Foy, Quebec	68,420
London, Ontario: City	223,270	Sarnia, Ontario	57,625
Metropolitan	286,270	Saskatoon, Saskatchewan	126,560
Longueil, Quebec	97,585	Sault Ste. Marie, Ontario	80,545
Markham, Ontario	36,690	Scarborough, Ontario	334,490
Mississauga, Ontario	156,085	Sherbrooke, Quebec	80,730
Moncton, New Brunswick	47,870	Sudbury, Ontario: City	90,515
Montreal, Quebec: City	1,214,375	Metropolitan	155,460
Metropolitan	2,743,235	Thunder Bay, Ontario:	
Montreal North, Quebec	89,135	City	108,445
New Westminster, British Columbia	42,895	Metropolitan	112,145
North Bay, Ontario	49,185	Toronto, Ontario: City	713,130
		Metropolitan	2,628,130

*As of January 1st, 1973, part of the new city of Cambridge.

Trois Rivières, Quebec	55,885	Waterloo, Ontario	36,615
Vancouver, British Columbia:		Welland, Ontario	44,395
City	426,265	Windsor, Ontario: City	203,370
Metropolitan	1,082,350	Metropolitan	258,655
Verdun, Quebec	74,700	Winnipeg, Manitoba:	
Victoria, British Columbia:		City	246,270
City	61,745	Metropolitan	540,260
Metropolitan	195,850	York, Ontario	147,270

LIST OF DIAGRAMS, GRAPHS, TABLES

LIST OF MAPS

HANDY CONCEPTS AND TERMS

Air drainage. The movement of cold air from higher to lower altitudes. Dense, cold air rolls down the mountainsides, "drains" through the orchards on the slopes, and comes to rest on the valley floor. Thus the trees are not too much affected by the cold temperatures.

Anadromous. Refers to fish that ascend a river to spawn.

Aquaculture. The raising of fish under controlled conditions; "fish farming."

Arable. Refers to land that can be made to produce; strictly, land that can be ploughed.

Arctic Circle. The parallel of latitude at 66½°N. At this latitude on one day of the year in the northern midsummer, usually about June 21, the sun does not set, and on one day of the year in the northern midwinter, usually on December 22, the sun does not rise. The number of such days increases as you move farther north, until, at the North Pole itself, there are six months of daylight and six months of night.

Arête. A sharp mountain ridge, often formed by the erosion of two adjoining cirques.

Atmospheric pressure. The pressure of the air all around us. It is measured by a barometer and is normally registered in millibars or kilopascals.

Banks. As icebergs met the warm North Atlantic Drift off the east coast of Canada, they melted. The debris they dropped have formed several huge underwater shoals.

Beneficiation. The process of crushing the ore and discarding the waste rock. The remaining ore contains a higher percentage of minerals and is therefore a higher-grade ore.

Block mountains. A mountain mass formed when faults occur, and huge parts of the earth's surface are elevated and tilted. (The Sierra Nevadas are block mountains.)

Boreal. Northern — after "Boreas," God of the North Wind.

Broken ecumene. Scattered blocs of settlement separated by considerable areas of uninhabited land.

Capital costs. Money required to set up an operation and bring it into production: costs of land, plant, machinery, equipment, etc.

Capital investment. Money invested in a project to make a profit.

Carapace. The shell of a crustacean; i.e., a lobster, a crab, etc.

Cereals. Grains — wheat, rye, oats, barley, etc.

Chernozem. Russian for "black earth."

Cirque. "Armchair" hollow gouged out of a mountainside by the head of the glacier. A valley glacier originates here.

Climate. The *average* weather conditions over a long period of time.

Close utilization. The use of all parts of the tree for some purpose: e.g., larger parts for building lumber; smaller, for pulp and paper.

Combine. A machine that reaps the grain, threshes it, winnows it, and collects it in a continuous process.

Commerce. Buying and selling goods and services on a large scale.

Commercial farming. Farming to grow and raise products for sale.

Coniferous. Refers to plants whose seeds are in the form of cones; generally have needle-like leaves.

Consumer goods. Goods bought to satisfy personal needs: e.g., food, clothing, appliances, automobiles, etc.

Continental shelf. The seabed along the edges of a continent.

Conurbation. A number of cities that grow

so large that they merge one into the other: e.g., the Mississauga Conurbation.

Cultural geography. Study of the way in which human beings have modified the natural landscape — roads, cities, dams, farms, and so on — and the effect of these modifications on human settlement.

Culture. The distinctive customs and habits of particular groups of people. In this broad meaning of the word, it includes language, religion, food, clothes, recreation — in short, way of life or life style. It can be applied specifically to a segment of a society (e.g., teenage culture), more broadly to people of a region or a nation (e.g., Maritime culture, Canadian culture), and even to a continent or hemisphere (North American culture, Western culture).

Deciduous. Refers to plants that lose their leaves at some season of the year — in monsoon forests, during the hot season, as protection against excessive loss of moisture by evaporation; in northern forests, during the autumn, as protection against the cold and frost of winter.

Dory. Small, flat-bottomed fishing boat manned by one or two men.

Dragger. A ship that drags an otter-trawl net to catch groundfish.

Drumlin. Elongated, oval-shaped hill (like half an egg cut lengthwise), composed mainly of till and formed by glacial action.

Ecosystem. A section of nature that makes up a "home," including all the things in it and their environment. This particular "home" is created and sustained by a number of interdependent factors: living (animals, plants, micro-organisms) and non-living (sunlight, climate, minerals). Within such a "home" system, all factors interact with one another. If one factor changes, the whole system breaks down.

Examples are: a pond, forest, ocean.

Ecumene. The inhabited or settled parts of the world.

Entrenched valley. A valley that has been deeply cut by a river.

Environment. The objects or region surrounding anything, the sum total of conditions under which any person, animal, or thing lives or is developed; can be human, animal, vegetation, soil, etc.

Escarpment. The abrupt face or cliff of a ridge or hill range.

Ethnic. Refers to particular groups of people, with their distinctive customs, habits, and points of difference. Generally, in any country, has come to mean minority groups or people not born in that country.

Evergreen. Refers to plants that do not cut off their flow of sap but drop leaves continuously. Thus there is no season when the tree is not in leaf. May have needle-like leaves or broad leaves.

Exploitation. The development of resources — mining, forestry, and so on.

Extrusion. Lava forced above the earth's crust.

Fault. Fracture due to forces in the earth's crust.

Flakes. Platforms on which fish are spread out to be dried by the wind and sun.

Fluid milk. Milk produced to drink.

Fold. Huge crumples in the earth's crust. (The Rockies are fold mountains.)

Front. The dividing line between two masses of air.

Cold front. The leading edge of a cold air mass. The passage of a cold front through a place is usually marked by a rise of atmospheric pressure, a fall of temperature, a shift of wind, a heavy shower, and, sometimes, thunder.

Polar front. In North America, the polar front is the dividing line between the Arctic air mass and the Gulf air mass.

Its position fluctuates north and south according to the season.

Warm front. The leading edge of a warm air mass. The passage of a warm front through a place is usually marked by a rise in temperature, a slackening of precipitation, and a shift of wind. Warm fronts occur mainly in high latitudes, especially during winter.

Frontier. A zone in transition, a zone of change; a zone that is in the process of being developed, where type of settlement and effective use of land have not yet been resolved. A society that is changing from an agricultural economy to an industrial economy is a frontier. An area of land that is changing from rural to urban settlement is a frontier.

Geographic region. An area consisting of physical and cultural features that unify it and set it apart from other regions — e.g., the Shield, Latin America.

Geology. The study of the composition of the earth's crust.

Gravimeter. An instrument for measuring variations in the gravitational field of the earth; used in prospecting for mineral deposits.

Heterogeneous communities. Settlements of peoples of different customs and habits; communities in which there is a mixture of languages, religions, ethnic origins, cultures.

Homogeneous communities. Settlements of people who share a common life style or culture: the same language, religion, ethnic origin, etc.

Horned peak. A mountain peak carved out by three or more cirques.

Humus. The organic top layer of soil.

Igneous rocks. Rocks formed of cooled magma or lava.

Industry. Organization of the production of everything from raw material to finished article.

Primary industry. Concerned with the exploitation of raw materials: e.g., mining, fishing, agriculture, forestry.

Secondary industry. Manufacturing: e.g., food processing, automotive, clothing.

Integrated industry. One that processes the raw materials into diversified products, usually on the same site: e.g., iron-and-steel mills, lumber and pulp-and-paper complexes, etc.

Inshore fishing. Fishing in coastal coves and bays, close to the shoreline.

Intrusion. Magma forced into cracks in the earth's crust.

Isobar. A line on a map joining places that have equal pressures during a specific period of time.

Isohyet. A line on a map joining places that have equal rainfall during a specific period of time.

Isotherm. A line on a map joining places that have equal temperatures during a specific period of time.

Laker. A merchant vessel plying the Great Lakes. They are generally very long and narrow. Before the building of the Seaway they were confined strictly to the Lakes. But today they can use the whole of the Seaway because of the larger locks.

Latitude. Suppose we make a line from the equator to the centre of the earth. Suppose we then draw another line from anywhere on the earth's surface north or south of the first line to the centre of the earth. The angle between these two lines is what we call latitude. And the *distance* between these two lines *at the earth's surface* we measure in degrees of latitude. If north of the equator, the reference is °N; if south of the equator, °S. Thus latitude is distance measured in degrees north or south of the equator. Lines on a map showing latitude are called *parallels of latitude*.

Livestock. The animals on a farm raised for human consumption.

Loess. Deposits of fine dust or silt transported by wind. Mixed with a high proportion of humus, it forms a large part of the fertile Prairie soils.

Logging:

Clear cutting. The felling of all trees in a stand; those trees that cannot be used because they are rotting or diseased are cut down and burned.

Patch logging. Clear cutting in patches, so that the logged patches can be re-seeded from the surrounding trees.

Selective cutting. Thinning out the forest to give younger and stronger trees more growing space.

Strip logging. Clear cutting in strips.

Longitude. Suppose we make a line from the *Greenwich* or *prime meridian* (the line of longitude – marked 0° – drawn from the North Pole, through Greenwich, England, to the South Pole) to the centre of the earth. Suppose we then draw another line from anywhere on the earth's surface east or west of the first line to the centre of the earth. The angle between these two lines is what we call longitude. And the *distance* between these two lines *at the earth's surface* we measure in degrees of longitude. If east of the prime meridian, the reference is °E; if west of the prime meridian, °W. Thus longitude is distance measured in degrees east or west of the prime meridian. Lines on a map showing longitude are called *meridians of longitude*.

Magma. The molten matter under the crust of the earth from which igneous rocks are formed. If a crack occurs in the crust, the release of pressure at that point causes the red hot magma to flow.

Magnetometer. An instrument for measuring the intensity of a magnetic field; used in prospecting for mineral deposits.

Manufacturing. Processing of raw materials into finished or semi-finished products.

Primary manufacturing. Production of semi-finished goods: lumber, pulp and paper, steel.

Secondary manufacturing. Production of finished goods: furniture, books, automobiles.

Marketing. All the activities involved in getting a product from the producer to the consumer: packaging, advertising, transportation, sales, etc.

Metamorphic rocks. Igneous and sedimentary rocks changed by great pressure and heat: e.g., granite ⟶ gneiss; shale ⟶ slate; limestone ⟶ marble; bituminous coal ⟶ anthracite.

Metropolis. Collection of municipalities, each with its own government, but under one metropolitan government for the purposes of administering those services common to all, e.g., transportation, police.

Mining region. A region in which mining operations expand outward from an initial core area and also develop within the area. Mining remains a major activity within the region.

Misfit stream. A stream that has shrunk remarkably so that it no longer fills the spillway (the flat, steep-sided valley carved out by glacial meltwater).

Mixed farm. One on which both stock and crops are raised: e.g., a combination of dairy cattle, hogs, grains, and poultry.

Moraine. Collection of weathered and ground debris within or deposited by a glacier.

Within a glacier:

Terminal. At the end, in the snout.

Medial. In the middle.

Lateral. Along the sides.

Deposited by a glacier:

End, Terminal, or *Recessional.* Till

(gravel, sand, clay, silt) deposited as rugged hills when the melting snout of the glacier remains stationary.

Ground. Till, comprised of boulder clay (clay containing boulders, stones, gravel "ground" down in the glacier) smeared on the bedrock by the base of the glacier and revealed as a rolling plain when the glacier recedes.

Muskeg. Algonquian word for bog or marsh.

Natural resources. Wealth supplied by nature used to satisfy human wants: mineral deposits, soils, timber, water, fish, wildlife, etc.

Offshore fishing. Fishing out at sea; generally refers to fishing on the banks.

Orogenesis or **Orogeny.** Creation of mountain ranges.

Parent material. The inorganic material from which soil has developed.

Pelletization. Making beneficiated ore into pellets for transportation to the blast furnaces.

Permafrost. Permanently frozen ground. The surface may thaw for a short time in summer, but the subsoil, i.e., the ground a foot or so below the surface, remains permanently frozen.

Petrochemical. Refers to the industry that makes chemicals from petroleum products — drugs, nylon, fertilizers, plastics, etc.

Physical geography. Study of the natural landscape (mountains, plains, rivers, lakes), climate, vegetation, and soil — the total characteristics of the earth's surface apart from human effort.

Plain. An extensive area of level or gently undulating land, usually of low altitude. (In Canada, the Prairies; in the Soviet Union, the steppes; in Argentina, the pampas.)

Till plain. A ground moraine (composed of boulder clay).

Clay plain. Fine particles of clay fall to the floor of a lake. When the lake recedes, these deposits are revealed as a flat plain.

Sand plain. As a lake recedes it creates a series of beaches. These remain as gently sloping plains.

Podzol. Russian for "underneath ashes." An acidic, generally infertile soil. Just below the humus is a layer of ashy-grey sand, hence the name.

Population density. The number of people per square kilometre.

Prairie. Actually "treeless plain." In this book, Prairie(s) with a capital "P" refers to the southern section of Manitoba, Saskatchewan, and Alberta.

Precipitation. Rain, snow, hail, sleet.

Production costs. Money required to produce and distribute goods: operating costs of labor, materials, maintenance, energy, transportation, etc.

Rain shadow. An area in the lee (the opposite direction to that from which the wind is blowing) of a mountain range. Thus, rainbearing winds drop their moisture on the windward side, and the leeward side is relatively dry.

Relief. The elevated parts of the landscape.

Scarp. Sometimes a synonym for escarpment, but more usually reserved for cliffs produced by faulting.

Sedimentary rocks. Sediments, nearly always deposited in huge seas millions of years ago, pressurized and cemented into layers of rock (strata): e.g., sandstone, shale, limestone.

Sediments. Debris (sand, gravel, silt, clay, fish bones, etc.) carried and deposited by any transporting agent.

Aeolian. Refers to sediments deposited by wind.

Alluvial. Refers to sediments carried and deposited by water.

Fluvial. Refers to sediments carried by a river.

Glacial. Refers to sediments deposited by a glacier.

Lacustrine. Refers to sediments deposited in a lake.

Marine. Refers to sediments deposited in a sea.

Seismograph. An instrument for measuring and recording the intensity of earth tremors and vibrations. In oil exploration, used to measure shock waves after explosive charge is set off.

Services. Work done for the help or benefit of others. People who deal in services are involved in every aspect of a product except its actual production: sales (shopkeepers, clerks, advertisers, etc.), maintenance and repair (drycleaners, plumbers, electricians, mechanics, etc.), transportation (truck drivers, dockers, etc.), and so on. Some services — medical, legal, educational — have little or nothing to do with a concrete product.

Shield. The part of the earth's crust that cooled and solidified first, billions of years ago; forms the core region of a continent. For example, in North America, the Cordillera, Plains, and Appalachians were formed from the Canadian Shield.

Soil. That part of the earth's surface that has developed from organic and inorganic material.

Sour soil. One that is extremely acidic; generally infertile and poorly drained.

Sweet soil. One that contains an adequate proportion of lime; generally fertile and well-drained.

Solid milk. Milk that contains a great deal of butter fat and used therefore in the production of butter and cheese.

Steppe. A treeless plain in the Soviet Union.

Strata. Layers of sedimentary rock.

Subsistence farming. Farming to grow and raise products to be consumed by the farm household. Most pioneer farming was of this type.

Sustained yield. The controlled harvesting of a resource so that it can renew itself: e.g., planting the same number of trees as are lost by logging, fire, disease, etc.; fishing in accordance with quotas, bans, and other regulations so that the fishery is not overfished and depleted.

Temperature average:

Daily or *diurnal average.* Add the highest and lowest temperatures that occur from 12 o'clock midnight to the following midnight and divide by two.

Monthly average. Total the daily averages and divide by the number of days in the month. If you total the averages for each month separately over a number of years and divide by that same number you can get a pretty good idea of the temperature conditions of each month.

Yearly average. Total the monthly averages and divide by twelve. Yearly averages are not of much use in describing climate because of seasonal differences. They certainly do not mean very much to a farmer.

Temperature range:

Daily or *diurnal range.* The range of temperature (coldest to hottest) from 12 o'clock midnight to the following midnight. The mean diurnal range is the mean difference between the highest and lowest temperatures for each day of a given period (a month being the usual period) over a number of years.

Annual range. The difference between the average temperatures of the highest and lowest months.

Threshing. Beating the grain to separate it from the stalk.

Topography. The shape of the surface features of the earth or their description (as in a topographic map).

Trash. What is left after the grain has been threshed and winnowed; today, spewed out by the combine on the fields and ploughed in by the farmer as a conservation measure.

Trawler. A ship, larger than a dragger, that drags a trawl to catch groundfish.

Tree line. The poleward, or high-altitude, limit of tree growth.

Tundra. Treeless plains of Arctic regions where the precipitation is so sparse and the temperature so cold that only mosses, lichens, and a few flowers can exist. There are no trees. The surface may be permanently frozen or frozen for only part of the year, but the subsoil, i.e., the ground about a foot below the surface, is permanently frozen.

Warp. Gentle fold.

Weather. The day-to-day state of the atmosphere — that is, raining, snowing, windy, hot, cold.

Wheat:

Fall or *winter wheat.* Wheat that is planted in the fall, lies dormant in the winter, generally under an insulating blanket of snow, grows in the spring, and is harvested in late spring. Also called *soft wheat* — high in moisture, low in gluten.

Spring wheat. Wheat that is planted in the spring and harvested in late fall. Also called *hard wheat* — low in moisture, high in gluten.

Winnowing. Separating the grains from the chaff.

RESOURCE MATERIALS

General

A Guide to Understanding Canada. Peters, James. Toronto: Guinness Publishing, 1968.

Atlas of Canada. Geographical Branch, Department of Mines and Technical Surveys. Ottawa: Queen's Printer, 1957.

Canada: A Geographical Interpretation. Warkentin, John, ed. Toronto: Methuen, 1970.

Canada: a regional geography, second edition. Tomkins, George S., and others. Toronto: Gage Educational Publishing, 1970.

Canadian Geographical Journal. Ottawa: The Royal Canadian Geographical Society.

Canada Year Book. Ottawa: Statistics Canada.

The Canadian Oxford School Atlas, third edition. Pleva, E. C., and Inch, Spencer, eds. Toronto: Oxford University Press (Canadian Branch), 1972.

Facts on Canada. Ottawa: Information Canada.

Gage World Atlas: A Canadian Perspective. Robinson, J. Lewis, ed., and others. Toronto: Gage Educational Publishing, 1972.

The National Atlas of Canada, fourth edition. Ottawa: Macmillan Co. of Canada Ltd., in association with the Department of Energy, Mines, and Resources, Ottawa, 1974.

Readings in Canadian Geography, revised edition. Irvine, Robert M., ed. Toronto: Holt, Rinehart and Winston, 1972.

Chapter 1

A Guide to Geology. Baird, David M. Toronto: Macmillan, 1974.

Canada Year Book. Ottawa: Statistics Canada. (The 1970 and 1971 editions are particularly helpful on the geology of Canada.)

The Canadian Landscape: Map and air photo interpretation. Blair, C., and Simpson, R. Toronto: Copp Clark, 1968.

Canadian Regions: a geography of Canada. Putnam, Donald F., ed. Toronto: J. M. Dent, 1957.

The Climate of Canada. Ottawa: Information Canada, 1973.

Patterns of Canada. Megill, W. J., ed. Toronto: McGraw-Hill, 1966.

Physiographic Subdivisions of Canada. Ottawa: Department of Energy, Mines, and Resources, 1970.

Readings in Canadian Geography. Irving, Robert M., ed. Toronto: Holt, Rinehart and Winston, 1972.

Wilderness Canada. Spears, Borden, ed. Toronto: Clarke, Irwin, 1970.

Chapter 2

The Canadian Family: a book of readings. Ishwaran, K., ed. Toronto: Holt, Rinehart and Winston, 1971.

The Canadian Indian. Ottawa: Information Canada, 1973.

Canadian Settlement Patterns. Trussler, Lloyd G. Toronto: J. M. Dent, 1972.

Communities in Canada: selected sources. Marsh, Leonard. Toronto: McClelland and Stewart, 1970.

Drum Dance: Legends, Ceremonies, Dances, and Songs of the Eskimos. Hofman, Charles. Toronto: Gage Publishing, 1974.

The Howling Arctic. Price, Ray. Toronto: Peter Martin, 1970.

The Other Canadians. Davis, Morris, and Krauter, Joseph. Toronto: Methuen, 1971.

Perspective Canada: A Compendium of Social Statistics. Ottawa: Statistics Canada, 1974.

Speaking Canadian English: An Informal

Account of the English Language in Canada. Orkin, Mark M. Toronto: General Publishing, 1970.

Chapter 3

Developing Water Resources: The St. Lawrence Seaway and the Columbia/Peace Power Projects. Richardson, Ronald E., and others. Toronto: McGraw-Hill, 1969.

Electric Power. Koegler, John. Toronto: J. M. Dent, 1972.

Impact of Oil: The Development of Canada's Oil Resources. Gray, Earle. Toronto: Ryerson Press and Maclean-Hunter Ltd., 1969.

The Story of Natural Gas. Don Mills, Ontario: The Canadian Gas Association.

Chapter 4

Atlantic Salmon. Ottawa: Department of Fisheries, 1965.

Canada's Pacific Herring. Ottawa: Department of Fisheries, 1965.

Fisheries Fact Sheet:
Number 1: Canada's Fisheries
Number 3: The Grand Banks
Number 4: The Sea Scallop
Number 5: The American Lobster.
Ottawa: Fisheries and Marine Service, Department of the Environment.

Chapter 5

About Pulp and Paper. Montreal: Canadian Pulp and Paper Association.

The Forest Book. Montreal: Canadian Pulp and Paper Association.

The Forest Industry of British Columbia. Vancouver: Council of Forest Industries of British Columbia.

Forest Regions of Canada. Ottawa: Information Canada, 1972.

Forestry Lessons. Ottawa: Information Canada, 1971.

Native Trees of Canada. Ottawa: Information Canada, 1970.

Chapter 6

Agriculture in Southern Ontario. Epp, Henry. Toronto: J. M. Dent, 1972.

The Agriculture of the Atlantic Provinces. Ottawa: Department of Regional Economic Expansion, 1970.

Farming in Canada. Ottawa: Information Canada, 1971.

Selected Agriculture Statistics for Canada. Ottawa: Agriculture Canada, 1973.

Wheat Farming. Henry, John C. Toronto: J. M. Dent, 1972.

Chapter 7

Canadian Minerals Yearbook. Ottawa: Information Canada.

Mining. Ottawa: The Mining Association of Canada, 1974.

Resources of the Canadian Shield. Robinson, J. Lewis. Toronto: Methuen, 1969.

Chapter 8

Man's Economic World: An introduction to economic geography. Balins, Arnolds, and others. Toronto: Holt, Rinehart and Winston, 1971.

Prices and Price Indexes. (A monthly publication issued by the Department of Consumer and Corporate Affairs.) Ottawa: Statistics Canada.

Studies in Canadian Economic Geography. Braund, W. Bruce, and Blake, William C. Toronto: McGraw-Hill, 1969.

Urban Areas. Winter, Eric. Toronto: Bellhaven House, 1971.

Urban Landscapes. Winter, Eric. Toronto: Bellhaven House, 1969.

Urban Prospects. Wolforth, John, and Leigh, Roger. Toronto: McClelland and Stewart, 1971.

Chapter 9

Building For People: Freeway and Downtown — New Frameworks for Modern Needs. Richardson, Ronald E., and others. McGraw-Hill Ryerson/Maclean-Hunter, 1970.

Communications. Skimson, Thomas C. Toronto: J. M. Dent, 1972.

Transportation: The Evolution of Canada's Networks. Schreiner, John. Toronto: McGraw-Hill Ryerson/Maclean-Hunter, 1972.

Chapter 10

Canada's North. Phillips, R. A. J. Toronto: Macmillan, 1967.

Essays on Mid-Canada. Mid-Canada Development Foundation. Toronto: Maclean-Hunter, 1970.

Northern Realities: the future of northern development in Canada. Lotz, Jim. Toronto: New Press, 1970.

The Northland: Studies of the Yukon and Northwest Territories. Wolforth, John. Toronto: McClelland and Stewart, 1969.

Chapter 11

American Investment: development or domination? Guenther, Victor J. Toronto: J. M. Dent, 1971.

Changing Values: The Human Impact of Urbanization. Smith, David C. Toronto: Bellhaven House, 1971.

The Future of Canadian Cities. Richardson, Boyce. Toronto: New Press, 1972.

Planning the Canadian Environment. Gertler, Leonard O., ed. Montreal: Harvest House, 1972.

Pollution: An ecological approach. Adamson, Robert C. Toronto: Bellhaven House, 1971.

The Pollution Guide. Bennett, Tiny, and Rowland, Wade. Toronto: Clarke, Irwin, 1972.

Regional and Resource Planning in Canada, revised edition. Krueger, Ralph R., ed., and others. Toronto: Holt, Rinehart and Winston, 1970.

FURTHER ACKNOWLEDGMENTS

Gage Educational Publishing Limited wishes to thank the following individuals and organizations for the use of material not acknowledged elsewhere in this book.

Cover photographs by Richard Harrington (front) and Fortunato Aglialoro (back). The opening pages of Chapter 1: Information Canada Photothèque for the photographs of Rocky Mountain foothills, eastern woodlands, and a sea coast; Richard Harrington for the photograph of hikers in the Chilkoot Pass area of British Columbia. Fortunato Aglialoro for the photographs on the opening pages of Chapter 2, and the Canada Post Office for the postage stamps in the same chapter. The Photographic/Art Division of the Government of Saskatchewan for the photograph on the opening pages of Chapter 6. The opening pages of Chapter 9: Transport Canada for the photograph of the Boeing 747; Freeman Patterson, from Information Canada Photothèque, for the photograph of rail lines; and the Ontario Ministry of Transportation and Communications for the highway scene. The opening pages of Chapter 10: Information Canada Photothèque for the photograph of Ottawa; Canadian Pacific for the photograph of Banff, Alta., and vicinity; and Richard Harrington for the photograph of the mining community of Tungsten, Northwest Territories.

INDEX

Feasibility factors, 213-214

Fishing: aquaculture, 130; Atlantic coast, 102-114; capelin, 110, 126; cod, 102, 110, 126; conservation in, 125-131, 328-329; fish ladders, 117; fish processing, 111-112, 119-122, 123; halibut, 121, 125, 129; herring, 112, 114, 121; inland waters, 123-124, 125, 126; inshore, 102, 110, 126; lobster, 106-109, 125; offshore, 102, 110, 126; Pacific coast, 115-122; pollution, 110, 125-126, 131; redfish, 110, 114; salmon, 110, 115-120; spawning grounds, 129-130; in Yarmouth County, 106-107

Foreign exchange, 170, 326

Foreign investment, 326-327

Forest: conservation of, 162-164; an environment, 138, 164; kinds of, 140, 141, 142, 143, 149; production areas, 143; regions, 140-142

Forest industries, 137-163; in British Columbia, 143, 151-155, 162-163; employees in, 137; exports, 150; primary manufacturing, 151-157. See also Logging; Lumber; Plywood; Pulp and paper

Fort McMurray, 310, 311

Frontier, 295, 296-297; agriculture in, 300-302; conflicts in, 297, 305, 307-308, 310, 311, 314; external, 313-315; hydro-electric development in, 305-309; industrial development in, 302-304; oil exploration in, 310-313; transportation in, 273-278, 287, 289

Geographic regions: Appalachian Canada, 33-37; Arctic Lowlands, 37-40; classifications of, 4-7; Great Lakes-St. Lawrence Lowlands, 14-17; Great Plains, 18-22; Pacific coast, 30-32; Shield, 8-14; Western Cordillera, 25-29

Golden Horseshoe. See Mississauga Conurbation

GO (Government of Ontario) Transit, 285-286

Grand Bank, Newfoundland, 62-65

Grand banks, 35, 102, 104-105, 108-109, 110

Great Clay Belt, 301-302, 310

Great Lakes-St. Lawrence Lowlands: climate of, 17; hydro-electric development in, 89; physiography of, 14-16; soils of, 17

Great Lakes-St. Lawrence waterway, 263-265

Great Plains: climate of, 23-25; physiography of, 18-22; soils of, 21, 25; vegetation, 25

Highway 401. See Macdonald-Cartier Freeway

Highways. See Roads and highways

Holland Marsh, 184-190

Hudson Bay Railway, 276-277

Hydro-electric development: in British Columbia, 88-89; in the frontier, 305-309; in the Great Lakes-St. Lawrence, 89; in the Saguenay Valley, 85-86; in the Shield, 87-88

Hydrologic cycle, 336, 337

Indians. See Native peoples

Industry. See individual industries; Manufacturing

Intensive farming, 170

International Commission of the Northwest Atlantic (ICNAF), 328

International North Pacific Fisheries Commission (NORPAC), 128

International Pacific Halibut Commission (IPHC), 129

Inuit (Eskimo). See Native peoples

Iron, 207, 209-210, 211, 223, 238-240

Labrador-Quebec mining region, 209-210, 275-276

Lake Iroquois, 16

Lake Superior mining region, 211

"Law of the Sea," 314, 328

Livestock. See Agriculture

Lobster fishing, 106-109, 125

Logging, 143-144, 146-149

Lumber, 143, 153-155, 159; sawmills, 158-159

Macdonald-Cartier Freeway, 283-284